Die Koranhermeneutik von Günter Lüling

Judaism, Christianity, and Islam – Tension, Transmission, Transformation

Edited by Patrice Brodeur, Alexandra Cuffel, Assaad Elias Kattan, and Georges Tamer

Volume 9

Die Koranhermeneutik von Günter Lüling

Herausgegeben von
Georges Tamer

DE GRUYTER

ISBN 978-3-11-060142-8
e-ISBN (PDF) 978-3-11-059917-6
e-ISBN (EPUB) 978-3-11-059884-1
ISSN 2196-405X

Library of Congress Control Number: 2018961674

Bibliografische Information der Deutschen Nationalbibliothek
Die Deutsche Nationalbibliothek verzeichnet diese Publikation in der Deutschen Nationalbibliografie; detaillierte bibliografische Daten sind im Internet über http://dnb.dnb.de abrufbar.

Dieser Band ist text- und seitenidentisch mit der 2019 erschienenen gebundenen Ausgabe.
Druck und Bindung: CPI books GmbH, Leck

www.degruyter.com

Inhalt

Georges Tamer

Günter Lüling: Leben, Werk und Fall

Der vorliegende Band ist Ergebnis einer Konferenz, die vom Lehrstuhl für Orientalische Philologie und Islamwissenschaft der Friedrich-Alexander-Universität Erlangen-Nürnberg am 19.–20. Juni 2015 unter dem Titel „Kritische Koranhermeneutik. Günter Lüling in Memoriam" organisiert wurde. Neun Monate nach seinem Ableben am 10. September 2014 stand Lülings Werk zum ersten Mal im Mittelpunkt objektiver wissenschaftlicher Auseinandersetzung, sachlich, kritisch, z. T. ablehnend, jedoch erstmals ernsthaft und jenseits von schlichtem Ignorieren oder billiger Polemik, frei von phantasievoller Mythenbildung und Verschwörungstheorien. Eine solche Auseinandersetzung war übrigens längst fällig, denn kaum ein anderer deutscher Islam- und Koranwissenschaftler sorgte mit seinen Thesen und den darauf folgenden akademischen und juristischen Reaktionen so sehr für Kontroversen und Medieninteresse und polarisierte die Fachkreise in den letzten dreißig Jahren des 20. Jahrhunderts so sehr, wie Günter Lüling es tat.

Wer war dieser Mann und was sind die zentralen Thesen seines höchst umstrittenen Werkes?

Günter Lüling wurde am 25.10.1928 als Sohn des konservativen evangelischen Pastors und Missionars Gerhard Lüling und seiner Frau Ilse, geb. Wilms, im bulgarischen Varna geboren. Pastor Gerhard Lüling war von September 1925 bis März 1935 hauptsächlich in Varna als Muslimenmissionar im Dienst des Frankfurter „Hilfsbundes für Christliches Liebeswerk im Orient" tätig. Zu seinen missionarischen Tätigkeiten gehörte u. a. die Entwicklung einer türkischen „Lesefibel mit bebilderten biblischen Geschichten." Nachdem die Nazi-Regierung die nötigen Mittel nicht mehr bewilligte, musste er seine Missionsarbeit in Bulgarien beenden und 1936 eine Pfarrstelle in Alt Belz bei Köslin in Ostpommern übernehmen. Von dort musste er nach kurzer polnischer Haft nach Braunschweig fliehen. Von 1946 bis zu seiner Pensionierung 1958 im Alter von 74 Jahren arbeitete er als Pfarrer der Braunschweiger Landeskirche. Danach widmete er sich im Ruhestand wieder eifrig missionarischen Tätigkeiten. Bis in sein hohes Alter hinein betreute er zum Protestantismus konvertierte türkische Muslime. Mit 96 Jahren starb er im November 1979.[1]

1 Die zusammengestellten Angaben zu Gerhard Lüling stammen aus zwei kurzen am 22.01.2013 datierten Berichten von seiner inzwischen verstorbenen Tochter Anneliese. Nach einer Mitteilung von Herrn Dr. Andreas Baumann, Geschäftsführer des Christlichen Hilfsbundes im Orient e.V., der Nachfolgeorganisation des oben erwähnten Hilfsbundes für Christliches Liebeswerk im Orient, vom 11.06.2018 lebte Anneliese Lüling in hohem Alter im Feierabendhaus für Missionarinnen in

https://doi.org/10.1515/9783110599176-001

Günter Lüling wuchs in einem konservativ-evangelischen, von missionarischem Engagement gegenüber Muslimen geprägten Elternhaus auf. Eigenen Angaben zufolge[2] besuchte er zwischen 1935 und 1939 die Grundschule in Bad Bibra in Thüringen und in Alt Belz. Darauf folgte bis 1943 der Besuch der Staatlichen Oberschule für Jungen in Köslin. Die Lülings waren keine Nazis. Günter Lüling lehnte es als 14-jähriger in Köslin ab, die Führerschaft der örtlichen Hitlerjugend zu übernehmen und wurde noch im März 1945, wenige Wochen vor Kriegsende, zu den Panzergrenadieren eingezogen.[3] Zum Kriegsende geriet er kurz in amerikanische Kriegsgefangenschaft. Nach seiner Freilassung erlernte er von 1945 bis 1947 das Maurerhandwerk in Braunschweig und Salzgitter. Im März 1949 bestand er die Reifeprüfung an der Großen Schule in Wolfenbüttel. Vom Sommersemester 1950 bis zum Wintersemester 1953/54 studierte er Evangelische Theologie, Klassische Philologie und Germanistik in Erlangen und Göttingen, wo er am 27.02.1954 das Theologische Examen mit der Gesamtnote „fast gut" bestand. Zu seinen „besonderen" Lehrern zählt er den Arabisten Hans Wehr, den Theologen Walther Zimmerli, den Theologen und Orientalisten Joachim Jeremias und den Religionshistoriker Hans Joachim Schoeps. Er fügt aber hinzu: „In dieser Zeit hat mich Martin Werner (Bern) ausschlaggebend beeinflußt."[4] Damit wird der erste ernsthafte Konflikt in Lülings Leben und Karriere angedeutet: aufgrund seiner anti-trinitarischen Ansichten konnte er damals weder den Kirchendienst antreten noch eine theologische Promotion anstreben.

Infolgedessen wechselte Günter Lüling das Fach. Vom Sommersemester 1954 bis zum Sommersemester 1957 studierte er in Erlangen Staatswissenschaften mit einem Zweitstudium der Soziologie im Hauptfach, Semitische Philologie mit Islamkunde und Religionsgeschichte im Nebenfach. Das Staatsexamen für Dipl. rer. pol. bestand er am 27.11.1957 mit der Gesamtnote „gut". Neben Schoeps und Wehr nennt er als besondere Lehrer in diesem Studienabschnitt den Soziologen Georg Weippert, den Juristen Gustav Clausing sowie die beiden Wirtschaftswissenschaftler Rudolf Stucken und Erich Thiess. Er erklärt weiter, dass in dieser Zeit „besonders die Sozialanthropologen Dietrich Bonhoeffer [sic!], Arnold Gehlen,

---

Waldwimmersbach. Die elektronische Mitteilung mit den angehängten Kurzberichten wurde mir von Herrn Prof. Dr. em. Stefan Wild (Universität Bonn) freundlicherweise zur Verfügung gestellt.

2 Die oben angeführten biographischen Angaben stammen aus dem von Günter Lüling am 07.06. 1973 angefertigten und unterschriebenen Lebenslauf, den er einen Tag später der Philosophischen Fakultät der Friedrich-Alexander-Universität Erlangen zusammen mit dem Antrag auf Einleitung eines Habilitationsverfahrens einreichte.

3 So gemäß brieflicher Mitteilung von Stefan Wild.

4 Zum Einfluss Martin Werners auf die Koranforschung Günter Lülings s. den Beitrag von Hartmut Bobzin im vorliegenden Band.

Adolf Portmann, Claude Lévi-Strauss und der Religionswissenschaftler Mircea Eliade“ ihn beeinflusst haben.

Im Sommersemester 1958 nahm Lüling in Erlangen das Studium der Semitischen Philologie mit Islamkunde im Hauptfach mit den Nebenfächern Soziologie und Religionsgeschichte auf und sollte mit einer Edition des arabischen pseudoaristotelischen Liber de pomo[5] promovieren. Die Nachricht von einer bereits vollendeten Edition des Werkes[6], der unerwartete Tod seines akademischen Lehrers Jörg Kraemer (1917–1961) und die darauf eingetretene Vakanz des Erlanger Lehrstuhls für Orientalische Philologie, der erst 1964 mit Wolfdietrich Fischer wiederbesetzt werden konnte, führten zu Lülings Abbruch des Studiums im Sommersemester 1961.

Am 01.01.1962 trat er den Dienst am Goethe-Institut an. Vom 01.09.1962 an war er drei Jahre lang Leiter des Goethe-Instituts in Aleppo. Zu Beginn des Wintersemesters 1965/66 nahm er seine Tätigkeit als wissenschaftlicher Assistent am Seminar für Geschichte der Medizin der Universität Erlangen auf mit der Aufgabe, in Zusammenarbeit mit dem Seminar für Orientalische Philologie „eine Editionsreihe alter arabischer, medizingeschichtlich relevanter Handschriften durch Vergabe entsprechender Dissertationen an arabische Medizinstudenten“ zustande zu bringen. Am 01.11.1967 übernahm Lüling die Assistentenstelle des Orientalistischen Seminars, wo er am 20. Februar 1970 im Hauptfach Islamwissenschaft mit Semitistik und den Nebenfächern Religionsgeschichte und Staatswissenschaften promovierte. Die danach folgenden, z.T. tragischen Ereignisse stehen im zitierten Lebenslauf nicht; ein Überblick darüber wurde infolge akribischer Erforschung von zahlreichen Dokumenten, u.a. Briefen, Gerichtsurteilen und wissenschaftlichen Gutachten, chronologisch rekonstruiert.[7]

In seiner Dissertation *Kritisch-exegetische Untersuchung des Qurʾantextes*, die erst am 10.11.1972 in Erlangen veröffentlicht wurde, vertritt Günter Lüling die Auffassung, dass beachtliche Teile des Korans spätere Rekonstruktionen von christlich-arabischen Hymnen seien, deren strophische Struktur in weiteren Tei-

---

5 Siehe: Jörg Kraemer, „Das arabische Original des pseudo-aristotelischen ‚Liber de pomo‘,“ in *Studi orientalistici in onore di Giorgio dell Vida*, Vol. I (Rom: Istituto per l'Oriente, 1956), 484–506. Der lateinische Text mit einer deutschen Übersetzung in: *Liber de pomo / Buch vom Apfel*. Eingeleitet, übersetzt und kommentiert von Elsbeth Acampora-Michel (Frankfurt am Main: Vittorio Klostermann, 2001). Weitere Angaben sind in: Maroun Aouad, „Aristote de Stagire: De Pomo,“ in *Dictionnaire des Philosophes Antiques*, Bd. 1 (Paris: CNRS, 1994), 537–541.

6 Eine solche Edition konnte ich bisher nicht finden.

7 Für umfangreiche Unterstützung dabei und überhaupt bei der Vorbereitung und Durchführung der oben erwähnten Konferenz möchte ich meinem damaligen Assistenten Herrn Dipl. Jur. Tibor Linke, M.A. meinen ausdrücklichen Dank aussprechen.

len des Korans noch erkennbar sind. Seine erstmals hier zum Ausdruck gebrachten Grundthesen führte er in seiner späteren umfangreichern Publikation *Über den Ur-Qurʾān*, erschienen 1974 im Erlanger Verlag seiner Frau Hannelore Lüling, weiter aus und versah sie mit zusätzlichen Beispielen.[8] Die in beiden Schriften vorgestellten Thesen lassen sich folgendermaßen knapp zusammenfassen:

- Der traditionelle Korantext verbirgt streckenweise „einen inhaltlich anderen, zum Teil in der Aussage ausgesprochen gegenteiligen Text, der sich aus einer Lesung des nackten Grundzeichentextes, des *rasm*-Textes, mit anderen Lesezeichen ergibt“[9]. Der dem Koran zugrundeliegende Text ist in jedem Fall poetisch verfasst und durchwegs strophisch gegliedert gewesen. Dieses Merkmal sowie grammatische, lexikalische und inhaltliche Kriterien werden als Schlüssel zur Wiederherstellung des Urtextes dargestellt. Der Ur-Qurʾān ist schon deutlich vor der Lebenszeit des Propheten Muhammad verfasst worden und hat seinen Ursprung in christlichen liturgischen Texten, die zum psalmodierenden Vortrag bestimmt waren.
- Der Korantext ist verwandt mit dem Strophenbau in den äthiopisch-christlichen Hymnen. Insbesondere ist die sog. „Šellāsē-Strophe“, ein Dreizeiler, im Koran nachweisbar. Zudem werden weitere, seltenere Strophenformen nicht ausgeschlossen.[10] Lüling verweist hier auf Adolf Grohmann [11], der festgestellt hatte, dass ein Teil der äthiopischen Hymnen nicht auf die inhaltlich parallel verlaufenden koptischen Hymnen zurückgeht, sondern auf eine arabische Übersetzung derselben. Weiterhin verweist er auf die Wahrscheinlichkeit, dass eines Tages die Vor- bzw. Nachstufe der koranisch-christlichen Hymnen aufgefunden werden würde.
- Im Gegensatz zum hochsprachlich gehaltenen Koran ist die Sprache des Ur-Korans das volkssprachliche Arabisch gewesen, das aus verschiedenen Richtungen auffallende Anklänge an das christliche Arabisch bietet. Dieses Arabisch ist eine christlich-arabische Koine, also eine Gemeinsprache, gewesen.

---

8 Während die Dissertation 185 Seiten umfasst, besteht das als Habilitationsschrift eingereichte Buch *Über den Ur-Qurʾān* aus 542 Seiten.

9 Günter Lüling, *Kritisch-exegetische Untersuchung des Qurʾantextes* (Erlangen-Nürnberg: Friedrich-Alexander-Universität Dissertation, 1970), VI.

10 Ebd., VIII.

11 Adolf Grohmann, *Äthiopische Marienhymnen.* Abhandlungen der philosophisch historischen Klasse der Sächsischen Akademie der Wissenschaften 33, No. 16 (Leipzig: Teubner, 1919) (insb. S. 10 ff. und 36 ff.). S. zu diesem Punkt die Kritik Holger Zellentins in diesem Band.

- Die vorgenommenen redaktionellen Umdeutungen am Ur-Koran bestehen in der abweichenden Vokalisierung des Grundzeichentextes (*ar-rasm*), der abweichenden Lesung von Konsonanten, der teilweise erfolgten Deformierung des Grundzeichentextes und in der Auslassung bzw. Hinzufügung oder Ersetzung einzelner Wörter, Sätze oder Abschnitte. Lüling nutzt in diesem Zusammenhang die schwankende Orthographie im Arabischen, die Konkurrenz verschiedener Bedeutungen eines Wortes im zeitgenössischen Hebräisch, Syrisch und Arabisch, die Umdeutung einzelner Wörter auf der Grundlage vager Assoziationen und schließlich die Missachtung grammatischer, insbesondere syntaktischer Normen, die dazu geführt haben soll, dass die Grammatik des „klassischen" Arabisch an den Koran angeglichen wurde, um nicht zur ursprünglichen Textbedeutung zurückkehren zu müssen.
- Infolgedessen gliedert sich der „überlieferte islamische" Korantext „in zwei Textarten, nämlich in zweitsinnige (dem Grundtext oktroyierte) Texte und einsinnige (originär-islamische) Texte". Lüling sieht in der von den islamischen Koranwissenschaften vertretenen Zweiteilung der Koranverse in „*mutašābihāt*" (gängig in „mehrdeutig" übersetzt) und „*muḥkamāt*" („eindeutig") eine Bestätigung seiner These.[12] Als ein Beispiel für die Umarbeitung des ursprünglichen Korantextes hebt Lüling hervor, dass „eine Fülle von Aussagen über das muslimische Paradies [...] ursprünglich negative Aussagen über den paganen Fruchtbarkeitshain" gewesen seien. Urkoranische Texte, die das „Heil in Christo" thematisieren, werden des Weiteren derart überarbeitet, „daß sie entweder positiv als auf den Qurʾān (statt auf Christus) bezogen wurden, oder aber mit (redaktionell hinzugefügten) negativen Vorzeichen versehen als gegen Gegner Muhammads gerichtet interpretiert wurden (so z.B. Sure 74,11ff)".[13] Unterschiedliche Lesearten des Korans stehen nach Lüling im Zusammenhang mit den verschiedenen Graden der Überarbeitung und könnten als eine Art verschiedener Auflagen verstanden werden.
- „Der überlieferte islamische Qurʾāntext ist das Endergebnis mehrerer aufeinanderfolgender redaktioneller Überarbeitungen."[14] Die formale Umarbeitung des Textes, d.h. die absichtliche Unkenntlichmachung des ursprünglichen Strophenbaues und die Umstilisierung der Sprache fand nach Lüling zur Lebenszeit Muhammads statt, nachdem dieser sich pagan-arabischen religiösen Vorstellungen annahm. Die Redaktionsarbeit ist in mindestens zwei

---

12 Q 3:7.

13 Günter Lüling, *Über den Ur-Qurʾān: Ansätze zur Rekonstruktion der vorislamisch-christlichen Strophenlieder im Koran* (Erlangen: Lüling-Verlag, 1974), 5–6.

14 Ebd., 9.

bis drei nachweisbaren Stufen vor sich gegangen. Die erste ist vor der Hinwendung Muhammads zum Heidentum geschehen und lässt sich nur andeutungsweise im Text feststellen. Die zweite Phase wird greifbar in der Polemik gegen die christlichen Gegner und in einer unverhohlenen „Verteidigung der heidnischen Positionen".[15] Die dritte Phase diente der formalen und inhaltlichen Verwischung der Auseinandersetzungen der zweiten Phase.
- „Die am Qur'ān gewonnenen Erkenntnisse werden durch eine Fülle außerqur'ānischer Nachrichten bestätigt, die bislang in ihrer Bedeutung nicht erkannt wurden oder unkritischerweise unbeachtet geblieben sind."[16] Lüling folgert, dass die gesamte frühislamische Primärliteratur von Grund auf in einem neuen Licht gesehen werden muss.

Methodisch hält Lüling eine ein- oder zweidimensionale Auseinandersetzung mit dem Korantext unter theologischen, religionswissenschaftlichen, philosophischen oder linguistischen Gesichtspunkten für inadäquat. Jede für seine Untersuchung relevante Koranstelle möchte er aus einer sich „für die Erschließung des Sinngehalts nützlich erweisenden Konstellation"[17] von theologischen, anthropologischen, religionswissenschaftlichen, dogmenhistorischen, überlieferungsgeschichtlichen, profanhistorischen, literatur-kritischen, sprachgeschichtlichen, morphologischen, syntaktischen, lexikalisch-etymologischen, metrischen sowie vers- und strophentechnischen Gesichtspunkten aus überprüfen.

In der Dissertation rekonstruiert Lüling die Passagen Sure 96:1–19, Sure 80:1–22, Sure 89 und Sure 101, um den strophisch-christlichen Hintergrund des Korans aufzuzeigen. Darüber hinaus behandelt er die behauptete Umdeutung des in den ursprünglichen Texten bekämpften paganen heiligen Hains zum muslimischen Paradies. Dafür wählt er den arabischen Ausdruck *ṯubūr* und die arabische Wurzel *z-l-f*. Der Begriff *ṯubūr* sei nach Lüling eine Umdeutung des Begriffs *ṯabūr*. Zum Beleg seiner These zieht er die Belegstellen Q 84:11; 25, 13; 25,14 als Beispiel heran. Lüling identifiziert mit *ṯabūr* einen biblischen Topos, den Berg Tabor[18] und lehnt die klassische Deutung des Begriffs *ṯubūr* als „Ach- und Wehklagen" ab.[19] Dann wendet er sich der von ihm behaupteten Umdeutung der arabischen Wurzel *z-l-q* zu *z-l-f* in Bezug auf das Paradies zu. Er argumentiert, dass die frühen arabischen Philologen mit dem Wortstamm *z-l-f* nichts anfangen

15 Lüling, *Kritisch-exegetische Untersuchung*, XII.
16 Lüling, *Über den Ur-Qur'ān*, 13.
17 Lüling, *Kritisch-exegetische Untersuchung*, XIII.
18 Siehe die Evangelien nach Matthäus 7:1–9, 17:1; Markus 9:2–13; Lukas 9:28–36.
19 Ebd., 80.

konnten und führt im Zuge dessen einige Belegstellen auf, in denen andere Autoritäten *z-l-q* statt *z-l-f* gelesen hätten. Lüling sieht hierin ein Indiz für eine absichtliche Umdeutung des Wortstamms *z-l-q* im Koran.[20] Dabei verlässt Lüling bei der Ausarbeitung dieser Abschnitte durchaus nicht immer den Weg der muslimischen Tradition. Vielmehr bezieht er sich auf Überlieferungen der Lesart *z-l-q* in Sure 26:64 und 90 bei Ibn Masʿūd, Ubai b. Kaʿb und Ibn ʿAbbās.[21] Die Arbeit bricht schließlich auf der letzten Seite etwas unvermittelt ab, eine Zusammenfassung oder ein Schlusswort fehlt.

In seiner Habilitationsschrift *Über den Qurʾān* erweitert Lüling quantitativ den in seiner Dissertation abgesteckten Rahmen: Kapitel 1 bis 3 sind eine überarbeitete Fassung der Dissertation u. a. unter Berücksichtigung der Kritik des Münchner Semitisten Anton Spitaler; in Kapitel 4 und 5 werden weitere Koranpassagen unter Anwendung derselben Methode rekonstruiert. Neben den bereits genannten Stellen behandelt er hier hauptsächlich die Suren 55, 77, 78[22] und 74[23], geht zugleich auch auf viele andere Koranverse ein.[24]

In beiden Arbeiten wollte Lüling beweisen, dass der Islam in einem christlich geprägten Umfeld entstanden ist, dass die Verkündigung Muhammads eine Kontinuität ursprünglicher, unitärer christlicher Lehren darstellt, Teil davon eine Engelchristologie, die der Trinitätslehre diametral widerspricht. Er rekonstruiert Passagen im Koran, um seine Thesen zu beweisen. Es kommt ihm freilich zugute, dass das arabische Grundkonsonantenschriftbild (*ar-rasm*) Ambiguitäten zulässt und durch Buchstabenverschiebung und diakritische Veränderungen andere Wortbildungen erlaubt.

Was geschah nach Einreichung der Dissertation? Die Dissertation von Günter Lüling erhielt von beiden Gutachtern (Prof. Dr. Fischer, Prof. Dr. Kienast) das höchste Prädikat *eximium opus*. Besonders im fachlich gewichtigeren Erstgutachten von Wolfdietrich Fischer wird die bahnbrechende Bedeutung der Untersuchung hervorgehoben, weil „Lüling methodisch einen völlig neuen Ansatz [bietet], indem er den vorliegenden Korantext grundsätzlich in Frage stellt und so eine neue Basis für [...] Interpretationsmöglichkeiten gewinnt." Die bislang in der Koranforschung dominierende „einseitig philologisch-linguistische und normengrammatische" Methode genüge nicht, dem Korantext neue Interpretationen

20 Ebd., 74 – 151.
21 Ebd., 123 mit Weiterverweisung auf S. 104.
22 Lüling, *Über den Ur-Qurʾān*, 297 – 346.
23 Ebd., 347 – 400.
24 Im Rahmen seiner Behandlung von *ṭubūr/ṭabūr:* Q 84:11; 25:10 – 15, ebd., S. 189 – 230, von *z-l-q* / *z-l-f:* Q 81:13; 67:27; 50;31; 26:64, 90; 34:37, ebd., 231 – 289.

abzugewinnen, denn der Koran sei „in erster Linie ein religiöses, d. h. theologisch-dogmatisches Werk“. Hingegen verbinde Lülings komplexer methodischer Ansatz die Philologie mit theologisch-dogmengeschichtlichen Gesichtspunkten. Seine Rekonstruktionsversuche koranischer Suren „sind in den Grundzügen akzeptabel und beweisen, daß der methodische Ansatz zutreffend und äußerst fruchtbar ist.“ Im Hinblick auf die Schwierigkeit des Forschungsgegenstands „bedarf es gewiß noch vieler Forschungen und vor allem vieler Diskussionen von einzelnen Problemen“, „ein erster Anstoß“ in die Richtung musste jedoch gegeben werden, was Lüling in seiner Untersuchung leistet. „Bei aller Kühnheit der Rekonstruktionsversuche im Einzelnen bleibt [er] [...] im Rahmen des philologisch Begründbaren.“ Weiter heißt es: „Ob alle vorgeschlagenen Thesen in der jetzt vorgetragenen Form haltbar sind, muß weiterer Forschung überlassen werden. Gewiß werden sie Korrekturen erfahren. Sicher bleibt jedoch, daß der methodisch-kritische Ansatz richtig und weiterweisend ist. Die Arbeit stellt die Entstehungsgeschichte des Islam und die Dogmengeschichte des frühorientalischen Christentums in neue Dimensionen.“

Ich habe ausführlich aus Fischers Gutachten vom 06. Februar 1970 zu Lülings Dissertation zitiert, weil er die Bedeutung der darin enthaltenen Thesen richtig einschätzt, indem er ihnen die Funktion zuschreibt, eine neue exegetisch-kritische Untersuchung des Korantextes in Gang zu bringen. Lülings kühnen, allenfalls diskutablen Thesen und Interpretationen sollte der notwendige Raum gegeben werden, damit sie zur Initiierung einer grundlegenden Erneuerung der orientalistischen Koranforschung beitragen können. Das hatte Wolfdietrich Fischer also anfangs durchaus erkannt.

Fischer konnte sein positives Urteil über Lülings Untersuchungsergebnisse jedoch nicht aufrechterhalten. Denn während er in Erlangen Lülings Dissertation mit dem bestmöglichen Prädikat bewertete, hielt sie der damalige Münchner Arabist und Semitist Anton Spitaler (1910 – 2003) zur ungefähr gleichen Zeit rundum für eine Fehlleistung. „Zu sehr ist sie auf falschen Voraussetzungen und methodischen Mängeln aufgebaut.“ Dieses Zitat stammt aus einem verheerenden Gutachten Spitalers, das er der Universität Göteborg im Rahmen eines Berufungsverfahrens am 29. Januar 1970 vorlegte. Auf Anregung seines Doktorvaters W. Fischer hatte sich Lüling dort um den Lehrstuhl für die arabische Sprache, die Nachfolge Bernhard Lewins, mit einem großen Teil seiner im Entstehen begriffenen Dissertation als repräsentativer Schrift beworben. Spitalers Urteil darüber fällt vernichtend aus: der Verfasser verfüge nicht „in ausreichendem Umfang“ über „die formalen Voraussetzungen zur Bewältigung seiner Aufgabe [...] im arabistisch-philologischen Bereich [...]. Es konnte infolgedessen [...] darauf verzichtet werden, die von ihm mit unzulänglichem Handwerkzeug gewonnenen Ergebnisse [...] einer detaillierten kritischen Würdigung zu unterziehen.“ Lüling verändere „den überlieferten Korantext nach Gutdünken [...]. Eine kritische Prüfung der sich [...] ergebenden Folgerungen wäre [...] zwecklos. [...] Würde sich aber dennoch die eine oder andere These bzw. Hypothese des Verf. als richtig erweisen [...], so ließe sich dadurch die Arbeit nicht retten." Das Gutachten wurde später veröffentlicht.[25] Lüling reagiert scharf und teilweise polemisch auf Spitalers harte Kritik im Einzelnen in Endnoten in seinem *Über den Ur-Qurʾān*, S. 414–420.

Als Fischer später von der Beurteilung Spitalers erfuhr, beeinflusste ihn das offensichtlich stark.[26] Der Münchener Kollege war schließlich nicht nur älter als er, sondern damals auch von großem Einfluss und wurde von vielen Fachkollegen geachtet und gefürchtet. Er war überdies ein sehr konservativer Mensch, dessen Weltanschauung in fast allem der Lülings diametral widersprach. Nach der damals geltenden Habilitationsordnung der Erlanger Philosophischen Fakultät hätte eine mit dem Prädikat *eximium opus* bewertete Dissertation als Habilitationsschrift eingereicht werden können. Lüling tat dies nicht. Stattdessen bat er zweimal um Verlängerung der Frist zur Abgabe der Pflichtexemplare der Dissertation, bis er sie schließlich 1972 einreichte. Mit einer um mehr als den doppelten Umfang erweiterten Fassung, jetzt unter dem Titel *Über den Ur-Qurʾān*, versuchte er die *Venia Legendi* in den Fächern Islamwissenschaft und Semitische Philologie zu erlangen. Bei Einsicht in die Unterlagen war deutlich zu erkennen, dass er sich damit dem Rat seines Doktorvaters und Vorgesetzten Wolfdietrich Fischer widersetzte, der ihm mehrfach nahelegte, sich mit einer Abhandlung zu einem anderen Thema zu habilitieren. Lülings Versuch, die Habilitation mit einer umfangreicheren Schrift zum selben Thema der Dissertation zu erlangen, scheiterte, da es sich bei der eingereichten Habilitationsschrift nicht um eine „selbstständige, zum Zwecke der Habilitation verfaßte Abhandlung" i.S.d. § 6 der Habilitationsordnung handelte.[27] Die von der Fakultät bestellten vier Gutachter: Wolfdietrich Fischer (Erlangen), Helmut Gätje (Saarbrücken), Erwin Gräf (Köln) und William Montgomery Watt (Edinburgh) beantworten die Frage nach der Anerkennung der von Lüling eingereichten Schrift als Habilitationsleistung allesamt negativ. Die Habilitationsordnung kenne zwar den Sonderfall der Habilitation auf Grund der Dissertation, nicht aber den Fall einer erweiterten Dissertation zum selben Thema. Außerdem bemängeln die Gutachter der Habilitationsschrift durchweg, dass die Grundthesen und die Argumente Lülings nicht überzeugten:

---

25 S. dazu: Lüling, *Über den Ur-Qurʾān*, 414, Anm. 8. Mir liegt eine freundlicherweise von Prof. Lutz Edzard übermittelte Kopie des Gutachtens vor.

26 Später zeigte Lüling Verständnis für Fischers Position unter dem Druck Spitalers: Günter Lüling, *A Challenge to Islam for Reformation* (Delhi: Motilal Banarsidass, 2003), XVIII, Fußnote 3.

27 Habilitationsordnung der Philosophischen Fakultät der Universität Erlangen-Nürnberg von 1968.

Er liefere keine sicheren Beweise für die Existenz eines christlichen Ur-Korans oder arabisch-christlicher Hymnen vor dem Islam und könne nicht zeigen, dass Muhammad und seine Gemeinde solche Materialien in ihrem Sinn umgewandelt hätten; trotzdem formuliere er seine Thesen so, als ob sie bereits bewiesen wären. Am 04.02.1974 entschied sich die Philosophische Fakultät, die von Lüling vorgelegte Abhandlung nicht als Habilitationsschrift anzuerkennen und das Habilitationsverfahren abzuschließen. Lülings Beamtenverhältnis auf Zeit wurde bereits am 31.12.1972 beendet. Der durch alle gerichtlichen Instanzen ausgetragene Rechtsstreit endete am 31.10.1979 mit einem Urteil des 7. Senats am Bundesverwaltungsgericht, in dem die Entscheidung der Fakultät bestätigt wurde. Formaljuristisch verlor Lüling den Fall, er wurde nicht habilitiert, seine akademische Karriere endete kläglich, bevor sie richtig beginnen konnte.

Der Intention, christliche Ursprünge des Islam nachzuzeichnen, entspringt ebenfalls die Untersuchung *Der christliche Kult an der vorislamischen Kaaba als Problem der Islamwissenschaft und christlichen Theologie*, erschienen 1977 in Erlangen. Auf frühere Arbeiten von Louis Cheikho und Tor Andrae gestützt vertritt Lüling darin die grundlegende These, dass die vorislamisch-arabische Dichtung echt sei und als Indiz für die Stärke des christlichen Einflusses im vorislamischen Zentralarabien dienen könne. Mit Bezug auf seine eigene Abhandlung *Über den Ur-Qurʾān* verweist er erneut darauf, dass der Koran mit der in ihm enthaltenen vorislamischen christlich-arabischen Literatur die Existenz eines vorislamischen zentralarabischen Christentums beweist. Die Architektur der Kaaba in Mekka sei Zeuge für die Christlichkeit des vorislamischen Kultes. Darin ließen sich Spuren einer christlichen Kirche entdecken, wie etwa die ursprüngliche Nord-West-Ausrichtung der Kaaba, welche zudem eine Apsis besessen haben soll.[28] Die Kaaba sei ausschließlich Ort des christlichen Kultes gewesen. In den islamischen Quellen sei die Entstehungsgeschichte des Islam umgedeutet worden. Grund dafür sei die Ablehnung des hellenistischen Dogmas der Christen und deren Christologie und Mariologie sowie des Heiligen- bzw. Bilderkultes gewesen. Als Beweis führt Lüling u. a. Johannes von Damaskus auf, welcher unmissverständlich darstelle, dass die Muslime die Christen als Hetäristen, d. h. *mušrikūn*, „Beigeseller", bezeichneten, weil sie Gott andere Götter beiordnen würden.[29] Dementsprechend seien die koranischen *mušrikūn*, Beigeseller, nicht pagane Heiden, sondern Christen wegen ihrer Trinitätslehre. Die Umdeutung der islamischen Frühgeschichte sei im poli-

28 Günter Lüling, *Der christliche Kult an der vorislamischen Kaaba als Problem der Islamwissenschaft und christlichen Theologie* (Erlangen: Lüling-Verlag, 1977), 49.
29 Ebd., 56.

tisch-dogmatischen Interesse der politischen Herrscher nach dem Tode des Propheten Muhammad geschehen. Diese hätten quasi in Notwehr gehandelt, da sie nicht die Mittel gehabt hätten, dem hellenistischen Christentum sein theologiegeschichtliches und dogmatisches Unrecht nachzuweisen. Denn „der Verzicht auf eine Auseinandersetzung mit der eigenen christlichen Vergangenheit hat natürlicherweise zugleich auch den Verzicht auf die Auseinandersetzung mit der jüdischen Vorgeschichte mit sich gebracht. [...] daher hat der Islam sowohl die eine Quelle seines geistigen Herkommens, das antitrinitarische Judenchristentum, als auch die andere Quelle, die Traditionen des semitischen Paganismus [...], die 'Religion Abrahams', versiegen lassen."[30]

Die Rückkehr des Propheten Muhammad zur Religion Abrahams – Lüling setzt sie gleich mit der Rückkehr zum archaischen Denken – „bedeutet modern und als Kritik an der überlebten Theologie der hellenistisch-christlichen Kirchentradition formuliert, dass es im globalen Horizont modernen, vernünftigen Denkens abgelehnt werden muss, dass christliche Theologie alle dem Christusgeschehen [...] in allen Zeiten und Erdteilen im Prinzip gleichenden Weltdeutungskonzepte", disqualifiziere.[31] Lüling meint also, dass sich der Islam diese historisch-kritische Rückbesinnung auf seine Urquellen leisten und sich so aus der selbstverschuldeten geistigen Selbstisolierung befreien und damit zugleich den Tendenzen moderner Wissenschaft zu einem Sieg über die reaktionären Kräfte in der Wissenschaft verhelfen könne.[32]

Dass im Zuge neuer Interpretation der Anfänge des Islam auch Kritik am christlichen Abendland, vor allem der institutionalisierten christlichen Theologie und Islamwissenschaft, formuliert werden kann, zeigt Lüling erneut in seinem Buch *Die Wiederentdeckung des Propheten Muhammad* von 1981 mit dem bezeichnenden Untertitel *Eine Kritik am „christlichen" Abendland.*[33] Auf S. 331, Anm. 5 dieses Buches stellt Lüling fest: „Unsere Kritik bezieht sich natürlicher Weise insbesondere auf die kirchlichen und theologischen Verhältnisse des bundesrepublikanischen Westdeutschland." Und weiter: „In dieser Situation will diese Abhandlung der seit langem präzisierten aber bislang unterdrückten wissenschaftlichen Kritik am abendländischen Christentum – und damit am Kern der abendländischen Gesellschaft – dadurch allgemeinere Aufmerksamkeit, größeres Gewicht und breitere Wirkung verschaffen, daß sie auf Grund der in Generationen von dogmenkritischen Protestanten erarbeiteten selbstkritischen Erkenntnisse

---

30 Ebd., 66.
31 Ebd., 76–77.
32 Ebd., 78.
33 Günter Lüling, *Die Wiederentdeckung des Propheten Muhammad. Eine Kritik am „christlichen" Abendland* (Erlangen: Lüling-Verlag, 1981).

über die Fehlentwicklung des hellenistisch-christlichen Dogmas das *erkennbare Recht des Propheten Muhammad* in seiner Verteidigung *urchristlicher Theologie* gegenüber dem hellenistisch-christlichen Dogma des Abendlands aufzeigt."[34] Und weiter: „Die Einladung an den Islam, an einer allgemeinverbindlichen wissenschaftlichen Kritik des abendländischen Christentums teilzunehmen, ist also zugleich eine Aufforderung an den Islam, die Verfälschung seines eigenen orthodoxen, nachprophetischen Geschichtsbildes zu erkennen und das wahre Bild vom Denken und Wirken seines auch unter wissenschaftlich-objektiven Gesichtspunkten wahrhaft großen Propheten wieder freizulegen."[35] In diesem Sinn versucht Lüling in diesem Buch des Weiteren zu zeigen, dass eine urchristliche Engelschristologie im Koran erhalten sei. Er präsentiert darin den Propheten Muhammad als den „bestens informierte[n] letzte[n] Kämpfer für die vom hellenistisch-christlichen Abendland um imperialistischer Interessen willen verlassene urchristliche Vorstellung von Christus".[36]

Als die bereits genannten Bücher veröffentlicht wurden, hatte der Fall Lüling juristisch schon hohe Wellen geschlagen und für viel Aufmerksamkeit gesorgt. Die schwere Krise, die Lüling durchmachen musste, hatte massiven Einfluss auf sein Schaffen: Es wurde davon definitiv beeinträchtigt, gleichzeitig aber auch sogar beflügelt. Trotz weitgehender Mittellosigkeit konnte er hartnäckig und zäh seine Bücher und Aufsätze weiter publizieren. Seine wichtigste Helferin war freilich seine Frau. In dem nach ihr genannten Verlag konnten seine Bücher erscheinen. Lülings Thesen wurden über Jahrzehnte von der deutschen Arabistik, Semitistik und Islamwissenschaft weitgehend totgeschwiegen.[37] So lässt sich beispielsweise beobachten, dass Spitalers Schülerin Angelika Neuwirth in einer Bestandsaufnahme der neueren Koranforschung auf dem XXI. Deutschen Orientalistentag 1980 (veröffentlicht 1983) Günter Lüling mit keinem Wort erwähnt.[38]

---

34 Ebd., 20 f. Die kursiv gesetzten Worte sind im Original in Sperrung.
35 Ebd., 22.
36 Ebd., 89. S. zu den oben erwähnten Ansichten Lülings den Beitrag von Klaus von Stosch in diesem Band.
37 Für einen Überblick über Rezensionen zu Lülings Büchern s. unten den Beitrag von Marianus Hundhammer.
38 Angelika Neuwirth, „Zum neueren Stand der Koranforschung," in *XXI. Deutscher Orientalistentag, vom 24. bis 29. März 1980 in Berlin, Supplement 5*, Hg. Fritz Steppat (Wiesbaden: Franz Steiner Verlag, 1983), 183–189. Lüling veröffentlichte 1984 eine äußert negative Besprechung der Habilitationsschrift von Angelika Neuwirth in der *Zeitschrift für Religions- und Geistesgeschichte* 36 (1984): 56–67. Im „Preface" seines bereits erwähnten Buches *A Challenge to Islam for Reformation*, XI–LXVIII, besonders S. XVIIIf., Fußnote 4, attackiert Lüling A. Neuwirth und ihren Lehrer A. Spitaler vehement.

Auch in ihrem Beitrag zum Koran in dem von Wolfdietrich Fischer herausgegebenen *Grundriss der arabischen Philologie* von 1987 taucht Lülings Name nicht einmal auf. Lüling galt in der gängigen deutschsprachigen Islam- und Koranforschung lange als ein querdenkender Außenseiter, dessen Thesen völlig falsch und daher nicht diskussionswürdig seien. Der zu jener Zeit bedeutendste deutsche Koranforscher Rudi Paret behandelt Lüling beiläufig und erklärt seine Thesen für abwegig.[39] Paret hatte übrigens abgelehnt, als Gutachter in Lülings Habilitationsverfahren zu fungieren mit der Begründung, dass er Lülings Thesen kenne, sie aber nicht für einschlägig halte und aus diesem Grund nur zu einem negativen Urteil gelangen könnte. In manchen Bibliographien fand Lülings Hauptwerk *Über den Ur-Qur'ān* Erwähnung.[40] Erst nach Veröffentlichung einer wiederum erweiterten englischen Übersetzung von *Über den Ur-Qur'an* unter dem Titel *A Challange to Islam for Reformation* (2003) stießen Lülings Thesen auf größeres Interesse im englischsprachigen Raum. In einigen Artikeln der *Encyclopaedia of the Qur'ān*, verfasst u. a. von Angelika Neuwirth, wird er kurz erwähnt. Auch in der deutschsprachigen Wissenschaft können in jüngster Zeit ähnliche Entwicklungen beobachtet werden.[41] Neuwirth geht auf Lüling in ihrem Buch *Der Koran als Text der Spätantike* von 2010 kurz ein.[42] Dass bisher keine angemessene Auseinandersetzung mit dem Werk Günter Lülings stattfinden konnte, regte zu dem Symposium an, dessen Beiträge dieser Band umfasst. Er soll einen wissenschaftlich-redlichen Umgang mit der Methode, den Thesen und Forschungsergebnissen von Günter Lüling bieten.

Dafür sprechen zahlreiche Gründe. Zunächst ruft der Gegenstand von Lülings wissenschaftlichem Interesse, der Korantext selbst, dazu auf, ja er drängt diejenigen, die sich mit ihm wissenschaftlich auseinandersetzen, regelrecht dazu, sich mit Lülings kühnen Thesen ernsthaft zu befassen: Ein in der ihn bewahrenden Tradition als göttliche Offenbarung verehrter Text, der unterschiedliche Entwicklungsschichten aufweist und eine heterogene Fülle früherer Ideen und Vorstellungen hellenistisch-orientalischer Religionen und Weltanschauungen der Spätantike in sich birgt, deutlich übernimmt, verändert oder negiert; der theologische, politische, gesellschaftliche und historische Diskurse unmittelbar offenlegt oder indirekt andeutet; dessen Sprache fasziniert, abstößt, zu Rätselraten

39 Rudi Paret, *Der Koran: Kommentar und Konkordanz* (Stuttgart: Kohlhammer Verlag, 1971).
40 Wie z. B. unter weiterführender Literatur in Hartmut Bobzin, *Der Koran. Eine Einführung* (München: Beck, 2000).
41 So wird z. B. Lülings Deutung der koranischen Entstehung von Reinhard Schulze in seinem Buch *Der Koran und die Genealogie des Islam* (Basel: Schwabe, 2015), 324–327, berücksichtigt.
42 Angelika Neuwirth, *Der Koran als Text der Spätantike* (Frankfurt: Verlag der Weltreligionen, 2010), 96–98.

einlädt und von Mehrdeutigkeiten behaftet ist. Der Koran fordert die Wissenschaftler, die sich mit ihm beschäftigen, heraus, mit Mut und Kühnheit an ihn heranzutreten, multiple Methoden einzusetzen und sich tiefschürfender Fragestellungen zu bedienen, wenn sie ihr hermeneutisches Geschäft ernstnehmen. Angesichts der koranischen Herausforderung sind alle für die Aufgabe einer kritischen Hermeneutik relevanten Disziplinen gleichberechtigt, in gegenseitiger Anerkennung zu diesem Unterfangen beizutragen. Dem Koran Erkenntnisse über seinen theologischen, kultischen, kulturellen, politischen, sozialen und literarischen Entstehungskontext, über den Prozess seines Werdens, seine dunklen Stellen, und über den frühen Islam mittels kritischer Hermeneutik abzugewinnen, ist nach wie vor ein wissenschaftliches Desiderat, dessen Erfüllung ein langwieriger komplexer Prozess ist, bei dem die Wissenschaft ziemlich noch am Anfang steht und auf Denkimpulse, methodische Anregungen und interdisziplinäre Herangehensweisen angewiesen ist. Günter Lüling gehörte zu den ersten Wissenschaftlern, die sich bei der Annäherung zum Korantext auf dem Kreuzweg der Disziplinen positionierten.

Auch die wissenschaftlichen Leistungen von Günter Lüling verdienen an und für sich kritische Würdigung. Er war ergriffen von dem, was er für wahr hielt. Er glaubte fest an die Wahrheit der Erkenntnisse, die er erlangte und wollte sich nicht auf Kompromisse einlassen. Das erschwerte offensichtlich die Kommunikation mit ihm über seine Thesen und wie er sie zu belegen versuchte. Er war jemand, der religiöse Dogmen, nicht nur im Islam und Christentum, gleichermaßen skeptisch radikalem Hinterfragen unterziehen wollte. Mit einem unbeirrt, quasi missionarischen Eifer sah er seine wissenschaftliche Aufgabe darin, durch eine brisante Mischung aus heftiger Kritik an westlich-christlicher Theologie zum einen, und zugespitzter Polemik gegen die islamische Tradition zum anderen, Muhammad als einen christlichen Theologen zu präsentieren, der gegen das trinitarische Christentum eine ur-christliche Lehre des reinen Unitarismus durchsetzen wollte.

Gleichzeitig war in Lüling die Faszination am Neuen, koranexegetisch Revolutionären so stark verankert, dass er der in Deutschland etablierten Orientalistik unangenehm wurde. Vor allem die deutsche Koranforschung, die seit den großen Leistungen Theodor Nöldekes über die Forschungen der folgenden Generationen seiner unmittelbaren und indirekten Schüler bis in unsere Zeit hinein den überlieferten Korantext philologisch nüchtern unter kritischer Berücksichtigung von muslimischer Historie und mithilfe literarischer Analyse zum Gegenstand sorgfältiger Untersuchung machte, fand in Lülings Forschungsmethode und den daraus resultierenden Ergebnissen einen Stein des Anstoßes. Lülings ungewöhnlich kühne Thesen stellten sich als „reine paradigmazerstörende Forschung“ dar, wie es ein Rezensent drastisch formulierte.[43] Nicht nur der überlieferte Korantext sollte damit auf den Kopf gestellt werden, sondern auch die bisher übliche Art, mit dem Koran wissenschaftlich umzugehen. Aus Sicht der etablierten Koranforscher musste Lüling deshalb gestoppt werden. Und in der Tat wurde damals von einem Spitaler-Schüler nach eigener Angabe der Spruch in die Welt gesetzt: „Stop Lüling now!“ Den einflussreichen Orientalisten in Deutschland ging Lüling zu weit mit seinen Behauptungen, der Koran bestehe z.T. aus Rekonstruktionen vorkoranischer christlich-arabischer Strophen, die Kaaba sei eine Kirche gewesen, Muhammads neue Religion sei aus seiner Wende von einer Form des Judenchristentums zu einem Paganismus der besonderen Art hervorgegangen usw. usw.[44]

Auf der anderen Seite blieb Lüling so manche Antwort schuldig. Nicht all seine Behauptungen überzeugen; seine philologischen Vorschläge sind meistens phantasievoll überzogen oder nach heutigem Kenntnisstand sogar falsch. Die Existenz einer christlich-arabischen Literatur aus vorislamischer Zeit ist genauso wenig belegt wie die Existenz einer arabischen Bibelübersetzung vor dem Islam. Die religiöse Gemengelage im vor- und frühislamischen Arabien liegt bislang weitgehend im Dunkeln; man kann darüber bestenfalls mutmaßen. Die ohnehin erst im zweiten islamischen Jahrhundert entstandenen Quellen geben Auskunft über christliche Formen in und um Mekka. Die islamischen Quellen, einschließlich des Korans, vermitteln den Eindruck, die religiöse Bewegung Muhammads sei einem christlichen oder jüdisch-christlichen Kontext entsprungen, ähnlich wie Jesus aus dem Judentum hervorgegangen ist. Das islamische und nicht-islamische Überlieferungsmaterial reicht jedoch nicht aus, um im Koran einen christlich-arabischen Ur-Koran verborgen zu sehen, dessen Herausarbeitung die ganze bisherige Koranforschung revolutionieren würde. Vom Reiz eines solchen Unternehmens war Lüling aber durch und durch ergriffen, während seine Gegner darin eine Erschütterung des ihnen genehmen wissenschaftlichen Status quo der Koranforschung sahen. Deutschland war nie das Land großer Revolutionen. Lüling entfaltete seine provokanten Thesen im falschen Land zum falschen Zeitpunkt.

---

43 Erhart Kahle, „Rezension zu *Über den Ur-Qur'ān*,“ *Zeitschrift der Morgenländischen Gesellschaft 132* (1982): 182–184, hier S. 182.

44 In einer brieflichen Mitteilung von Stefan Wild am 07.06.2018 heißt es: „Es muss zu denken geben, dass die wissenschaftlichen Kollegen im englisch- und französisch-sprachigen Raum die Lüling'schen Texte bedeutend weniger hart attackierten als seine deutsch-sprachigen Kollegen, und dass auch eine Anzahl in namhaften deutschen Zeitungen erschienene Kritiken seiner Bücher nicht nur so rigoros urteilten wie die deutschen Experten, sondern auch Positives darin entdeckten. Ein wichtiger Durchbruch waren dabei seine in englischer Sprache publizierten Werke.“

Die revisionistischen Thesen von John Wansbrough[45] sowie Patricia Crone und Michael Cook[46], die nur wenige Jahre später veröffentlicht wurden, erfuhren ein anderes Schicksal, obwohl sie nicht weniger gewagt sind. Auch das Werk von Christoph Luxenberg konnte zum Beginn des dritten Jahrtausends ausführlich diskutiert werden, obwohl es über weite Strecken jegliche solide philologische Grundlage vermissen lässt.[47] Lülings Werk hätte es eher verdient, Gegenstand ernsthafter wissenschaftlicher Auseinandersetzung zu werden, die seine Stärken und Schwächen sachlich analysiert.

Trotz nicht wegzuwischender Ungereimtheiten in Lülings Rekonstruktion von koranischen Passagen muss ihm zugutegehalten werden, dass seine Suche nach einem christlich-arabischen Hintergrund des Korantextes richtungsweisend war, wie Jahrzehnte nach der Veröffentlichung seiner Werke begonnene Projekte und publizierte Bücher deutlich machen.[48] Mit seinen Arbeiten hat Lüling darüber hinaus die islamwissenschaftliche Behandlung des Korans zu anderen Fachdisziplinen hin geöffnet. Seine Thesen erwiesen sich interessant für christliche Theologien, Byzantinisten und Historiker des christlichen Orients. Auch hier hat er Pionierarbeit geleistet. Er gehört zu den ersten Islamwissenschaftlern, die im Zuge der Beschäftigung mit dem Koran und der Entstehung des Islam tragfähige Brücken zu anderen wissenschaftlichen Disziplinen schlugen. Die Verbindung von philologischer Akribie, breitem religionsgeschichtlichen Spektrum und historischen Konstellationen ist ein markantes Zeichen seiner Arbeiten, das die Koranforschung in dem Maße nach wie vor vermisst.

Dass Lülings Werk nach wie vor unterschiedliche, z.T. widersprüchliche Urteile sowie harte Kritik hervorruft, demonstrieren deutlich die im vorliegenden Band gesammelten Beiträge. Nach einem von persönlicher Erfahrung mit Günter Lüling als Lehrer geprägten Beitrag von Fred Donner stellt Hartmut Bobzin die Einflüsse von Martin Werner und Albert Schweitzer auf die Entwicklung von Lülings religionsgeschichtlichem Denken dar. Im Anschluss an Lülings Forschungen diskutiert Sidney Griffith spätantike Christologien aus koranischer

45 John Wansbrough, *Quranic Studies: Sources and Methods of Scriptural Interpretation* (Oxford: Oxford University Press, 1977); ders. *The Sectarian Milieu: Content and Composition of Islamic Salvation History* (Amherst: Prometheus Books, 1978).

46 Patricia Crone and Michael Cook, *Hagarism: The Making of the Islamic World* (London [u.a.]: Cambridge University Press, 1977).

47 Christoph Luxenberg, *Die Syro-aramäische Lesart des Korans: Ein Beitrag zur Entschlüsselung der Koransprache* (Berlin: Schiler, 2000). Lüling wird von manchen Kritikern als Ideengeber Luxenbergs gesehen.

48 So z.B. das Projekt *Corpus Coraniqum* an Berlin-Brandenburgischen Akademie der Wissenschaften und die jüngsten Publikationen von Angelika Neuwirth.

Perspektive und stellt fest, dass sich die koranische Polemik gegen den christlichen Glauben an Jesus von Nazareth als den Messias und Sohn Gottes weniger gegen griechisch-theologische Begrifflichkeit als homiletische Darstellungen dieses Glaubens in syrischen *mêmrê* richtet, die unter arabischen Christen vor dem Islam großen Einfluss genossen. Klaus von Stosch setzt sich kritisch mit Lülings Behauptung einer urchristlichen Engelchristologie im Koran auseinander. Gerald Hawting diskutiert Lülings Thesen zur Kaaba in Mekka und hebt hervor, dass Lüling in seinen Arbeiten auf signifikante Probleme in der Erforschung der vorislamischen Geschichte des islamischen Heiligtums hinwies, auch wenn er nicht in allen Fällen richtige Lösungen anbieten konnte. In ihrem Aufsatz gewinnt Cornelia Horn dem Werk von Günter Lüling hermeneutische Ansätze für den Bereich der Intertextualität und der interreligiösen Diskurse ab. Von Lülings skeptischer Herangehensweise an den Koran geleitet, beleuchtet Fred Donner die koranischen Begriffe *dīn*, *islām* und *muslimūn*, um daraus Schlüsse für die Identität der frühen Muslime zu ziehen. Die drei aufeinanderfolgenden Beiträge fallen in ihrer Behandlung des Lülingschen Werkes sehr kritisch aus. Marianus Hundhammer zeigt Schwächen in Lülings Methodologie und deren Anwendung. Unter Berücksichtigung jüdischer und christlicher Quellen unterzieht Holger Zellentin Lülings Rekonstruktion von Sure 96:1–19 rigoroser Untersuchung und zeigt seine falschen Deutungen. Gestützt auf einer kolometrischen Darstellung des Korantextes äußert sich schließlich Lutz Edzard negativ zu Lülings Deutung derselben Sure.

Die Vorbereitung der Konferenz war von intensiven Gesprächen zur causa Lüling mit aktiv Beteiligten und unmittelbaren Beobachtern begleitet, die mir Hinter- und Beweggründe mancher Entscheidungen erläuterten. Allen Gesprächspartnern, insbesondere Prof. Dr. em. Otto Jastrow, Herrn Ltd. RD a.D. Karl-Ernst Merker, Herrn Thomas A. H. Schöck, Kanzler der FAU Elangen-Nürnberg a.D., und Prof. Dr. em. Stefan Wild möchte ich für freundlichen und informativen Austausch danken. Die Philosophische Fakultät und Fachbereich Theologie stellte mir die umfangreiche Lüling-Akte vorbehaltlos zur Verfügung. Dem Dekan der Fakultät Prof. Dr. Rainer Trinczek danke ich für seine Unterstützung.

Bei der Vorbereitung des vorliegenden Bandes erhielt ich Unterstützung von meiner Wissenschaftlichen Mitarbeiterin Jarmila Geisler, M.A., und meinen studentischen Hilfskräften Frau Saskia Pilgram und Herrn Jonas Knoblach, wofür ich mich bedanken möchte.

Fred M. Donner

Günter Lüling (1928 – 2014) als Lehrer

Ich besuchte die Universität Erlangen während des Wintersemesters 1970 und des Sommersemesters 1971, um meine Ausbildung in islamisch-orientalischen Studien fortzusetzen. Ich hatte das Bachelorstudium in Orientalistik an der amerikanischen Princeton University schon 1965 angefangen (B.A. 1968), aber mein weiteres Studium war von dem Vietnamkrieg und von meiner damals unvermeidlichen Einberufung zum amerikanischen Militärdienst unterbrochen worden. Weil ich schon ziemlich gute Kenntnisse im Arabischen hatte, besonders dank eines Jahres intensiver Sprachausbildung im Libanon (1966 – 67), hatte ich an der Universität auch Deutsch studiert, weil mein Studienberater mir klar gemacht hatte, dass ich unbedingt Deutsch brauchte, wenn ich mit dem Doktorgrad in Islamwissenschaft promovieren wollte. Dieser Rat hat vielleicht mein Leben gerettet, und nicht nur in wissenschaftlichlicher Hinsicht: Als ich 1968 den amerikanischen Militärdienst antreten musste, glaubte ich, ich könnte den Vietnamkrieg vermeiden, indem ich als arabischer Linguist nach Asmara in Äthiopien geschickt würde, wo der amerikanische Sicherheitsdienst in jener Zeit Horchposten hatte, die die Militärrundfunksendungen der kommunistischen Regierung im Südjemen heimlich abhörten. Aber entgegen meinen Erwartungen hatte die amerikanische Armee damals zufällig einen Überfluss an Arabisten, aber es mangelte an Soldaten mit Deutschkenntnissen. Glücklicherweise wurde ich deshalb im amerikanischen Sicherheitsdienst als deutscher Linguist eingezogen, und

Der vorliegende Text ist eine erheblich erweiterte Version des ersten Teils meines Keynote-Vortrags beim Symposium „Kritische Koranhermeneutik", das vom 19.–20. Juni 2015 in Erlangen unter der Leitung von Prof. Dr. Georges Tamer stattgefunden hat. Der zweite, wissenschaftliche, Teil meines Vortrags erscheint in fast unveränderter Form separat in diesem Band. Der erste Teil in seiner Originalfassung, nach Äußerung meiner Dankbarkeit für die Einladung an die Universität Erlangen-Nürnberg und an Herrn Professor Tamer für die Einladung zu sprechen, enthielt manche kurze Erinnerungen an Günter Lüling, wie ich ihn durch mein Studium bei ihm vor 45 Jahren kannte; damals beim Symposium war es mir offensichtlich nicht möglich, ihm mehr Zeit zu widmen. Mit der Entscheidung, die Beiträge des Symposiums zu veröffentlichen, hat sich die Möglichkeit eröffnet, Ausführlicheres über Lüling zu schreiben, was, wie ich glaube, berechtigt und sogar empfehlenswert ist, weil ich wahrscheinlich der einzige seiner Schüler bin, welcher einer akademischen Karriere nachgegangen ist. Bei der Vorbereitung dieser Fassung konnte ich meine alten Notizbücher aus dem Unterrichtssaal leider nicht mehr finden. Ich habe aber meinen Briefwechsel mit Günter, der sich von 1985 bis 2006 erstreckt, nachgelesen. Diese Briefe hoffe ich im Archiv der Universität zu hinterlegen.

https://doi.org/10.1515/9783110599176-002

nach mehreren Monaten technischer Ausbildung zur U.S. Army Security Agency Field Station Herzogenaurach, etwa 8 km von Erlangen, geschickt.

Es war deshalb reiner Zufall, dass ich mich am Ende meines Militärdienstes im Sommer 1970 in der Nähe der Friedrich-Alexander Universität Erlangen-Nürnberg befand, und bald entdeckte ich, dass die Uni eine Abteilung für Orientalische Philologie hatte, und zwar eine berühmte, Erbin einer stolzen Tradition, welche zurück bis zu Friedrich Rückert (1788 – 1866), Dichter, Orientalist, und ehemaliger Vorstand der Abteilung, reicht (Rückert war Professor in Erlangen 1826 – 1841). Ich dachte, es wäre gut, meine praktischen Kenntnisse des Arabischen durch weitere Studien in der berühmten deutschen Tradition der Philologie und der vergleichenden Semitistik zu vervollständigen, und habe mich deshalb für das Wintersemester 1970 eingeschrieben.

Zufall war es auch, dass die zwei Semester, in denen ich die Universität Erlangen besuchte, dieselben waren, in denen Günter Lüling Unterricht angeboten hat; mein altes Studienbuch bestätigt mir, daß sein Kurs „Koran-Lektüre" hieß. (Leider kann ich mein altes Heft, mit Notizen zu seinen Unterrichtstunden, nicht mehr finden). Es war kurz nachdem Günter seine eigene Doktorarbeit abgeschlossen hatte, oder als er sie eben noch fertigschrieb. Wir waren wenige Studenten – ich erinnere mich mit Sicherheit nur an zwei andere – meine ehemalige Frau und einen pensionierten evangelischen Pfarrer, Herr Dr. Pastor Heinrich Ringel, der seine orientalistisch-arabistische Ausbildung in Erlangen viele Jahre vorher unter der Betreuung von Prof. Josef Hell (Rektor der FAU 1926 – 27) abgeschlossen hatte. Lüling, wie die anderen Kollegen in der Abteilung für orientalische Philologie, war sehr ermutigend, und für zwei Semester hat unsere kleine Gruppe verschiedene Suren des Korans gelesen, sie philologisch und theologisch ausgelegt und diskutiert.

Günter Lüling war ein sehr höflicher und netter Mensch, freundlich und ermunternd jedem Studenten oder jeder Studentin gegenüber. Er war auch sehr freigebig, trotz seiner beschränkten Umstände. Mehrere Jahre nach meiner Studienzeit mit ihm haben er und seine Frau Hannelore die Güte gehabt, mir Unterkunft anzubieten, als ich einen kurzen Besuch in Erlangen gemacht habe. Wir haben damals natürlich über seine Ideen und über die deutsche Orientalistik und seine unglücklichen Erfahrungen damit gesprochen, aber auch über die Geschichte Erlangens als „Hugenottenstadt" über die fränkische Umgangssprache, über seine Erfahrungen als Jugendlicher in den letzten Jahren des Zweiten Weltkriegs, über seine Zeit als Direktor des Goethe-Instituts in Aleppo, über Musik (er war ganz stolz darauf, dass er als Sänger einst Schuberts *Winterreise* aufgeführt hatte), und über vieles andere. Er war, trotz mancher schwierigen Lebenserfahrungen, kein verbitterter Mensch, sondern jemand, der immer das Positive im Leben sah. Auch in diesem Sinne war er ein vorbildliches Beispiel und ein guter Lehrer.

Im Unterrichtssaal war Günter lebhaft und begeisternd, und er hat meine Augen geöffnet für die Komplexität des Korantextes. Ich verstand zum ersten Mal, dass der Koran nicht einfach ein „offenes Buch" ist, sondern ein Text, der die tiefsten und faszinierendsten Themen und Probleme enthält. Ich hatte als roher Anfänger bisher keine Ahnung von diesen vielfältigen Aspekten des Korans gehabt. Er hat uns in eine ganze Reihe neuer Fragen eingeführt, und auf neue Wege hingewiesen, auf denen man sich dem Koran annähern könnte. Einen solchen Lehrer früh in seiner akademischen Ausbildung zu haben, ist für jeden ein glückliches Ereignis, weil es den Weg zu neuen Denkensmöglichkeiten und Originalität öffnet.

Günter Lüling hatte viele ungewöhnliche Ansichten über den Koran, wie jedermann jetzt weiß. Manche erscheinen im Rückblick problematisch, andere deuten positive Möglichkeiten an, wie man anhand der sorgfältigen Behandlung der Schwächen und Stärken in Lülings Arbeiten und Arbeitsweisen in den Beiträgen von Zellentin, Horn, und Hundhammer in diesem Band sehen kann. Ihre Analysen erlauben uns ein verfeinertes und ausgewogeneres Bild von Günters Arbeit zu erhalten.

Ich möchte hier noch einen besonderen Aspekt von Lülings Unterricht kurz unterstreichen. Im Gegensatz zu fast allen anderen Koranwissenschaftlern jener Zeit – um 1970 – erkannte Günter die Wichtigkeit von eschatologischen, und sogar apokalyptischen, Konzepten in der koranischen Gedankenwelt.[1] Es ist wohl bekannt, dass der französische Orientalist Paul Casanova schon am Anfang des 20. Jahrhunderts sein interessantes Buch *Mohammad et la fin du monde* verfasst hat,[2] in dem er einen apokalyptischen Anstoß als Triebkraft der neuen Gemeinde Muḥammads gesehen hat; seine Ideen wurden aber im Allgemeinen vernachlässigt, oder einfach mit Schweigen übergangen, und Islamwissenschaftler der nächsten Generation haben von seiner Arbeit kaum gesprochen – es sei denn, um sie als Beispiel eines idiosynkratischen und wahrscheinlich irreführenden Ge-

---

1 Ein typisches Beispiel der allgemeinen Vernachlässigung von Apokalyptik um 1970 ist William Montgomery Watt, *Bell's Introduction to the Qur'ān* (Edinburgh: Edinburgh University Press, 1970); Watt war ohne Zweifel einer der führenden Wissenschaftler seiner Zeit für die Erforschung von Muḥammads Leben und das Studium des Korans. Das Buch enthält ja eine kurze Behandlung des Themas „Jüngstes Gericht" (S. 158 – 62), welches z. B. eine vorläufige Liste der koranischen Termini für den Jüngsten Tag bietet: *yawm al-dīn, al-yawm al-ākhir, al-sāʿa*, usw., ohne aber irgendeinen Hinweis auf das Vorhandensein eines apokalyptischen Konzepts in der koranischen Gedankenwelt. Die Wörter „apocalypse", „apocalyptic" und sogar „eschatology" sind auch im Index des Buches nicht zu finden.

2 Paul Casanova, *Mohammad et la fin du monde, étude critique sur l'Islam primitif*, 2 Bde (Paris: P. Geuthner, 1911 – 1924).

dankengangs zu erwähnen.[3] Die Apokalyptik stand nicht im Mittelpunkt von Günters Unterricht – Brennpunkt war vielmehr die Frage der Wiederherstellung von dem, was er für die arabisch-christlichen Vorlagen des Korans hielt, und die philologische und theologische Umgestaltung des Texts. Ich erinnere mich auch nicht, ob Günter die Werke Casanovas im Unterricht besprochen hat oder nicht – ich glaube, er kam durch seinen Kontakt mit dem Theologen Martin Werner und durch sein Studium des frühen Christentums zu diesen Ideen. Aber ich erinnere mich wohl, dass Günter einmal über die Sure 101, *sūrat al-qāriʿa*, gesprochen hat, und sagte, daß *qaraʿa* „zerreißen" bedeutet und *al-qāriʿa* der Moment ist, in dem der Vorhang des Tempels in Jerusalem zerrissen wird, d. h. am Jüngsten Tag. Als junger Student ohne bedeutsame theologische Ausbildung habe ich damals die Wichtigkeit von Lülings wiederholten Erwähnungen des Jüngsten Tags nicht komplett verstehen können. Erst viele Jahre später „entdeckte" ich sozusagen für mich selber die Idee, dass der Prophet und die frühste Bewegung der Gläubigen vielleicht – wahrscheinlich, würde ich jetzt sagen – von eschatologischen, ja apokalyptischen Sorgen getrieben waren. Günter war aber schon 1970 auf den Spuren apokalyptischen Denkens im Koran.

In mancher Hinsicht also war Günter Lüling seiner Zeit voraus. Fast ein Jahrzehnt vor den Veröffentlichungen über den frühen Islam von Mitgliedern der „britischen Schule" (vor allem der Amerikaner John Wansbrough, die Dänin Patricia Crone, und der Engländer Michael Cook[4]), welche die Basis der traditionellen Sicht des Ursprungs des Islams erschütterten, hat Günter Lüling seine eigene weitreichende Herausforderung dieser Sicht vorgestellt. Freilich wurden manche seiner Ideen zurückgewiesen, aber in den letzten Jahren haben manche eine erneuerte Annahme gefunden, z. B. dass Teile des Qur'āns vielleicht auf vorislamische Vorlagen zurückgehen.[5] Seine innovativen Beiträge verdienen also weite Anerkennung als wichtige Schritte zu einem sichereren Verständnis des Ursprungs des Islams.

---

3 Das allgemeine Urteil der Arbeit Casanovas ist knapp zusammengefasst in der englischen Übersetzung von *Jean Sauvaget's Introduction to the History of the Muslim East: A Bibliographical Guide, Based on the Second Edition as Recast by Claude Cahen* (Berkeley and Los Angeles: University of California Press, 1965), 118–19, wo *Mohammed et la fin du monde* als „drawing conclusions which have not been widely adopted" abgelehnt wird.

4 John Wansbrough, *Qur'ānic Studies* (Oxford: Oxford University Press, 1977); Patricia Crone und Michael Cook, *Hagarism. The making of the Islamic world* (Cambridge: Cambridge University Press, 1977).

5 Zum Beispiel, siehe Patricia Crone, „What do we actually know about Mohammed?" *Open Democracy* (10 June 2008), gefunden auf: https://www.opendemocracy.net/faith-europe_islam/mohammed_3866.jsp. Sie erwähnt Lülings Idee, der Qur'ān sei „adapting or imitating ancient texts," und äußert das Urteil „there is much to be said for it."

Hartmut Bobzin

Martin Werner und Albert Schweitzer und ihre Bedeutung für die Arbeiten von Günter Lüling

Martin Werner und Albert Schweitzer – das waren zwei Männer, auf deren Werke sich Günter Lüling in seinen Arbeiten – vor allem zum „Urkoran"[1] – recht häufig berief. Dabei zitiert er jedoch Martin Werner wesentlich häufiger, – was schon mit der Widmung des „Urkorans" an Werner beginnt:

MARTIN WERNER
(*17.11.1887 †23.3.1964)
Professor für Dogmatik, Dogmengeschichte und
Geschichte der Philosophie zu Bern
ZUM GEDENKEN

Doch zunächst einmal: wer waren diese beiden Männer?

Martin Werner[2] ist wohl nur in Theologenkreisen bekannt. Und zwar war er einer der bekanntesten *liberalen* Theologen seiner Zeit. Sein Wirkungskreis blieb aber im wesentlichen auf die Schweiz beschränkt, genauer gesagt, auf die Universität Bern, an der er auch – bis auf ein Auslandssemester im Sommer 1913 in Tübingen[3] – seine gesamte Ausbildung absolvierte[4]. Werners theologische Bedeutung liegt, in aller Kürze gesagt, vor allem in zweien seiner Werke, und zwar in

---

1 Der folgenden Untersuchung liegt die 2., korrigierte Auflage zugrunde: Günter Lüling, *Über den Urkoran. Ansätze zur Rekonstruktion der vorislamisch-christlichen Strophenlieder im Koran, korrigierte jedoch im Haupttext (1–542) seitengleiche 2. Auflage* (Erlangen: Verlagsbuchhandlung Hannelore Lüling, 1993); vgl. dort im Register S. 527. Die erste, 1974 im gleichen erschienene Auflage hat übrigens einen sowohl in Wortlaut als auch in Schreibung leicht veränderten Titel: „Über den Ur-Qurʾān. Ansätze zur Rekonstruktion vorislamischer christlicher Strophenlieder im Qurʾān".

2 * 17.11.1887 Bern – † 23.3.1964 ebd. Vgl. zu ihm *Historisches Lexikon der Schweiz*, Bd. 13 (Basel: Schwabe, 2014), 411 (Max Ulrich Balsiger).

3 Vgl. H. Guggisberg, „Martin Werners Werk im Spiegel seines Briefwechsels," in *Weg und Werk Martin Werners. Studien und Erinnerungen*, Hg. F. Sciuto (Bern u. Stuttgart: Paul Haupt in Komm., 1968), 9. Während dieser Zeit lernte er Schweitzers Werk *Von Reimarus zu Wrede*, d. h. die erste Auflage des ab der zweiten Auflage *Geschichte der Leben-Jesu-Forschung* genannten Werkes kennen (s. u. S. 25), das für seinen weiteren Lebensgang von entscheidender Bedeutung werden sollte.

4 Und zwar von 1910 bis 1921.

https://doi.org/10.1515/9783110599176-003

dem 1941 publizierten Werk *Die Entstehung des christlichen Dogmas problemgeschichtlich dargestellt* [5] sowie dem zweibändigen Werk *Der protestantische Weg des Glaubens*, das 1955 und 1962 erschien[6].

Martin Werner wurde am 17.11.1887 in Bern geboren als Sohn eines Stadtmissionars. Nach einer Ausbildung zum Primarlehrer am evangelischen Seminar Muristalden in Bern[7] unterrichtete Werner in Heimenschwand (entfernungsmäßig ziemlich genau zwischen Bern und Interlaken) und bereitete sich dabei auf das Abitur vor. Mit dem Theologiestudium begann er 1910 in Bern. Ein Auslandssemester verbrachte er 1913 in Tübingen, wo er vor allem bei Adolf Schlatter[8] hörte. 1916 wurde er reformierter Pfarrer in Krauchthal (Verwaltungskreis Emmental des Kantons Bern). 1921 erlangte er den Titel eines Lic. theol. – wie damals der theologische Doktorgrad bezeichnet wurde, und im Jahr darauf folgte die Habilitation und er wurde Privatdozent für Neues Testament. Fünf Jahre später, also 1927, wählte ihn das Gremium des Berner Regierungsrates zum Professor an der Universität Bern, und zwar für die Fachgebiete systematische Theologie sowie Geschichte der Philosophie. In der Folgezeit war er sehr aktiv als Förderer der Volkshochschule und als Mitbegründer einer Bildungsstätte für soziale Arbeit. Daneben war er lange Zeit Präsident einer Fürsorgestelle für Alkoholkranke. 1945 wurde er Ehrendoktor der Universität Chicago.

Für Martin Werners Denken wurde die Lektüre der theologischen Werke von Albert Schweitzer von entscheidender Bedeutung, vor allem in dem, was in ihnen als „liberal" bezeichnet wird. Zur Begriffsklärung zitiere ich hier aus einem (ungedruckten) Vortrag von H. Zoss über „Martin Werner als Wegbereiter für das Denken Albert Schweitzers". Da heißt es: „Die liberale Theologie hat ihre Wurzeln in der Aufklärung. Es ist eine theologische Strömung im evangelischen Christentum. Sie betreibt Theologie auf Grund selbständigen, humanistischen und geisteswissenschaftlichen Denkens. Sie will dadurch unabhängig sein von Dogmen, kirchlicher Tradition und vorgegebenen Glaubensinhalten. Die liberale Theologie will ein offenes, befreiendes und tolerantes Christentum, ohne geisti-

---

5 Bern: Haupt 1941; 2. Auflage Bern: Haupt und Tübingen: Katzmann 1954. Eine Taschenbuchausgabe erschien 1959 im Verlag Kohlhammer, Stuttgart („Urban Bücher", Nr. 38), eine gekürzte englische Fassung in London 1957 im Verlag A. & G. Black sowie eine amerikanische Ausgabe im gleichen Jahr in New York im Verlag Harper & Brothers.

6 Bern: Haupt und Tübingen: Katzmann, 1955 – 1962.

7 Vgl. dazu Jacob Aellig, *Evangelisches Seminar Muristalden: Jubiläumsschrift 1854 – 1954. Ein Beitrag zur bernischen Kirchen- und Schulgeschichte* (Muristalden: Verlag des Seminars, 1954).

8 1852 – 1938. Vgl. zu ihm *Religion in Geschichte und Gegenwart. Handwörterbuch für Theologie und Religionswissenschaft*, vierte, völlig neu bearbeitete Auflage, Bd. 7 (Tübingen: Mohr Siebeck, 2004), 902. In bestimmten Kreisen des Protestantismus wird Schlatter nach wie vor viel gelesen.

gen Zwang. Sie will Glauben und Vernunft aussöhnen. Denken und Glauben widersprechen sich nicht." Diesem Ideal blieb Martin Werner zeit seines Lebens verpflichtet.

Demgegenüber ist Albert Schweitzer[9] weltweit berühmt geworden als *Urwalddoktor* in Lambarene (Gabun)[10], sodann als begnadeter *Organist* und *Bachkenner*[11], und schließlich als *Friedensnobelpreisträger*[12] und Denker der *„Ehrfurcht vor dem Leben"*, sowie als *Neutestamentler*, von dem zwei Werke nach wie vor zu *Klassikern* der Disziplin gehören, nämlich die *Geschichte der Leben-Jesu-Forschung* (1913 u. ö.) sowie *Die Mystik des Apostels Paulus* (1930) – beide erschienen übrigens im bekannten Tübinger Verlag von J. C. B. Mohr & Paul Siebeck. Auf beide Werke werde ich in meinem Vortrag eingehen, auf das *Leben Jesu* etwas ausführlicher, weil es eine weit größere Wirkung entfaltet hat als das Buch über Paulus. Allerdings möchte ich schon hier bemerken, dass das Wort „Klassiker" in diesem Zusammenhang so zu verstehen ist, dass man beide Bücher nicht mehr unbedingt benötigt, um sich über den heutigen Forschungsstand der neutestamentlichen Wissenschaft zu informieren. In der *Einleitung in das Neue Testament* des früheren Marburger Neutestamentlers Werner Georg Kümmel[13] (Heidelberg 1965 u. ö.) sind sie jedenfalls *nicht* genannt. Allerdings geht Kümmel ausführlich auf sie ein in seinem vorzüglichen Buch *Das Neue Testament. Geschichte der Erforschung seiner Probleme*[14].

Interessant ist nun die Begründung, warum Lüling sein Buch *Über den Ur-Qur'ân* dem Gedenken Martin Werners gewidmet hat:

> In erster Linie ist es der Wunsch, mit dem Verweise auf ihn sein [d. h. Werners; HB] grundlegendes Verdienst an der Gewinnung der hier vorgelegten islamwissenschaftlichen Forschungsergebnisse gebührend hervorzuheben. Dabei liegt sein Verdienst sowohl in den von ihm geschaffenen wissenschaftlichen Voraussetzungen, – jedoch auch die wesentlichen Voraussetzungen, die Hans-Joachim Schoeps[15] mit seiner „Theologie und Geschichte des Judenchristentums[16]" und anderen theologiegeschichtlichen Arbeiten schuf, müssen hier

---

9 * 14.1.1875 Kaysersberg/Oberelsaß – † 4.9.1965 Lambarene/Gabun.

10 Vgl. dazu Mary Woytt-Secretan, *Albert Schweitzer baut Lambarene* (Königstein: Langewiesche, 1959), („Die Blauen Bücher"), mit eindrücklichen Illustrationen.

11 Vgl. dazu Erich Gräßer, *Schweitzer, Albert*, in *Deutsche Biographische Enzyklopädie der Musik*, Bd. 2 (München, 2003), 791ff. (mit weiteren Literaturangaben).

12 Und zwar im Jahr 1952.

13 1905–1995; vgl. zu ihm Deutsche Biographie, https://www.deutsche-biographie.de/gnd118567640.html.

14 München/Freiburg: Karl Alber 1953; ^{2}1970. Zur Leben-Jesu-Forschung und Albert Schweitzers Beitrag dazu vgl. dort 298–309.

15 * 30.1.1909 Berlin, † 8.7.1980 Erlangen; vgl. *Deutsche Biographische Enzyklopädie* 9, 103.

16 Tübingen: J.C.B. Mohr, 1969.

> genannt werden! – als auch besonders in der Ermutigung, die er allenthalben durch sein Beispiel geduldiger Arbeit einerseits und *unerschrockenen Auftretens gegen reaktionäre Restauration* (Hervorhebung H.B.!) andererseits gegeben hat. Zum Zweiten ist ihm die Widmung deshalb zugeeignet, um in Anbetracht der zu erwartenden Auseinandersetzungen über die hier vorgetragenen islamwissenschaftlichen Thesen mit der Nennung Martin Werners und seines wissenschaftlichen Werkes die Basis des hier eingenommenen wissenschaftlichen Standpunktes zu bezeichnen, wie auch die Bestimmtheit, mit der dieser Standpunkt vertreten wird. (Seite V).

Doch nun zu Albert Schweitzer! Er hat eine *Autobiographie* geschrieben unter dem Titel *Aus meinem Leben und Denken*, die 1931 im Richard-Meiner-Verlag (Bern u. Leipzig) erschien. Seine Kindheit verlebte Schweitzer im Dorf Günsbach im Münstertal im Oberelsaß, wohin sein Vater kurz nach Alberts Geburt als Pfarrer versetzt wurde. Der Vater starb in hohem Alter im Jahr 1925. Schweitzers Mutter war bereits während des 1. Weltkrieges auf tragische Weise ums Leben gekommen, denn schon 1916 wurde sie von Militärpferden auf dem Weg von Günsbach in den Nachbarort Weier zu Tode getrampelt. Bereits im Alter von fünf Jahren – also ab 1880 – bekam Schweitzer von seinem Vater Klavierunterricht, und mit acht Jahren, als – wie Schweitzer schreibt – „die Füße lang genug waren, um die Pedaltasten zu erreichen“[17], begann er Orgel zu spielen. Mit neun Jahren durfte er zum ersten Mal in Günsbach den Organisten vertreten.

Im Herbst 1885 wechselte er auf das Gymnasium zu Mühlhausen im Elsaß. Er konnte dort bei seinem Onkel Ludwig Schweitzer und dessen Frau – sie waren kinderlos – unterkommen: andernfalls hätte er aus finanziellen Gründen das Gymnasium nicht besuchen können. In besonderer Weise gedenkt Schweitzer seines Klassenlehrers Dr. Wehmann, den er ab der Quarta (entspricht heute der 7. Klasse) hatte[18]. Dieser erzog ihn zum „richtigen Arbeiten“ und gab ihm „einiges Selbstvertrauen“. Schweitzer schreibt, dass er ihn „immer und immer wieder besucht“ habe. Aber, so schreibt er, „als ich gegen Ende des Krieges nach Straßburg kam, wo er zuletzt wohnte, und alsbald nach ihm fragte, erfuhr ich, daß er durch das Hungern nervenkrank geworden sei und sich das Leben genommen habe“ (S. 9). Auf dem Gymnasium war Schweitzer vor allem an Geschichte und Naturwissenschaften interessiert. Seine Schullaufbahn beschloss er mit einer eher mittelmäßigen Abgangsprüfung.

---

17 Albert Schweitzer, *Aus meinem Leben und Denken* (Stuttgart: Stuttgarter Hausbücherei, o. J., 7.) Nach dieser Ausgabe wird auch im folgenden immer zitiert.

18 Vgl. zu ihm Andreas Fritzsch, „Langzeitwirkungen eines altsprachlichen Unterrichts. Zum 30. Todestag von Albert Schweitzer,“ in *Mitteilungsblatt des deutschen Altphilologenverbandes* 3 (1995), 91 ff.

In Straßburg, wo er seit 1893 studierte, wohnte er im theologischen Studienstift (Collegium Wilhelmitanum[19]), das unmittelbar bei der Kirche St. Thomas gelegen war. Dessen Leiter war zur damaligen Zeit der überaus gelehrte Pfarrer Alfred Erichson[20], der während Schweitzers Studienzeit in Straßburg mit der Herausgabe der (z.T. noch heute gültigen) Ausgabe der Werke des Reformators Johannes (Jean) Calvin (1509–1564) beschäftigt war[21]. Daneben widmete sich Erichson besonders der Straßburger bzw. überhaupt der elsässischen Kirchengeschichte[22], und hier besonders der Reformationszeit. An Arbeiten bleibender Bedeutung von ihm möchte ich nennen: *Das Marburger Religionsgespräch über das Abendmahl im Jahre 1529 nach ungedruckten Straßburger Urkunden*[23], *Zwingli's Tod und dessen Beurtheilung durch Zeitgenossen*[24]; *'Ein feste Burg'. Entstehung, Inhalt und Geschichte des Lutherliedes dem protestantischen Volk erklärt*[25] und *L' Eglise Française de Strasbourg au seizième siècle d'après des documents inédits*[26].

Nebenbei möchte ich – vor allem für die Musikliebhaber unter Ihnen – noch erwähnen, dass Schweitzer in Straßburg an der Orgel in St. Thomas spielen durfte; gebaut worden war sie von dem berühmten süddeutschen Orgelbauer Andreas Silbermann[27], der seit 1701 in Straßburg ansässig war und dort 1713–16 auch die Orgel im Straßburger Münster erbaut hatte. An der Orgel in St. Thomas hatte einstmals übrigens auch Mozart (und zwar im Jahr 1778 auf dem Weg nach Paris) gespielt[28].

---

19 *Das theologische Studienstift Collegium Wilhelmitanum 1544–1894 zu dessen 350 jährigen* [sic] *Gedächtnisfeier* (Straßburg: J.H.E. Heitz, 1894).

20 1843–1901; vgl. zu ihm *Religion in Geschichte und Gegenwart*² II, 236.

21 Erschienen unter dem Titel: *Joannis Calvini opera quae supersunt omnia*. Vol. I – LIX, ediderunt Guilielmus Baum, Eduardus Cunitz, Eduardus Reuss et Alfred Erichson (Braunschweig und Berlin: C. A. Schwetschke und Sohn, 1863–1900).

22 Z. B. *Das Straßburger Universitätsfest vom Jahr 1621. Ein Rückblick am Tage der Einweihung der neuen Universitätsgebäude zu Straßburg, den 27. Oktober 1884* (Straßburg: C.F.Schmidt's Buchh. Friedrich Bull, 1884).

23 Straßburg, 1880 (ohne Verlagsangabe).

24 Straßburg: Schmidt, 1883.

25 Straßburg: Schmidt, 1883.

26 Straßburg: Schmidt, 1886.

27 1678–1734; vgl. zu ihm *Deutsche Biographische Enzyklopädie der Musik*, Bd. 2, Hg. Bruno Jahn (München: Saur, 2003), 804; vgl. ferner *Die Musik in Geschichte und Gegenwart*, Bd. 12 (München: Saur, 1965), 694 f.

28 Das geht aus einem Brief Mozarts an seinen Vater vom 26. Oktober 1778 hervor, vgl. dazu *Mozart. Briefe und Aufzeichnungen*. Gesamtausgabe, herausgegeben von der Internationalen Stiftung Mozarteum Salzburg, gesammelt und erläutert v. Wilhelm A. Bauer und Otto Erich Deutsch, Bd. II: 1777–1779, Nr. 503, S. 504: „ich habe auf die 2 hier besten orgeln von Silbermann

Schweitzers erstes Semester – so beschreibt er es in seiner Autobiographie – wurde durch das „Hebraicum" „verdorben", ich zitiere: „Da ich auf dem Gymnasium nur die *Anfänge* des Hebräischen gelernt hatte, wurde mir das erste Semester durch die Arbeit auf das „Hebraicum" (das Vorexamen in Hebräisch) hin verdorben, das ich am 17. Februar 1894 mit Mühe und Not bestand. Später, wieder durch das Bestreben angespornt, auch das mir *nicht* liegende zu bewältigen, eignete ich mir dann gediegene Kenntnisse in dieser Sprache an."

Mit dem Alttestamentler Karl Budde[29] besaß Straßburg übrigens einen vortrefflichen und in seinem Fach äußerst vielseitigen Professor, der u. a. durch seine zahlreichen Kommentare zu biblischen Büchern – zu ihnen zählt ein hervorragender Hiob-Kommentar (1896; 1913²) – bleibenden Ruhm erworben hat.

Für unser Thema wichtiger ist nun allerdings die damalige Besetzung der neutestamentlichen Lehrstühle. Die seit der Reformationszeit bestehende Straßburger sog. „Hohe Schule" (seit 1538) wurde erst im Jahr 1621 zur Universität erhoben[30]. Mit der Übernahme des Elsaß durch das Deutsche Reich im Jahre 1870 war der Universität die Möglichkeit eröffnet worden,

a) vielversprechende *junge* Gelehrte zu berufen – als Beispiel nenne ich hier den Semitisten und Arabisten Theodor Nöldeke[31], dessen Werk *Geschichte des Qorâns* – erstmals 1860 erschienen – bis heute das maßgebliche Grundwerk moderner Koranforschung geblieben ist[32], und
b) neue Wege im Fächer*zuschnitt* zu gehen – als Beispiel könnte hier genannt werden, dass der traditionell seit Universitätsgründung vorhandene Lehrstuhl für „Orientalische Philologie" in einen solchen für *Semitistik* umgewandelt wurde.

öfentlich gespiellt, in der lutherischen Kirchen; – in der Neükirche, und thomaskürche." [NB: Originalschreibung von Mozart!].

29 1850–1935; vgl. zu ihm *Die Religion in Geschichte und Gegenwart*, dritte Auflage, Bd. 1 (Tübingen: Mohr, 1957) Sp. 1468 f., *Neue Deutsche Biographie*, Bd. II, 714 ff. Daneben war Budde übrigens ein hervorragender Kenner des Malers und Zeichners Ludwig Richter (1803–1884).

30 Zur Geschichte der Universität Straßburg vgl. August Schricker: *Zur Geschichte der Universität Straßburg*, Straßburg 1872; zur älteren Universitätsgeschichte vgl. Anton Schindling, *Humanistische Hochschule und freie Reichsstadt. Gymnasium und Akademie in Straßburg 1538–1621* (Wiesbaden: Steiner, 1977) (= Veröffentlichungen des Instituts für europäische Geschichte Mainz, Band 77).

31 1836–1930; vgl. zu ihm Hartmut Bobzin, „Theodor Nöldekes Biographische Blätter aus dem Jahr 1917," in *„Sprich doch mit deinen Knechten aramäisch, wir verstehen es!": Festschrift für Otto Jastrow zum 60. Geburtstag*, Hgg. Werner Arnold und Hartmut Bobzin (Wiesbaden: Harrassowitz, 2002), 91–104; Bernhard Maier, *Gründerzeit der Orientalistik. Theodor Nöldekes Leben und Werk im Spiegel seiner Briefe* (Würzburg: Ergon, 2013) (= Arbeitsmaterialien zum Orient, Bd. 29).

32 Nachdruck der 2. Auflage 1970, Teile I – III (Hildesheim und New York: Georg Olms).

Der maßgebliche Straßburger *Neutestamentler* war zu Schweitzers Studienzeit Heinrich Julius Holtzmann[33], der hier von 1874 bis 1904 lehrte. In der Frage des zeitlichen Verhältnisses der drei synoptischen Evangelien zueinander (nämlich: Matthäus, Markus, Lukas) hat er 1863 in seinem Buch *Die synoptischen Evangelien*[34] die (zeitliche) „Priorität des Markusevangeliums und die Annahme einer eigenen Quelle (sog. „Logienquelle") als Grundlage der Reden bei Matthäus und Lukas (die sog. Zweiquellentheorie) erfolgreich vertreten"[35]. Eine weitere wichtige Veröffentlichung von Holtzmann war die 100seitige, im Jahre 1907 erschienene Schrift *Das messianische Bewußtsein Jesu. Ein Beitrag zur Leben-Jesu-Forschung*[36], die mit folgenden Worten beginnt:

> Ein rückläufiges Buch eines alternden Theologen. So wird man vielleicht da und dort empfinden und urteilen. Alt genug bin ich allerdings, um den Vor- und Rücklauf des Pendels an der Uhr unserer gemeinsamen theologischen Lebensarbeit in seiner konstanten Gesetzmäßigkeit soweit beobachtet und begriffen zu haben, als mit einer gewissen Sicherheit jeweils hier auf *Rückschläge*, dort auf *neue Anläufe* zu rechnen ist. Wie auf dem weitesten Kampffeld Metaphysik und Historismus, Deduktion und Induktion, vorauseilende Intuition und nachrechnende Reflexion sich abwechselnd gegenseitig verdrängen, so steigen auch am gesonderten Horizont der Spezialforschung immer dieselben Sterne auf und nieder. Wie steht es um Paulus? Ist er nicht *heute* der Mann unerbittlicher Konsequenz eines überall Zusammenhänge anstrebenden Denkens, *morgen* der unerschöpfliche Produzent religiöser Ergüsse und eruptiver Bekenntnisse, die man vielleicht auf Einheitlichkeit und Übereinstimmung ihrer Motive und Ziele, aber ja nicht auf logische Kompatibilität der jeweils zur Verwendung kommenden Vorstellungen und Begriffe ansehen und prüfen soll? Zuerst sind die Ausgänge seiner Gedankenwelt rein jüdisch gewesen, dann wurden sie zum guten Teil *griechisch*, weiterhin lieber *„hellenistisch"*, bald genug wieder *alttestamentlich* usw. Bald bildet er die geradlinige Fortsetzung des Lebenswerkes Jesu, bald einen dieses im Grunde ignorierenden neuen Anfang. Und nicht viel anders als um diesen „zweiten Stifter des Christentums" steht es um den ersten. Auch hier wechseln, und zwar nicht ganz ausser Zusammenhang mit jeweiligen theologischen Stimmungen, die auf Gesetzlichkeit oder Gesetzesfreiheit, auf Nationalismus oder Universalismus, auf Gegenwartshorizont oder Zukunftsperspektive lautende Urteile.

Als Schweitzer sich nun, wie er in seiner Autobiographie recht ausführlich beschreibt, „an einem Ruhetage im Dorfe Guggenheim mit dem 10. und 11. Kapitel

---

33 1832–1910; vgl. zu ihm Werner Georg Kümmel, *Das Neue Testament. Geschichte der Erforschung seiner Probleme*, zweite, überarbeitete und ergänzte Auflage (Freiburg und München: Alber, 1970), 185–192 u.ö.; *Deutsche Biographische Enzyklopädie*, Bd. 5 (2001), 157.

34 Vollständiger Titel: *Die Synoptischen Evangelien, ihr Ursprung und geschichtlicher Charakter* (Leipzig: Engelmann, 1863).

35 *Die Religion in Geschichte und Gegenwart*, zweite Auflage, Bd. II (Tübingen, 1928), Sp. 1999 f.

36 Tübingen: Mohr, 1907.

des Matthäus beschäftigte", wurde er „auf die Bedeutung des in ihnen enthaltenen, nur von Matthäus, nicht auch von Markus gebotenen Stoffes aufmerksam." (S. 12). Das Problem wurde für Schweitzer im Zusammenhang mit seiner ersten theologischen Prüfung 1897 wieder virulent, bei der sich die Prüfungsfrage auf die Abendmahlslehre von Friedrich Schleiermacher[37], dem „Säulenheiligen der protestantischen Theologie des 19. Jahrhunderts", wie ich ihn nennen möchte, bezog. Schleiermacher nämlich „macht darauf aufmerksam, daß nach den Berichten über das Abendmahl bei Matthäus und Markus Jesus die Jünger nicht aufgefordert habe, das Mahl *zu wiederholen*, und wir uns also möglicherweise mit dem Gedanken vertraut machen müssen, daß die Wiederholung der Feier in der urchristlichen Gemeinde auf die Jünger und nicht auf Jesum selber zurückgehe... Dieser ... Gedanke arbeitete an mir, auch als ich mit jener Kandidatenthese schon fertig war"[38].

Hintergrund ist: Wenn die Feier *nicht* wiederholt werden soll, dann wird die Erwartung des „unmittelbar bevorstehenden Weltendes" unausgesprochen *vorausgesetzt!* Das heißt, gedanklich liegt hier die Wurzel von Schweitzers Überzeugung einer „konsequenten Eschatologie".

Schweitzer widmete sich nun zunächst seiner *philosophischen* Promotion. Sein Urteil über den Betrieb in der Bibliothèque Nationale in Paris kann ich übrigens aus eigener Erfahrung nachvollziehen: „Literatur über Kants Religionsphilosophie einzusehen, erwies sich *wegen des schwerfälligen Betriebs auf dem Lesesaal* als undurchführbar. So entschloß ich mich kurzerhand, die Arbeit zu machen, ohne mich mit der Literatur abzugeben und zu sehen, was sich mir bei einem Vergraben in die Kantschen Texte ergäbe."[39]. Die Dissertation erschien 1899 als Buch mit dem Titel: *Die Religionsphilosophie Kants von der Kritik der reinen Vernunft bis zur Religion innerhalb der Grenzen der bloßen Vernunft*[40]. Entgegen dem Rat seines Doktorvaters Theobald Ziegler[41] habilitierte sich Schweitzer dann aber in der *Theologischen* und nicht in der *Philosophischen* Fakultät.

---

37 1768–1834; vgl. zu ihm *Die Religion in Geschichte und Gegenwart*, vierte Auflage, Bd. 7 (Tübingen, 2004), Sp. 904–919 (Eberhard Jüngel).

38 *Das messianische Bewußtsein*, 18.

39 *Aus meinem Leben und Denken*, 23.

40 Freiburg i. Br., Leipzig u. Tübingen: Mohr; ein Nachdruck erschien 1974 (Hildesheim u. New York: Olms).

41 * 9.2.1846 in Göppingen, † 1.9.1918 in Sierentz (Sierenz) im Elsaß; vgl. zu ihm *Meyers Konversations-Lexikon*, fünfte Auflage, Bd. 17 (Leipzig und Wien: Bibliographisches Institut, 1897), 1017. Er ist nicht zu verwechseln mit dem Philosophen Leopold Ziegler (* 30. April 1881 in Karlsruhe, † 25. November 1958 in Überlingen).

Mit einer Arbeit über das Abendmahlsproblem – *Das Abendmahl im Zusammenhang mit dem Leben Jesu und der Geschichte des Urchristentums.* Erstes Heft: *Das Abendmahlsproblem auf Grund der wissenschaftlichen Forschungen des 19. Jahrhunderts und der historischen Berichte*[42] erwarb Schweitzer den Grad eines Lizentiaten der Theologie (Lic. Theol.), was eine ältere Bezeichnung für den theologischen Doktortitel ist. Mit dem zweiten Heft: *Das Messianitäts- und Leidensgeheimnis. Eine Skizze des Lebens Jesu*[43] wurde Schweitzer zum Privatdozenten der Theologischen Fakultät.

Nachdem Schweitzer 1904 zunächst sein Werk über Bach veröffentlicht hatte[44], brachte er im folgenden Jahr die Ergebnisse seiner Leben-Jesu-Forschung heraus, und zwar zunächst unter dem Titel: *Von Reimarus zu Wrede. Eine Geschichte der Leben-Jesu-Forschung*[45]; von 1913 an erschien das Buch dann unter dem knapperen Titel *Geschichte der Leben-Jesu-Forschung.* Zwei Jahre zuvor – also 1911 – waren seine Paulus-Forschungen unter dem Titel *Geschichte der paulinischen Forschung von der Reformation bis auf die Gegenwart*[46] erschienen, was dann in veränderter Form erst 1930 unter dem Titel *Die Mystik des Apostels Paulus*[47] veröffentlicht wurde, zu einem Zeitpunkt also, in dem sich die Forschungslage derart gewandelt hatte, dass Schweitzer „eine Zustimmung fand, wie er sie vor dem Ersten Weltkrieg schwerlich hätte finden können“[48]. Der uns schon bekannte Holtzmann hatte nämlich 1897 in seinem *Lehrbuch der Neutestamentlichen Theologie*[49] erklärt, dass Paulus, indem er das Christentum „hellenisierte“, zum „secundären Religionsstifter“ geworden sei und „den Anschluß der christlichen Dogmengeschichte an das Urchristentum ... ermöglicht“ habe[50]. Dem widersprach jedoch Schweitzer und verlangte, dass man zum geschichtlich richtigen Verständnis des Paulus „vom Griechischen her in jeder Form und in jeder Mischung absieht und die Einseitigkeit wagt, die Lehre des Heidenapostels ausschließlich aus dem Jüdisch-Urchristlichen begreifen zu wollen“ und so „die Mystik der Erlösungslehre und das Sakramentale aus dem Jüdisch-Eschatologischen zu erklären“[51].

---

42 Tübingen u. Freiburg: Mohr, 1901, Nachdruck ebd. 1929.

43 Tübingen u. Freiburg: Mohr, 1901, Nachdruck ebd. 1929.

44 *Jean Sébastien Bach, le musicien poète* (Leipzig: Breitkopf & Härtel, o.J. [Vorwort 1904 datiert; zahlreiche Nachdrucke]; deutsche Fassung ebd., 1908).

45 Tübingen: J.C.B. Mohr.

46 Tübingen: J.C.B. Mohr.

47 Tübingen: J.C.B. Mohr.

48 So Kümmel (wie Anm. 13), 95.

49 Tübingen: J.C.B. Mohr 1911.

50 Kümmel (wie Anm. 13), 93.

51 *Geschichte der paulinischen Forschung*, 187 f.

Diese Position – also das Festhalten an der sogenannnten „konsequenten Eschatologie“ – war für Lülings Denken von großer Bedeutung, jedoch nicht in dem Sinne, dass es einzelne Auslegungen betraf, sondern es war die bewußt gewählte Position eines Außenseiters, der den *mainstream* der Forschung ablehnte. Das heißt, im Hintergrund von Lülings Denken und seiner Beschäftigung mit dem Koran steht der alttestamentliche, gewissermaßen „heidnische“ Gedanke einer autochthonen Religion, so wie sie im alten Israel üblich war – im Gegensatz zum Brauch der aus Ägypten eingewanderten Juden, die ihren Kultus auf den Höhen (bāmot) ausübten.

Sidney H. Griffith

Late Antique Christology in Qurʾānic Perspective

I

There have been many scholarly studies of the Christology of the Qurʾān done over the past century and more. Almost all of them have been composed by scholars of Islam who studied the relevant passages in the Qurʾān from the hermeneutic perspective of the later Islamic interpretive tradition.[1] For the most part, albeit that their focus has been on the text of the Qurʾān, many authors have nevertheless taken their cue for studying the Qurʾān's Christology from the commentaries of later Muslim exegetes, Muslim jurists, Muslim theologians and interreligious controversialists. Ultimately, they have presented accounts of the Muslim Jesus or the Jesus of Islam, but they normally have not approached the topic of the Qurʾān's Christology taking into account the wider historical and cultural framework of the Qurʾān in its origins. That is to say, scholars have not normally read the Qurʾān's passages featuring 'the Messiah, Jesus, son of Mary, God's Messenger' (*an-Nisāʾ* 4,171), with an eye to the Qurʾān's awareness of contemporary Christian discourse about him that would have been current, especially but not exclusively in Syriac, in the first third of the seventh century in the Qurʾān's immediate circumambient Arabian milieu. Rather, most scholars, seemingly seeking sources for the Qurʾān's own Christological positions, have heretofore looked for their precedents in Jewish and Christian heresiographical literature; but they have scarcely ever considered mainline Christian, Christological discourse current in Greek, Syriac, and even in Arabic-speaking churches in

1 A representative selection of important studies on the topic would include: Michel Hayek, *Le Christ de l'Islam* (Paris: Éditions du Seuil, 1959); Claus Schedl, *Muhammad und Jesus: Die christologisch relevanten Texte des Koran neuübersetzt und erklärt* (Wien, Freiburg, Basel: Herder, 1978); Giuseppe Rizzardi, *Il problema della cristologia coranica: Storia dell'ermeneutica Cristiana* (Milano: Istituto Propaganda Libraria, 1982); Kenneth Cragg, *Jesus and the Muslim; an Exploration* (London: George Allen & Unwin, 1985); Tarif Khalidi, *The Muslim Jesus; Sayings and Stories in Islamic Literature* (Cambridge, MA: Harvard University Press, 2001); Geoffrey Parrinder, *Jesus in the Qurʾān* (New York: Oxford University Press, 1977); Neal Robinson, *Christ in Islam and Christianity* (Albany, NY: State University of New York Press, 1991); Oddbjørn Leirvik, *Images of Jesus Christ in Islam*, 2nd ed. (New York: Continuum, 2010); Mona Siddiqui, *Christians, Muslims, & Jesus* (New Haven, CT: Yale University Press, 2013); Zeki Saritoprak, *Islam's Jesus* (Gainesville, FL: University Press of Florida, 2014).

https://doi.org/10.1515/9783110599176-004

the first third of the seventh century as in any way being within the purview of the Qur'ān.[2]

The work of Günter Lüling has been something of an exception to the foregoing. He saw in certain passages of the Qur'ān the remnants of an earlier Christian hymnody in Arabic translation that he supposed reflected a theme that was actually once very popular in Early Christian thought, featuring an Angel Christology with its roots in a Christian reading of Old Testament precedents. While Lüling looked in the wrong place for the Late Antique Christianity that had spread into the Arabic-speaking milieu by the early seventh century CE, his instinct was nevertheless correct in discerning the presence of a Christian discourse with which the Qur'ān was in fact in conversation about Jesus the Messiah.[3] The thesis proposed in the present study is that the Late Antique Christology that was within the Qur'ān's purview was that of the Syriac-speaking churches whose presence on the peripheries of Arabia and within the cultural and religious ambience of the Arabic-speaking communities at the origins of Islam is well attested historically.

A considerable controversy has arisen among recent historians of Islamic origins about the Christian denominational identity of the "Nazarenes" (*an-naṣārā*), the Qur'ānic term for "Christians", of whom the Qur'ān speaks some fourteen times. On the basis of what the Qur'ān has to say about Jesus the Messiah and his mother, Mary, many researchers have taken the evidence of the relevant passages as a warrant for postulating the existence in the Arabian ḥijāz in the first third of the seventh century of groups known from earlier Christian heresiographical texts, whose Christology most nearly approximates that of the Qur'ān, whose views could then be considered as sources for the Arabic scripture. It is in this way that a number of historians have taken the further step of postulating the active presence in Arabia of various branches of Jewish Christians, principal-

2 A notable recent exception has been the work of Frank van den Velden, "Konvergenztexte syrischer und arabischer Christologie: Stufen der Textentwicklung von Sure 3, 33–64," *Oriens Christianus* 91 (2007), 164–203; *idem*, "Relations between Jews, Syriac Christians and Early Muslim Believers in Seventh-Century Iraq," *The Bulletin of Middle East Medievalists* 19 (2007): 27–33; *idem*, "Kontexte im Konvergenzstrang – die Bedeutung textkritischer Varianten und christlicher Bezugstexte für die Redaktion von Sure 61 und Sure 5, 110–119," *Oriens Christianus* 92 (2008): 130–173.

3 Lüling's bibliography is long; a comprehensive presentation of his thought is available in Günther Lüling, *A Challenge to Islam for Reformation: The Rediscovery and Reliable Reconstruction of a Comprehensive Pre-Islamic Christian Hymnal Hidden in the Koran under Earliest Islamic Reinterpretations* (New Delhi: Motilal Banarsidass Publishers, 2003). This book is an English translation and expansion of Lüling's *Über den Ur-Koran: Ansätze zur Rekonstruktion vorislamischer christlicher Strophenlieder im Koran* (Erlangen: H. Lüling, 1974 & 1993).

ly the so-called "Ebionites", "Elkasaites", and "Nazarenes", albeit that no other shred of evidence for their survival in Arabia in the early seventh century has come to hand. Having thus postulated their presence and actual influence on the emerging Qur'ānic teaching, these scholars have not hesitated as a consequence to cite them as present sources contributing to and even determining the Christology of the Arabic scripture.[4] By way of contrast, the present writer has argued that the hermeneutically more plausible approach to discerning the denominational and creedal identity of the Christians within the Qur'ān's purview, along with the Christology which the Qur'ān challenges, is to consider the Qur'ān's pertinent objections in reference to the views of the Christian communities actually historically discoverable within its early seventh century milieu, namely the so-called "Melkites", "Jacobites", and "Nestorians", who, along with the Manichees, flourished along the Arabian periphery and within Arabia proper at the very moment of the Qur'ān's origins.[5]

The methodological turn toward the Late Antique Christian intellectual, cultural, and religious horizons circumambient to the Arabic-speaking milieu of the Qur'ān in its origins, especially in regard to Christology, widens both the chronological and geographical parameters within which one would read and interpret the passages that refer to Christians and Christian beliefs and practices.[6] This

4 See in particular François De Blois, "*Naṣrānī (Ναζωραιος)* and *ḥanīf (εθνικος)*: Studies on the Religious Vocabulary of Christianity and of Islam," *Bulletin of the School of Oriental And African Studies* 65 (2002): 1–30; *idem*, "Elchasai – Manes – Muḥammad: Manichäismus und Islam in religionshistorischen Vergleich," *Der Islam* 81 (2004): 31–48; Édouard-Marie Gallez, *La messie et son prophète: Aux origins de l'islam*, Studia Arabia 1 & 2, 2nd ed. (Paris: Éditions de Paris, 2005); Joachim Gnilka, *Die Nazarener und der Koran: Eine Spurensuche* (Freiburg: Herder, 2007). On the proposed Jewish Christian background see now the comprehensive article by Patricia Crone, "Jewish Christianity and the Qur'ān (Part One)," *Journal of Near Eastern Studies* 74 (2015): 225–253; See also Guy G. Stroumsa, "Jewish Christianity and Islamic Origins," in *Islamic Cultures, Islamic Contexts: Essays in Honor of Professor Patricia Crone*, eds. Behnam Sadeghi et al. (Leiden: Brill, 2015), 72–96.

5 See Sidney H. Griffith, "*Al-Naṣārā* in the Qur'ān: A Hermeneutical Reflection," in *New Perspectives on the Qur'ān: The Qur'ān in its Historical Context 2*, ed. Gabriel Said Reynolds (London & New York: Routledge, 2011), 301–332; *idem*, "The Qur'ān's 'Nazarenes' and Other Late Antique Christians: Arabic-Speaking 'Gospel People' in Qur'ānic Perspective," in *Christsein in der islamischen Welt: Festschrift für Martin Tamcke zum 60. Geburtstag*, eds. Sidney H. Griffith and Sven Grebenstein (Wiesbaden: Harrassowitz, 2015), 81–106.

6 See in particula Garth Fowden, *Empire to Commonwealth: Consequences of Monotheism in Late Antiquity* (Princeton, NJ: Princeton University Press, 1993); *idem*, *Before and after Muḥammad: The First Millennium Refocused* (Princeton, NJ: Princeton University Press, 2014); Greg Fisher, *Between Empires: Arabs, Romans, and Sasanians in Late Antiquity* (Oxford: Oxford University Press, 2011); Angelika Neuwirth, *Der Koran als Text der Spätantike* (Berlin: Verlag der Weltreligionen im

widening of the interpretive horizons removes the hermeneutic restraints that had for a long time focused historians' attention almost exclusively on the Bedouin culture of the Arabian ḥijāz and its environs prior to the rise of Islam as the principal point of reference for the exegesis of Qur'ānic passages, a chronological and cultural horizon that both Muslim and non-Muslim scholars, borrowing a virtually dogmatic term from the Qur'ān itself, have long called the "Time of Ignorance" (*al-jāhiliyyah*, e.g., *'Āl 'Imrān* 3,54). This limited perspective effectively focused the Qur'ān's interpreters' attention solely on pre-Islamic poetry and Bedouin culture, effectively emptying the ḥijāz of all other cultural and religious currents of thought and expression,[7] thereby creating the cultural and religious vacuum into which many scholars then introduced otherwise historically unattested groups locally, such as Jewish Christians, Ebionites, Elkasaites, and Nazarenes, as we have seen, who were thought to have served as sources or to have provided sub-texts for the Qur'ān's own distinctive Christology.[8]

Reading the Qur'ān within the wider perspective of Late Antiquity means taking into account the Arabic scripture's interaction not only with the Bedouins and settled Arabs of the "Empty ḥijāz", but also with other contemporaries, both at home and abroad, whose views circulated in the Arabic-speaking milieu of the first half of the seventh century. And since both the number and the identities of the Qur'ān's interlocutors are thus seen to be both more numerous than the local Arab tribes and more varied in their cultural and religious commitments, including a significant presence of Jews and Christians in its audience, in addition to the more numerous adherents of the traditional Arabian traditions, the reader must be more alert to the Qur'ān's various modes of speaking in its interaction and intercourse with the devotees of other religious traditions, Jews and Christians in particular, living within the ambience of its Arabian homeland.[9] For ex-

Insel Verlag, 2010); Aziz al-Azmeh, *The Emergence of Islam in Late Antiquity* (Cambridge, UK: Cambridge University Press, 2014). See also the numerous studies by Christian Robin and his associates on the history and culture of South Arabia in Late Antiquity, summarily presented in Christian Julien Robin, "Ethiopia and Arabia," in *The Oxford Handbook of Late Antiquity*, ed. Scott Fitzgerald Johnson (Oxford: Oxford University Press, 2012), 247–332.

7 See James E. Montgomery, "The Empty *ḥijāz*," in *Arabic Theology, Arabic Philosophy; from the Many to the One: Essays in Celebration of Richard M. Frank*, ed. J. E. Montgomery, Orientalia Lovaniensia Analecta, 152 (Leuven: Uitgeverij Peeters en Departement Oosterse Studien, 2006), 37–97.

8 See in this connection the bibliographical references cited in n. 4 above.

9 See Angelika Neuwirth, "Locating the Qur'ān in the Epistemic Space of Late Antiquity," in *Christsein in der islamischen Welt*, eds. Griffith and Grebenstein, 65–79. See also, *eadem*, "From Tribal Genealogy to Divine Covenant: Qur'ānic Re-figurations of Pagan Arab Ideals Based on Biblical Models," in *Scripture, Poetry and the Making of a Community: Reading the*

ample, on the one hand the Qur'ān can be seen to be actively concerned with the lore of the biblical Patriarchs and Prophets whose stories circulated among the contemporary "Scripture People" (*'ahl al-kitāb*), whom the Qur'ān mentions some fifty-four times. On the other hand the Qur'ān not only participates in evoking the memory of the narratives of those whom the Scripture People speak of as Patriarchs and Prophets, it does so within the framework of its own interpretive paradigm, construing the significance of its reminiscences of those same figures, whom it calls God's Messengers and Prophets,[10] in a way considerably at variance with the Jewish, and especially with the contemporary Christian construal of the same narratives,[11] as we shall see below. The Qur'ān of course presents its distinctive message in a rhetorical discourse that is geared both to commend the veracity of its own message and to contend with and to counter teachings it critiques, censures and regards as "false" or a "lie" (*kadhib, kidhāb*), or tantamount to "ungrateful disbelief" (*kufr*).[12]

II

There is no surviving record outside of the Qur'ān itself of any response to its teaching on the part of the Syriac or Arabic-speaking Christians who lived within Arabia proper or on its periphery in the seventh century. The first Christian theologians outside of Arabia to record their opinions of the Qur'ān and its teachings about Christian belief and practice were the Palestinian monks, Anastasios of Sinai (d.c.700) and John of Damascus (c.655–c.750), both of whom wrote in Greek, and both of whom were deeply concerned with the contemporary Christological controversies. So too was Christology a major concern of the now unknown eighth century author of the earliest Christian theological tract written in Arabic, the *Treatise on the Triune Nature of God.*[13] Recognizing the Qur'ān's

Qur'ān as a Literary Text, ed. Angelika Neuwirth (Oxford: Oxford University Press/ London: The Institute of Ismaili Studies, 2014), 53–75.

10 See W. A. Bijlefeld, "A Prophet and More than a Prophet? Some Observations on the Qur'ānic Use of the Terms 'Prophet' and 'Apostle'," *Muslim World* 95 (1969): 1–28.

11 See Sidney H. Griffith, *The Bible in Arabic: The Scriptures of the "People of the Book" in the Language of Islam* (Princeton, NJ: Princeton University Press, 2013), esp. 55–96.

12 See Mehdi Azaiez, *Le contre-discours coranique*, Studies in the History and Culture of the Middle East, vol. 30 (Berlin: Walter de Gruyter, 2015).

13 On this important text, see Margaret Dunlop Gibson, ed., *An Arabic Version of the Acts of the Apostles and the Seven Catholic Epistles from an Eighth or Ninth Century MS in the Convent of St Catharine on Mount Sinai, with a Treatise on The Triune Nature of God, with Translation, from the Same Codex*, Studia Sinaitica, no. VII (Cambridge: Cambridge University Press, 1899), 1–36 [Eng-teaching about Jesus the Messiah to be at the heart of its censure of the beliefs of the Christians, i.e., the Qur'ān's "Nazarenes", these writers were quick to characterize it as a heretical doctrine and to declare it to be Arian in its origins.[14] So too was the eighth century, "Jacobite" author of the Syriac *Disputation between a Muslim and a Monk of Bēt ḥālē* concerned, like his "Melkite" contemporaries, to refute the Qur'ān's teaching about Jesus the Messiah.[15] And in another, later, Syriac / Arabic text, the now unknown ninth-century author of the *Legend of the Monk Baḥîrâ* was likewise concerned to accredit the Qur'ān's teaching to a renegade Christian monk.[16] But the Late Antique Greek and Syriac-speaking Christian scholars of the seventh century, be they Chalcedonians or non- Chalcedonians, were seemingly totally unaware of the Arabic Qur'ān and its Christology during the first half of the seventh century, the era of its initial oral proclamation and of its appearance as the first Arabic book.

By way of contrast, while neither Jews nor Christians living within or just beyond the Qur'ān's Arabian homeland left any written notice of having taken cognizance of the new Arabic scripture or its contents in the era of its origins, the Qur'ān for its part, as many scholars have shown for a century and more now, discloses a wide-ranging awareness of the religious lore of the Jews and Christians of Late Antiquity, especially but not exclusively reminiscences of the stories and legends of the biblical Patriarchs and Prophets.[17] And it is within the frame-

---

lish], 74–107 [Arabic]; Maria Gallo, trans., *Palestinese anonimo; Omelia arabo-cristiana dell'VIII secolo* (Roma: Città Nuova Editrice, 1994). See Samir Khalil Samir, "The Earliest Arab Apology for Christianity (c.750)," in *Christian Arabic Apologetics during the Abbasid Period (750–1258)*, eds. Samir Khalil Samir and Jørgen S. Nielsen, Studies in the History of Religions, vol. 63 (Leiden: E.J. Brill, 1994), 57–114.

14 See Sidney H. Griffith, "The Melkites and the Muslims: The Qur'ān, Christology, and Arab Orthodoxy," *Al-Qanṭara: Revista de Estudios Arabes* 33 (2012): 413–443.

15 See now David G.K. Taylor, "The Disputation between a Muslim and a Monk of Bēt Ḥālē: Syriac Text and Annotated English Translation," in *Christsein in der islamischen Welt*, ed. Griffith/ Grebenstein (Wiesbaden: Harrassowitz Verlag, 2015), 187–242.

16 See Barbara Roggema, *The Legend of Sergius Baḥīrā: Eastern Christian Apologetics and Apocalyptic in Response to Islam*, The History of Christian-Muslim Relations, vol. 9 (Leiden: Brill, 2009).

17 From the early nineteenth century until today, many scholars have been busily searching out biblical, apocryphal, and pseudepigraphical passages in Jewish and Christian sources that in their opinion might be thought to lie behind passages in the Qur'ān, beginning with Abraham Geiger, *Was hat Mohammed aus dem Judenthume aufgenommen?*, 1st ed. (Bonn: Baaden, 1833) and Heinrich Speyer, *Die biblischen Erzälungen im Qoran* (Gräfenhainichen/Breslau: Schulze, 1931), and reaching the present day in, e.g., Gabriel Said Reynolds, *The Qur'ān and Its Biblical Subtext*, Routledge Studies in the Qur'ān (London & New York: Routledge, 2010), to name only a few.

work of just these recollections that the Qur'ān's distinctive view of God's Messenger, the Messiah, Jesus, the son of Mary, most clearly emerges. In fact, for the Qur'ān, Christology, or what one says is the truth about Jesus of Nazareth, is the main point of the Arabic scripture's critique of the doctrine of those it calls "Nazarenes". So one might not unreasonably make the case that while contemporary Christians outside of Arabia knew virtually nothing of the Qur'ān in its origins and first publication in writing, the Qur'ān itself was nevertheless at the same time making a bid of its own to stake out a position in the very matter of Christology that was itself then at the heart of the current, church-dividing controversies, of which it seems the Qur'ān was well aware; it speaks of Christian doubts about the Qur'ān's truth regarding Jesus and their differing factions (see, e.g., *Maryam* 19, 34–37; *az-Zukhruf* 43, 63–65, see also *al-Baqarah* 2, 253).

Scholars of the Qur'ān's Christology ancient and modern have long and closely studied the fifty-some passages in the Arabic scripture that expressly concern Jesus and his mother, Mary. Many if not most of them have interpreted the Qur'ānic view of Jesus the Messiah expressed in these passages in reference to the doctrines of earlier, often Jewish Christian groups, as mentioned above.[18] A few scholars, including the present writer, have interpreted the principal verses as criticisms and corrections from the Qur'ān's perspective of the doctrines and liturgical expressions of the major, contemporary, seventh century, Christian denominations, the so-called "Melkites", "Jacobites", and "Nestorians", whose presence within Arabia and on its periphery in the seventh century is well attested.[19] But heretofore scholars have neglected to take a careful account of the fact that the Qur'ān voices its own view of Jesus the Messiah almost entirely in terms of the vocabulary, and within the framework of its own distinctive "prophetology". And what is more, the Qur'ān can be seen to display this distinctive "prophetology" most evidently in its reminiscences and recollections of the accounts of the biblical Patriarchs and Prophets whose stories it recalls in a patterned discourse that highlights its different construal of the significance of the prophetic mission of the Patriarchs and Prophets vis-à-vis that of its contemporary Jews and Christians.[20]

---

18 See the studies cited in n. 4 above.

19 In addition to the valuable studies of Frank van den Velden, cited in n. 2 above, see also Griffith, "*Al-Naṣārā* in the Qur'ān," and Sidney H. Griffith, "Syriacisms in the Arabic Qur'ān: Who Were 'Those who said Allāh is Third of Three', according to *al-Mā'idah* 73?" in *A Word Fitly Spoken: Studies in Mediaeval Exegesis of the Hebrew Bible and the Qur'ān Presented to Haggai Ben-Shammai*, eds. Meir M. Bar-Asher *et al.* (Jerusalem: The Ben-Zvi Institute, 2007), 83–110.

20 See the discussion in Griffith, *The Bible in Arabic*, 54–89; Sidney H. Griffith, "The '*Sunna* of Our Messengers': The Qur'ān's Paradigm for Messengers and Prophets; a Reading of Sūrat ash-

The argument to be advanced here is that in its rhetorically carefully worded critique of the Christian confession that Jesus of Nazareth is both the Messiah and the Son of the living God (Mt. 16:16), the Qurʾān very much had Late Antique Christology within its purview. However, it related to it not so much if at all in terms of the technical, creedal formulae in the Greek academic parlance current in the contemporary Christological disputes, often in fact translated into Syriac in fifth and sixth century dogmatic treatises, but very much in response to the popular, homiletic presentation of Christian teaching about Jesus that was transmitted in the scriptural reasoning characteristic of the widely circulated Christian homiletic literature of the period, and especially in the very popular Syriac *mêmrê*, or verse homilies, composed originally by the major writers of the Syriac-speaking churches, such as St. Ephraem the Syrian (d. 373), Narsai of Nisibis (d. 503), and Jacob of Serūg (d. 521). Due to the customary presentation of selections from these *mêmrê* in the liturgy, they became the medium that largely informed the Christological faith of the Syriac and Arabic-speaking Christian communities on the Arabian periphery and within Arabia proper in the seventh century.[21]

Syriac *mêmrê* were composed in verse and they were meant to be recited by a speaker in an ecclesial setting, albeit that they might also have an afterlife as a written text. The verse structure is characteristically isosyllabic, featuring in most instances a more or less self-contained line, usually composed of two (sometimes three) "half lines" with an equal number of full syllables in the wording of each of the "half lines". For example, Ephraem the Syrian characteristically composed *mêmrê* in which each "half line" featured seven syllables, or fourteen syllables to the line, whereas Narsai of Nisibis (d.c.501) and Jacob of Serūg (c.451–521) usually wrote in twelve syllable "half lines", twenty-four in the full line, while the fifth century Syriac poet Balai favored the five syllable per half-line meter.[22] *Mêmrê* typically went on for hundreds of lines without any stanzas or other textual divisions. The speaker, who would often address

Shuʿarāʾ (26)," in *Qurʾānic Studies Today*, eds. Angelika Neuwirth and Michael Sells (London & New York: Routledge, 2016), 203–223.

21 See Theresia Hainthaler, *Christliche Araber vor dem Islam*, Eastern Christian Studies, vol. 7 (Leuven: Peeters, 2007). See also the important studies contained in Joëlle, Françoise Briquel-Chatonnet and Christian Julien Robin, eds., *Juifs et Chrétiens en Arabie aux Ve et VIe siècles: regards croisés sur les sources*, Collège de France – CNRS, Centre de Recherche d'Histoire et Civilisation de Byzance, Monographies, 32 (Paris: Association des amis du Centre d'Histoire et civilization de Byzance, 2010).

22 See S.P. Brock, "Poetry," in *Gorgias Encyclopedic Dictionary of the Syriac Heritage*, eds. S.P. Brock *et al.*, Beth Mardutho The Syriac Institute (Piscataway, NJ: Gorgias Press, 2011), 334–336.

the congregation directly, would readily move from topic to topic, theme to theme, even person to person in line groupings marked off only by rhetorical devices, voice modulations, or subtle shifts in reference, for example from one biblical verse to another, one liturgical theme to another, or one addressee to another, not unlike what one also finds in the Qur'ān. In the hands of the classical authors of Syriac religious discourse, the *mêmrô* was a performance genre; and when these writers were exploring the meanings of biblical passages in their *mêmrê* they were in fact engaging in scriptural exegesis within a particular tradition of biblical interpretation. In the Syriac-speaking milieu, this tradition was inevitably the one that came to its classical and clearest expression first in the works of Ephraem the Syrian,[23] whose authority and even whose modes of expression hovered over the works of later Syriac writers even as they adhered to the doctrinal commitments of rival ecclesial communities. Given the widespread popularity of the *mêmrê* among Syriac-speaking Christians of Late Antiquity, who played a major role in disseminating their faith among the neighboring, Arabic-speaking peoples, one must inevitably consider the Syriac *mêmrê* in relation to the Arabic Qur'ān, not in the sense of their being in any way sources for the Qur'ān, but in view of the likelihood of their being readily present evidence for the modes of popular Christian, religious discourse that would have been available in the first third of the seventh century, albeit in all likelihood in oral translation, in the Christian precincts of Arabia, to which the Qur'ān seems to have been particularly attentive in its origins. Interestingly, the biblical and many of the non-biblical figures of Jewish and Christian lore whose words and deeds the Qur'ān recalls, particularly the Patriarchs and Prophets, are the very ones whose stories are also rehearsed at great length in the Syriac *mêmrê*. Sometimes the sequence of events narrated or alluded to in the two texts featuring the same figures mirror one another and the Qur'ān can be seen to comment on, to change the focus, or even to critique the points made in the *mêmrê*.[24] For example, while the Syriac authors are ever alert to what they perceive to be the presence of types for Christ in the biblical texts of the

---

23 See Sidney H. Griffith, *'Faith Adoring the Mystery': Reading the Bible with St. Ephraem the Syrian*, The Père Marquette Lecture in Theology 1997 (Milwaukee, WI: Marquette University Press, 1997); *idem*, "Ephraem the Exegete (306–373): Biblical Commentary in the Works of Ephraem the Syrian," in *Handbook of Patristic Exegesis: The Bible in Ancient Christianity*, ed. Charles Kannengiesser, 2 vols. (Leiden: Brill, 2004), vol. II, 1395–1428.

24 See, e.g., Sidney H. Griffith, "Christian Lore and the Arabic Qur'ān: the 'Companions of the Cave' in *Sūrat al-Kahf* in Syriac Christian Tradition," in *The Qur'ān in Its Historical Context*, ed. Gabriel Said Reynolds, Routledge Studies in the Qur'ān (London & New York: Routledge, 2008), 109–137.

Old Testament, which in their estimation can be seen to preview or set the pattern for events in the later life and career of Jesus of Nazareth that would mark him out as the promised Messiah, the Qur'ān for its part highlights what it calls the "signs" (*'āyāt*) and "clear indications" (*bayyināt*) of the action of the one God in the careers of these same individuals, Jesus of Nazareth included, which in its view mark them out as God's Messengers and Prophets. And it is in these very passages that evoke the scriptural lore of Jews and Christians that one encounters numerous Arabized Syriac words and turns of phrase that are so familiar to readers of the Syriac *mêmrê*.[25] The further fact that the *surahs* of the Qur'ān were meant to be chanted in cadenced, metrical tones in liturgical assemblies, just like the Syriac *mêmrê*, only heightens the suggestion of a shared cultural milieu between the Arabic Qur'ān and the classical Syriac *mêmrê*.

III

A prominent feature of the very numerous Syriac *mêmrê* that have survived from Late Antiquity is their authors' preference for a mode of discourse that can best be described as a form of *lectio divina*, an exercise in reading and reasoning with passages from the scriptures rather than a discourse in the discursive style of an academic treatise or dogmatic letter addressed primarily to intellectuals and church leaders in their communities. For the *mêmrê* were intended for popular presentation. Their language is cadenced, composed in a poetic style that shifts almost imperceptibly from one theme to another as the author explores the meanings and implications of a passage of scripture, of episodes in the lives of the patriarchs and prophets, events in the life and teaching of Jesus the Messiah, or even the highlights of a saint's life.

As it happens, there are many *mêmrê* in the collections attributed to Ephraem, Jacob of Serug and Narsai of Nisibis that focus their attention on the biblical narratives and popular traditions about the same Patriarchs and Prophets whose stories the Qur'ān recollects, particularly accounts of Noah, Abraham, Joseph, Moses, David and Solomon, to mention only the most prominent of them. The exegetical method that the authors of the Syriac *mêmrê* most often employed in their verse homilies, in which they intended to disclose the Christian understanding of the stories of these Old Testament figures, is that of "typology". In the hands of these Syriac Christian readers of the Old Testament, it was a distinctive interpretive strategy akin to "allegory", by means of which an interpreter

25 See, e.g., Griffith, "Syriacisms in the Arabic Qur'ān."

reads passages in the Old Testament and extra-biblical traditions through the lens of the Gospel; a person, event, or institution in the Old Testament narrative (the "type"), is said to correspond to another in the New Testament (the "anti-type").[26] Unlike "allegory", which is "a narrative which uses symbolic figures and actions to suggest hidden meanings behind the literal words of the text,"[27] "typology" requires the integrity of both the literal and the historical dimensions of the biblical text.[28] For the composers of Syriac *mêmrê*, this typological method of interpretation involved discerning and explicating how moments in the lives and exploits of the Patriarchs and Prophets could be seen to anticipate, in a patterning way, corresponding moments in the life and achievements of the Messiah as depicted in the Gospel. The Old Testament narratives could then be thought to have prepared the mind of the rightly guided believer to discern the truth about the Messiah and his mission in the world by providing both the paradigm and the vocabulary for disclosing the truth about him. The authors of the Syriac *mêmrê* called such revelatory moments *râzê* (sing. *râzâ*), a term that suggests "signals", "signs", "symbols", even "secrets" and "mysteries".[29] As the term was used in the Syriac *mêmrê* under discussion its demonstrative capacity is more kinetic than that of the parallel Greek terms, "types" or "verbal icons", which Greek-speaking, early Christian writers employed in parallel exegetical circumstances. In the Syriac *mêmrê*, the *râzê* are seen to bespeak the "mysteries" they signify; for the Christian reader they disclose the real presence of God in Christ, acting and speaking in the patriarchal and prophetic narratives of salvation history. Christ himself is said to be the "Lord of the *râzê*";[30] for the Christian they reveal Christ himself directing the course of events in the biblical narratives of patriarchs and prophets, preparing the minds of believers to see in the Gospel's presentation of Jesus, the Messiah, the Christ, the Son of the living God,

---

26 Adapted from Friedbert Ninow, "Typology," in *Eerdmans Dictionary of the Bible*, ed. David Noel Freedman (Grand Rapids MI: William B. Eerdmans Publishing Company, 2000), 1341.

27 William R. Goodman, "Allegory," in *Eerdmans Dictionary of the Bible*, Freedman, 43–44.

28 Jean-Noël Guinot, "La frontier entre allégorie et typologie: école alexandrine, école antiochenne," *Recherches de Science Religieuse* 92 (2011): 223 (207–228).

29 For the full range of meaning of this term, see Michael Sokoloff, *A Syriac Lexicon: A Translation from the Latin, Correction, Expansion, and Update of C. Brockelmann's Lexicon Syriacum* (Winona Lake, IN & Piscataway, NJ: Eisenbrauns & Gorgias Press, 2009), 1424; R. Payne Smith, *Thesaurus Syriacus* (Oxford: Clarendon Press, 1897), fascicle, X, cols. 3871–33875, in reprint edition; Hildesheim: Georg Olms Verlag, vol. II, cols 3871–3875.

30 Edmund Beck, *Des heiligen Ephraem des Syrers Paschalhymnen; (de Azymis, de Crucifisione, de Resurrectione)*, CSCO, vols. 248 & 249 (Louvain: Peeters, 1964), *De Azymis*, III:1.

himself both God and man,[31] the very vision of Jesus the Messiah that the Qur'ān critiques and corrects.

In its counter discourse, the Qur'ān's critique of Christian belief about Jesus the Messiah may be seen to challenge it precisely by undermining the understanding of the biblical narratives of the patriarchs and prophets proposed in the Syriac *mêmrê*. The Qur'ān's Christology is determined principally by its own distinctive master narrative, its paradigmatic "prophetology", the "*Sunnah* of Our Messengers", as the Qur'ān itself called it (cf. *al-'Isrā'* 17, 77). As we have seen above, it is an interpretive paradigm that yields a Christology framed neither in the dogmatic idiom of Late Antique Greek logic and philosophy, nor in the typological, scriptural reasoning of the Syriac *mêmrê*, but rather in terms of its own construal of the significance of the sequence and experience of those whom it presents as God's prophets and messengers, expanded to include both biblical and non-biblical, Arabian messengers of God. This paradigmatic "prophetology" is most clearly displayed in the Qur'ān, as mentioned above, in *surah ash-Shu'arā'* 26, where not all the biblical prophets and messengers are mentioned, not even Jesus the Messiah, but where the Qur'ān's prophetic paradigm is most readily in evidence. And it is of course reprised in other passages in the Qur'ān where the lists of God's prophets and messengers are more complete. The parameters of the Qur'ān's "*Sunnah* of Our Messengers" indicate the framework within which the distinctive, Qur'ānic Christology is expressed. So it will come as no surprise that the Qur'ān's view of Jesus the Messiah, as we shall see, accords precisely with its prophetology. However, it is important first to briefly describe that prophetology more closely.

IV

As was just mentioned, the distinctive Qur'ānic *sunnah* of God's messengers and prophets, which is articulated in a number of places in the Qur'ān, is well schematized in a recurring, probably liturgical, pattern of recall, most clearly displayed in *surah ash-Shu'arā'* 26. In the text, God addresses Muḥammad's concerns about the reception of the message from God he had been called to deliver to his contemporaries, probably in the later Meccan phase of his public

---

31 For more discussion on the function of 'typology' in the Syriac *mêmrê*, see Sidney H. Griffith, "Disclosing the Mystery: The Hermeneutics of Typology in Syriac Exegesis: Jacob of Serūg on Genesis XXII," in *Interpreting Scriptures in Judaism, Christianity, and Islam: Overlapping Inquiries*, eds. Mordechai Cohen, Adele Berlin *et al.* (Cambridge, UK: Cambridge University Press, 2016), in press.

career, when he seems first to have engaged in controversy with Christians. The *surah* provides a concentrated insight into the conceptual framework within which the Qur'ān recalls more particular moments of pre-Islamic Arabian and biblical prophetic history. It provides a schematic view of the interpretive horizon within which particular biblical stories are recalled, and it exemplifies the features of prophetic experience that according to the Qur'ān's "*sunnah* of Our messengers" determine which specific aspects of a given biblical story are selected for approving recollection throughout the Qur'ān. Several repeated phrases intone the basic features of the apostolic, prophetic vocation, articulated in such a way as to assure Muḥammad of his own heritage as one of God's messengers and prophets. The following outline highlights the schematic aspects that are readily evident in the *surah*.

ash-Shu'arā' 26
A Paradigm for God's Messengers and Prophets

I – Proemium: 1–6

"These are the signs (*'āyāt*) of the manifest scripture." (vs. 2)

"No new remembrance comes to them from the Compassionate One that they do not spurn." (vs. 5)

II – The Earth: 7–9

"In that there is a sign (*'āyah*); but most of them are not believers. Your (2ms) Lord is indeed mighty and merciful." (vss. 8–9)

III – Moses: 10–68

"[Remember] when (*'idh*) your (2ms) Lord called out to Moses ... ." (vs. 10)

Moses' dialogue with Pharaoh (vss. 16–62)

"In that there is a sign (*'āyah*); but most of them are not believers. Your (2ms) Lord is indeed mighty and merciful." (vss. 67–68)

IV – Abraham: 69–104

"Recite to them the account of Abraham, when (*'idh*) he said to his father." (vss. 69–70)

Abraham's testimony: vss. 77–102.

"In that there is a sign ('*āyah*); but most of them are not believers. Your (2ms) Lord is indeed mighty and merciful." (vss. 103–104)

V – Noah: 105–122

"Noah's people called the messengers liars when ('*idh*) their brother Noah said to them ... ." (vss. 105–106)

"Indeed I am a trustworthy messenger (*rasūl*) to you, so fear God and obey me." (vss. 107–108)

"*I ask of you no wage for it; my wage is only on the Lord of the Worlds.*" (vs. 109)

"In that there is a sign ('*āyah*); but most of them are not believers. Your (2ms) Lord is indeed mighty and merciful." (vss. 121–122)

VI – Hūd > 'Ād: 123–140

"'Ād called the messengers liars when ('*idh*) their brother Hūd said to them ... ." (vss. 123–124)

"Indeed I am a trustworthy messenger (*rasūl*) to you, so fear God and obey me." (vss. 125–126)

"*I ask of you no wage for it; my wage is only on the Lord of the Worlds.*" (vs. 127)

"In that there is a sign ('*āyah*); but most of them are not believers. Your (2ms) Lord is indeed mighty and merciful." (vss. 139–140)

VII – Ṣāliḥ > Thamūd: 141–159

"Thamūd called the messengers liars when ('*idh*) their brother Ṣāliḥ said to them ... ." (vss. 141–142)

"Indeed I am a trustworthy messenger (*rasūl*) to you, so fear God and obey me." (vss. 143–144)

"*I ask of you no wage for it; my wage is only on the Lord of the Worlds.*" (vs. 145)

"In that there is a sign ('*āyah*); but most of them are not believers. Your (2ms) Lord is indeed mighty and merciful." (vss. 158–159)

VIII – Lot: 160–175

"Lot's People called the messengers liars when ('*idh*) their brother Lot said to them ... ." (vs. 161)

"Indeed I am a trustworthy messenger (*rasūl*) to you, so fear God and obey me." (vss. 162–163)

"*I ask of you no wage for it; my wage is only on the Lord of the Worlds.*" (vs. 164)

"In that there is a sign (ʾ*āyah*); but most of them are not believers. Your (2ms) Lord is indeed mighty and merciful." (vss. 174–175)

IX – Shuʿayb > Aṣḥābu l-Aykah: 176–191

"The companions of the forest called the messengers liars when (ʾ*idh*) Shuʿayb said to them ... ." (176–177)

"Indeed I am a trustworthy messenger (*rasūl*) to you, so fear God and obey me." (vss. 178–179)

"*I ask of you no wage for it; my wage is only on the Lord of the Worlds.*" (vs. 180)

"In that there is a sign (ʾ*āyah*); but most of them are not believers. Your (2ms) Lord is indeed mighty and merciful." (vss. 190–191)

X – Muḥammad and the Qurʾān: 192–217

"The trustworthy spirit has brought down (*nazala*) the revelation (*tanzīl*) of the Lord of the Worlds upon your (2ms) heart so that you might become one of those who warn with a clarifying Arabic tongue; it (i.e. the revelation) is indeed in the books (*zubur*) of the ancients." (vss. 192–196)

"Put your confidence in the Mighty One, the Merciful One, Who sees you (2ms) when you stand [for prayer] and your circulation among the worshippers (*as-sājidīna*); He is the All-Seeing, the All-Knowing One." (vss. 217–220)

XI – The Satans' Minions and the Poets: 221–227

Of the Satans' minions: "Most of them are liars." (vs. 223)

Of the poets: "They say what they do not do; except for those who believe and do good deeds and remember God much, and who are vindicated after having been wronged." (vss. 226–227)

Qurʾānic "prophetology" thus displayed is: *catholic* (God's messengers have come to both biblical and non-biblical people); *recurrent* (the pattern of apostolic and prophetic experience recurs in the sequence of messengers and prophets); *dialogical* (the messengers and prophets interact in dialogue with their people); *singular* in its message (the one God, who rewards good and punishes evil on the Day of Judgment; no divinizing of creatures); *vindicated* (God vindicates His messengers and prophets in their struggles, i.e., the so called "punishment stories"). In this connection one must take cognizance of the fact that the several passages in the Qurʾān that charge the Jews with being killers of the prophets (e.g., *al-Baqarah* 2, 61; *ʾĀl ʿImrān* 3, 21), do not contradict this feature of "the *sunnah* of Our messengers", whereby the messenger or prophet is vindicated over his adversaries in the end. Rather, the polemical charge against the Jews of having killed the prophets echoes a theme in earlier Jewish and Christian polemical lore, finding a place already in the New Testament in the Christian instance (e.g., Mt. 23:37; Lk. 13:34). It is noteworthy in this connection that none of the prophets whose names are mentioned in these Jewish and Christian traditions as having been killed by their adversaries are ever named in the Qur'ān, and in the case of John the Baptist, who is named in the Qur'ān (e.g., *al-Baqarah* 3, 39–41; *Maryam* 19, 7, 12–15), his execution at the hands of Herod Antipas as reported in the Gospel (Mt. 14:1–12; Mk. 6:14–29; Lk. 9:7–9) is also never mentioned in the Islamic scripture.[32]

These same marks of "prophecy" and "messengership" are evident in other places in the Qur'ān that present the sequence of prophets and messengers (e.g., *al-'A'rāf* 12; *Hūd* 11etc.). While no single sequence anywhere in the Qur'ān includes the names of all of the messengers and prophets recognized in the Arabic scripture, their *sunnah* or the paradigmatic program of their careers is remarkably consistent, often expressed in the same vocabulary found in the formulaic phrases quoted in the outline of *ash-Shu'arā'* 26 presented here; notice in particular that the much-repeated phrase in reference to the significance of a given messenger/prophet's mission to his people, "In that there is a sign (*'āyah*)," is repeated eight times in the *surah* in connection with God's vindication of the messenger.

Many other *surahs* offer insights into Qur'ānic "prophetology" and even provide fuller lists of the pre-Islamic messengers and prophets, including the biblical ones. In this connection, consider the following long passage from *surah al-'An'ām* 6, 83–90, which, like *ash-Shu'arā'* 26 , is addressed by God to Muḥammad in view of the opposition to his admonitions he was receiving from his contemporaries.

> This is our argument that we brought to Abraham against his people. We raise in rank whomever we wish. Indeed, your (2ms) Lord is all-wise, all-knowing. And we gave him Isaac and Jacob and guided each of them. And Noah we guided before, and from his offspring, David and Solomon, Job, Joseph, Moses and Aaron – thus do we reward the virtuous – and Zechariah, John, Jesus and Ilyās, – each of them among the righteous – and Ishmael, Elisha, Jonah and Lot – each we graced over all the nations – and from among their fathers, their descendants and brethren – we chose them and guided them to a straight path. That is God's guidance: with it he guides whomever

32 On the 'punishment stories' in the Qur'ān, see David Marshall, *God, Muhammad, and the Unbelievers: A Qur'ānic Study* (Richmond, Surrey, UK: Curzon Press, 1999).

> he wishes of his servants. But were they to ascribe any partners [to God], what they used to do would not avail them. They are the ones to whom we gave the scripture, the judgment and prophethood (*an-nubuwwah*). So if these disbelieve in them, we have certainly entrusted them to a people who will never disbelieve in them. They are the ones whom God has guided. So follow (sing.) their guidance. Say (sing.), "*I do not ask of you (2mp) any wage for that.*" It is but a recollection (*dhikrā*) for the worlds. (*al-'An'ām* 6, 83–90)[33]

But when all is said and done, *surah ash-Shu'arā'* 26, with its highly structured format and ritualistically repeated refrains puts the basic features of prophetic recall in the Qur'ān into high relief. And the presence of three non-biblical messengers, Hūd, Ṣāliḥ, and Shu'ayb, in this *surah's* short list of messengers and prophets immediately calls attention to the fact that for the Qur'ān, prophecy is more than a biblical phenomenon, albeit that the high profile of the recollections of biblical prophets in the Qur'ān can seem to dominate the others. The fact remains that in the Qur'ān, the recollection of biblical prophets does not determine the "prophetology". Rather, the "prophetology" structures the biblical reminiscences; memories of biblical prophets are folded into a sequence that extends beyond the Bible's reach.[34] Some figures who do appear in the Bible, but who are not normally considered prophets in the biblical tradition, are nevertheless included among the messengers in the Qur'ān, e.g., Ishmael, Isaac, Jacob and the Tribes, Joseph, Jesus, Job, Jonah, Aaron, Solomon and David among others. Consider the following passage addressed to Muḥammad:

> We have indeed revealed to you (2ms) as we revealed to Noah and the prophets (*an-nabiyyīn*) after him, and [as] we revealed to Abraham and Ishmael, Isaac, Jacob, and the Tribes, Jesus and Job, Jonah, Aaron, and Solomon, – and we brought David the Psalms – and messengers (*rusulan*) we have recounted to you (2ms) earlier and messengers (*rusulan*) we have not recounted to you (2ms), – and to Moses God spoke directly – messengers (*rusulan*), as bearers of good news and warners so that men may not have any argument against God, after the [sending of] messengers (*ar-rusul*); and God is mighty and wise. (*an-Nisā'* 4, 163–165)[35]

The Qur'ān envisions a hierarchy among the messengers and prophets. Addressing Muḥammad again, God says:

---

33 Translation adapted from Sayyid 'Ali Quli Qara'i, *The Qur'an: With a Phrase-by-Phrase English Translation*, 2nd US Edition (Elmhurst, NY: Tahrike Tarsile Qur'an, Inc., 2011), 186–187.

34 See Griffith, *The Bible in Arabic*, esp. 54–96.

35 Translation adapted from 'Ali Quli Qara'i, *The Qur'an*, 140–141.

> These are God's signs (*'āyāt Allāh*) We are reciting to you (2ms) in truth. You (2ms) are one of those sent (*mursalīn*). We have favored some of these messengers (*rusul*) over others. There are those of them with whom God has conversed; some of them He has raised in rank. We brought Jesus, son of Mary, clear signs (*al-bayyināt*) and aided him with the holy spirit (*rūḥ al-qudus*). (*al-Baqarah* 2, 252–253)

On the basis of the pattern presented in *ash-Shuʿarā'* 26 and other *surahs*, the Qur'ān's distinctive "prophetology", its *sunnah* as the Qur'ān itself speaks of it,[36] has a certain paradigmatic profile; it features a paradigm shift from earlier descriptions of prophecy among the "Scripture People", principally the Jews, Christians, Jewish Christians and the Manichees.

By the time of the Qur'ān, Jews, Christians and others had long spoken of a sequential series of spokesmen who under divine inspiration summoned people to the worship of the one God and to right religion. The distinctiveness of the Qur'ān's "prophetology" was not so much in the idea of prophecy as such, or even in the idea of a sequence of patriarchs and prophets, but in the structure of the sequence and in the comprehension of the message, identical in each instance, along with the paradigmatic, prophetic pattern of warning, summons to fear the one God, opposition, and vindication. This paradigm pares down the prophetic profile familiar to Jews and Christians and focuses it more intensely on the Qur'ān's single-minded message and its phenomenological template of prophetic behavior. It has analogues with other Late Antique prophetic profiles, such as that to be found in certain Judeo-Christian texts, like the Pseudo-Clementine literature, and in Manichaean theology.

Judeo-Christian prophetology, like that of the Qur'ān, envisions a sequence of prophets, usually seven, which would culminate in the coming of the True Prophet, the Messianic Prophet, who is said to have come in the person of Jesus, to lead the Gentiles to the reformed Covenant of Sinai (in this view, Moses and Jesus are related as type to anti-type). According to the Pseudo-Clementines, the sequence included: Enoch, Noah, Abraham, Isaac, Jacob, Moses, and Jesus the Messiah, in whom the Spirit of revelation became incarnate.[37]

---

36 In reference to the messengers prior to Muḥammad, God speaks of "the *sunnah* of our messengers whom We have sent before you; you will not find that our *sunnah* has any turning away."*al-Isrā'* 17, 77. In other places the Qur'ān refers to this *sunnah* of the prophets and the '*sunnah* of the ancients' (*sunnat al-awwalīn*), as in *al-ḥijr* 15, 13; *Fāṭir* 35, 43.

37 See Hans Joachim Schoeps, *Theologie und Geschichte des Judenchristentums* (Tübingen: J.C.B. Mohr/Paul Siebeck, 1949), 87–116; *idem*, *Jewish Christianity: Factional Disputes in the Early Church*, trans. Douglas R. A. Hare (Philadelphia, PA: Fortress Press, 1969), 61–73.

Hans Joachim Schoeps and others have considered Judeo-Christian prophetology to be an ancestor to the Qur'ān's prophetology,[38] but it should be already clear from the present exposition that the idea of a succession of prophets bearing the same idea of a primordial religion (*Urreligion*) is the limit of the comparability; the Qur'ānic paradigm shares only the names of some of the prophet messengers with Judeo-Christian prophetology. For the Qur'ān, the messenger is not more important than the message.

Manichaeism, which was inaugurated by Mani (c. 216 – 276) in the third century, who was raised in the Judeo-Christian community of the Elkasaites in lower Mesopotamia, also features a succession of messengers and prophets with a universal message. And it is clear that Manichaean ideas were widespread in the Greek and Aramaic-speaking worlds of the first half of the seventh century and later, and they had long been familiar to the Arabs on the Arabian periphery.[39] In all likelihood, Manichaean lore circulated along with Jewish and Christian religious thought and practice throughout Late Antiquity, and particularly within the Aramaic and Syriac-speaking communities that were channels of so much religious culture into the Arabic-speaking milieu. It is entirely possible, even likely, that Manichaeism was known in the immediate surroundings of Muḥammad and the Qur'ān. But once again, the Qur'ān's distinctive "prophetology" has a different profile than that of the Manichees, albeit that one can find common features in the two scenarios.

As one recent scholar has put it:

> Mani located himself and his teachings at the final point in a line of divinely-commissioned apostles (*apostoloi, shlîḥê*); a tradition that formed part of the theology of the community in which Mani was raised the so-called Elchasaites, who looked to a cast of biblical forefathers as the divine revealers of teachings to their ancestors…. Mani, possibly as a reaction against his Elchasaite upbringing, extended the range of his succession to include figures who were unlikely to have been acknowledged by his former Jewish-Christian coreligionists as apostles or prophets. "Wisdom and deeds have always from time

---

38 See Schoeps, *Theologie und Geschichte*, 334 – 342; *idem*, *Jewish Christianity*, 136 – 140; Tor Andrae, *Mohammed: The Man and His Faith*, trans. T. Menzel (New York: Scribner's, 1936), esp. 99 – 113; and Patricia Crone, "Jewish Christianity and the Qur'ān." See also Samuel Zinner, *The Abrahamic Archetype: Conceptual and Historical Relationships between Judaism, Christianity and Islam* (Bartlow, Camb. UK: Archetype, 2011).

39 See Moshe Gil, "The Creed of Abū 'Amīr," *Israel Oriental Studies* 12 (1992): 9 – 57; Robert Simon, "Mānī and Muḥammad," *Jerusalem Studies in Arabic and Islam* 21 (1997): 118 – 141; François de Blois, "Elchasai – Manes – Muḥammad: Manichäismus und Islam in religionshistorischen Vergleich," *Der Islam* 81 (2004): 31 – 348.

> to time been brought to mankind by the messengers of God. So in one age they have been brought by the messenger, called Buddha, to India, in another by [Zoroaster] to Persia, in another by Jesus to the West. Thereupon this revelation has come down, this prophecy in this last age through me, Mani, the messenger of the God of truth to Babylonia."[40]

Mani's sequence of apostles and messengers according to most sources included: Adam, Seth, {Enoch}, Noah, {Abraham}, Zoroaster, Buddha, Jesus, {Paul}, and finally Mani, the Paraclete, and the "the seal of the prophets."[41] Notably absent from the lists are Moses and the Hebrew prophets. The sequence clearly indicates "a genealogy of divinely-sanctioned prophets and apostles."[42] And it is clear that "the role of prophetic personalities was essential to the overall meaning of the religion's teachings."[43] Mani may well have been inspired by the Judeo-Christian idea of the "True Prophet" coming at the end of a sequence of seven predecessors, a concern that was probably on the minds of his native community of Elchasaites in Babylonia. It has also been noted that the biblical messengers on the list, i.e., Adam, Seth, Enosh, Shem, and Enoch, are figures who are "all drawn from apocalyptic texts which had been presented as if composed by these primeval, legendary figures."[44]

One readily recognizes the parallels between the Manichaean prophetic genealogy and the Qurʾān's "prophetology". And as Arthur Jeffery remarked years ago, there are "striking coincidences" to be seen in "how Mani, who had had no human teacher or Master, was called to his mission by an angelic visitant who brought him Divine wisdom, and of how Elchasai was called to his preaching of the One God and an imminent Day of Judgment by an enormous angelic visitant who filled the horizon and brought him sheets of a heavenly book."[45] These matters will sound very familiar to readers of the biographic traditions of Muḥammad. But these Islamic narratives all come from well after the time of the

40 Nicholas J. Baker-Brian, *Manichaeism: An Ancient Faith Rediscovered* (London: T & T Clark, 2011), 27, including a quotation from *The Chronology of Ancient Nations*, 207; trans. C.E. Sachau 1879, 190.

41 See the lists in the several sources discussed by Michel Tardieu, *Manichaeism*, trans. M.B. De Bevoise (Urbana & Chicago: University of Illinois Press, 2008), 13–19. On the epithet, 'seal of the prophets,' see Gedaliahu G. Stroumsa, "'Seal of the Prophets': The Nature of a Manichaean Metaphor," *Jerusalem Studies in Arabic and Islam* 7 (1986): 61–74; Yohanan Friedmann, "Finality of Prophethood in Sunnī Islam," *Jerusalem Studies in Arabic and Islam* 7 (1986): 177–215.

42 Baker-Brian, *Manichaeism: An Ancient Faith Rediscovered*, 42.

43 Baker-Brian, *Manichaeism: An Ancient Faith Rediscovered*, 34.

44 Baker-Brian, *Manichaeism: An Ancient Faith Rediscovered*, 50.

45 Arthur Jeffery, *The Qur'ān as Scripture* (New York: Russell F. Moore Company, 1952), 8.

Qur'ān. As for the features of the story that actually appear in the Qur'ān, one might best think that they supply evidence that the author/speaker of the Arabic scripture was consciously addressing an audience known to be familiar with the concept of prophetic genealogy. It was presumably this realization that prompted Arthur Jeffery to say that Muḥammad was convinced that "he was called to bring to the Arabs, who had had no prophet sent them, the same religion which the prophets had brought to those other religious communities whom he referred to as the People of the Book."[46] But the matter is not so simple; the Qur'ān's "prophetology" suggests that the composer/speaker of this Arabic scripture has employed the readily available vocabulary and syntax of messengership and prophethood both to critique and to correct current ideas about the message of the earlier messengers and prophets, and clearly to present its own teaching about the one God, with whom other contemporary communities perversely persist in associating creatures as divine equals, principally those who say that God has a Son.

When one considers the lists of messengers and prophets that circulated among the so-called Judeo-Christian groups, principally the Ebionites and Elchasaites, and the Manichees, it is clear that the Qur'ān rejects any hint of a Judeo-Christian or Marcionite view of earlier scriptures and the prophets whose message they transmit. The Qur'ān says, "God chose Adam, and Noah, and the family of Abraham and the family of 'Imrān over the peoples (*'alā l-'ālamīn*)" (*'Āl 'Imrān* 3, 33). So Moses and the Hebrew patriarchs and prophets down to John the Baptist and Jesus are included in the Qur'ān's sequence, right along with earlier biblical messengers and a selection of non-biblical messengers. Notably absent from the Qur'ān's list are Zoroaster, Buddha, Paul, and Mani himself. And Muḥammad is notably present as the culminant prophetic figure, indeed as "the messenger of God and the seal of the prophets." (*al-'Aḥzāb* 33, 40). Moreover it is clear in the Qur'ān that the dominant personal profile for those sent by God is that of the "messenger" (*rasūl*, pl. *rusul*), the "apostle", a designation that altogether occurs some 331 times in the Arabic scripture, whereas with the exception of Muḥammad himself, only those who are mentioned in the Jewish and Christian biblical traditions are called "prophet", a designation occurring 75 times all told, sometimes a title accorded to those who are also called "messenger". Muḥammad, who is said to be the "seal of the prophets," seems, again like Mani,[47] to have preferred the title "messenger". But his mission also has prophetic over-

46 Jeffery, *The Qur'ān as Scripture*, 9.

47 See the remark of G. Stroumsa, "Mani does not seem to have considered himself only, or mainly, a prophet. In his own eyes, he was, more than a prophet, an apostle." Stroumsa, "Seal of the Prophets," 74.

tones, and Muḥammad is a number of times called simply "prophet" (*nabīy*) in the Qur'ān.[48] The Arabic scripture seems to enroll him as one among the "messengers" who had also taken on the role of a biblical prophet. In the Qur'ān God says of the Jews and Christians: "As for those who follow the Messenger, the *ummī* Prophet,[49] whom they find inscribed among them in the Torah and the Gospel, he bids them to do good and to forbid evil." (*al-'A'rāf* 7, 157) Muḥammad is thus the "messenger" whose status the Qur'ān is affirming by enrolling him in its sequence of messengers and prophets, recognized by this scripture's distinctive "prophetology".[50] What is more, the Qur'ān presents Muḥammad and his mission within the horizon of the history of the prophets and messengers who came before him to the "Scripture People" as the paradigmatic "messenger" of God, whose message critiques and corrects the distorted beliefs and practices of those communities, Jews, Christians, and *mushrikūn* among other Arabic-speakers, who, in the Qur'ān's view, had lapsed from the right guidance they had previously received.

V

The Qur'ān's distinctive "prophetology" entailed a corresponding, distinctive presentation of the commonly circulating stories of the biblical Patriarchs and Prophets who appear in the sequence of the Qur'ān's Messengers and Prophets; in the text they are presented as closely following the "*sunnah* of Our Messengers". In the telling there is a notable pattern of counter discourse, counter to that of the Christians and others, even a corrective dimension to the Qur'ān's recollection of the biblical and other narratives of the Jews and Christians in its milieu. The Qur'ān means not so much to retell the biblical stories but to recall them, and to recollect them within the corrective framework of its own discourse. For this reason, with the exception of the quotation of a portion of Ps. 37:29 in *al-'Anbiyā'* 21, 105, the Qur'ān does not in fact ever actually quote the Bible. Rather,

---

48 See, e.g., the dozen times the title 'prophet' is accorded to Muḥammad in *al-'Aḥzāb* 33, including the famous verse, "Muḥammad is not the father of any of your men, but he is the Messenger of God and the 'seal of the prophets'" (vs. 40). See also the interesting sequence in *at-Taḥrīm* 66, 1–9.

49 See the important study by Sebastian Günther, "Muḥammad, the Illiterate Prophet: An Islamic Creed in the Qur'ān and Qur'ānic Exegesis," *Journal of Qur'anic Studies* 4 (2002): 1–26.

50 See in this connection the aforementioned important article by Willem A. Bijlefeld, "A Prophet and More than a Prophet? Some Observations on the Qur'anic Use of the Terms 'Prophet' and 'Apostle'," *The Muslim World* 59 (1969): 1–28.

the Qur'ān re-presents the stories of many of the Bible's major figures within the parameters of its own, distinctive "prophetology", "the *sunnah* of Our messengers", which is in effect an apologetic and corrective counter discourse vis-à-vis that of the Jews and Christians about the significance and role of the same biblical figures. In particular, it also supplies the discursive framework that determines the idiom in which the Qur'ān proclaims its own view of the truth about Jesus the Messiah. It is very much in contrast to the Christology one finds commended in contemporary, particularly Syriac, Christian homiletic texts that primarily explore and elucidate the types and functional symbols (*râzê*) of the Christ of the Gospels in the stories of the Bible's Patriarchs and Prophets, the Messiah who is proclaimed to be both human and divine, who died on the cross and who rose again to sit at the right hand of His Father in heaven.

In notable contrast to the Syrian Christian exegetical practice of highlighting the so-called *râzê*, the typological symbols discerned in the narratives of the Bible's Patriarchs and Prophets that pre-figure the Gospel's proclamation of the coming of the Messiah in the person of Jesus of Nazareth, the Qur'ān's concern with the same narratives of Patriarchs and Prophets, is to discern in them and to highlight not the *râzê* of Jesus the Messiah, but the active presence of the "signs" (*'āyāt*) that God has displayed in connection with their witness, to signal the authenticity of their testimony to the truth that God is one and that He rewards good behavior and punishes wickedness. In *surah ash-Shuʿarāʾ* 26, where the Qur'ān presents the clearest and most detailed exposition of its distinctive "prophetology", the paradigm or *sunnah* of all God's Qur'ānic Messengers and Prophets, the term *'āyah* (pl. *'āyāt*) occurs some fourteen times all told. Eight of them, as we mentioned above, refer to God's vindication of His Messengers and Prophets after their rejection by the people to whom they were sent. The Qur'ān commonly refers to the punishment of these disobedient people in some formulation of the phrase, "In this there is surely a sign (*'āyah*), but the majority of them will not believe" (*ash-Shuʿarāʾ* 23, 8, 67, 103, 121, 139, 158, 174, 190). More positively, in reference to the Qur'ān itself and to some people in its audience who refuse to accept its message, God says to Muḥammad, "Is it not a sign (*'āyah*) for them that the Israelite scholars are acquainted with it? Even if We had sent it down to a non-Arabic speaker and he recited it to them, they would not believe it" (*ash-Shuʿarāʾ* 23, 197). On the face of it, the verse avers that the Israelites in the Qur'ān's audience, that is to say the Jews and the Christians, recognize the Arabic scripture's reminiscences of the experiences of the biblical Patriarchs and Prophets in Muḥammad's recitations and that in itself is a "sign" (*'āyah*) of the authenticity of his recollection of them.

The Qur'ān veritably teems with references to the "signs" of the authenticity of God's Messengers and Prophets and their unvarying message; the term *'āyah* (pl. *'āyāt*) itself occurs almost four hundred times in this connection, some sixty times along with the companion term *bayyinah* (pl. *bayyināt*) in the sense of "manifest" or "evident" signs. The Qur'ān presents them as evidentiary, even miraculous "signs" produced by God, or by God's permission, not only in testimony to the veracity of God's revelatory message, but also as indicative of God's presence and action.[51] In this connection, God's *'āyāt* have a cognitive function; they are meant to elicit a person's recognition, albeit that the Qur'ān most often reports that the people to whom His Messengers have been sent have turned aside from His *'āyāt*, and they have even regarded them as false, even though God "would diversify the *'āyāt*, so that they perhaps would understand" (see *al-'An'ām* 6, 65, 98, 105), or He displays His *'āyāt* so that people may perhaps understand (see *al-Baqarah* 2, 73, 164; *al-Ḥadīd* 57, 17).

Here is not the place to expand on this very important theme, save only to say that the disclosure of God's *'āyāt* is an integral feature of the Qur'ān's distinctive "prophetology" in action. In fact, at one place in a Medinan *surah*, in reference to Muḥammad's mission to his own Arabic-speaking people, the Qur'ān says of God, "It is He who has raised up among unlettered people (*al-'ummiyyīn*) a Messenger from among them to recite His signs (*'āyāt*), to purify them, and to teach them Scripture and Wisdom" (*al-Jumu'ah* 62, 2). And just as reports of the role of God's *'āyāt* thus have a prominent place in the Qur'ān's affirmation of Muḥammad and of all of God's Messengers and Prophets, so too is the invocation of them prominent in the Qur'ān's proclamation of Jesus, the Messiah, as God's Messenger (*an-Nisā'* 4, 171) and Prophet (*Maryam* 19, 30).

VI

It is clear from a number of passages that the Qur'ān's hermeneutically most significant title for Jesus the Messiah, Mary's son, is "Messenger of God" (*rasūl Allāh*); it explicitly accords him this title five times in crucial passages, and in one such place the text specifies that, "The Messiah, Mary's son, is only a Messenger, before whom Messengers have passed away." (*al-Mā'idah* 5, 75) Further, in a remarkable passage, laden with significant vocabulary, the Qur'ān says that Jesus, Mary's son, like God's other Messengers, was sent to his own people, the Israelites:

---

51 See Binyamin Abrahamov, "Signs," in Jane Dammen McAuliffe, *Encyclopaedia of the Qur'ān*, 6 vols. (Leiden: Brill, 2001–2006), vol. V, 2–11.

> [Remember] when the angel said, 'O Mary, God is announcing to you a word (*kalimah*) from Him, whose name is the Messiah, Jesus, Mary's son, a notable person in this world and the next, one of those close [to God]. He will converse with people both in the cradle and as a a mature adult, one of the righteous.' She said, my Lord, how will I have a child; no man has touched me?' He said, 'So it is that God creates what He wills; when He determines something, He just says to it, 'Be', and it comes to be. He will teach him the scripture, the Wisdom, the Torah, and the Gospel.' As a messenger (*rasūlan*) to the Israelites, [he will say,] 'I have brought you a sign (*ʾāyah*) from your Lord. With God's permission, I am going to create for you the form of a bird from clay and I am going to breathe into it, and it will become a bird. I will cure the blind and the lepers, and I will revivify the the dead, with God's permission. I will announce to you what you will eat and what you will store in your houses. If you are believers, that will be a sign (*ʾāyah*) for you. Confirming what was before me of the Torah, I will allow for you some of what was forbidden to you. I bring you a sign from your Lord, so fear God and obey me.[52] God is my Lord and your Lord, so worship Him; this is the straight path.' (*ʾĀl ʿImrān* 3, 45–51).

Similarly, in *surah Maryam* 19, in a passage revealed earlier than the one quoted just above, for which it served as a template in the early collection and recension of the Qurʾān,[53] the same prophetic paradigm is evident. After recalling Mary's story in terms reminiscent of the Annunciation scene in the Gospel according to Luke 1:26–38 and of the legends about her that circulated widely among Late Antique Christians, which survive in Christian apocryphal literature,[54] the Qurʾān says:

> Remember Mary in the scripture, when she went away from her people to the east. She took on a veil out of their sight and We sent down Our spirit to her and to her he seemed like a comely man. She said, 'I seek refuge with the Compassionate One from you, if you are a [God-]fearer.' He said, 'I am only your Lord's

52 The phrase, "So fear God and obey me," recurs in accounts of God's Messengers, cf., e.g., *ash-Shuʿarāʾ* 26, 126, and again in reference to Jesus in *az-Zukhruf* 43, 63.
53 In this connection, see the studies of Frank van den Velden cited in n. 2 above.
54 See, e.g., Suleiman Mourad, "On the Qurʾānic Stories about Mary and Jesus," *Bulletin of the Royal Institute for Inter-Faith Studies* 1 (1999): 13–24; *idem*, "From Hellensim to Christianity and Islam: The Origin of the Palm-Tree Story concerning Mary and Jesus in the Gospel of Pseudo-Matthew and the Qur'ān," *Oriens Christianus* 86 (2002): 206–216; *idem*, "Mary in the Qurʾān: A Reexamination of Her Presentation," in *The Qurʾān in Its Historical Context*, ed. Gabriel Said Reynolds (London & New York: Routledge, 2008), 163–174.

> Messenger, to grant you a pure boy.' She said, 'How can I have a boy? No man has touched me and I am not a harlot.' He said, 'Thus has your Lord spoken, 'For Me it is easy; let Us make of him a sign (*'āyah*) for people and a mercy from Us.' And it was so decreed. She became pregnant and she went off with him to a distant place.... [From the cradle] he said, 'I am God's slave (*'abd*); He has given me the scripture and made me a Prophet, He has made me blessed where ever I may be, and He has mandated prayer and alms-giving as long as I live, and piety toward my mother (*wālidatī*), and He did not make me wretchedly overweening. Peace be on the day I was born, the day I will die, and the day I will be brought back alive.' That is Jesus, Mary's son, the statement of the truth about which they are in doubt. It is not for God to take any son. Praise be to Him, when He determines anything He just says to it, 'Be' and it comes to be. God is my Lord and your Lord, worship Him; this is a straight path. The partisans disagree among themselves. Woe be to those at the time of witness on a mighty day who will have disbelieved (*Maryam* 19, 16–37).

As for the actual way in which God brought about Mary's pregnancy with Jesus, the Qur'ān elsewhere reports God's saying regarding "the one who guarded her womb," "We breathed into her of Our spirit and We made her and her son a sign (*'āyah*) for the worlds." (*al-'Anbiyā'* 21, 91; see also *at-Taḥrīm* 66, 12) One readily recognizes in these passages words and phrases already familiar from the formulaic language that describes the role of God's Prophets and Messengers in other passages in the Qur'ān. There could hardly be clearer statements of the Qur'ān's Christology and we find it reprised elsewhere in the Arabic scripture. It is important to notice in these passages how the Qur'ān uses words, phrases, and concepts well-known also in Christian parlance, but the Qur'ān deploys them within an interpretive framework that reinterprets them within the hermeneutic horizon of its own message.

An important element of the Qur'ān's message about Jesus the Messiah is that he came in a sequence of God's Messengers, each with the same distinctive message for his own people. So having spoken of Moses and the other prophets and their mission to the Israelites, the Qur'ān reports God's saying about Jesus,

> We caused Jesus, Mary's son, to follow in their footsteps, confirming what was before him of the Torah. We gave him the Gospel, in which there is guidance and light, confirming what was before it of the Torah, guidance and warning for the [God-]fearers. Let the Gospel People judge by what God has sent down in it. Whoever does not judge by what God has sent down, they are the wicked (*al-Mā'idah* 5, 46–47).

Other passages also emphasize Jesus' place in the sequence of messengers, emphasizing the role of God's spirit in aiding him and calling attention to God's "signs" (*'āyāt*) evident in his mission. "We brought the scripture to Moses and caused messengers to follow him; We gave Jesus, Mary's son, clear signs (*al-bayyināt*) and We aided him by means of the holy spirit" (*al-Baqarah* 2, 87). And the sequence of messengers extends beyond Jesus himself to anticipate the coming of another and final messenger after him, whose name is Aḥmad, whom commentators have consistently identified with Muḥammad. The Qur'ān says:

> [Remember] when Jesus, Mary's son, said, 'O Israelites, I am God's messenger to you, confirming what was before me of the Torah and announcing a Messenger who will come after me, whose name is Aḥmad. When he comes to them with clear signs (*bayyināt*), they will say this is manifest sorcery.[55] (*aṣ-Ṣaff* 61, 6).

Interestingly, in the sequence of Prophets and Messengers, only Moses, Jesus, and Muḥammad seem to have been accorded both titles, "Messenger" and "Prophet",[56] in all probability because all three of them addressed their messages to the Israelites. And among the Israelites to whom he was sent, according to the Qur'ān, Jesus had both helpers as well as adversaries. In a passage that follows upon Jesus' miraculous statement of his mission while still in the cradle as quoted above, the Qur'ān goes on to say,

> When Jesus perceived disbelief on the part of some of them, he said, 'Who are my helpers (*'anṣārī*) unto God?' The apostles (*al-ḥawāriyyūn*)[57] said, 'We are God's helpers (*'anṣār Allāh*); we believe in God. Testify that we are submitting.[58] O Lord, we

---

55 It is interesting to note in passing that the Qur'ān says the same thing about the Israelites' reception of Jesus as God's messenger, "This is just manifest sorcery," (*al-Mā'idah* 5, 110). In the Talmud Jesus is regularly accused of sorcery. See Peter Schäfer, *Jesus in the Talmud* (Princeton, NJ: Princeton University Press, 2007).

56 For Moses see *at-Tawbah* 9, 51; for Jesus see *at-Tawbah* 9, 30; Muḥammad is called 'prophet'12 times in *al-'Aḥzāb* 33, 1–59.

57 This term is alternatively translated as 'disciples' or 'apostles'. Given the fact that the Ethiopic term that seems to lie behind the Arabic word is regularly used to mean 'apostle', that option seems the best one here. See Arthur Jeffery, *The Foreign Vocabulary of the Quran* (Baroda: Oriental Institute, 1938), 115–116.

58 The term in the Qur'ān is *muslimūn*, i.e., muslims; it is used here in its common, lowercase sense of those who submit and not in its technical, uppercase sense of Muslims.

> believe in what You have sent down and we follow the Messenger.[59]
> So inscribe us among those testifying (*'Āl 'Imrān* 3, 52–53).

These words are echoed in another place in the Qur'ān, where the text is addressed to "those who believe", i.e., Muḥammad's community, the Muslims, who are bidden to emulate Jesus' apostles:

> O you who believe, become God's helpers (*'anṣār Allāh*), as Jesus, Mary's son, said to the apostles (*al-ḥawāriyyīn*), 'Who are my helpers unto God?' The apostles said, 'We are God's helpers.' So a group of the Israelites believed and a group disbelieved. So We aided those who believed over their enemy and they prevailed (*aṣ-Ṣaff* 61, 14).

And finally, like all God's Messengers mentioned in the Qur'ān, Jesus faced disbelieving adversaries who threatened his life, but according to the Qur'ān they did not prevail against him. The Qur'ān says of the Israelite "Scripture People" that they say, "We killed the Messiah, Jesus, Mary's son, God's messenger.... They certainly did not kill him. Rather, God raised him up to Himself" (*an-Nisā'* 4, 157–158). While there is much discussion among the commentators on the Qur'ān both ancient and modern about the full meaning of these verses,[60] on the face of it, at the very least the text denies the Israelite boast of responsibility for Jesus' death, and it thereby affirms, following the "*sunnah* of Our Messengers", that his disbelieving, Israelite adversaries did not prevail against him. As a matter of fact, in another passage in the Qur'ān in which God is addressing Jesus, He says, "[Remember] when I held the Israelites back from you when you came to them with clear signs (*bayyināt*)" (*al-Mā'idah* 5, 110). Already the earliest Muslim commentators on the Qur'ān argued that Jesus's Israelite adversaries did not prevail against him because someone else, a look-alike, was by God's design crucified and killed in his stead,[61] a position that has become a constant point of controversy ever since. What is not in controversy is that in the Qur'ān's view,

59 The Messenger here is doubtless Jesus.
60 See Todd Lawson, *The Crucifixion and the Qur'ān: A Study in the History of Muslim Thought* (Oxford: One World, 2009); Gabriel Said Reynolds, "The Muslim Jesus: Dead or Alive?" *Bulletin of the School of Oriental and African Studies* 72 (2009): 237–258; Suleiman Mourad, "The Death of Jesus in Islam: Reality, Assumptions, and Implications," in *Engaging the Passion: Perspectives on the Death of Jesus*, ed. Oliver Larry Yarbrough (Minneapolis, MN: Fortress Press, 2015), 357–379.
61 See, e.g., Abū l-Ḥasan Muqātil ibn Sulaymān, *Tafsīr Muqātil ibn Sulaymān*, ed. Aḥmad Farīd; 3 vols. (Beirut: Dār al-Kutub al-'Aqliyyah, 2002), vol I, 269.

Jesus the Messiah is God's Messenger, whose adversaries did not prevail against him.

In addition to proclaiming Jesus the Messiah, Mary's son, to be God's Messenger and Prophet, the Qur'ān also states that he is God's "word" (*kalimatuhu*) "that He cast into Mary and a spirit (*rūḥun*) from Him" (*an-Nisā'* 4, 171). While both of these terms, "word" and "spirit" familiarly appear in the Qur'ān in connection with the activities of Messengers and Prophets, as we shall see, they are unique as titles for Jesus the Messiah.

As for the designation of Jesus the Messiah as a "spirit" from God, it recalls in particular the Qur'ān's view of God's "spirit" as a created, almost personalized being, often accompanied by angels, who at God's bidding (*'amr*) brings life to His creatures, and both life and revelation to His Prophets and Messengers.[62] And strikingly, in conjunction with God's creative command to both Adam and Jesus "to be" (*kun*; *'Āl 'Imrān* 3, 47 & 59), the Qur'ān says that God breathed of His "spirit" into Adam (*al-Ḥijr* 15, 29; *Ṣād* 38, 72) and also to have breathed of "Our spirit" into Mary when she became pregnant with Jesus (*al-'Anbiyā'* 21, 91 & *at-Taḥrīm* 66, 12). With this same "holy spirit", or "spirit of holiness" (*rūḥ al-qudus*),[63] God also aided Jesus, Mary's son, having brought him "clear signs" (*al-bayyināt*) in evidence of his role as God's Messenger (*al-Baqarah* 2, 87, 253), just as God instructs Muḥammad to say to those questioning him, "Say, 'The spirit of holiness has brought [the message] down with the truth from your (2ms) Lord so that He might affirm those who believe, and as guidance and good tidings for those who submit (*muslimīn*)'" (*an-Naḥl* 16, 102). Finally one might say that according to the Qur'ān, Jesus the Messiah, Mary's son, is a "spirit" from God in the same way as was the one who seemed to Mary to be "a proper human being" when God sent His spirit to her: "We dispatched Our spirit to her and he seemed to her to be like a proper human being (*tamaththala lahā basharan sawiyyan*)" (*Maryam* 19, 17). In the Qur'ān's view a created human being like Jesus, Mary's son, and God's Messenger, can therefore be seen as the human face of God's created spirit. In this way the Qur'ān critically presents its own doctrine of God's "holy spirit" vis-à-vis the Christian doctrine of the "Holy Spirit" and simultaneously articulates a distinctive aspect of its own positive Christology, which then serves as a critical correction of current, Late Antique Christian Christology.

---

62 See esp. Thomas O'Shaughnessy, *The Development of the Meaning of Spirit in the Koran*, Orientalia Christiana Analecta, 139 (Rome: Pont. Institutum Orientalium Studiorum, 1953).

63 See Sidney H. Griffith, "Holy Spirit," in *Encyclopaedia of the Qur'ān*, ed. Jane Dammen McAuliffe, 6 vols. (Leiden: Brill, 2001–2006), vol. II, 442–444.

When the Qur'ān says that God breathed of "Our spirit" into Mary (*al-'Anbiyā'* 21, 91) and spoke the imperative word, *kun* ("be"), so that Jesus the Messiah might actually come into created being (*'Āl 'Imrān* 3, 47), the text goes on to say that Mary and her son Jesus himself are then to be seen as a "sign (*'āyatan*) for the ages" (*al-'Anbiyā'* 21, 91). That the Qur'ān speaks of Jesus, God's Messenger, and his mother as one of God's "signs" is not surprising given the fact that so too generally does the Qur'ān speak of the careers of all the messengers and prophets, as we have seen. In the typology of Prophecy and Messengership set out in *surah ash-Shu'arā'* 26, as discussed above, some eight times at the conclusion of the accounts of the several Prophets and Messengers whose mission to their people is mentioned there one finds it said in reference to their prophetic careers and their people's response to them the phrase, "In that there is certainly a sign (*'āyatan*), but most of them did not become believers" (*ash-Shu'arā'* 26, 8, 67, 103, 121 139, 174, 190).

But the designation of Jesus as being himself God's created and creating "word" (*kalimah*), which "He cast into Mary," (*an-Nisā'* 4, 171) is a Christological title specific to him among the Messengers whose careers are recalled in the Qur'ān, who only transmit God's "word" and "words" (*kalimah*, pl., *kalimāt*) and "scriptures" (*kutub*) to their people.[64] One also finds reference to Jesus as God's "word" in two other passages. In the first one, speaking in anticipation of the coming of Jesus the Messiah, God's "word", in *surah 'Āl 'Imrān* 3, the angels say to Zachary, John the Baptist's father, "God is announcing John to you, one of the righteous ones, a Prophet, a celibate, a master, one who will confirm a "word" (*kalimah*) from Him" (*'Āl 'Imrān* 3, 39). The earliest Muslim commentators recognized the reference to Jesus' unique title here, i.e., God's "word" (*kalimah*), whom John would be the first to recognize,[65] and not uncommonly in later times, they also recalled Jesus' being a "spirit" from God, who had breathed of His spirit into Jesus at his creation. Commentators thereafter not infrequently said that Jesus was named God's "word" because he was created by means of God's spoken "word", i.e., *kun* ("be"), addressed to him at the moment when he came into being.[66] Then in a subsequent verse in the same *surah*, in a word pattern that echoes the angels' announcement to Zachary quoted just above, the angels address Mary: "O Mary, God announces to you a "word"

---

64 See, e.g., passages such as *al-A'rāf* 7, 137; *Yūnus* 10, 33; *Ibrāhīm* 14, 24; *al-Kahf* 18, 109; *Luqmān* 31, 27; *at-Taḥrīm* 66, 12.

65 See Muqātil ibn Sulaymān, *Tafsīr*, vol. I, 167–168.

66 See, e.g., Jalāl ad-Dīn al-Maḥallī and Jalāl ad-Dīn as-Suyūṭī, *Tafsīr al-Jalalayn li Imāmayn al-Jalīlayn*, ed. Ṣafī ar-Raḥmān al-Mubārakfūrī, 2nd ed. (Riyadh, Saudi Arabia: Dār as-Salām lil-Nashri wat-Tawzī', 2002/1422), 64.

from Him (*kalimatun minhu*), whose name is the Messiah, Jesus, Mary's son, one of those come nigh [unto Him], eminent in this world and the next" (*ʾĀl ʿImrān* 3, 45). So one might say that for the Qurʾān, just as Jesus the Messiah is the human face of God's created "spirit", so too is he the human face of God's created "word", addressing the Israelites as God's Messenger to them. In this way, the Qurʾān critically presents its own doctrine of the word of God vis-à-vis the Late Antique, Christian doctrine of Jesus the Messiah as the incarnate "Word of God", one of the "Three" of whom the Qurʾān bids its hearers to stop speaking (*an-Nisāʾ* 4, 171).

VII

Read within the horizon of the Late Antique context of its origins in the early seventh century CE, the Qurʾān thus readily appears to legitimate its message, including in particular its understanding of the role of Jesus the Messiah as God's Messenger and Prophet, by recalling the experiences of God's earlier Messengers and Prophets according to the pattern its own prophetic *Sunnah* of God's Messengers. The reminiscence includes the stories of the biblical Patriarchs and Prophets as they would have been available orally in the Arabic-speaking milieu of the time. In its select recollection of the events of their prophetic careers, the Qurʾān highlights what it constantly represents as God's evidentiary "signs" (*ʾāyāt*) perceptible already in the traditional accounts of the Patriarchs and Prophets, "signs" deemed by the Qurʾān to be indicative of the divine warrant for both their messengership and their message.

Within the Late Antique cultural context of Graeco-Aramean Palestine, Syria, Mesopotamia, and Arabia, while Syriac-speaking Christians within this milieu were in their own scriptural reasoning customarily contemplating the *râzê* they discerned in the biblical accounts of the patriarchs and prophets, which for them disclosed the mysteries of the coming of the Messiah proclaimed in the Gospel, the Qurʾān of a sudden appeared commending a different construal of the very same traditional and biblical lore. The Qurʾān proposed a different and distinctive, scriptural profile for the Messengers and Prophets of whom it speaks, which according to its own criteria disclosed a recurrent paradigm for the careers of God's Messengers and Prophets, "the *sunnah* of Our messengers", as the Qurʾān calls it that included Jesus the Messiah as the last but one in a series of Messengers and Prophets, culminating in the coming of Aḥmad/Muḥammad, the "seal of the prophets" (*al-ʾAḥzāb* 33, 40), whose advent Jesus himself is said to have foretold (*aṣ-Ṣaff* 61, 61). Instead of the *râzê* or "types" of Christ, "the Son of the living God" that Syriac-speaking Christians saw in the biblical narratives of the Patriarchs and Prophets, the Qur'ān called attention to the *'āyāt Allāh* recorded in these same narratives that in its view warranted its own understanding of Christ's role in salvation history, disclosed it its own distinctive prophetology. The Qur'ān's Jesus the Messiah is thus not the Jewish Christian, angelomorphic "True Prophet, the Messianic Prophet", nor is he the Manichaean "Jesus of Light, the Messiah, Jesus *patibilis*", as the Manichees described him. Rather in the Qur'ān, Jesus' identity-profile as *rasūl Allāh*, God's "word" and a "spirit" from Him, is presented fully in accordance with the typological pattern schematically displayed in *surah ash-Shu'arā'* 26, and often repeated in the phrasing of prophetic narratives elsewhere in the Arabic scripture.

Similarly, the Qur'ān's Jesus the Messiah, Mary's son, *rasūl Allāh*, is not the divine "Son of God", whose prophetic *râzê* Syriac-speaking, Christian writers were wont to find strewn throughout nature and scripture. Nor, according to the Qur'ān, is he the only-begotten Son, consubstantial (*homousios*) with God the Father who begot him, in whom divinity and humanity are united in a single, individual "person", as the several propositional Christologies current in the main-line church communities of the seventh century expressed it, each according to its own understanding of the implications of the technical Greek terms used in the several confessional and creedal formulae that symbolized their disunity on the topic. Rather, the Qur'ān explicitly critiques and expressly disowns any talk of Jesus the Messiah being in any way accurately described as "Son of God". Nevertheless, one can discern in the Qur'ān's own Arabic language of critique of contemporary Christian doctrine and practice, and especially in its Christology, numerous evidences of the Arabic scripture's familiarity with customary Christian Theology and Christological parlance, especially in Syriac. In other words, it is clear that Late Antique Christology was fully within the purview of the Qur'ān's counter discourse.

Everywhere in the Qur'ān, early and late, in both Meccan and Medinan *surahs*, one finds the clear expression in one formulation or another of the Arabic scripture's basic creedal proclamation of strict monotheism (*at-tawḥīd*). Perhaps the most succinct expression of this article of faith and fundamental, theological principle is the statement in *sūrat al-'Ikhlāṣ* 112, 1–4, with its echo of the Jewish *Shema*^{c} (Deuteronomy 6:4): "Say, 'God is one, the eternal God," and even possibly its counter claim to the Christian Nicene Creed: He has not given birth, nor is He born; and being one, He has no coequal'."[67] The point is reinforced throughout the Qur'ān in phrases such as, "There is no God but He, (2:163)" "He has no

67 See Angelika Neuwirth, *Der Koran als Text der Spätantike: ein europäischer Zugang* (Berlin: Verlag der Weltreligionen im Insel Verlag, 2010), 761–768.

associate (6:163)," and "He has not gotten any offspring (*walad*)" (17:111). In one passage the Qur'ān identifies the one God with the God of the biblical patriarchs, just as do the Torah and the Gospels. Recalling God's words to the Israelites, the verse asks, "Were you witnesses when death came to Jacob, when he said to his sons, 'What will you worship after me?' They said, 'We will worship your God, and the God of your fathers, Abraham, Ishmael, and Isaac, one God, we shall be submitters (*muslimūn*) to Him'." (*al-Baqarah* 2, 133)

In addition to proclaiming its own view of the truth about Jesus the Messiah in a discourse that counters Late Antique, Christian Christology in terms of Qur'ānic "prophetology", the Qur'ān also polemically critiques and directly contradicts Christian affirmations about Christ. The Qur'ān mounts this critique polemically both in the direct discourse of denying the validity of Christian affirmations of the divinity of Jesus the Messiah, as well as by means of rhetorical ploys that highlight what from the Qur'ān's point of view illustrates the absurdity of Christian doctrine. In particular, as we shall see in several instances, the Qur'ān seems at times, from a Christian point of view, rhetorically to misconstrue the customary Christian expression of belief about Jesus the Messiah in order to censure it more forcefully. For example, as we shall discuss in more detail below, in rejecting the Christian belief that Jesus the Messiah is God, the Son of God, the Qur'ān says, "They have disbelieved who say that God is the Messiah, Jesus, Mary's son" (*al-Mā'idah* 5, 17 & 72). No Christians of the seventh century who confessed the divinity of Jesus the Messiah ever said, "God is the Messiah", a claim that would have been as repugnant to them as it was to the Qur'ān. This is why the Qurān knowingly, we may surmise, expressed its critique as it did, namely to suggest that what the Christians did say about Jesus, that he is the Son of God, might be taken logically to entail the blasphemy ("God is the Messiah"), a formula that Christians would themselves reject.

The Qur'ān's constant designation of Jesus the Messiah as "Mary's son", repeated some 22 times, seems calculated rhetorically to counter the usual Christian confession that Jesus is the Son of God, albeit that Christians would have had no objection to the title, "Mary's son" as such, save in as much as it would be used to deny his divine son-ship. As for Mary herself, in the Christological controversies of the early seventh century, the title "Mother of God" for her was still rejected by members of the so-called "Nestorian" Church of the East, who, although they confessed Jesus to be the Son of God, they nevertheless preferred titles for Mary such as "Mother of Jesus" or "Mother of the Messiah", as in the Qur'ān. Meanwhile the title "Mother of God" functioned effectively at the same time as a creedal statement of the Christology of both the "Jacobite" and "Melkite" churches, a usage that doubtless lay behind the Qur'ān's report of God's rhetorical question to Jesus, "Did you say to people, 'Take me and my mother to be two gods instead of God?'" (*al-Mā'idah* 5, 116). As for the Qur'ān's own view of Mary, it says, "[Remember] when the angels said, 'O Mary, God has chosen you and purified you above the women of the world'" (*'Āl 'Imrān* 3, 42). And in another place she is described as "sincerely truthful" (*siddīqah*; *al-Mā'idah* 5, 75). The language used here and in *al-Mā'idah* 5, 17 & 116 clearly indicate both the Qur'ān's high esteem for her and, at the same time, its disavowal of any divinity associated with her. In God's name, the Qur'ān also puts Mary forward as a woman who was a model (*mathalan*) for those who believe, "And there was Mary, the daughter of 'Imrān, who safeguarded her womb, so We breathed of Our spirit into it and she credited the truth of her Lord's words (*kalimāt*) and of His scriptures. She was one of the devout ones." (*at-Taḥrīm* 66, 12; see also *al-'Anbiyā'* 21, 91)[68]

According to the Qur'ān, while the basic "infidelity" (*al-kufr*) of the polytheists of old consisted in wrongly ascribing partners to God (*al-mushrikūn*), so too, according to the Qur'ān, did the infidelity of the Christians among the "scripture people" (*'ahl al-kitāb*) consist in ascribing a partner to God in their confession of the divinity of Jesus the Messiah, the Son of God. In fact, in one passage that occurs precisely within the context of the Qur'ān's most significant critique of Christian views of Jesus the Messiah, the suggestion is made that their error is that the Christians make the same mistake in their beliefs about Jesus as the ancient polytheists did in regard to the partners they ascribed to God. "Say, O People of the Book, do not go to excess in your religion untruthfully (*lā taghlu fī dīnikum ghayra l-ḥaqq*), and do not follow the fancies of a people who went astray in the past and led others astray and they strayed from the Right Path" (*al-Mā'idah* 5, 77). The Qur'ān most explicitly applies this principle to Christology in its succinct and most comprehensive passage in critique of Christian doctrine:

> O People of the Book, do not go to excess in your religion, and do not say about God aught but the truth. The Messiah, Jesus, son of Mary, is only God's messenger (*rasūl Allāh*) and His word (*kalimatuhu*) that He cast into Mary, and a spirit from Him (*warūḥun minhu*). So believe in God and His messengers and do not say 'three'. Stop it, as something better for you! God is only one God. Praised be He that He would have a son (*waladan*), neither in the heavens nor on the earth. God suffices as one in whom to place trust (*an-Nisā'* 4, 171).

68 See Angelika Neuwirth, "Imagining Mary, Disputing Jesus: Reading *Sūrat Maryam* (Q. 19) and Related Meccan Texts in the Context of the Qur'anic Communication Process," and, "Mary and Jesus: Counterbalancing the Biblical Patriarchs: A Re-reading of *Sūrat Maryam* (Q. 19) in *Sūrat 'Āl 'Imrān* (Q. 3)," in *Scripture, Poetry and the Making of a Community*, Neuwirth, 328–358, 359–384. See also Neuwirth, *Der Koran als Text der Spätantike*, 472–489.

This passage provides a succinct summary statement of the Qur'ān's Christology both negatively and positively. Negatively, in that along with many other passages, it declares that God has no son, nor is Jesus the Messiah God's son. Positively in that it declares that Jesus, son of Mary, is but God's messenger, God's word, and a spirit from God. As for the admonition, "Say not three"; this succinct phrase reminds the reader that in the Qur'ān's view it is precisely what Christians say and believe about Jesus the Messiah that leads them to speak and think mistakenly, in the Qur'ān's view, about the one God in terms of three persons or hypostases. For this reason, unlike later Islamic critiques of Christian faith, little is said in the Qur'ān about the doctrine of the Trinity as such. Rather it is what the Christian believes and says about Jesus the Messiah that is the Qur'ān's central issue in its critique of Christian faith.

What is there finally to say about the Qur'ān's participation in Late Antique conversations about Christology? On the basis of the matters discussed in the present essay, it seems that the Qur'ān is an Arabic scripture that suddenly appeared in the first third of the seventh century proposing a new understanding of the biblical tradition's prophetic history that highlights the strict construction of what one might hesitantly call "Abrahamic monotheism". In the parts of the Qur'ān that critique Christian thought and practice, the dominant concern is with what Christians say and believe about Jesus of Nazareth. Noting the current controversies among the contemporary Christian communities on this very topic, the Qur'ān can be seen to present a distinctive Christology of its own, albeit one that seventh century Christians were slow to notice. It is a Christology dictated by the Qur'ān's own master narrative, its paradigmatic "prophetology". In the process of formulating its Christology, the Qur'ān knowingly critiques Christian beliefs about Jesus by means of a polemical counter rhetoric that recasts current Christian christological language in a way that highlights its absurdity from the point of view of the Qur'ān's reconstruction of prophetic history. In the end, one sees that the Qur'ān carried the Late Antique Christological controversies into Arabia and there it made its own contribution to them by articulating a markedly different view of Jesus of Nazareth from that espoused by any of the Arabic-speaking Christian communities within its purview. For the Qur'ān, Jesus the Messiah is not the Son of the living God, as the Christians in its milieu would have it, but he is the son of Mary, God's Messenger, His "word" cast into Mary, and a "spirit" from Him (*an-Nisā'* 4, 171), a view expressed in terms immediately recognizable as a re-construal of Late Antique Christian parlance, critiqued in a Qur'ānic counter discourse.

There remains only one further point to make and it is that in my view, the Arabic-speaking Christians living within the Qur'ān's immediate purview, those whom it calls "Nazarenes" some fourteen times, whose views of Jesus the Messiah the Qur'ān strongly critiques, were associated with the mostly Syriac-speaking, main-line "Melkite", "Jacobite", and "Nestorian" ecclesial communities of the seventh century, whose presence both on the Arabian periphery and within the peninsula, even in the Ḥijāz at the time, is historically well attested. Consequently there is no reason to suppose, as many present day scholars have done, as we have seen, that the Qur'ān's Christians were members of ancient Gnostic or "Jewish Christian" groups such as the Ebionites or the Elchasaites, who had long ago found refuge in the desert. Those who postulate the otherwise historically unattested presence of such groups in seventh century Arabia, do so on the basis of what I consider to be a hermeneutical mistake in their reading of the principal Qur'ānic passages that criticize Christian faith. As I have argued in some detail elsewhere,[69] they typically fail to recognize the Qur'ān's polemical rhetoric in these passages. They mistake the Qur'ān's ironical, polemical formulations, meant to reduce the adversary's positions to absurdity, for statements of a theological position. Or they make the unwarranted assumption that the congruence of the Qur'ān's view of Jesus of Nazareth with that of an earlier sect, otherwise historically unattested in the Qur'ān's milieu, constitutes evidence of the current presence of such a group in Arabia, from whom the Qur'ān is then supposed to have taken its position. That is to discount the Qur'ān's own integrity and the parameters of its own distinctive frame of reference, namely its distinctive "prophetology", the "*sunnah* of Our Messengers".

---

69 See the studies cited in nn. 4, 19, 20, 24, above.

Klaus von Stosch

Eine urchristliche Engelchristologie im Koran?

1 Die urchristliche Engelchristologie nach Günter Lüling und Martin Werner

Eine zentrale These von Günter Lülings *Die Wiederentdeckung des Propheten Muhammad*[1] besteht in der Behauptung, dass die Christologie des Koran die Wiederaufnahme einer urchristlichen Engelchristologie vornimmt. Die These geht davon aus, dass Jesus Christus für das Urchristentum nichts weiter war als „ein geschöpflicher immanenter, und sei es auch höchster Engel"[2]. So meint Lüling festhalten zu müssen: „Das Selbstverständnis Jesu und das Christusverständnis der Urgemeinde bestand darin, dass der endzeitlich erwartete Messias der ‚Engel des Hohen Rates (Gottes)' ist."[3] Der sterbliche Mensch Jesus wird

> durch Leiden und Tod verwandelt [...] in die überirdische und dennoch *geschöpfliche* Gestalt des Christus Angelus. Diesem Verständnis der Seinsweise Jesu nach seinem Tode als eines *geschöpflichen Engels* des Hohen Rates steht das Verständnis seines Seins *vor seiner Geburt* gegenüber, das generell mit dem Begriff ‚Präexistenz als Engel des Hohen Rats vom Beginn der Schöpfung an' umschrieben ist.[4]

Ausgehend von dieser Basisannahme ergeben sich neue Deutungsmöglichkeiten für eine ganze Reihe von neutestamentlichen Forschungsproblemen. So erklärt Lüling beispielsweise das Messiasgeheimnis dadurch, dass Jesus sich als Engel weiß.[5]

1 Günter Lüling, *Die Wiederentdeckung des Propheten Muhammad. Eine Kritik am „Christlichen" Abendland* (Erlangen: Verlagsbuchhandlung Hannelore Lüling, 1981).

2 Ebd., 53, mit Verweis auf die Tradition von Albert Schweitzer und Martin Werner. Wörtlich spricht Lüling an dieser Stelle auch davon, dass dies „die abendländische selbst- und dogmenkritische Wissenschaft eindeutig festgestellt hat."

3 Ebd., 55, mit Verweis auf Jes. 9,5 f. in der Version der LXX.

4 Ebd., 55–56.

5 Lüling 86. In der heutigen Exegese wird das Messiasgeheimnis in der Regel als bewusste redaktionelle Gestaltung des Mk. angesehen, der damit deutlich machen wollte, dass Jesus nur vom Glauben und damit auch vom Leiden und Kreuz her richtig verstanden wird. Vgl. etwa Hans Conzelmann und Andreas Lindemann, *Arbeitsbuch zum Neuen Testament* (Tübingen: Mohr, [10]1991), 289. Bei einer solchen Deutung erübrigt sich eine engelchristologische Interpretation.

https://doi.org/10.1515/9783110599176-005

Derartige Deutungsversuche widersprechen allerdings in zentralen Punkten dem heutigen Stand der Einsichten der historisch-kritischen Forschung, sodass erst ein Blick auf die theologische Forschungsgeschichte der ersten Hälfte des 20. Jahrhunderts erhellt, auf welche exegetischen Traditionen sich Lüling beruft. Offenkundig ist die Hauptquelle all seiner Überlegungen der Berner liberale, reformierte Theologe Martin Werner, der seit den 1920er Jahren als einer der engagiertesten Gegner Karl Barths galt. Wie viele liberale Exegeten seiner Zeit ging er davon aus, dass im Neuen Testament und der vornizänischen Theologie ein deutlicher Subordinatianismus vertreten wird.[6]

Auf der Linie dieser recht weit verbreiteten Urteile entwickelt Werner die Behauptung einer uralten Engelchristologie im Neuen Testament, die vor allem durch das apokalyptische Schrifttum – wie etwa die Henochapokalypse – inspiriert gewesen sei. Und in der Tat stellt beispielsweise die Himmelfahrt Jesajas eine jüdisch-christliche Apokalypse dar, die aus der Perspektive des Jesaja eine angelomorphe Christologie vertritt[7] und Christus ebenso wie den Heiligen Geist ausdrücklich als Engel bezeichnet.[8] Vermutlich handelt es sich hier um eine Reaktion auf und Korrektur von älteren Engelchristologien[9], so dass man davon ausgehen kann, dass angelomorphe Traditionen bereits in den ältesten Strängen des Christentums eine Rolle gespielt haben.[10] Werner selbst meint zeigen zu können, dass „der Christus des ältesten christlichen Dogmas gerade wie der philonische Logos ein hohes Engelwesen ist“[11] – eine These freilich, bei der ihm kaum Fachkollegen gefolgt sind und die heute von der überwältigenden Mehrheit der exegetischen Wissenschaftler völlig abgelehnt wird.[12]

---

6 Martin Werner, *Die Entstehung des christlichen Dogmas. Problemgeschichtlich dargestellt. Mit einer Bildbeilage* (Stuttgart: Kohlhammer, 1959), 78.

7 Charles A. Gieschen, *Angelomorphic Christology. Antecedents and early evidence* (Leiden-Boston–Köln: Brill, 1998), 229.

8 Ebd., 244.

9 Vgl. Darrell D. Hannah, *Michael and Christ. Michael traditions and Angel Christology in early Christianity* (Tübingen: Mohr Siebeck, 1999), 218.

10 Nach Lüling gibt es ähnlich angelomorphe christologische Hinweise auch bei den apokryphen Schriften, die den Koran beeinflusst haben – eine Vermutung, auf die wir im Rahmen dieses Beitrags nicht weiter eingehen können. Lüling weist als Beispiel auf das arabische Kindheitsevangelium hin, das „sogar im Stern von Bethlehem (Mt. 2) die Erscheinung eines Engels [sehe], der dann gelegentlich von anderen Autoren irgendwie auf Christus selber gedeutet wird“ (Lüling, 90) – ein Hinweis, der in seiner Vagheit allerdings wenig belastbar ist.

11 Werner, *Die Entstehung*, 84.

12 Vgl. Johann Ev. Hafner, *Angelologie: Gegenwärtig Glauben denken 9* (Paderborn u.a.: Schöningh, 2010), 11, sowie Hannah, *Michael and Christ*, 185.

Bereits ein Jahr nach der Erstveröffentlichung seines Buches legt der Berner Exeget Wilhelm Michaelis eine Widerlegung vor, die einen weitgehenden Konsens über die Verfehltheit von Werners Thesen zur Folge hat, so dass erst Jahrzehnte später seine These von einer Engelchristologie im Urchristentum wieder ernsthaft geprüft wird.[13] So zeigt Michaelis detailliert, dass bereits die Behauptung der Existenz einer Engelchristologie im apokalyptischen Spätjudentum nicht belegt werden könne.[14] Allerdings macht es sich Michaelis bei seiner Widerlegung Werners gelegentlich etwas leicht, so dass es sich durchaus lohnt, die von ihm so wirkungsmächtig verworfene Fragestellung neu aufzurollen. Ich möchte im vorliegenden Beitrag also überlegen, ob man nicht doch von angelomorphen Tendenzen in der urchristlichen Christologie ausgehen kann (2.) und ob diese Tendenzen Einflüsse auf den Koran gehabt haben können. Um letztere Frage klären zu können, muss ich einerseits überlegen, wie angelomorphe christologische Traditionen in die muslimische Tradition vermittelt worden sein könnten (3.) und nach ihren Spuren im Koran suchen (4.).

2 Engelchristologische Spuren im Urchristentum

2.1 Grundlagen im Neuen Testament?

Auch wenn man in der Forschung heute – anders als noch Werner und Lüling – nicht mehr von einer ausdrücklichen Engelchristologie im Neuen Testament sprechen würde, so gibt es doch einige neuere Studien, die zu zeigen versuchen, dass angelomorphe Traditionen wirkmächtigen Einfluss auf die Ausbildung wichtiger neutestamentlicher Christologien hatten. So verteidigt beispielsweise Charles A. Gieschen die Einsicht, dass an der Wurzel von neutestamentlichen Christologien wie der Weisheitschristologie oder der Menschensohnchristologie angelomorphe Traditionen stehen.[15] Wörtlich schreibt er:

> Angelomorphic traditions, especially those growing from the Angel of the Lord traditions, had a significant impact on the early expressions of Christology to the extent that evidence of

---

13 Vgl. Gieschen, *Angelomorphic Christology*, 13. Michaelis war einer der exegetischen Kollegen aus Werners eigener Fakultät. Da Werner selbst Systematiker war, kann man gut verstehen, dass die vernichtende Kritik seines Kollegen nicht ohne Folgen für die Rezeption Werners exegetischer Einlassungen geblieben ist.

14 Vgl. Wilhelm Michaelis, *Zur Engelchristologie im Urchristentum. Abbau der Konstruktion Martin Werners* (Basel: Verlag Heinrich Majer, 1942), 86.

15 Vgl. Gieschen, *Angelomorphic Christology*, 5–6.

> an Angelomorphic Christology is discernible in several documents dated between 50 and 150 CE.[16]

Um diese Einschätzung angemessen würdigen zu können, ist es wichtig, den Engel des Herrn, von dem Gieschen hier spricht, von gewöhnlichen, geschaffenen Engeln zu unterscheiden – eine Unterscheidung, die Werner und Lüling leider nicht in dieser Deutlichkeit treffen, so dass in ihrer Wahrnehmung jede Engelchristologie der dogmatischen Entwicklung nach Nicäa widersprechen muss. Wir werden im Folgenden sehen, dass es sich bei dieser Vorentscheidung der beiden um eine unzulässige Verengung angelomorpher Traditionen handelt. Denn Jesus Christus – so Charles Gieschen in seinen spannenden Analysen – sei sicher nicht ein geschaffener Engel neben anderen Myriaden.[17] Entscheidend für die frühe Christologie sei vielmehr die Tradition des Engels des Herrn.[18] Dieser Engel des Herrn (hebr. MALACH JHWH) macht eine prominente Deutungsgeschichte in der Zeit des entstehenden Christentums durch. Wird er zunächst als eine Weise des Daseins JHWHs und damit als eine Ausweitung und Konkretisierung göttlicher Gegenwart verstanden, wird er in späteren Texten immer mehr als individuelles Mitglied der himmlischen Heerscharen angesehen.[19] Erst diese letztere Tradition depotenziert den Engel des Herrn in einer Weise, dass er kaum für die nicänische Christologie anschlussfähig erscheint. Die Deutung des Engels des Herrn als Gegenwart Gottes dagegen lässt sich gut mit alttestamentlichen Texten belegen – man denke etwa an die Gegenwart Gottes im Engel, der mit Jakob ringt (Gen 32,23–32) – und ist für eine christologische Rezeption auch nach Nicäa hochinteressant.

Eben diese Rezeptionslinie des Engels des Herrn aus dem Alten Testament ist es nun aber, die urchristlich mit Christus identifiziert worden zu sein scheint.[20] „In the texts where God and the angel are indistinguishable, the Angel of the Lord is understood to be God's visible form, but not distinct, in any substantive way, from God. In other texts this angel is a distinct figure who functions with divine authority and power."[21] D. h. in der ursprünglichen Tradition kann man durchaus

16 Ebd., 6.
17 Vgl. ebd., 349.
18 Vgl. ebd., 350.
19 Vgl. Hannah, *Michael and Christ*, 24: „The term MALACH JHWH, then, underwent a profound development during biblical history. In the earliest texts it denotes, not a separate being, but an extension of Yahweh, an expression of the divine presence." Später sei dann die Entwicklung erfolgt „toward an understanding of him as an individual member in the heavenly host."
20 Vgl. Gieschen, *Angelomorphic Christology*, 16.
21 Ebd., 68.

eine göttliche bzw. ungeschaffene Natur im Engel des Herrn annehmen; „this angel was a ‚person' distinct from God who, in a significant way, shared in God's ‚substance' through the possession of the Divine Name."[22] Hat man diese Tradition erst einmal vor Augen, kann man die Rezeption angelomorpher Tendenzen in der Christologie des Neuen Testaments an einigen Stellen wahrnehmen. So kommt Gieschen etwa zu dem gut belegten Schluss, dass ausgerechnet im Johannesevangelium angelomorphe Terminologie, Traditionen und Funktionen ein integraler Teil der Christologie des Evangelisten sind.[23] Auch bei Paulus meint er zeigen zu können, dass Christus mit dem Engel des Herrn identifiziert wird[24] und dass im Hintergrund der paulinischen Christologie Vermittlungsfiguren wie Engel von großer Bedeutung sind.[25] Noch deutlicher sind die engelchristologischen Einflüsse in der Offenbarung des Johannes, so dass beispielsweise Stuckenbruck vermutet, dass die Verehrung von Engeln in einigen jüdischen Gruppierungen ein Modell geboten haben mag, um den monotheistischen Glauben mit der Christologie zu vermitteln.[26] Jedenfalls werde das Wort Gottes in diesem Buch angelomorph beschrieben.[27]

Von daher haben Werners und Lülings Thesen einer Engelchristologie im Urchristentum durchaus mehr Evidenz für sich als ihre Kritiker zu sehen bereit waren. Allerdings geht es hier zunächst einmal um eine Form von Engelchristologie, die durchaus im Einklang mit der nicänischen Entscheidung gelesen werden kann. Diese gewissermaßen orthodoxen Rezeptionsmöglichkeiten angelomorpher Traditionen in der Christologie werden allerdings durch die bereits innerbiblisch ansetzende Uminterpretation des Engels des Herrn hin zu einem individuellen, geschaffenen Engel fragwürdig. So grenzt sich Hebr. 1,4–14 deutlich gegen eine Gleichsetzung Christi mit den Engeln ab[28], verliert aber dabei offenkundig auch die Tradition vom Engel des Herrn als ungeschaffener Präsenzweise Gottes aus dem Blick. Denn wenn der Engel des Herrn als Weise des Daseins Gottes verstanden wird, lässt sich dieser problemlos mit dem heutigen christlichen Bekenntnis zusammenbringen. Von daher kommt bei der Bewertung ange-

22 Ebd., 69.
23 Vgl. ebd., 293.
24 Vgl. ebd., 346.
25 Ebd., 22 mit Verweis auf Andrew Chester.
26 Vgl. ebd., 24.
27 Vgl. ebd., 269. Vgl. zur intensiven neueren Diskussion über die Bedeutung der Engelchristologie in der Literatur zur Offenbarung den Literaturbericht bei Konrad Huber, *Einer gleich einem Menschensohn. Die Christusvisionen in Offb 1,9–20 und Offb 14,14–20 und die Christologie der Johannesoffenbarung* (Münster: Aschendorff, 2007), 51–64.
28 Vgl. Hafner, *Angelologie*, 186.

lomorpher Tendenzen in der Christologie alles darauf an, in welcher Weise die Tradition des Engels des Herrn aufgenommen wird.

2.2 Rezeption in der Christologie des zweiten Jahrhunderts

In der Christologie des zweiten Jahrhunderts ist an dieser Stelle offensichtlich noch keine Entscheidung gefallen. Kritische Stimmen gegen engelchristologische Deutungsversuche wie im Hebräerbrief finden sich genauso wie die selbstverständliche Aufnahme angelomorpher Traditionen in der Christologie. „Offensichtlich dienten im zweiten Jahrhundert der Titel und die Funktion des Erzengels als angemessener Titel für Christus."[29] So entwickelte bereits der allererste große Apologet und Kirchenvater Justin der Märtyrer eine dezidierte Engelchristologie, in der er davon ausgeht, dass der Logos in vorchristlicher Zeit genauso real in Engeln erschienen ist, wie er in Jesus Christus Mensch geworden ist.[30] „Vor allem aber erscheint der Logos als Herrenengel ANGELOS KYRIOU, wenn er mit Jakob ringt, aus Jakobs Träumen spricht, zu Mose aus dem Dornbusch spricht oder den Israeliten als Wolkensäule voran geht."[31] Die Bezeichnung als Engel erscheint in diesem Sinne bei Justin als einer der ersten Titel, den der Messias durch die Propheten erhalten hat[32], wobei hier Engel des Herrn nichts anderes meint als „the visible manifestation of the Father"[33].

Offenkundig war es unter den Kirchenvätern der vornicänischen Christologie eine weit verbreitete Ansicht, dass „der Logos im Alten Testament gerade als Engel auftritt"[34], so dass es ausgesprochen naheliegend war, diese Tradition für die Entwicklung der Christologie zu nutzen. Entsprechend erhalten die Engel und Christus im Frühchristentum ähnliche Aufgaben und Titel[35] – etwa bei Tertullian, Cyprian und Novatian, wobei gerade bei Novatian herausgestellt wird, dass Jesu

---

29 Ebd., 182.

30 Vgl. ebd., 183. Genauso wie schon Philo benutzt auch Justin den Logosbegriff, um verschiedene abstrakte Konzepte, die im Judentum auf Gott angewendet wurden, mit seiner Einheit zusammenzudenken, und zwar „Name, Glory, Wisdom, Word, Spirit, and Power", die sonst jeweils als Aspekte des einen Gottes gedacht wurden, die unterschiedliche Grade von Personalität haben (Gieschen, *Angelomorphic Christology*, 122).

31 Hafner, *Angelologie*, 183.

32 Vgl. Gieschen, *Angelomorphic Christology*, 189.

33 Ebd. 189 – 190.

34 Joseph Barbel, *Christos Angelos. Die Anschauung von Christus als Bote und Engel in der gelehrten und volkstümlichen Literatur des christlichen Altertums. Zugleich ein Beitrag zur Geschichte des Ursprungs und der Fortdauer des Arianismus* (Bonn: Peter Hannstein, 1941), 4.

35 Vgl. Hafner, *Angelologie*, 185.

Engelsein nicht gegen sein Gottsein spricht, weil die Tradition des Engels des Herrn ja an den zweiten Gott Israels erinnert, der hier manifest wird.[36] Auch Origenes sehe Jesus als den Engel des Hohen Rates an.[37] Die Brücke sei hier immer der Engel des Herrn aus dem Alten Testament, der in einer Weise mit Christus identifiziert werden kann, dass dabei die göttliche Natur Christi keineswegs in Frage gestellt wird.[38]

2.3 Rezeption im Judenchristentum

Besonders beliebt scheinen angelomorphe Traditionen bei ursprünglich jüdischgläubigen Christen gewesen zu sein, für deren Bezeichnung sich in der Forschung der etwas merkwürdige Begriff der Judenchristen eingebürgert hat. Als Judenchristen bezeichnet man Christen jüdischen Ursprungs in der Antike, die die Messianität Jesu anerkannt und die weiterhin die Tora befolgt haben. Unter ihnen war umstritten, ob man auch die Gottheit Christi anerkennen solle.[39]

Schon Wilhelm Bousset hat in seinen religionsgeschichtlichen Studien deutlich gemacht, wie wichtig, die Engel als Mittlerwesen für die Vermittlung von Gottes Transzendenz für die Menschen im jüdischen Denken der Zeit des Neuen Testaments waren.[40] Bereits dieser Befund legt es nahe, dass sich gerade bei frühen judenchristlichen Strömungen angelomorphe Traditionen in der Christologie ausbildeten. Und tatsächlich hat bereits Jean Daniélou gezeigt, „how early Jewish Christians drew on angelomorphic traditions in order to articulate their understandings of Christ and the Holy Spirit."[41] Offensichtlich diente die jüdische Angelologie schon sehr früh dazu, um die Präexistenz und Sichtbarkeit Gottes in Jesus verständlich zu machen.[42]

In den Pseudo-Klementinen sei Christus beispielsweise als größter Erzengel genannt, ja als Herr aller Engel verehrt. Er gilt als derjenige der Erzengel, der mit der Führung des Volkes betraut ist, gewissermaßen als „‚god of princes' under the

---

36 Margaret Barker, *The great angel. A study of Israel's second God* (London: Westminster John Knox Press, 1992), 197.

37 Vgl. ebd., 207.

38 Vgl. ebd., 200.

39 Folker Siegert, „Das Judenchristentum in der Antike: ein neuer Ansatz zu seiner Erforschung," in *Grenzgänge. Menschen und Schicksale zwischen jüdischer, christlicher und deutscher Identität. Festschrift für Diethard Aschoff.* Münsteraner Judaistische Studien 11, Hg. Ders. (Münster, 2002), 117–128, hier 118.

40 Vgl. Gieschen, *Angelomorphic Christology*, 8–9.

41 Ebd., 15.

42 Vgl. ebd., 351.

authority of the ‚Most High God'"[43]. Zugleich wird der Engel des Herrn in den Pseudo-Klementinen auch immer wieder gerne mit dem wahren Propheten gleichgesetzt. Die Lehre vom wahren Propheten, der sich seit Adam und Mose immer wieder manifestiert und der schließlich in Jesus Christus offenbar geworden ist, gilt als Herzstück der Theologie der Pseudo-Klementinen. Insgesamt gebe es in diesem judenchristlichen Zugang zum wahren Propheten „acht Erscheinungsweisen des Adam-Christus unter den Menschen in der Schrift"[44]: Adam, Henoch, Noah, Abraham, Isaak, Jakob, Mose und Jesus, allerdings mit Variationen in den verschiedenen Schriften. Der wahre Prophet sei also „der nach dem Bilde Gottes Gestalt gewordene ideale Mensch, der mit heiligem Geist gesalbt worden ist."[45] Wenn eben dieser wahre Prophet wie in den Pseudo-Klementinen mit dem Engel des Herrn identifiziert wird, ergibt sich in der Christologie automatisch eine angelomorphe Färbung, aber auch der Prophetentitel erhält eine Bedeutung, die er in den heidenchristlichen Traditionen nie innehatte.

Waren die angelomorphen Traditionen in der Frühzeit auch im judenchristlichen Milieu in einer Weise in die Christologie integriert, dass sie durchaus mit den weiteren dogmatischen Entwicklungen der Christologie vermittelt werden können, so scheint sich unter späteren Judenchristen, den sog. Ebioniten und Elkesaiten mit der Zeit die Auffassung von der Geschaffenheit aller Engel und damit auch der Geschöpflichkeit Christi durchgesetzt zu haben. Diese scheinen vom Glauben geprägt gewesen zu sein, dass Jesus so geschaffen wurde, wie die Erzengel.[46]

Von daher sind Werners Diagnosen im Blick auf die Ebioniten durchaus zutreffend: Jesus wird von ihnen offensichtlich mit einem geschaffenen Engelwesen gleichgesetzt.[47] Im Vordergrund steht hier eine apokalyptisch-eschatologisch geprägte Form der Christus- bzw. Menschensohnerwartung, bei der der im zukünftigen Äon siegreiche Erzengel Christus dem Teufel bereits jetzt als dem Herrn dieser Welt gegenübersteht. „Denn in den ‚Kyrios über die Engelheere', ja in den über alle Kreatur eingesetzten Erzengel ist der nach seiner natürlichen Erzeugung und Geburt ‚bloße Mensch' Jesus erhöht und verwandelt worden."[48] Aus der Sicht des Konzils von Nicäa war eine solche Christologie natürlich adoptianistisch und

43 Vgl. ebd., 210.
44 Hans Julius Schoeps, *Theologie und Geschichte des Judenchristentums* (Tübingen: Mohr Siebeck, 1949), 106.
45 Ebd.
46 Vgl. Peter R. Carrell, *Jesus and the Angels. Angelology and Christology of the Apocalypse of John* (Cambridge: CUP, 1997), 102–103.
47 Schoeps, *Theologie und Geschichte*, 80.
48 Schoeps, *Theologie und Geschichte*, 82.

subordinatianistisch, so dass eine ebionitisch konzipierte Engelchristologie leicht, im Sinne arianischer Auffassungen gelesen werden konnte, wie ja auch Werner und Lüling festhalten.

3 Das Konzil von Nicäa als Ende der Engelchristologie?

3.1 Die unglückliche Verbindung von Arianismus und Engelchristologie

Martin Werner vertritt in seiner Vorlage für Lülings Überlegungen die These, dass die Kirchenväter vor Nicäa ganz selbstverständlich mit einer subordinatianistischen Engelchristologie unterwegs gewesen seien.[49] Den Arianismus bewertet er entsprechend als Versuch, „die bisher zwar immer noch vorhandene, aber doch problematisch gewordene Engelchristologie in einer der fortgeschrittenen Entwicklung der neuen, andersartigen Christologie entsprechenden Weise zu vertreten und zu verteidigen."[50] Jesus Christus wird hier angeblich im Einklang mit Paulus unter die Engelmächte gezählt – allerdings als größte dieser Mächte –, die Gott in der Welt präsent machen.[51]

Dagegen bestehe Athanasius auf der Göttlichkeit Jesu, weil er den christlichen Erlösungsglauben gefährdet sah, wenn Jesus Christus nur ein Engel gewesen sei. Denn – so die Argumentation des Athanasius: *„Ein Engelwesen vermag uns ebenso wenig zu erlösen wie ein Mensch."*[52] Werner echauffiert sich, dass Athanasius Erlösung ganz unpaulinisch mit der Vergottung des Menschen gleichsetze.[53] Dabei übersieht er, dass es bei der Erlösung des Menschen bei Athanasius ursprünglich darum geht, dass wir Gemeinschaft mit Gott haben, gewissermaßen von ihm berührt und verwandelt werden. Eben dies vermag durchaus auch ein Engel zu leisten, wenn dieser wie der Engel des Herrn als Daseinsweise Gottes gedacht wird. Wenn er dagegen wie im Arianismus als Mittlerwesen gedeutet wird, das selbst nur eine geschaffene Natur besitzt, kann er keine Gemeinschaft mit Gott mehr ermöglichen und der christliche Erlösungsglaube wird hinfällig. Von daher ist es auch aus Sicht heutiger christlicher Theologie mehr als verständlich, dass

49 Vgl. Werner, *Die Entstehung*, 86–87.
50 Ebd., 93.
51 Vgl. ebd., 94.
52 Ebd., 100.
53 Vgl. ebd.

sich Athanasius gegen die Depotenzierung der Engelchristologie im Arianismus zur Wehr setzt und diese Deutungsmöglichkeit Jesu Christi bekämpft.

Leider wollen weder Werner noch Lüling die tieferen Beweggründe des Athanasius verstehen, und so nimmt es kein Wunder, dass sie die spannende Ambiguität übersehen, die der Engelchristologie *ab ovo* innewohnt. Lüling sieht im nicänischen Christentum nichts als eine imperiale Ausbreitung der hellenistisch-römischen Kultur, die „unter dem Einfluss des Nichteintreffens der urchristlichen eschatologischen Voraussagen ein neues Verständnis von der Person Jesu entwickelt, indem es sich dem magischen Volksglauben des hellenistisch-römischen imperialen Kulturkreises anpasste."[54] Im Gefolge des Johannesevangeliums setze sich eine „*dekadente magische* Auffassung des Abendmahls" durch, die „*zugleich* die imperiale Hierarchie der Reproduzenten der mysteriösen Materie begründet, denn in *einer* Gemeinde kann nur *ein* besonders eingeweihter und legitimierter Magier diese Reproduktion vollziehen."[55]

Mit dieser maßlosen Polemik nimmt sich Lüling nicht nur jede Rezeptionschance seiner Thesen im Mainstream des Christentums, sondern auch die Möglichkeit einer produktiven Anknüpfung an die neuere historisch-kritische Forschung. Diese hat nämlich längst eingesehen, dass die sogenannte hohe Christologie keineswegs eine Erfindung des dritten und vierten Jahrhunderts ist. Vielmehr wissen wir durch die neueren Forschungen gerade im Dialog mit der Judaistik, dass die sogenannte hohe Christologie nicht das Ergebnis einer späten heidnischen Überformung des Christentums darstellt, sondern bereits im Verständnis des Monotheismus des Judentums des Zweiten Tempels angelegt war.[56]

Das Judentum dieser Zeit hat sich deutlich als monotheistisch verstanden und hielt es um der Souveränität und der alleinigen Herrschaft Gottes willen für völlig ausgeschlossen, dass andere Wesen als der *eine* Gott selbst an Gottes Herrsein über die Schöpfung teilhaben. Für gottähnliche Wesen, wie sie der Arianismus konzipiert, ist in einem solchen Denken kein Platz. JHWH alleine wurde angebetet und so konnten geschaffene Engel oder die Patriarchen und Propheten niemals etwas mit Gottes Identitätsbestimmung zu tun haben und auch nicht seine Menschenfreundlichkeit erweisen. Dagegen werden der Geist, das Wort und die Weisheit Gottes als hypostasierte Aspekte Gottes selbst angesehen[57], die in un-

---

54 Lüling, *Die Wiederentdeckung*, 57.

55 Lüling, *Die Wiederentdeckung*, 59.

56 Vgl. Richard Bauckham, *God crucified. Monotheism and Christology in the New Testament* (Grand Rapids-Cambridge: Eerdmans, 1998), viii.

57 Ebd., 17.

terscheidbarer Weise am Schöpfungswirken Gottes teilhaben[58] und damit verbindlich Gott selbst zur Sprache bringen können.

Bereits in jüdischer Perspektive gibt es also Hypostasen Gottes, in denen der eine Gott seine Fürsorge für uns erfahrbar macht. Eben als eine solche Hypostase wird ja auch in der älteren Engelchristologie der Engel des Herrn angesehen, wie wir weiter oben gesehen haben. Unabhängig davon, ob man es für hilfreich hält, angelomorphe Traditionen in die Theologie einzubeziehen, ist es bei dieser Explikationsweise des Monotheismus jedenfalls so, dass der Glaube an den einen Gott Raum lässt für ungeschaffene Präsenzweisen seiner Wirklichkeit in unterschiedlichen Hypostasen.

An diese Denkmöglichkeit konnte bereits die früheste Christologie anschließen. Von daher setzt sich in der Exegese mehr und mehr die Auffassung durch, dass die sogenannte hohe Christologie bereits ganz am Anfang des Christentums steht und dass also die neutestamentliche Christologie von Anfang an versucht, Jesus in die göttliche Identität des einen Gottes hineinzudenken bzw. zu sagen, „that Jesus Christ is intrinsic to the unique and eternal identity of God."[59] Für alle Schriften des Neuen Testaments gehört Jesus fest zur Identität Gottes; er macht erfahrbar, *wer* Gott ist[60], nämlich ein sich radikal hingebender und den Menschen zugewandter Gott, der sich vom Schicksal der Menschen berühren und verändern lässt.[61] Dieses Gottesbild steht ganz im Einklang mit dem jüdischen Gottesglauben, so dass es weniger das jüdische als das griechische Denken ist, das das Erkennen der Gottheit Jesu für seine Zeitgenossen so schwierig gemacht hat.[62]

Die hellenistische Entfremdung vom wahren Kern christlich-jüdischer Identität, die Lüling nicht nur bei den Nicänern, sondern auch bei den mekkanischen Gegnern des Propheten zu entdecken meint[63], ist also eigentlich gar keine Entfremdung vom jüdischen Gottesglauben, sondern eine Irritation seiner üblich gewordenen griechischen Überformung. Entsprechend stellt die – übrigens his-

---

58 Vgl. ebd., 21.
59 Ebd., viii; vgl. ebd. 26.
60 Vgl. ebd., 45.
61 Vgl. ebd., 68–69.
62 Vgl. ebd., 78.
63 Gegen alle neueren Erkenntnisse der Forschung sieht Lüling diese mekkanischen Gegner Muhammads als hellenistische Christen an. Vgl. Lüling, *Die Wiederentdeckung*, 94; zum Stand der historischen Forschung zu diesem Punkt vgl. einstweilen Klaus von Stosch, „Jesus im Qur'ān. Ansatzpunkte und Stolpersteine einer qur'ānischen Christologie," in *Handeln Gottes – Antwort des Menschen. Beiträge zur Komparativen Theologie 11*, Hg. Ders./ Muna Tatari (Paderborn, 2014), 109–133, hier 125–127.

torisch gesehen marginale[64] – arianische Inanspruchnahme angelomorpher christologischer Traditionen nicht etwa eine moderne Neudeutung der klassischen Engelchristologie dar, sondern ihre häretische Fortschreibung. Der Arianismus rettet nicht die jüdisch geprägten angelomorphen Traditionen, sondern verwendet sie in völlig neuer Absicht: „traditions and texts that had been used to express a pre-existent creator Christology were now being employed to assert a subordinate first-created Christology."[65] Von daher kann man sagen: Erst der Arianismus zerstört durch die Verfremdung angelomorpher Elemente in seiner Christologie die Möglichkeit, sich im Rahmen der Orthodoxie auf engelchristologische Traditionsbestände zu beziehen, und hat so auch die Entfremdung der Christologie von ihren jüdischen Wurzeln vorangetrieben.[66]

Spielen angelomorphe Traditionen in der reichskirchlichen Christologie nach dem Konzil von Nicäa keine Rolle mehr, weil sie durch deren arianische Usurpation ihre ursprüngliche Deutungsoffenheit verloren haben, so ist die Lage in judenchristlichen Kreisen außerhalb des Einflussbereichs des römischen Reiches eine andere. Allerdings sind wir hier in einer recht unsicheren Quellenlage, so dass es schwer ist, in der unübersichtlichen Debattenlage festen Stand zu gewinnen.

3.2 Judenchristentum als Brücke zum Islam?

In der neueren Forschung findet immer wieder die These Erwähnung, dass Elemente des Judenchristentums bzw. der ebionitischen Theologie in die Entwicklung des Islams miteinflossen.[67] Lüling greift diese Forschung auf und nimmt insbesondere auf die oben bereits kurz referierten Überlegungen von Schoeps Bezug. Wörtlich schreibt er:

64 Michaelis meint sogar zeigen zu können, dass im Arianismus gar keine Engelchristologie vorliegt (Michaelis, *Zur Engelchristologie*, 173). Wenn Christus beispielsweise von den Arianern als „Herr der Dynameis" bezeichnet werde, dann gerade nicht, um ihn als Engel zu bezeichnen (Michaelis, *Zur Engelchristologie*, 180 gegen Werner, *Die Entstehung*). Dagegen meint auch Gieschen, dass Arius' Subordinatianismus durch die Engelchristologie beeinflusst war und er eine angelomorphe Terminologie benutzt (Gieschen, *Angelomorphic Christology*, 187).

65 Gieschen, *Angelomorphic Christology*, 188.

66 Vgl. ebd., 350.

67 Vgl. Jürgen Wehnert, „Art. Ebioniten," *LThK 3* (^{3}1995), 431; Georg Strecker, „Art. Judenchristentum," *TRE 17* (1988): 323; Francine E. Samuelson, „Messianic Judaism: church, denomination, sect, or cult?," *Journal of ecumenical studies 37* (2000): 162; Simon Claude Mimouni, *Le judéo-christianisme ancien. Essais historiques* (Paris: Cerf, 1998), 22.

> Hans-Joachim Schoeps hat die zahlreichen Elemente aufgezählt, die aus dem urchristlichen semitischen Judenchristentum stammend sich im Islam erhalten haben: die täglichen Waschungen, die Gebetsrichtung nach Jerusalem, [...] , die Ablehnung anthropomorpher Vorstellungen von Gott und die Vorstellung, dass die Juden ihre alttestamentlichen Schriften verfälschten, eine gewisse Abhängigkeit der koranischen Speisegesetzgebung von den Vorschriften des neutestamentlichen Aposteldekrets, schließlich die antipaulinische Tendenz [...] und die Ablehnung des Islam gegen die großen Schriftpropheten des Alten Testaments.[68]

Auch die oben bereits vorgestellte Tradition der wahren Propheten und die Art der Aufzählung zentraler prophetischer Figuren hat große Parallelen zur Prophetologie des Koran. Schon Schoeps selbst sind die Ähnlichkeiten dieser Prophetenrezeption im Koran und im Judenchristentum aufgefallen, zumal in beiden Fällen eher die Patriarchen als die großen Schriftpropheten rezipiert werden[69]; so kommt er zu dem Schluss, „die indirekte Abhängigkeit Muhammeds vom sektiererischen Judenchristentum [sei; Vf.] doch über jeden Zweifel erhaben. [...] Die ebionitische Kombination von Moses und Jesus hat in Muhammed ihre Erfüllung gefunden."[70] Gerade im Blick auf den schiitischen Islam kann man an dieser Stelle im Anschluss an Henry Corbin noch ergänzen, wie sehr die schiitische Vorstellung der Imamologie mit dem judenchristlichen Denken verwandt ist.[71]

Aber genügen diese in der Tat verblüffenden Parallelen um von einem Fortleben des Judenchristentums im Islam zu sprechen oder zumindest eine gemeinsame Traditionsgeschichte beider behaupten zu können? Leider lässt sich diese Frage nur schwer beantworten. Lange Zeit ging die Forschung davon aus, dass sich die Spuren des Judenchristentums nach dem 5. Jahrhundert verlieren, so dass jegliche Überlegung über Einflüsse über diese Zeit hinaus als reine Spekulation erschien.[72] Doch in der neueren Forschung wird zwar weiterhin akzeptiert, dass ein Teil des Judenchristentums – oft wird es auch als nazoräisches Christentum bezeichnet – im vierten oder fünften Jahrhundert verschwunden ist, weil es von der Großkirche absorbiert wurde. Zugleich wird angenommen, dass es ein stärker mit der Synagoge verbundenes Judenchristentum gab – die *Ebioniten* und *Elkesaiten* –, das von der Großkirche als Sekte bezeichnet wurde und möglicherweise bis ins 8. Jahrhundert Bestand hatte und Einfluss auf den Islam gehabt haben könnte.

---

68 Lüling, *Die Wiederentdeckung*, 60 mit Verweis auf Schoeps, *Theologie und Geschichte*, 334 ff.

69 Vgl. Schoeps, *Theologie und Geschichte*, 336.

70 Schoeps, *Theologie und Geschichte*, 342.

71 Vgl. Lüling, *Die Wiederentdeckung*, 61.

72 So noch Ernst Dassmann, *Kirchengeschichte I. Ausbreitung, Leben und Lehre der Kirche in den ersten drei Jahrhunderten* (Stuttgart-Berlin-Köln: Kohlhammer, 1991), 63.

Wir haben allerdings keine direkten Quellen, die dieses Fortbestehen belegen. Nimmt man die Kennzeichen des Judenchristentums als Beleg für seine Fortexistenz im Islam, so müsste man nicht nur die offenkundigen Ähnlichkeiten, sondern auch die großen Unterschiede zwischen beiden verständlich machen können – etwa den Vegetarismus oder die Ablehnung der Jungfräulichkeit Mariens, die wir beide bei den Ebioniten, nicht aber im Koran finden. Allerdings kennen wir viele Kennzeichen der Ebioniten nur aus der polemischen Darstellung der Kirchenväter, so dass ihr Quellenwert begrenzt ist.

Konzentriert man sich deshalb auf die älteren judenchristlichen Schriften, ergibt sich ein klareres Bild mit wichtigen Konvergenzen zum Islam, ohne dass man genau sagen könnte, ob es judenchristliche Gruppen mit solchen Glaubensvorstellungen nach dem vierten Jahrhundert tatsächlich noch gab. Holger Zellentin hat jüngst dafür argumentiert, dass sich aus dem Koran im Vergleich mit älteren judenchristlichen Schriften wie den Klemens-Briefen und der Didaskalia Apostolorum eine jüdisch-christliche Rechtskultur rekonstruieren lässt, die gerade für die längeren Suren des Koran von großer Bedeutung ist.[73] Zellentin geht hierbei nicht von getrennt judenchristlichen Gemeinden aus, sondern von einer besonderen jüdisch-christlichen Wirksamkeit sowohl im syrischen Christentum als auch im rabbinischen Judentum.[74] Fest machen kann er diese gemeinsame Rechtskultur an gemeinsamen Speisevorschriften, die etwa in der Didaskalia und im Koran sehr ähnlich sind,[75] und an gemeinsamen rituellen Regelungen.[76] So kommt er zu dem Schluss, dass es eine gemeinsame Rechtskultur zwischen dem vierten und siebten Jahrhundert gab, die sich folgendermaßen charakterisieren lässt: „ritual washing after intercourse and before prayer, the prohibition of intercourse during the menses, the strict and expanded prohibition of carrion, and the avoidance of pork."[77]

Von daher lassen auch diese neuesten Forschungen den Schluss zu, dass sich im Koran ein judenchristliches Erbe niedergeschlagen hat, das im Christentum selbst untergegangen ist.[78] Entsprechend ist es auch nicht von vornherein von der Hand zu weisen, dass die im Koran erwähnten Nazaräer (*an-naṣārā*; Q 22:17) als

73 Vgl. Holger Michael Zellentin, *The Qur'ān's legal culture. The Didascalia Apostolorum as a point of departure* (Tübingen: Mohr Siebeck, 2013), X.
74 Vgl. ebd., 50.
75 Vgl. ebd., 170.
76 Vgl. ebd., 178.
77 Ebd., 200.
78 Vgl. ebd., 197: „Muhammad kept alive part of the Jesus movement that Christianity did not."

Judenchristen zu identifizieren sind, wie etwa François De Blois vermutet.[79] Hieraus leitet er ab, dass es durchaus möglich ist, einen Kontakt der frühen muslimischen Gemeinde mit judenchristlichen Strömungen anzunehmen.[80] Eine andere interessante Spur judenchristlicher Einflüsse auf den Koran könnte über das äthiopische Christentum vermittelt sein, das ebenfalls stark judenchristlich geprägt war.[81]

Die Judenchristen könnten also durchaus eine Brücke sein, durch die die Engelchristologie Eingang in den Koran gefunden hat. Einige Tendenzen in der neueren Forschung geben hier einer zentralen These Lülings Recht. Allerdings kann man die Behauptung einer judenchristlichen Beeinflussung des Korans immer noch mit guten Argumenten bestreiten, wie etwa Sidney Griffith gezeigt hat.[82] Und selbst wenn man eine solche Beeinflussung konzedieren möchte, ist damit noch nichts darüber gesagt, welche Form von Engelchristologie es ist, die im siebten Jahrhundert kolportiert wird. Viel spricht dafür, dass es sich um eine aus nicänischer Sicht häretische Form von Engelchristologie handelt, die Jesus im arianischen Sinn zu einem besonderen Werkzeug Gottes macht, aber nur als Geschöpf zu denken vermag. Doch gibt es tatsächlich Spuren einer solchen arianischen Engelchristologie im Koran? Wenn man nicht nur wie Zellentin eine gemeinsame Rechtskultur von zentralen judenchristlichen Schriften und dem Koran annehmen will, sondern auch gemeinsame Theologumena, so müssten diese zuallererst im Koran selbst nachgewiesen werden. Diese Facette scheint mir nun allerdings der schwächste Teil von Lülings Argumentation zu sein.

4 Rezeption der Engelchristologie im Koran?

Lüling stützt sich bei seiner Diagnose einer Engelchristologie im Koran auf zwei Koranstellen. Ich gebe diese jeweils zunächst in der Übersetzung Bobzins wieder, um sie dann auf ihre engelchristologischen Implikationen hin zu überprüfen.

---

79 Vgl. François de Blois, „Naṣrānī (Ναζωραῖος) and ḥanīf (ἐθνικός): Studies on the Religious Vocabulary of Christianity and of Islam,“ *Bulletin of the School of Oriental and African Studies 65* (2002): 27. Zellentin argumentiert ähnlich und kommt zu dem Schluss: „Yet it seems to me that the group that most closely corresponds to the Qur'ān's *naṣārā* is that of the Didascalia's Christian authors“ (Zellentin, *The Qur'ān's legal culture,* 189).

80 Vgl. de Blois, „Naṣrānī (Ναζωραῖος) and ḥanīf (ἐθνικός)“ 27–28.

81 Vgl. Theresia Hainthaler, „La foi au Christ dans l'Eglise éthiopienne. Une synthèse des élèments judéo-chrétiens et helléno-chrétiens,“ *Revue des sciences religieuses 71* (1997): 330–331.

82 Vgl. Sidney H. Griffith, *„Al Naṣārā* in the Qur'ān. A hermeneutical reflection,“ in *New perspectives on the Qur'ān. The Qur'ān in its historical context 2,* ed. Gabriel Said Reynolds (London-New York, 2011), 301–322.

Danach werde ich noch eine dritte von Lüling selbst nicht untersuchte Stelle diskutieren, die in der muslimischen Tradition in einem seltenen Ausnahmefall engelchristologisch gedeutet wurde.

> Q 3:79 – 80a „Keinem Menschen steht es zu, dass Gott ihm das Buch, die Urteilskraft und die Prophetengabe gibt und er dann zu den Menschen sagt: ‚Seid *meine,* nicht nur Gottes Knechte!' Seid vielmehr Gelehrte Gottes, weil ihr ja das Buch gelehrt und darin geforscht habt!
> Und auch nicht, dass er euch befiehlt, die Engel und Propheten als Herren anzunehmen."

Der erste Teil von Vers 79 warnt Menschen davor, sich als Herr anderer Menschen aufzuführen und diese als die eigenen Knechte anzusehen. Sie wendet sich damit gegen eine Vorstellung, in der ein Herr neben Gott gesetzt wird, weil Gott allein die Herrschaft zusteht. Vers 80a macht zudem explizit deutlich, dass auch Engel und Propheten nicht als Herr anerkannt werden dürfen. Statt uns einem anderen Herrn als Gott zu unterwerfen, sollen wir – so der Gedanke des zweiten Versteils von Vers 79 – autonom handeln und uns mit Hilfe von Vernunft und Offenbarung im Leben und Glauben orientieren. Die Textpassage ist also ausgesprochen machtkritisch und wendet sich gegen jede Form von Engelchristologie, die einen Engel als Macht neben Gott denkt – auch wenn diese Macht eine geschöpfliche Macht ist. Sie könnte also tatsächlich gegen ebionitische Gruppen gerichtet sein, die ja auch Christus als Herrn anerkannten – nur eben als geschöpflichen Herrn. Einen solchen Herrn darf es dem Text zufolge nicht geben. Wenn der Text also irgendetwas mit einer Engelchristologie zu tun haben sollte, dann sicher in kritischer Absicht. Er wendet sich also genau wie das Judentum des Zweiten Tempels gegen jede Einführung von Zwischenwesen, die irgendwie an der Herrschaft Gottes teilhaben.

Lüling meint in seiner Exegese der Verse zeigen zu können, dass genau das Gegenteil dieser Schlussfolgerung richtig ist. Um diese ausgesprochen kontraintuitive Sicht zu plausibilisieren, führt er die These ein, dass der Text nach dem Tod des Propheten redaktionell verändert wurde und in Vers 80 ursprünglich lautete: „Sondern *es waren Herrschaftsengel, durch die* euch das Buch *gelehrt wurde* und *durch die ihr unterrichtet wurdet.* Und ER befiehlt euch nicht, dass Ihr die Engel euch zu Herren nehmt." Ganz davon abgesehen, dass diese textkritische Operation auf tönernen Füßen steht, ändert sie nichts an der Stoßrichtung gegen jede Gruppierung, die die Engel als Herrn nehmen. Eben das tun die Judenchristen aber mit Christus, so dass auch in dieser veränderten Gestalt keine judenchristlich rezipierbare Engelchristologie entsteht.

Der andere Vers, auf den sich Lüling für seine Diagnose einer Engelchristologie im Koran stützt, lautet folgendermaßen:

Q 4:172 „Christus wird es nie verschmähen, ein Knecht Gottes zu sein, und auch die Engel, die ihm nahestehen, nicht. Wer es jedoch verschmäht, ihm zu dienen, und sich erhaben dünkt, die wird er allesamt zu sich versammeln."

Dieser Vers ist aus zwei Gründen irritierend und scheint zunächst einmal Lülings Deutung stark zu machen. Zunächst einmal ist es auffällig, dass hier der Messias, also Jesus Christus, in einem Atemzug mit den Engeln genannt wird. Diese Nennung liegt aber noch durchaus auf der Linie der soeben betrachteten Koranstelle, da es bei Christus wie den Engeln darum geht, dass sie sich als Knechte Gottes verstehen. Insofern kann auch dieser Versteil als Kritik an der judenchristlichen Engelchristologie verstanden werden. Im zweiten Versteil scheint nun aber auf den ersten Blick ausdrücklich der Gedanke stark gemacht zu werden, dass man Christus dienen soll; in der Übersetzung Lülings ist sogar vom Anbeten Christi die Rede.

Falls sich das Personalsuffix -hu des entsprechenden arabischen Wortes (ʿibādatihi) tatsächlich auf Christus bezieht, ist eine solche Übersetzung wie die von Lüling an dieser Stelle durchaus möglich. Allerdings kann mit dem Personalsuffix auch Gott gemeint sein, was den ganzen Vers viel einfacher verständlich machen würde und auch der gängigen Übersetzungspraxis entspricht. Es würde dann um eine Gerichtsdrohung für all die gehen, die es nicht wie Christus und die Engel machen und die also Gott nicht anbeten. Zu dieser Standardübersetzung passt auch die Fortsetzung der Gerichtsdrohung in Vers 173,[83] die die in Vers 171 beginnende Anrede an die Buchbesitzer sinnvoll abschließt.

Lüling sieht in V. 173 dagegen einen späteren redaktionellen Zusatz, der die ursprünglich engelchristologische Aussage von V. 172 vertuschen soll. V. 174[84] bildet in Lülings Lesart den ursprünglichen Abschluss zur Sequenz Q 4:171 f. und liest sich dann als feierliche Beglaubigung der Engelchristologie. In der Tat könnte das klare Licht, von dem der Vers spricht auf einen Engel gedeutet werden. Aber die Anrede „O ihr Menschen!", die die Anrede aus V. 170 wiederholt, scheint mir doch eher darauf hinzuweisen, dass die Verse 171–173 als Einheit zu lesen sind, der man nur schwer diesen Vers 174 hinzufügen kann.

83 „Doch denen, welche glauben und gute Werke tun, wird er ihren Lohn in vollem Maße geben und ihnen noch mehr Huld gewähren. Die aber, welche es verschmähen und sich erhaben dünken, wird er mit schmerzhafter Pein bestrafen, die werden gegen Gott weder Freund noch Helfer finden."

84 „O ihr Menschen! Zu euch kam ein Beweis von eurem Herrn, und wir sandten zu euch ein klares Licht herab."

Dennoch hat Lüling Recht, dass V. 172 rein philologisch mehrere Deutungen zulässt und auch seine Übersetzung möglich ist. Was spricht nun also für seine engelchristologische Deutung des Verses?

Sein Hauptargument besteht darin, dass der hier begegnende arabische Terminus „*al-muqarrabūn*" – von Bobzin übersetzt als „die ihm nahestehen" – „zweifelsfrei der Terminus für die *Engel des Hohen Rates* ist"[85]. Im Verein mit Q 3:45, wo Jesus als „einer von den Nahestehenden" bezeichnet wird, sei klar, dass sich dieser Ausdruck auch auf Jesus beziehe und der Vers also einschärfe, dass Jesus als Engel verehrt, aber nicht angebetet werden soll.[86]

Philologisch gesehen ist die Sache aber nicht so klar, wie Lüling behauptet. Wenn man die koranischen Verse über *muqarrabūn* bzw. *muqarrabbīn* insgesamt anschaut, so ergibt sich ein vielschichtiges Bild. Die Nahestehenden sind diejenigen, die (beim Gericht?) die Vorauseilenden sind (Q 56:10 f.) und die (ebenfalls beim Gericht?) Zeugnis für ein mit Sorgfalt geschriebenes Buch abgeben (Q 83:20 f.) – beides Eigenschaften, die durchaus auch Engeln zukommen könnten. In Sure 83 spricht der Kontext aber eher dafür, dass fromme Menschen gemeint sind, zumal die Nahestehenden in Q 83:28 aus einer Quelle trinken – eine Tätigkeit, die bei Engeln nur begrenzt Sinn ergibt. Noch deutlicher gegen eine angelomorphe Deutung scheint mir allerdings die Verwendung des Begriffs in Q 56:86–89 zu sprechen, die die Nahestehenden in einer Weise in das Gericht einbezieht, die doch sehr deutlich macht, dass hier von Menschen die Rede ist.[87]

Von daher ist schon der koranische Befund nur schwer mit der von Lüling vorgeschlagenen Interpretation vereinbar. Hinzu kommt, dass auch fast[88] in allen Korankommentaren der Tradition der Begriff *muqarrabūn* auf Menschen hin gedeutet wird, die aufgrund ihres Glaubens und Handelns Gott nahestehen. Schließlich werden auch in großen Teilen der islamischen Gebetspraxis mit den Nahestehenden, den *muqarrabūn*, die Gott nahestehenden Menschen bezeichnet.

Die Nahestehenden können im Koran also an einigen Stellen als Engel verstanden werden, und Q 4:172 ist sicherlich eine solche Stelle. Aber der Ausdruck ist nicht zwingend mit Engeln zu verbinden, so dass Jesu Bezeichnung als Nahestehender in Q 3:45 kein Beleg dafür ist, dass Jesus vom Koran als Engel an-

---

85 Lüling, *Wiederentdeckung*, 70.

86 Lülings Argumentation ist an dieser Stelle etwas irritierend, weil der Wortlaut des Koranverses bei seiner eigenen Übersetzung ja gerade die Möglichkeit des Anbetens Jesu zulässt.

87 Im Arabischen ist hier allerdings von *muqarrabīn* die Rede und nicht von *muqarrabūn*

88 Einzige Ausnahme ist meines Wissens der schiitische Tafsir, Nūr aṯ- ṯaqalayn, von Ḥuweizi, aus dem 17. Jahrhundert, der in Bd 1., 578 eine Überlieferung des Propheten Muhammad wiedergibt, in der die *muqarrabūn* als die beiden Engel Gabriel und Michael gedeutet werden.

gesehen wird. Trotzdem ist diese Deutungsmöglichkeit nicht ausgeschlossen, falls das Personalsuffix in Q 4:172b tatsächlich auf Christus zu beziehen ist.

Übernehmen wir also rein hypothetisch einmal Lülings Übersetzungsvorschlag und überlegen wir, welche Deutung sich daraus ergibt: Um verstehen zu können, warum Christus hier gedient / angebetet wird, müsste man berücksichtigen, dass der vorangehende Vers Christus als Wort und Geist Gottes auszeichnet, zugleich aber davor warnt von drei Göttern zu sprechen oder von einem Sohn Gottes zu sprechen (Q 4:171). Der Vers argumentiert hier ganz auf der Linie des oben referierten Monotheismus des Zweiten Tempels. „Gott genügt als Anwalt", heißt es am Ende, d. h. ein Zwischenwesen oder ein besonderer Engel oder auch ein Prophet darf nicht etwa als Anwalt bei Gott verstanden werden, überhaupt darf nichts zwischen Gott und den Menschen gestellt werden und die Einheit und Einsheit Gottes muss gewahrt bleiben. Eben deshalb darf Jesus weder neben Gott noch zwischen Gott und Mensch gestellt werden.

All das könnte als Kritik an einer ebionitischen Engelchristologie zu verstehen sein. Wenn dann dennoch die Möglichkeit eingeräumt wird, Christus anzubeten, so könnte dies den paradoxen Gedanken nahelegen, dass Christus wie in der älteren Engelchristologie eben in die Identität Gottes hineingedacht werden muss. Er wäre dann so sehr nichts als Gesandter und Diener Gottes, dass er in all seinem Sein Gottes Wort und Geist selbst ist und damit in Gottes Identität gehört, gewissermaßen als Gottes Dasein für uns. Man kann Q 4:171 f. also leichter im Einklang mit der orthodoxen älteren Engelchristologie verstehen als im Kontext einer ebionitisch-häretischen Auffassung. Die ganze Deutung beruht allerdings auf einer eher kontraintuitiven Übersetzung, die erst dann wirklich überzeugen könnte, wenn man noch mehr Koranstellen beibringen könnte, die eine engelchristologische Deutung nahelegen.

Im vorliegenden Beitrag kann ich die an dieser Stelle erforderliche Spurensuche nicht vollständig leisten, sondern will es bei einem letzten Hinweis auf einen weiteren Koranvers bewenden lassen. Der hanbalitische Theologe Naǧm al-Dīn al-Ṭūfī (14. Jahrhundert), der als erster Muslim zugleich einen Kommentar zur Bibel und zum Koran geschrieben hat, entwickelte eine Engelchristologie, indem er Jesus als einen Engel in menschlicher Gestalt identifiziert. Lejla Demiri verdanke ich den Hinweis, dass er sich dabei auf Q 6:9 und Joh 3,12 f. beruft.[89]

---

89 Vgl. Lejla Demiri, Muslim Exegesis of the Bible in Medieval Cairo: Najm al-Dīn al-Ṭūfī's (d. 716/1316) Commentary on the Christian Scriptures. A Critical Edition and Annotated Translation with an Introduction, HCMR (The History of Christian-Muslim Relations) series vol. 19 (Leiden: Brill, 2013), 74, 310–312; Lejla Demiri, A Medieval Muslim Commentary on the Bible: Najm al-Dīn al-Ṭūfī's Response to the Christians (PhD Thesis: University of Cambridge), Cambridge, 2008, 182–193. Unter dem Titel „Angelic Jesus: A Medieval Quest for an Alternative Christology?" hat Demiri

Letzteren Vers erklärt er so, dass Jesus als Engel eben wisse, wie es im Himmel zugehe, so dass der Menschensohntitel hier engelchristologisch gedeutet wird. Außerdem erkläre Jesu engelhafte Natur gut, dass er zölibatär und auch sonst sehr einfach lebte. Ähnlich wie Ṭūfī hatte bereits Ibn Isḥāq in Jesus eine engelhafte Natur sehen wollen – allerdings erst nach seiner Himmelfahrt. Ich kann diesen spannenden Hinweisen hier allerdings nicht weiter nachgehen und konzentriere mich allein auf die Frage, ob man ausgehend von Q 6:9 eine Engelchristologie entwickeln kann.

Der Vers muss im Zusammenhang zitiert werden, um ihn richtig zu verstehen:

> Q 6,8 f,: „Sie sprechen: ‚Warum wurde denn kein Engel zu ihm herabgesandt?' Doch hätten wir einen Engel herabgesandt, wäre die Sache ja entschieden, und sie hätten dann keinen Aufschub zu erwarten. Hätten wir ihn zu einem Engel gemacht, dann hätten wir ihn in männlicher Gestalt gemacht und sie in Verwirrung über das gebracht, worüber sie schon in Verwirrung waren."

Gewöhnlich wird dieser Satz als rhetorisches Statement verstanden: Selbst wenn Gott Engel geschickt hätte, hätten sich die Herzen der Menschen verhärtet. Entsprechend wird auch traditionell als Offenbarungsanlass für diesen Vers die vorwurfsvolle Anfrage einiger in Mekka gesehen, die Muhammad gesagt haben sollen, sie würden ihm glauben, wenn er ein geschriebenes Buch ihnen vorlege bzw. wenn ihnen ein Engel als Bote Gottes erscheinen würde (vgl. hierzu Vers 10). Diese Verse sehen die Kommentatoren als eine Antwort, die sowohl den Propheten beruhigen soll, weil er nicht der erste Gesandte ist, dem die Menschen nicht glauben wollen, und die zum anderen eine Antwort auf die Menschen bieten, die einen Engel als Boten haben wollten. Der Konjunktiv ist ein Hinweis darauf, dass auch dann die Menschen nicht bereit wären zu glauben, weil sie auch dann nach Ausreden suchen würden.

Allerdings ist es laut Q 6:9 ja nicht die Schuld der Menschen, dass sie dem Engel nicht Glauben schenken, sondern Tat des sie in Verwirrung bringenden Gottes. Gott selbst will also offenbar Ambiguität in der Offenbarung, um dem Menschen Freiraum zur Antwort zu lassen und Aufschub gewähren zu können. Wie immer man diesen Punkt zu deuten hat, so ist jedenfalls in kontrafaktischer Weise von dem Schicken eines Engels die Rede und der Vers gibt keinen direkten Hinweis darauf, dass er auf Christus zu beziehen ist. Der Vers scheint einfach nur deutlich zu machen, dass die Menschen auch dann irritiert und verwirrt gewesen

---

2014 noch detaillierte Überlegungen hierzu vorgetragen, die mir bei der Abfassung dieses Artikels sehr geholfen haben.

wären, wenn ein Engel zu ihnen kommen würde, um ihnen die Offenbarung zu bringen.

Laut Ṭūfī hat sich dieses Wort in Christus erfüllt. Christus ist für ihn der Engel in Gestalt eines Menschen, der für Verwirrung gesorgt hat, sodass er der lebendige Beweis für die Richtigkeit der Argumentation von Q 6:9 ist. Die im Koran immer wieder thematisierten Streitigkeiten der Christen wären dieser Lesart zufolge ein Ergebnis der Verwirrung, die über sie gekommen ist, weil sie es mit einem Engel in Menschengestalt zu tun bekommen haben.

Diese Deutungsmöglichkeit ist philologisch nicht völlig ausgeschlossen, und es ist theologiegeschichtlich hochinteressant der Frage nachzugehen, wie Ṭūfī auf sie gekommen ist. Immerhin ist die Engelchristologie ja auch im Christentum des 14. Jahrhunderts nicht gerade gängig, so dass sein enger Gesprächskontext mit Christen noch keine zureichende Erklärung für seinen Deutungsvorschlag ist.[90]

Exegetisch gesehen ist sein Vorschlag allerdings so ungewöhnlich, dass er einer engelchristologischen Deutung der Koranstellen über Jesus keine zusätzliche Plausibilität verleiht. Bedenkt man, dass eine Durchsicht durch über 130 bekannte und weniger bekannte muslimische Korankommentare der Geschichte, die dankenswerterweise meine Kollegin Hamideh Mohagheghi vorgenommen hat, keinen einzigen Kommentar ergab, der auch nur ansatzweise für einen der drei hier diskutierten Verse die Deutung ins Auge fasst, Jesus als Engel zu verstehen, müsste man meines Erachtens stärkere Indizien für angelomorphe Traditionen in der koranischen Christologie nennen können, wenn man Lülings Thesen stark machen möchte.

Immerhin weist er uns auf einen spannenden Themenkomplex hin, der durchaus genauere Nachforschungen verdient. Diese sollten zwei Aspekte im Auge behalten.

---

90 J. Hafner meint ikonographische Nachwirkungen der Engelchristologie im vierten Fresko der Basilika von Assisi (um 1290) finden zu können, in der Franziskus die Stigmata von einem Christusengel erhält (Hafner, *Angelologie*, 189). Hier sei ganz offenkundig „Christus in Engelsgestalt" (Hafner, *Angelologie*, 191) gegeben. Bei genauerer Betrachtung der franziskanischen Tradition ist aber klar, dass hier entweder ein Seraph oder Christus gemeint ist und nicht etwa ein Mischwesen. Eine engelchristologische Tradition scheint sich lediglich bei den Katharern zu finden, die interessanterweise ihre Ursprünge bei den Bogomilen im Osten (10. Jahrhundert) haben könnten, also wohl im Byzantinischen Reich. Bei den Katharern gab es wohl Auffassungen, wonach Luzifer und Christus Brüder seien und durchaus als Engel angesehen wurden – eine Auffasssung, die starke Parallelen zur ebionitischen Gegenüberstellung von dem Teufel als dem Herrn dieser Welt und dem Engelwesen Christus hat (vgl. Schoeps, *Theologie und Geschichte*, 82). Dies sind allerdings nur erste grobe Hinweise für eine noch zu leistende Spurensuche, wie sich engelchristologische Traditionen bis zu Ṭūfī haben halten können.

Einerseits gibt es in der islamischen Tradition eine Überlegung, der zufolge alle Propheten in der Offenbarung engelhafte Qualitäten empfangen, um Gottes Botschaft verstehen und weitergeben zu können. So hat Ǧalāl ad-Dīn as-Suyūṭī (gest. 1505)[91] in seinem Werk *al-itqān fī ʿulūm al-qurʾān* die These verteidigt, dass Muḥammad im Offenbarungsgeschehen Engelsqualitäten annahm, also selber über eine bipolare Natur verfügte, deren eine Seite für die göttliche Offenbarung ansprechbar war.[92] Um für Gottes Offenbarung empfänglich zu sein, würde der Mensch dieser Deutung zufolge eine „innermenschliche Engelsnatur" als vermittelnde Qualität zwischen Unbedingtem und Bedingtem entwickeln – eine Denktradition, die möglicherweise mit Lülings Thesen vereinbart werden kann und seine engelchristologischen Konzepte dann plausibilisiert, wenn sie entsprechend der judenchristlichen Tradition auf alle wahren Propheten ausgedehnt wird.

Allerdings besteht bei diesem Denkstrang immer die Gefahr, dem Engel bzw. dem Propheten zu sehr eigenständige Bedeutung zu geben, so dass es mir eine noch plausiblere Deutung zu sein scheint, an die ältesten Traditionen der Engelchristologie anzuknüpfen, die Christus gerade nicht als Mittler und Zwischenwesen, sondern als Dasein Gottes für uns begreift. Diese Denktradition im Gefolge der Rede vom Engel des Herrn wird jedenfalls an keiner Stelle des Koran abgelehnt, und es wäre eine spannende Aufgabe für eine umfassendere Untersuchung aller christologischen Bezüge des Korans zu klären, ob eine solche hohe Christologie mit den koranischen Aussagen vermittelbar ist.[93]

Anders als Lüling meint, scheint mir eine Engelschristologie in ebionitischer und damit antinicänischer Stoßrichtung klar dem Wortlaut des Koran zu widersprechen. Wenn Lüling Muhammad also zum „letzte[n] theologische[n] Verteidiger urchristlicher Theologie gegen ihre hellenistisch-abendländische Entstellung" hochstilisiert, die auch in Mekka und Zentralarabien dominant gewesen sei[94], so bleibt er Gefangener seiner eigenen dogmatischen Vorentscheidung gegen jede rationale Adaption der klassischen christlichen Christologie und Trinitätslehre. Hier werden seine Ausführungen ideologisch und verlieren ihre inspi-

---

91 Ǧalāl ad-Dīn as-Suyūṭī war ein ašʿaritischer Exeget und Theologe, der zur schafiʿitischen Rechtschule gehörte.

92 Vgl. Ǧalāl ad-Dīn as-Suyūṭī, *al-Itqān fī ʿulūm al-qurʾān*, Madīna, o.J., 289 – 297.

93 Im Rahmen eines DFG-Projekts bin ich derzeit dabei, in Zusammenarbeit mit verschiedenen muslimischen Kolleginnen und Kollegen eine solche Untersuchung zu leisten. Vgl. einstweilen Klaus von Stosch, „Jesus im Qurʾān. Ansatzpunkte und Stolpersteine einer qurʾānischen Christologie," in *Handeln Gottes – Antwort des Menschen. Beiträge zur Komparativen Theologie 11*, Hg. Ders. and Muna Tatari (Paderborn, 2014), 109 – 133.

94 Vgl. Lüling, *Die Wiederentdeckung*, 21.

rierende Kraft. Wenn Lüling uns dagegen einlädt, die christologischen Verse des Korans neu zu lesen und bisher unbedachte Deutungstraditionen ins Auge zu fassen, ist er ungemein innovativ und anregend. Vielleicht ist seine grundlegende Hypothese einer Engelchristologie im Koran ja doch bei einer bestimmten Lesart der koranischen Verse zu verteidigen. Allerdings führt dies gerade nicht zur Rehabilitierung einer urchristlichen Theologie gegen die spätere dogmatische Gestalt des christlichen Glaubens. Vielmehr öffnet uns diese spätere Gestalt für neue Quellen und Inspirationen – eben auch für solche, die aus angelomorphen Traditionen schöpfen.

Gerald Hawting

Sanctuary and Text: How Far can the Qur'ān Throw Light on the History of the Muslim Sanctuary?

1 Lüling's work on the Ka'bah

Günter Lüling was one of a relatively small number of scholars who have engaged critically with the traditional Islamic material about the history of the Meccan sanctuary in pre-Islamic and early Islamic times. In his *Die Wiederentdeckung des Propheten Muhammad*,[1] he proposed a radical reinterpretation of that traditional material and consequently of the history of the Ka'bah at Mecca. The conclusions he advocated are driven by a thesis about Jewish Christianity which predetermined his choice and interpretation of evidence, and in some demonstrable instances led to the suppression of conflicting evidence, or to the misinterpretation of evidence in order to support the wider thesis.

I do not want here to try to refute his views in detail but to focus on something that is surprisingly absent from his discussion, given his work on the Qur'ān: examination of passages in the Muslim scripture that seem relevant to the Meccan sanctuary. Only once in his discussion of the Ka'bah in *Die Wiederentdeckung*, so far as I can see, does he cite the Qur'ān, when he mentions a few Qur'anic allusions to circumambulation (*ṭawāf*) in the course of his argument that the Prophet supported a closed Ka'bah and a cult outside it – in opposition to what Lüling claimed was the pre-Islamic Christian use of the building as a house of worship.[2]

Before we come to the issue of the Qur'anic material on the sanctuary, however, a few broader comments about Lüling's work on the Ka'bah are in order, beginning with something that was a significant contribution to the topic.

1 Erlangen: Verlagsbuchhandlung Hannelore Lüling, 1981; see too G. Lüling, *Der christliche Kult an der vorislamischen Kaaba als Problem der Islamwissenschaft und christlichen Theologie* (Erlangen: Verlagsbuchhandlung Hannelore Lüling, 1977).
2 Lüling, *Wiederentdeckung*, 154.

https://doi.org/10.1515/9783110599176-006

Form and Function

Lüling related the form of a building to its function. That may seem obvious but, to the extent that Muslim tradition offers explanations for the changes to the form of the Kaʿbah, they are accidental and inconsequential, unrelated to its function.

The tradition reports details of a number of re-buildings of the Kaʿbah from the time when Muhammad was still young and had not yet been called to be a prophet, through the period when Ibn az-Zubayr claimed the caliphate and challenged the power of the Umayyads (ca. 683 – 4), until the killing of Ibn az-Zubayr by the Umayyad general al-Ḥaǧǧāǧ in 692. On each occasion changes were made to the form of the building.

Those changes concerned, first, whether the area lying to the northwest of the Kaʿbah known as the *ḥiǧr* should be included in the Kaʿbah or not, and, second, the issue of the door or doors.

When Qurayš re-built the Kaʿbah during Muḥammad's youth, we are told, they left the *ḥiǧr* out because they did not have enough money or material to build over it. Ibn az-Zubayr then included it, because he had heard that the Prophet would have included it if he had had the opportunity. Sometimes it is explained that the Prophet would have included it because the foundations on which Abraham had built the Kaʿbah extended into the *ḥiǧr*, and he wished to restore the building to Abraham's foundations. Finally, al-Ḥaǧǧāǧ again excluded the *ḥiǧr* from the Kaʿbah. That is not explained, although one assumes that it was because of his wish to undo the work of the defeated rival to the Umayyads.

As for the doors, tradition reports that Qurayš provided just one door, slightly to the north of the eastern corner, and that door was raised up considerably above ground level so that anyone entering the Kaʿbah had to ascend a set of steps that could be moved into place. The motive for this is again obscure, although different reports sometimes contain different explanations: it was so that they could keep out anyone to whom they wished to deny entrance; it was to prevent water entering the Kaʿbah when, as often happened, there were flash floods; it was to prevent theft from the Kaʿbah treasury.[3] Ibn az-Zubayr then provided two doors: one in the same place as that made by Qurayš, although at ground level; the other opposite it, north of the western corner of the Kaʿbah. He did so, again, because he had heard that that was in accordance with the wishes of the Prophet, who had spoken of a door for people to go in by

3 See, e.g., Azraqī, *Aḫbār Makkah*, ed. Rušdī ṣ-Ṣāliḥ Malḥas, 2 vols. (Beirut: Dār al-Andalus, 1389/1969), 1: 157–79.

and another for them to exit. Al-Ḥağğāğ then closed up the western door and restored the eastern one to its position above ground level, as Qurayš had positioned it.[4]

All of this vacillation between a Kaʿbah that included the *ḥiğr* and one that did not, and one with one door above ground level and one with two doors at ground level, is quite confusing, especially given the lack of substance in the explanations given by Muslim tradition for the changes. Lüling's attempt to provide an understanding involves a thesis-driven reinterpretation of what the tradition tells us about the various re-buildings, but he was the first, I believe, to draw attention to the importance of the connection between the *ḥiğr* and the idea that Abraham was the builder of the Kaʿbah, and to propose a relationship between the details about the various changes and competing concepts of the place of the Kaʿbah in ritual.

His broad argument – that the various re-buildings transformed the Kaʿbah from a Christian church to a closed cube where the main ritual consisted of an external circumambulation (*ṭawāf*) – involves an extensive revision of the traditional reports. While that revision is open to criticism, he was surely correct in seeing that a building with two doors for entry and exit (some reports also refer to its raised height and apertures for light in the roof) implies worship taking place inside, whereas one with a door raised up higher than the height of a man, and needing steps to be brought into place, is not consistent with the idea that entrance into it would be a normal occurrence.

In that connection he also cited material that stresses the function of the Kaʿbah as a building to be venerated by circumambulation and that it was not intended to be entered.[5] Here too one might criticise him for the selective use of evidence and failure to deal seriously with conflicting evidence (although he does acknowledge that there is conflicting evidence), but at least his work has the, perhaps by him unintended, consequence of indicating that there is a significant tension in Muslim tradition: On the one hand, there is the dominant idea of the Kaʿbah as a closed building around which circumambulation is to be performed and on the other hand, there is material which reports it being en-

4 Lüling discusses, and provides helpful plans and diagrams for, these and other features of the traditional accounts of the re-buildings of the Kaʿbah in Lüling, *Wiederentdeckung*, 126–61 (Chapter 3, part a: Die Nachrichten über die vor- und frühislamische Kaaba Mekkas als Beweis für ihre vorislamische Nutzung als christliches Kirchengebäude).

5 Lüling, *Wiederentdeckung*, 153–4.

tered and prayed in.[6] Lüling's understanding that whether the *ḥiğr* was included or not, whether the door or doors were elevated or at ground level, and whether divine worship took place within or without the Kaʿbah, are not inconsequential issues of style and aesthetics seems right.

The Nature of the Evidence

A wider point may be made about the evidence Lüling used. Detailed accounts of the history of the Kaʿbah are found only in the Muslim literary tradition, especially in the works the titles of which refer to them as histories of Mecca. Of those, the best known is that of Abū l-Walīd Muḥammad al-Azraqī (d. after 244/858), whose book has a complex compositional history. Lüling cites Azraqī frequently but has no concern for the reasons why his work and others like it came into existence. He simply treats it as a mass of reports some of which may be accepted as reflecting historical reality but the majority of which he judges to be the distortions and inventions of Islamic orthodoxy, aiming to conceal the true nature of conditions in Mecca in the time of Muḥammad. He does not propose any method for distinguishing between authentic or valid reports and the falsifications of orthodoxy, apart from occasionally saying that valid material is likely to be contained in asides or incidental details that are not the main concern of a particular report.

The most obvious importance of works like al-Azraqī's is that they reflect and support the development of Mecca as the cultic centre of Islam, a process which was by no means uncontested or obvious.[7] If that is their main purpose and function, then it is likely they will emphasize the role of Mecca and its sanctuary in pre-Islamic and early Islamic times, casting back the significance they came to have for Islam. To use their material about Mecca and the Kaʿbah in the rather positivist way that Lüling does is to underestimate its complexities and to overestimate what we can learn from it about early Mecca.

---

6 It should also be noted that he assumes that *ṭawāf* always indicates external circumambulation, as it does in Muslim practice. In itself the word could refer to circumambulation inside a building.

7 The early Umayyad caliphs seem to have regarded Medina as the locus of the religious authority that they wished to transfer to Syria, and ʿAbd al-Malik's Dome of the Rock is unlikely to have been conceived of as second in importance to the Kaʿbah built in Mecca by his rival Ibn az-Zubayr.

Lüling's concern only with the Kaʿbah at Mecca

One of the results of his reliance on works like that of Azraqī is that Lüling conveys the impression that Muḥammad and his followers, insofar as they were concerned with their sanctuary, were solely interested in the Kaʿbah at Mecca. The discussion focuses entirely on the Kaʿbah and the rituals it might have been used for, and while that largely reflects the material that one finds in the traditional histories of Mecca, it ignores or distorts the fuller picture provided in Muslim traditional literature in at least two ways.

First, Lüling plays down the tradition that before turning to face the Kaʿbah in prayer (adopting the Kaʿbah as the *qiblah*) the Prophet and his community prayed towards Jerusalem. The obvious importance of this tradition is that it is another sign that emerging Islam's adoption of the Meccan sanctuary was not a simple or uncontested process. Lüling undermines that by his insistence that praying towards Jerusalem was not intended to signify a break with Meccan Kaʿbah. He argues that the Kaʿbah itself, like early Christian churches in Syria-Palestine, was orientated towards Jerusalem, and the Prophet, therefore, was simply maintaining the practice of his fellow Meccans who worshipped in the church of the Kaʿbah.[8]

Secondly, he pays no attention to the fact that, in the *ḥaǧǧ* rituals, the Kaʿbah and the rites associated with it are a secondary part of a much larger complex. Although, popularly, there may be a tendency to focus on the Kaʿbah as the House of God, in the rituals of the *ḥaǧǧ* neither the Kaʿbah nor Mecca itself are really of central importance. It is, as Wellhausen showed, the complex of rites that take place outside Mecca – at places such as ʿArafah and Minā – that really constitute the *ḥaǧǧ*. According to some Islamic scholars, it is the standing ceremony (*wuqūf*) at ʿArafah that is at the heart of the *ḥaǧǧ* – if one misses the *wuqūf* one's *ḥaǧǧ* is not valid. The *ʿumrah*, on the other hand, consists only of rituals performed at and around the Kaʿbah.[9]

Generally, it may be said that Lüling's reliance on the traditional histories of Mecca results in attention to the Kaʿbah to the exclusion of other features of the sanctuary, emphasis on continuity in terms of institutions and sites, and an approach to the formation of the Muslim sanctuary at Mecca that lacks complexity. I suggest here that attention to sanctuary material in the Qurʾān would have at least raised different questions.

8 Lüling, *Wiederentdeckung*, 135–39.

9 On this, see further below (97–99).

2 The Qur'ān and the Sanctuary

Lüling's focus on the history of the Kaʿbah itself, and his lack of sustained reference to the Muslim scripture, which rarely provides straightforward historical information, may be explicable to some degree, but in the following, I shall draw attention to a number of Qur'ānic passages that do not seem to be consistent with Muslim tradition or practice. Going beyond that, to offer explanations for the apparent disparity between Qur'anic material and the material of Muslim tradition outside the Qur'ān, is more difficult, but some possibilities will be considered.

Tensions between Qur'ānic passages and Muslim tradition

Of course, one would not expect to find obvious and indisputable cases of disjunction between tradition, scripture and practice that the Islamic scholars themselves have not noted and found ways of reconciling, at least to their own satisfaction.

One example would be the reference to aṣ-Ṣafā and al-Marwah in Q 2: 158. There we are told that no blame is to be attached to anyone who, making *ḥağğ* or *ʿumrah*, performs the *ṭawāf* of aṣ-Ṣafā and al-Marwah (*fa-lā ğunāḥ*[a] *ʿalayhi an yaṭṭawwafa bihimā*). At first sight, the verse conveys the impression that it is allowing, but hardly making mandatory, a practice that some regarded as of questionable legitimacy. In Islamic law and practice, on the other hand, virtually all the schools do see this *ṭawāf* (classically better known as *saʿy*) as an obligation and, if it is omitted, the pilgrim must either go back to perform it, or compensate for it with an animal offering.[10]

The apparent difference in valuation of this *ṭawāf* between the Qur'anic verse and Muslim practice was overcome by a number of variant and even conflicting traditions. Most frequently it is said that the verse was revealed to reassure a particular group which had avoided making the *ṭawāf* of aṣ-Ṣafā and al-Marwah because the two places were associated with the worship of idols before Islam, and now that the group had accepted Islam it was hesitant about performing it. The verse was revealed to reassure them that there was no blame imputed

10 Muḥibb ad-Dīn aṭ-Ṭabarī, *Al-Qirā li-qāṣid Umm al-Qurā*, ed. Muṣṭafā as-Saqqā (Cairo 1390/1970), 361–4, especially 362–3.

to those who made it, because their association with idolatry no longer remained.[11]

While reports of that sort might be convincing within the terms of Muslim tradition, from an outsider perspective they could be understood as secondary attempts to loosen the tension between the Qur'an and an established practice, and it is clear from the commentaries on the verse that many found its wording problematic.

One obvious answer to the question of why there is a tension between the verse and Islamic practice would be that the Qur'ān here reflects a stage in the development of the Muslim sanctuary and the rituals associated with it that predates the stabilisation of ritual in that respect. It seems likely that the Qur'anic verse reflects a situation in which pre-existing rituals and holy places in Mecca (assuming that the names aṣ-Ṣafā and al-Marwah refer to the same entities as they do in Islam) were in the process of being assimilated into emerging Islam's sanctuary, and that there was some doubt about the validity of some of them. That still leaves the details of the process of assimilation rather vague, however.

Few examples of the tension between the Qur'anic text, Muslim tradition and Muslim practice are quite so obvious as the one just summarised, but it is certainly not unique, and the same verse, Q 2: 158, in fact displays another, which raises a bigger issue.

The verse refers to "those who make *ḥaǧǧ* of the *bayt* or make *'umrah* (*man ḥaǧǧa l-bayt awⁱ 'tamara*)", implying that the focus of *ḥaǧǧ* is the sacred "house" or *bayt*, which would be understood in Islam as a term for the Ka'bah. The idea that the destination of *ḥaǧǧ* is the *bayt* is also implicit in Q 3: 97, which proclaims that *ḥiǧǧ al-bayt* is a duty that men owe to God. In other words, it would seem that the purpose of *ḥaǧǧ* is visiting the Ka'bah.[12] That may not seem surprising and would be consistent with the fact that in Islam most pilgrims see visiting and circumambulating the Ka'bah as the central experience of the *ḥaǧǧ*.

According to Islamic law, however, the essence of the *ḥaǧǧ* is not visiting the Ka'bah, but participation in rites that occur away from Mecca. Frequently it is asserted that it is the "standing" ceremony at 'Arafah (the *wuqūf*) which is at the heart of the *ḥaǧǧ*: "he who has missed the *wuqūf* has missed the *ḥaǧǧ*".

11 Muḥibb ad-Dīn aṭ-Ṭabarī, *Qirā*, 361–4; Abū Ǧa'far aṭ-Ṭabarī, *Tafsīr*, ad Q 2: 158 (*Ǧāmi' al-bayān 'an ta'wīl āy al-Qur'ān*, ed. Maḥmūd Šākir, 30 parts in 16 vols. (Beirut, 1421/2001), vol. 2: 53–64).

12 *Ḥiǧǧ* is explained as simply a variant of *ḥaǧǧ*. Traditional philologists frequently explain *ḥaǧǧ* and *'umrah* as words meaning "a journey to" and "a visit". See E.W. Lane, *Lexicon*, s.vv.

"The day of the great *ḥaǧǧ*" (Q9: 3), usually reformulated as "the great day of the *ḥaǧǧ*", is variously explained as the day of the *wuqūf* or that of the slaughters at Minā (*yawm al-naḥr*), but is not usually associated with the Kaʿbah.[13]

That the Kaʿbah does not have a central role in the *ḥaǧǧ* of Islam, is supported by numerous *ḥadīṯ* and dicta of companions and successors. For example, Ibn ʿUmar said, "Whoever has not stood at ʿArafah, from the night of Muzdalifah before the dawn appears, has missed the *ḥaǧǧ*". The Prophet is reported to have told a group of Naǧdīs who asked him about the *ḥaǧǧ*, "The *ḥaǧǧ* is ʿArafah, and whoever comes there on the night of Ǧamʿ before the dawn appears has achieved the *ḥaǧǧ* (*qad adraka l-ḥaǧǧ*)". Saʿīd b. al-Musayyab said, "The *ʿumrah* is circumambulation (*ṭawāf*) and the *ḥaǧǧ* is ʿArafāt". In other words, it is *ʿumrah* that is the ritual associated with the Kaʿbah, whereas *ḥaǧǧ* is associated with the place outside Mecca where the *wuqūf* takes place.[14]

Wellhausen saw that point more than a century ago when he argued that the Islamic *ḥaǧǧ* consists of two originally distinct elements that have been combined – the *ʿumrah*, centred on rituals performed at the Kaʿbah in Mecca, and the pre-Islamic *ḥaǧǧ*, which originally took place at sites outside Mecca. He thought that the amalgamation of the two had been carried through by the Prophet himself with the intention of Islamising the Kaʿbah, part of the same process that identified the Kaʿbah as an Abrahamic foundation. By bringing the Kaʿbah into an association with the *ḥaǧǧ*, with which it originally had nothing to do, and by identifying it as built by Abraham, who had also initiated – on God's command – the rituals of the *ḥaǧǧ*, Muḥammad established the previously pagan shrine as a monotheist foundation and part of the *ḥaǧǧ* rituals.[15]

There is some evidence that suggests the process had not been completed by the time of the Prophet's death.[16] However, to explore the circumstances that

---

13 Abū Ǧaʿfar al-Ṭabarī, *Tafsīr*, ad. Q9: 3, cites an unusually large number of traditions on this issue, the majority supporting its identification as *yawm al-naḥr.*

14 Muḥibb ad-Dīn aṭ-Ṭabarī, *Qirā*, 388–92 for material of this sort.

15 Julius Wellhausen, *Reste arabischen Heidentums*, 2nd edition (Berlin: Reimer, 1897), 68–73, 79–84.

16 In his account of the *ḥaǧǧ* during the siege of Ibn al-Zubayr in Mecca in 72/692 by the Umayyad general al-Ḥaǧǧāǧ, Ṭabarī tells us that al-Haǧǧāǧ led the *ḥaǧǧ* but he did not circumambulate the Kaʿba or go there. Ibn az-Zubayr slaughtered animals in Mecca on the Day of Sacrifices, but neither he nor his men made the *ḥaǧǧ* in that year because they were not present at the "standing" ritual (*wuqūf*) at ʿArafah. See Ṭabarī, *Taʾrīḫ*, 2: 830; cf. Ibn al-Aṯīr, *Kāmil*, 3: 399 (s.a. 73!) who adds that in addition to not circumambulating the Kaʿbah, al-Ḥaǧǧāǧ was unable to make the ritual of running (*saʿy*) between the two hills in Mecca called al-Ṣafā and al-Marwah; furthermore, Ibn az-Zubayr could not make *ḥaǧǧ* because, as well as missing the *wuqūf* at ʿArafah, he was unable to perform the stone throwing rite at the Ǧimār.

brought the Kaʿbah into an association with the *ḥağğ* would take us too far from the present topic, and here I want to focus on the tension between those Qurʾānic verses that suggest that the *ḥağğ* is fundamentally concerned with the *bayt*, and Islamic law, which seems to deny that.

It would be possible, perhaps, to argue that the Qurʾānic verses are deliberately phrased as they are in order to create or support the idea that the *ḥağğ* is a ritual focused on the Kaʿbah, and that they are part of an attempt to associate *ḥağğ* with the Kaʿbah in the way that Wellhausen envisaged.

However, while I accept that the development envisaged by Wellhausen did occur, albeit probably at a date later than he thought, I am not sure that the two Qurʾānic verses we are concerned with here, verses that imply that *ḥağğ* or *ḥiğğ* are closely connected with the *bayt*, have anything to do with it.

In spite of the popular association of the *ḥağğ* with the Kaʿbah, in Islamic law and tradition there is no sustained attempt to link them – indeed, the essential disjunction between them is clear. The two Qurʾanic verses that use the phrases *man ḥağğa l-bayt* and *ḥiğğ al-bayt* seem quite anomalous in that respect, therefore. It seems worth considering, then, whether the *bayt* alluded to in each case is the Kaʿbah at Mecca, or whether the phrases have been carried over from some other context in which a *bayt* really was the focus of a *ḥağğ* or *ḥiğğ*. We will return to this.

Another area where there seems to be tension between the Qurʾanic material on the *bayt* and Islamic practice is that of the ritual slaughtering of animals. Several verses seem to envisage the *bayt* as the place for the slaughter of the animal offerings that are an important ingredient of *ḥağğ* and *ʿumrah.*

Q48: 25, refers to the animal offering (*hady*) being held back from the place where it will be slaughtered (its *maḥill*), by the enemies of the Believers, who bar them from *al-masğid al-ḥarām*, and the same term (*maḥill*) occurs in Q22:196: if you are prevented from carrying out the command, "fulfil the *ḥağğ* and the *ʿumrah* for God", you should send an animal offering and not desacralize "until the *hady* reaches its *maḥill*". Q22: 33 is more specific about the *maḥill*: it is *ilā l-bayt al-ʿatīq* (to the ancient/noble house). Q 5: 2 exhorts the Believers to respect God's signs, the sacred month, the animal offerings (*hady*) and the garlands that mark them out, and those people going towards *al-bayt al-ḥarām.*[17] Q 5:95 tells us that the compensation for killing game while in a state of *iḥrām* is a domestic animal equivalent to the one killed, "as a *hady* to reach the Kaʿbah".

17 The subsequent command not to go beyond the bounds in hatred of those who barred you from *al-masğid al-ḥarām* may indicate that it refers to a situation in which the Believers' opponents were continuing to make *ḥağğ*.

The implication of all this is that the animal offerings are to be slaughtered at or near the *bayt* (identified as the Kaʿbah in Q5: 95).

In the Islamic *ḥaǧǧ* and *ʿumrah*, on the other hand, animals are not slaughtered at or near the Kaʿbah. Indeed, it is not usual to offer an animal at all when making an *ʿumrah*, and the animals that are slaughtered as part of the *ḥaǧǧ* ritual are killed at Minā outside Mecca. Minā is not mentioned in the Qur'ān. The disjunction here between the Islamic practice at Minā and the Qur'anic verses that imply that the *bayt* was the place for the animal offerings to be killed, was naturally obvious to the commentators, who sought to reconcile the scripture with the practice in various ways.

For example, regarding Q 22: 33 (*ṯumma maḥilluhā ilā l-bayt al-ʿatīq*), while most did accept that this is a reference to the slaughter of animal offerings, some read it as an allusion to the pilgrims who would complete their rites by circumambulating the Kaʿbah. For those who accepted what seems the more obvious sense (that it concerns the animal offerings), some say that *ilā l-bayt al-ʿatīq* means "all of the *ḥaram*" just as al-*masǧid al-ḥarām* in Q9: 28 (the *mušrikūn*... shall not approach *al-masǧid al-ḥarām*) means that non-Muslims are barred from the whole of the *ḥaram*, the sacred area in which some certain things are prohibited or constrained, which extends considerably beyond the bounds of Mecca. Thus, Minā could be intended by the wording of the verse.[18]

Another approach is to theorise that the notion of the animals' *maḥill* as the *bayt* is to some extent symbolic: because of the importance of the *bayt* for those making *ḥaǧǧ*, the references to it as the destination for the animals to be slaughtered is not to be understood literally. That seems to the position of Yusuf Ali, translator of the Qur'an into English, who renders *ilā l-bayt al-ʿatīq* in Q22: 33 as "their place of sacrifice is near the Ancient House" and adds a note that "the actual sacrifice is not performed in the Kaʿba, but at Minā".

Again, it is tempting for the outsider to understand these procedures as secondary attempts to align the text with Islamic practice, and that in these passages the Qur'ān really does envisage that the animal offerings are to be slaughtered at the *bayt* or Kaʿbah.

That would be explicable in terms of the process suggested by Wellhausen, although again there is evidence from Muslim tradition and historical material to support the view that the *bayt* was regarded as a place of animal sacrifice (the place where the *hady* was slaughtered) in early Islam and remained so for some time after the death of the Prophet. For example, in the accounts of al-Ḥaǧǧāǧ's siege of Ibn az-Zubayr in Mecca in 73/692 it is reported that the latter and

18 E.g., Ṭabarī, *Tafsīr*, ad Q22: 33 (vol. 17: 185–9).

his companions slaughtered animals at the Ka'bah at the time of the *ḥaǧǧ*, although they could not leave the town to make *ḥaǧǧ*.[19]

If we do take the Qur'ān literally in those passages that suggest the *bayt* is the place for the slaughter of animal offerings, and if we accept that the *bayt* referred to was the Ka'bah at Mecca, one way of explaining it would be that the amalgamation of the Ka'bah into the *ḥaǧǧ*, as theorised by Wellhausen, led to the gradual abandonment of animal sacrifice at the Ka'bah and its displacement to Minā, where it was perhaps one of the rituals of the pre-Islamic *ḥaǧǧ*. The Qur'anic material presenting the *bayt* as the place of animal slaughter could be a residue of the time before it had been displaced to Minā.

Do all references to the sanctuary in the Qur'ān relate to that at Mecca?

So far, then, some of the tensions, discrepancies, or disjunctions between the Qur'ān and Islamic practice and tradition concerning the sanctuary and the *ḥaǧǧ* may be explained as reflections of the sort of development envisaged by Wellhausen – the deliberate conflation of two originally distinct and independent institutions: *'umrah* with its focus on the Ka'bah at Mecca and *ḥaǧǧ* associated with sites in the vicinity of Mecca but not involving the Ka'bah.

However, although those verses (Q 2: 158 and 3: 97) that present *ḥaǧǧ* or *ḥiǧǧ* as focused on the *bayt* could possibly be understood also as reflections of that development, another explanation of them, that they reflect ideas associated with another *ḥaǧǧ* and *bayt*, is also possible. Is there anything to strengthen that latter possibility? Does *bayt* in the Qur'ān always refer to the Ka'bah at Mecca, and do words relating to *ḥaǧǧ* always refer to those rites performed in the vicinity of Mecca and eventually incorporating the rituals at the Ka'bah, as Wellhausen theorised?

The term *al-ka'bah* occurs only twice in the book, in the course of a single passage, Q5: 95–97. That is concerned with the prohibition of killing game by those who are in the state of ritual purity necessary for the performance of *ḥaǧǧ* or *'umrah* (*wa-antum ḥurum*). In verse 95 it is said that, if one kills game while in this state, a compensatory offering must be brought "to the Ka'bah". In verse 97, the Ka'bah is then characterized as the sacred house: (*ja'ala llāhu l-ka'bah al-bayt al-ḥarām qiyāman li-n-nās*). It is not clear whether *al-bayt al-*

19 See note 14 above.

ḥarām here is merely an honorific epithet or a gloss. The latter would raise the question why the identity of the Kaʿbah with the *bayt* needed to be stated.

Equally, if one merely had the Qurʾān, it is likely that one would conclude that the most common name for the sanctuary was *al-masǧid al-ḥarām*. Many references to *al-masǧid al-ḥarām* in the Qurʾān are concerned with the Believers being barred from it by their opponents, and some with fighting there. In a few passages, the Believers seem to have obtained control of it themselves and then they bar their opponents from it. But nowhere, it seems, is there any mention of being barred or barring from the *bayt*.[20] This material gives the impression that *al-masǧid al-ḥarām* was the name for a place of worship that was in dispute between the Believers and their opponents.

A few passages suggest a relationship between *al-masǧid al-ḥarām* and the *bayt*, although its details are not clear. Q 8: 34–5 for example, refers to the opponents barring the Believers from *al-masǧid al-ḥarām* and is immediately followed by mockery of the opponents' prayer (*ṣalāt*) by or at (*ʿinda*) the *bayt:* it is no more than whistling and clapping of hands (*mukāʾ wa-taṣdiya*). That could suggest that the *bayt* is part of, or near, the *masǧid*.

Other verses refer to *al-masǧid al-ḥarām* in the context of material concerning *ḥaǧǧ*. For example, Q 2: 196 specifies that certain regulations concerning *ḥaǧǧ* only apply to "he whose family is not present in *al-masǧid al-ḥarām* (*lam yakun ahluhu ḥāḍirī l-masǧidi l-ḥarām*) ". Other verses that associate *al-masǧid al-ḥarām* with *ḥaǧǧ* include Q 9: 19, which regards the provision of drink for those making *ḥaǧǧ*, together with "abiding in" *al-masǧid al-ḥarām*, (*siqāyat al-ḥāǧǧi wa-ʿimārat al-masǧidi l-ḥarām*), as less worthy of praise than belief in God and the Last Day; and Q 48: 25, which links the opponents' barring the Believers from *al-masǧid al-ḥarām* with the animal offering being prevented (*maʿkūf*) from reaching "the place where it is to be slaughtered" (*maḥilluhā*).

Other notable occurrences of *al-masǧid al-ḥarām* in the text are in the verses naming it as the direction to be faced in prayer (*qiblah*) and when it is named as the starting point of the night journey alluded to in Q 17: 1.

---

20 Q 2: 191: "Do not fight them by (*ʿinda*) *al-masǧid al-ḥarām* until they fight you in (*fī*) it"; 2: 217: "fighting in the sacred month is a grave matter, but barring from ... *al-masǧid al-ḥarām* and expelling its people from it is graver with God"; 5: 2: "do not let hatred of a people who barred you from *al-masǧid al-ḥarām* cause you to transgress"; 8: 34: "why should God not punish them when they bar you from *al-masǧid al-ḥarām?* "; 9: 28: "the *mušrikūn* are just filth and shall not approach *al-masǧid al-ḥarām* after this year of theirs"; 22: 25 promises divine punishment for the unbelievers who bar from God's path and *al-masǧid al-ḥarām*; 48: 25 following a verse that talks of God having restrained the hands of the opponents from the Believers in the *baṭn* of Mecca, refers to the opponents' disbelief and their "having barred you from *al-masǧid al-ḥarām*".

The prominence and frequency in the Qur'an of the expression *al-masǧid al-ḥarām* suggests that it was the common name for the sanctuary contested between the Believers and their opponents. Now, according to Muslim tradition, before Islam the name was given to the empty space surrounding the Kaʿbah in Mecca. It had no buildings and no walls, and was merely the space around the Kaʿbah, extending as far as the ordinary houses of the Meccans. Only in the early caliphate was it subject to architectural embellishment and extension. It may seem to be another example of the sort of tensions we have been considering that a name figuring so prominently in the Qur'ān should be applied to an empty space without any apparent function.

Two more points maybe made about *al-masǧid al-ḥarām* and the traditional association of it with Mecca and the Kaʿbah.

Firstly, one would assume the name indicates that the rivals for the use of it were monotheists, in spite of propaganda in which the opponents of the Qur'ānic party are labelled as *mušrikūn*. The word *masǧid* (literally place of prostration), is attested in Aramaic and Nabatean forms long before Islam, and always seems to be used by monotheists.[21] One also notes the reference to the *ṣalāt* of the opponents in Q 8: 34–35. It seems as though according to the Qur'ānic evidence two opposed groups, each identifying itself as monotheist, contested possession of a sanctuary known as *al-masǧid al-ḥarām.*

Secondly, there is sometimes a tension between *al-masǧid al-ḥarām* as it appears in the Qur'ān and the Islamic application of that name.

One example concerns the so-called *qiblah* verses (Q 2: 142–52), which specify that one should turn to face *al-masǧid al-ḥarām* in prayer. In tradition and law, on the other hand, it is the Kaʿbah that is the *qiblah* and there is discussion about which precise point of the Kaʿbah is the exact point of it. That the scripture refers here to *al-masǧid al-ḥarām* can be ignored or glossed over.

For example, discussing Q 2: 144 in his *Tafsīr*, Ṭabarī understands "We have seen you turning your face to the heavens" as an allusion to the fact that, before he was told by God to turn to face *al-masǧid al-ḥarām*, the Prophet had longed to turn to the Kaʿbah in prayer, and he reports various views on why he had wanted to face the Kaʿbah. Then he comes to different views about the part of *al-masǧid al-ḥarām* which God ordered the Prophet to face (the verse has said nothing about facing a part of it, merely "Turn your face to *al-masǧid al-ḥarām*") and what precisely "a *qiblah* that shall please you" means. Some favour the water

---

21 Its earliest appearance seems to be in the papyri from Elephantine (5th century BCE). See Bezalel Porten, ed., *The Elephantine Papyri in English: Three Millennia of Cross-Cultural Continuity and Change* (Leiden: E.J. Brill, 1996), 266.

spout (*mīzāb*) that projects from the roof of the Kaʿbah, others say that all of the *bayt* is a *qiblah* and that it is the door of the Kaʿbah which is the *qiblah* of the *bayt* itself. From that sort of material one might have expected that the verse would have told the Prophet to turn to face the Kaʿbah or the *bayt.*

Some tension is also apparent between the traditional reports of Muḥammad's Night Journey and Ascension (*miʿrāǧ*) and Q 17: 1, viewed traditionally as an allusion to it. In the verse, the phrase *man asrā bi-ʿabdihi mina l-masǧidi l-ḥarām ilā l-masǧidi l-aqṣā* has been understood to designate the starting point and destination of the journey.

Some of the traditional reports about the event have details difficult to reconcile with the standard Muslim understanding of *al-masǧid al-ḥarām* as the empty space around the Kaʿbah. For example, some accounts say that the Prophet was sleeping in the house of his cousin Umm Hāniʾ when he was taken on his journey, and that led some commentators to define *al-masǧid al-ḥarām* in a way that was wider than usual: "all of the *ḥaram* (the restricted area of which Mecca is a part) is a *masǧid*".

Other stories about the event were more easily compatible with the standard understanding of the term as the area around the Kaʿbah. Thus, for instance, we are told that Muḥammad was sleeping "by the *bayt*" or "in the *ḥiǧr*" when he was transported.[22] Again, it seems possible that we are witnessing attempts in the tradition to interpret the Qurʾānic *al-masǧid al-ḥarām* in a way that makes it compatible with the Muslim sanctuary at Mecca, and the need to do that could indicate that in Q 17: 1 it may have a different significance.[23]

---

22 For the various understandings of *al-masǧid al-ḥarām* in Q17: 1, see, e.g., Ṭabarī, *Tafsīr* ad loc.; the *ḥiǧr* is most often identified in tradition as the semi-circular area enclosed by a low wall adjoining the northwestern wall of the Kaʿbah.

23 Cf. Ibn Abī Šaybah's chapter headed: "What is to be said when entering *al-masǧid al-ḥarām*" (*Muṣannaf* 4/2, 97). The five reports collected there use the following formulae indicating what is meant by "entering *al-masǧid al-ḥarām*": "the first time you enter Mecca and reach the Stone (or *al-ḥiǧr?*)"; "when you see the *bayt*"; "when he entered the *masǧid* of the Kaʿbah"; "when he saw the *bayt*"; "when he entered the *bayt.*" There is nothing there to indicate that the expression *al-masǧid al-ḥarām* was ever commonly used to mean "all of the *ḥaram*," or even the whole of Mecca.

What might it mean to say that the Qur'ān's sanctuary material relates to places other than Mecca?

Of course, it has been understood for some time that some passages in the Qur'ān are adaptations or re-workings of material from other sources, and much research has gone into identifying those related texts.

For example, in the Qur'ān the *bayt* is often associated with Abraham. In Q 2: 125 God reminds us that He has made the *bayt* as a refuge and sanctuary (*maṯāba wa-amn*) for men, that we should take Abraham's "place" (*maqām*) as a place of prayer, and that He commanded Abraham and Ishmael to purify it for those performing acts of worship there. Q 2: 127 reminds us that Abraham raised the foundations (*al-qawāʿid*) of the *bayt* together with Ishmael. Q 3: 96–7 tells us that the first *bayt* established for men was that at Bakkah, and that in it are clear signs, the "place" of Abraham. In Q 22: 26 God refers to His having pointed out to (*wa-iḏ bawwaʾnā li*) Abraham the place of the *bayt* and repeats the command to him to purify it for those worshipping there.

Academic scholars have seen the material in these verses as midrash-like developments of, ultimately, Biblical verses. Joseph Witztum has persuasively argued that there a link between Q 2: 125–7 and the account of Abraham's aborted sacrifice of his son, Isaac, in Genesis 22, and provides parallels and similarities sometimes in Jewish texts and sometimes in Syriac Christian ones to substantiate his argument. In particular, he notes that the altar on which Abraham was to sacrifice Isaac according to the account in Genesis is referred to in some pre-Islamic Syriac developments of the story as a *baytā*. In various versions of the story Abraham is pictured as a master builder and the son he is about to sacrifice willingly helps him in constructing the altar, details that have echoes in the Qur'ān and Muslim tradition.[24]

Whether he is right in all the details of his argument is not the issue here, for it seems clear that there are many passages in the Qur'ān that have originated in that way – as developments of Biblical materials and of Jewish and Christian reworkings of them. The question here is whether it is a purely literary phenomenon? By that, I mean how far were ideas and institutions subject to a similar process of transfer?

In the case of the sanctuary, could we envisage that not merely texts, but a pre-Islamic sanctuary, or features of it, with which the texts were associated, have been carried over into nascent Islam and left their residue in the Qur'ān

24 Joseph Witztum, "The Foundations of the House (Q 2: 127)," *Bulletin of the School of Oriental and African Studies* 72 (2009): 25–40.

and early tradition? For example, could the notion of Abraham as the builder of the *bayt* involve not merely the transfer and adaptation of literary material, but also of features of a pre-Islamic sanctuary at a place associated with Abraham?

We know that, for example, in Jewish tradition the land of Moriah, where Abraham was to build the altar on which he was to slaughter his son in Genesis 22, came to be identified with the place of the Temple in Jerusalem – it may be that one of the traditions about the rock in Jerusalem over which ʿAbd al-Malik built his Dome is that it was the altar on which the offering was made before God provided the ram as a substitute.[25] According to Muslim historical reports, both the Dome of the Rock and the Kaʿbah claimed to possess the horns of the ram slaughtered on the altar.[26]

Many have referred also to the place near Hebron where, according to the 5th century Sozomen, there was a sanctuary at the site thought to be Mamre, at the oak of which Abraham had the famous theophany described in Genesis 18.[27] At an annual festival and fair people of diverse ethnicities and religions had gathered there, worshipping in different ways and with different understandings of the holiness of the place, until Constantine the Great ordered that it be exclusively for Christians. Nevertheless, it seems clear from Sozomen's account that the Christianization of the site had not been achieved by his time.

Given that these sanctuaries were associated with Biblical materials which we find taken over and developed in the Qurʾān and Muslim tradition, it is reasonable to think that ideas and features of such sanctuaries are also reflected both in Muslim literature and in the set-up of the Muslim sanctuary. How far one could take that further, to theorise that nascent Islam regarded as its own a sanctuary situated somewhere other than Mecca – presumably further north,

---

25 For the identification of the land of Moriah (Genesis 22:2) with Mount Moriah and the site of the Jerusalem Temple, see 2 Chronicles 3:2; Josephus, *Antiquities of the Jews*, I, 13:1. For the association of the rock in Jerusalem with Abraham's aborted sacrifice of Isaac, see Oleg Grabar, *The Formation of Islamic Art* (New Haven: Yale University Press, 1987), 50. Note that Nāṣir-i Khusraw (middle of the 11th century) associated the rock in the Dome with Abraham and Isaac (cited by Grabar, *The Shape of the Holy* (Princeton: Princeton University Press, 1996), 156).

26 See the references in Amikam Elad, *Medieval Jerusalem and Islamic Worship. Holy Places, Ceremonies, Pilgrimage* (Leiden, 1995, 52) notes 5 & 6.

27 Sozomen, *Ecclesiastical History*, 2, ch.4. On the site, see Elizabeth K. Fowden, "Sharing Holy Places," in *Common Knowledge* 8 (2002): 124–46, especially 125–29. She refers to it as a classical *ḥaram* and refers to archaeological evidence for its survival at least until the fifth century as a place where both pagan and monotheist rituals were carried out. See too Arieh Kofsky, "Mamre: a case of regional cult?" in *Sharing the Sacred: Religious Contacts and Conflicts in the Holy Land, First-Fifteenth Centuries*, eds. Arieh Kofsky and Guy G. Stroumsa (Jerusalem: Yad Ben-Zvi Press, 1998), 19–30.

in Palestine or the borders of Arabia and Syria – would depend on broader ideas about the geography of Islam's origins and when the Ḥiǧāz became established as its holy land.

I suggest, then, that the Qur'ān reflects a stage where the process of formation of the Islamic sanctuary at Mecca was still taking place. Some of its material can be interpreted in the light of Wellhausen's theory about the amalgamation of *ʿumra* and *ḥaǧǧ*. Other passages have to be understood as developments of texts that ultimately go back to the Bible, but have found their way into the Qur'ān through Jewish and Christian re-workings of them. Finally, it is likely that it refers to ideas, institutions, and practices that originated in the context of sanctuaries other than that at Mecca. We should not assume that references in the Qur'ān to *ḥaǧǧ*, *bayt*, *al-masǧid al-ḥarām*, and other expressions that we now associate with the Islamic sanctuary at Mecca (such as *maqam Ibrāhīm*) always referred to that sanctuary, although, of course, that is how they came to be understood in Muslim tradition. The Qur'ān then reflects a process still ongoing at the time of its composition.

Cornelia Horn

Hermeneutische Dimensionen der Intertextualität und Interreligiöse Kontexte des Korans

Eine Neueinschätzung der Bedeutung des Beitrags Günter Lülings für die Entwicklung der modernen Koranforschung

Umfang und Definition des Fragehorizontes

Das Herzstück und Zentrum der philologischen Methode, die Günter Lüling in seinen Arbeiten anwandte, wie überhaupt das Kernstück eines jeden methodischen Vorgehens, ist im Begriff der Kausalität verankert.[1] Dies lässt sich auch in diesen hier vorzulegenden Überlegungen sagen, die nicht beabsichtigen, genauer auf die Frage einzugehen, in welchem Umfang Günter Lülings persönliche Motive und dogmatisch-historische Kritik einen Einfluss auf sein methodisches Vorgehen genommen haben oder wie diese Faktoren andere in ihrer Beurteilung Lülings beeinflusst haben mögen.[2] Das zentrale, treibende Moment jeglicher Methode ist

---

1 Den Forschungsarbeiten für diesen Artikel konnte ich während meines Heisenbergstipendiums (GZ HO 5221/1–1) sowie im Rahmen meiner Heisenberg-Professur „Sprachen und Kulturen des Christlichen Orients" an der Martin-Luther-Universität Halle-Wittenberg, Halle (Saale) (GZ HO 5221/2–1) Zeit widmen. Für die finanzielle Unterstützung hierfür bin ich der Deutschen Forschungsgemeinschaft (DFG) sehr dankbar.

2 Die hier vorgelegten Untersuchungen und Überlegungen gehen nur auf einen Ausschnitt aus dem wissenschaftlichen Oeuvre Günter Lülings ein. Genauer betrachtet wurde ein Teil der Schnittmenge aus seinen Veröffentlichungen zum Koran und seinen Bemühungen um die Identifizierung der diesem möglicherweise unterliegenden christlich-arabischen Hymnen. Hier sind an Arbeiten zu nennen: Günter Lüling, „Kritisch-exegetische Untersuchung des Qurʾantextes," Inaugural-Dissertation, Philosophische Fakultät der Friedrich-Alexander-Universität Erlangen-Nürnberg (Erlangen, 1970); Günter Lüling, *Über den Ur-Qurʾān. Ansätze zur Rekonstruktion vorislamischer christlicher Strophenlieder im Qurʾān* (Erlangen: Verlagsbuchhandlung Hannelore Lüling, 1974); Günter Lüling, *Über den Urkoran. Ansätze zur Rekonstruktion der vorislamisch-christlichen Strophenlieder im Koran* (Erlangen: Verlagsbuchhandlung Hannelore Lüling, 1974), korrigierte, jedoch im Haupttext (S. 1–542) mit den Auflagen 1 und 2 seitengleiche, 3. Auflage, 2004; und Günter Lüling, *A Challenge to Islam for Reformation. The Rediscovery and reliable Reconstruction of a comprehensive pre-Islamic Christian Hymnal hidden in the Koran under earliest Islamic Reinterpretations* (Erlangen: Verlagsbuchhandlung Hannelore Lüling, 2. Auflage [engli-

https://doi.org/10.1515/9783110599176-007

der Gedanke der Kausalität. Doch welchen einzelnen Elementen und welchen Regeln gewährt man Zutritt und Mitspracherecht, wenn es darum geht, Abschnitte in einem Text zu erklären, die, egal an welchen objektiven Maßstäben gemessen, für den jeweiligen Lesenden keinen Sinn zu ergeben scheinen? Wem daran gelegen ist, eine wissenschaftliche Einschätzung der Vorgehensweise Lülings zu versuchen, der kommt nicht daran vorbei zuzugestehen, dass Lüling darin korrekt handelte, dass er bei seinen Untersuchungen von der Voraussetzung ausging, dass alle Fragen der Religion, Theologie und Dogmatik einer jeweiligen Tendenz unterliegen, die die sorgfältig angewandte philologische Methode zutage fördern kann. Bei jeglichem Studium religiöser oder religiös-politischer Texte stehen wir einer Wahlmöglichkeit und Wahlnotwendigkeit gegenüber: Entweder gestatten wir göttlichem Handeln Zutritt zur Welt unseres Diskurses, oder wir gehen ohne dieses vor und gewinnen die Ideen und Vorstellungen des Göttlichen auf der Ebene des Textes. Lüling entschied sich für die zweite Option. Genauer betrachtet hat seine Arbeit den Koran für ein systematisches, wissenschaftliches Untersuchen erschlossen, das den interreligiösen literarischen Kontext des Korans über das einfache Zugeständnis der Präsenz biblischer oder der Bibel an der Seite stehender Texte hinaus nutzt, um zu einem Verständnis der ersten Schritte einer islamischen Tendenz zu gelangen.

Der Zugang zum Koran über den Weg intertextueller Untersuchungen stellt nicht nur ein vielseitiges und effektives Instrumentarium bereit, mit dem es sich dem Studium des Korans selbst zuzuwenden lohnt. Die intertextuelle Methode und Fragestellung ist auch in hervorragender Weise dazu geeignet, die Verortung des Korans in Beziehung zu und im Austausch mit den verschiedenen spätantiken literarischen, sozialen, kulturellen und religiösen Schichten und Kontexten, in denen der Koran in Erscheinung tritt, anzugehen. Der hier vorgelegte Beitrag stellt Lülings grundlegende Arbeit in den Kontext eines bemerkenswerten Aufschwungs im Bereich der intertextuellen Studien des Korans, der sich in den neueren Forschungen zur Islamwissenschaft, und etwas enger gefasst zum Koran,

---

sche Übersetzung, umgearbeitet und erweitert, der 2. deutschen Edition (1993) der Studie *Über den Ur-Koran*], 2011). Lülings weitere Arbeiten konnten für die hier anstehende Fragestellung noch nicht genauer betrachtet werden, wären jedoch zur Berücksichtigung in einer umfangreicheren Arbeit relevant. Diese Arbeiten bestehen, soweit mir bekannt, aus den folgenden Veröffentlichungen: Günter Lüling, *Der christliche Kult an der vorislamischen Kaaba als Problem der Islamwissenschaft und christlichen Theologie* (Erlangen: Verlagsbuchhandlung Hannelore Lüling, c. 1977); Günter Lüling, *Die Wiederentdeckung des Propheten Muhammad. Eine Kritik am ‚christlichen' Abendland* (Erlangen: Verlagsbuchhandlung Hannelore Lüling, 1981); und Günter Lüling, *Sprache und archaisches Denken. Aufsätze zur Geistes- und Religionsgeschichte* (Erlangen: Verlagsbuchhandlung Hannelore Lüling, 2., um zwei Aufsätze erweiterte Auflage, 2005).

beobachten lässt. In einem ersten Schritt untersucht und evaluiert dieser Beitrag, wenn auch nur kurz, die Legitimität, Berechtigung und Angemessenheit der Methoden, derer sich Lüling bei seinem Studium des Korans bediente. In einem zweiten Schritt bietet diese Untersuchung einen begrifflichen, grundlegenden Rahmen und eine dreifache Klassifizierung der intertextuellen Studien, besonders im Blick darauf, wie diese sich auf den Koran hin angewendet darstellen. Innerhalb dieses Rahmens wird es möglich, Lülings Identifizierung einer Untergruppe von Texten, von denen er als Ur-Koran spricht, als einen grundlegenden Beitrag zur Suche nach den intertextuellen Dimensionen des Korans und seiner Lokalisierung in der Spätantike wahrzunehmen und wertzuschätzen.

Hermeneutik und Methoden in Lülings Koranuntersuchung

Die Hermeneutik und Methoden, die Günter Lüling bei seinen Untersuchungen des Korans anwandte, lassen sich nicht völlig isoliert vom Stand und den Konventionen der Wissenschaft und Wissenschaftslandschaft seiner Zeit betrachten. Weiter gefasste Untersuchungen werden es künftig noch notwendig machen, einige der speziellen Probleme in den exegetischen und interpretativen Prozessen zu betrachten, die aus der besonderen Natur und Gestalt der akademischen Disziplinen erwachsen, die zum Studium des Korans beitragen, und die aus den Interaktionen dieser Disziplinen, oder aus einem Fehlen solcher Interaktionen, entstehen. Da Lülings Werk mehreren akademischen Disziplinen zugehörte und sich bewusst an mehreren Disziplinen beteiligte, wird man erwägen müssen, ob und in welchem Ausmaß die interdisziplinäre Natur seines Projektes die Grenzen einzelner Disziplinen über das hinausgehend herausgefordert hatte, was diese zur damaligen Zeit hätten bereitwillig bewältigen können oder wofür diese ohne allzu große Veränderungen hätten Platz schaffen können.

Günter Lülings Einsicht war es, die Einzelmanifestationen textlicher Probleme im Koran als ein System von Problemen wahrzunehmen, das eine integrierte und vereinheitlichte Lösung erfordert und durch eine solche optimal behandelt werden kann. Er verstand diese Textprobleme nicht als einzelne Unbekannte, sondern als ein zusammengehörendes Set oder eine Menge von Unbekannten, die in einem einzigen, einheitlichen Raum existieren. Dieses Herangehen an die Thematik verdankte sich ohne Zweifel dem Einfluss von Religionswissenschaftlern wie Albert Schweitzer und Martin Werner.[3] Die anzuwendende Methode bestand darin, die theologische Tendenz einer biblischen Erzählung durch sorgfältiges und genaues Untersuchen und Verstehen der Art und Weise, mit der die Erzählung Wort für Wort aufgebaut worden war, offenzulegen. Dieses Vorgehen schien beinahe so konzipiert worden zu sein, dass man annahm, dass das Göttliche, worüber diese Texte vorgeblich sprachen, aus der sorgfältigen, kritischen Arbeit hervortrat und sich fast als Begleiterscheinung der wissenschaftlichen Untersuchung offenbarte. Solch ein methodisches Vorgehen, bei dem kritische und textkritische Probleme und ihre Lösungen die Bedeutung eines Textes und somit auch die Realitäten und Wirklichkeiten seiner diskursiven Welt festlegen, mag bei der Suche nach Wahrheit und Schönheit in der gängigen Theologie nicht gerade hoch im Kurs stehen. Im Kern seiner Untersuchung und vielleicht auch in stärkerem Maße als andere Wissenschaftler, die ihm vorangegangen waren, misstraute Lüling dem Text, den er vor sich sah. Er misstraute auch den *ad hoc* Schlussfolgerungen der wissenschaftlichen Tradition, die diesen Text als ihren Ausgangspunkt und ihre Grundlage genommen hatte. Anstatt den Text als „dunkel" und „mysteriös" zu verurteilen und abzuschreiben und dann im nächsten Schritt Bedeutung für den Text zu schaffen oder zu erfinden, die mit späteren Traditionen in eine Linie fallen konnte, ist es klar, dass es für Lüling als Forschungsantrieb von größter Wichtigkeit war, eine Erklärung zu finden und bereitzustellen, Ursachen von einer Grundlage her anzusprechen, die auf der Logik von Sprache, Schrift, Diskurs, Erzählung und den jeweiligen Hintergründen und Kontexten des Verfassers und seines Publikums aufgelagert waren und von daher weiterentwickelt werden konnten. Ob es nun Lülings Absicht war oder nicht, von seiner Entdeckung her und durch seine Entdeckung eines christlichen Ur-Korans erlaubt Lüling es uns, in den Textproblemen des Korans nicht irgendwelche Fehler zu sehen, die es zu korrigieren gilt, sondern sie als Fenster eines systematischen Transformationsprozesses wahrzunehmen, der vielleicht gut mit der Gelegenheit verglichen werden könnte, die sich einer Biologin bietet, wenn sie in die Chrysalis einer Larve gerade zu dem Zeitpunkt blicken darf, an dem sich diese Larve in einen Schmetterling verwandelt.

Es scheint ironisch, dass sich die Herangehensweisen derer, die Lüling am heftigsten kritisierten, auch darum bemühten, eine holistische Methode zu finden, indem sie den Koran als ein islamisches Dokument verstanden, mit seiner eigenen Tendenz, die wiederum aus der Bewahrung eigener Besonderheiten heraus zu verstehen ist und im Gegensatz zu einer Perspektive steht, die den

3 Günter Lüling widmete sein Hauptwerk „Über den Ur-Koran" ausdrücklich dem Gedächtnis Martin Werners.

Koran lediglich als ungeordnete Ansammlung nur halb verstandener und verarbeiteter Anspielungen auf jüdische und christliche Texte sieht, ohne System oder Akzentsetzung. Lülings philologische Rekonstruktion vorislamischer christlich-arabischer Hymnen, die den Ur-Koran konstituieren, bietet eine solide Theorie für das, was den Besonderheiten des Textes des Korans zugrunde liegt. Seine Erläuterungen der Transformation dieses christlich-arabischen Dokumentes blieben unvollständig; die Kritiker ergriffen die Gelegenheit dieser Unvollständigkeit und sahen in Lülings Vorgehen einen Versuch, dem Koran eine eigenständige Identität zu verweigern. Doch ist eine solche eigenständige Identität nicht im Urtext zu suchen, sondern in der Adaptation dieses Urtextes. Anders gesagt gilt es zu erkennen, dass die Identität vom Urtext als Intertext herrührt, den die koranischen Redaktoren umformten, um ihre eigene, bestimmte religiöse und kulturelle Vorstellung widerzuspiegeln. Die Arbeit der Enthüllung der frühesten Stufen des Islams liegt im Verständnis dieser Transformation als Transformation begründet, und nicht in der Abwertung dieser Transformation als sklavisches Ausleihen. Es geht hier um die Akkulturation des zur Hand liegenden Materials in ein neues System. Hier liegt auch genau die gleiche Betonung, für die Lülings Kritiker selbst argumentiert haben, wenn auch zeitweilig auf eher unproduktive Weise.

Der hier vorgelegte Beitrag zur Diskussion und Einschätzung der Arbeiten Lülings kann keine erschöpfende Auswertung der redaktionellen Veränderungen, und hier speziell der Redaktionen des *rasm*s, also des Konsonantenskeletts des Korantextes, bieten, die nach Lülings Einschätzung durch die Hand eines oder mehrerer, zeitgenössischer oder chronologisch sukzessiver islamischer Bearbeiter oder Redaktoren an einer Sammlung von Texten ausgeführt wurden, die ursprünglich zu einem wesentlichen Teil aus christlich-arabischen Hymnen bestand. Doch legt eine Klassifizierung der Arten von Veränderungen, von denen man annimmt, dass sie durch die Hand von Redaktoren ausgeführt wurden, offen, dass die Veränderungen in vielen Fällen auf Transformationen begrenzt sind, die die grammatische Zahl oder die Zeitstufe eines Verbs betreffen, woraus schließend man sich vorstellen könnte, der oder die islamische(n) Redaktor(en) hätten Prädikate beispielsweise aus der dritten Person Singular in Verbformen der ersten Person Plural und Imperfektverbformen in Perfektverbformen umgewandelt. An mehreren Stellen geht Lülings Analyse von ähnlichen Modifikationen mit einem Blick auf Veränderungen des Numerus von Pronomina, beispielsweise wieder von der dritten Person Singular zur ersten Person Plural, aus. Es wird auch angenommen, dass islamische Redaktoren deklinierte Verbformen gegen die ihnen entsprechenden Nomina und Partizipialformen ausgetauscht haben. An manchen Stellen nimmt die Analyse an, dass ein Vokal oder ein Halbvokal aus einem Wort in einem voranliegenden Text entfernt oder diesem zugefügt wurde, was in einem Fall die Existenz eines dem Text unterliegenden Wortes, das auf dem Aramäischen basierte, verschleierte.[4] An einer Stelle schwächte die angenommene Eliminierung eines kurzen Nomens, hier des Wortes جسد (Körper), die Möglichkeiten eines Lesers des überlieferten Korantextes, den Textabschnitt als Hinweis auf die Gemeinde als den Körper der Gläubigen oder den Körper Christi zu verstehen.[5] Zur Unterstützung seiner Rekonstruktion dieser Stelle führte Lüling paralleles Material aus der alten christlich-arabischen Dichtung an. In relativ wenigen Fällen nahm Lüling an, dass der oder die Redaktor(en) die Anordnung zweier Wörter oder zweier Zusammenstellungen von Ausdrücken im Text geändert hätte(n).[6] Bei der hier vorgestellten, recht kurzen Liste handelt es sich nicht um eine erschöpfende Darstellung aller von Lüling angeführten Fälle. Dennoch können die genannten Beispiele gut als repräsentativ für die Arten von Veränderungen des Konsonantentextes (*rasm*) gelten, die nach Lülings Argumentation notwendig waren, um den vorhergehenden Text eines jeweiligen Verses offenzulegen. Dieses Vorgehen zeigt in der Tat, dass Lüling die Ansicht vertrat, dass eine Rekonstruktion und ein kritisches Lesen des Korantextes so vorgehen können, dass das Konsonantenskelett des Textes modifiziert werden kann, besonders an Stellen, an denen solche Änderungen Widersprüche im Inhalt oder in der logischen Abfolge von Themen oder Ideen, die in aufeinanderfolgenden Versen ausgedrückt werden, auflösen. Unter der Annahme menschlichen intentionalen Handelns und menschlicher Ursächlichkeit könnten die Veränderungen, die Lüling vorschlug und deren Wirkung er dahingehend verstand, dass durch sie vorhergehende Veränderungen und Modifikationen einzelner Wörter durch islamische Redaktoren wieder rückgängig gemacht würden, als insgesamt geringfügige Eingriffe in und Anpassungen des Konsonantentextes klassifiziert werden. Sie machen einzelne Ausdrücke des Korans verständlich und schaffen einen harmonischen Bedeutungskontext in ihrer jeweiligen textlichen Umgebung. Doch scheinen die Vorwürfe gegen Lülings Methode eher von der Bedeutung dieser kumulativ zu betrachtenden Veränderungen für die Identifizierung größerer Abschnitte des Korans herzurühren.

Wenn Lüling in der Tat einen Ur-Koran rekonstruiert haben sollte, gibt es dennoch keinen Grund anzunehmen, dass das Endprodukt, nämlich der Koran in der Gestalt, in der er jetzt existiert und angenommen wird, also der *textus receptus* des Korans, kein eindeutig und vollständig islamisches Dokument ist. Diese letztgenannte Tatsache steht ganz unabhängig davon fest, welchen konfessionellen Standpunkt jemand vertritt bezüglich der Natur des Ursprungs des

4 Lüling, *Über den Urkoran*, 112–113.
5 Lüling, *Über den Urkoran*, 127–128.
6 Lüling, *Über den Urkoran*, 168 und 271–272 und 279–280.

Korans oder seiner Bedeutung für eine bestimmte Gruppe von Menschen, die sich an bestimmte religiöse Glaubenswahrheiten, die auf dem Inhalt dieses Buches aufbauen, halten. Da Wissenschaft eine logische Vorstellung von Kausalität fordert, die Bezüge auf *ad hoc* Vorstellungen wie die eines *deus ex machina* ausschließt, muss also auf jeden Fall auch schon von Anfang an die Vorstellung eines *librum ex coelis* verworfen werden. Dennoch kommt auch die Forschung, die Lüling betrieb, am Ende zu einem islamischen Koran, hier jedoch durch die Anwendung einer sorgfältig und behutsam vorgehenden philologischen Methode, da es dies ist, was die Beweislage fordert, und nicht das, was bestimmte Annahmen diktieren. In einem echten und tiefen Sinn hat Lüling somit den islamischen Koran wiederentdeckt. Er hat dies auch in einem realeren Sinn als frühere Forscher, beispielsweise Heinrich Speyer, getan, die damit zufrieden waren, nach Punkten der Gemeinsamkeiten zwischen dem Judentum und dem Islam zu suchen, und es der Leserschaft überließen anzunehmen, der Islam sei ein Produkt der Ableitung aus dem Judentum. Demgegenüber hat Lüling gezeigt, dass der Koran, wenn er auch zum Teil auf christlichen Texten aufbaut, nicht einfach eine Übernahme dieser Texte oder ihrer Ideen ist, sondern ein Produkt der Inkulturation dieses Materials, das eine eigenständige islamische Vorstellung und Vorstellungswelt widerspiegelt. Es scheint also, dass dies genau das erwünschte Resultat vieler ist, die Lüling angegriffen und bloßgestellt haben, sowie anderer, die ähnlich enge Vorstellungen von Philologie und den Grenzen der Kausalität vertraten oder vertreten.

Wenn Lülings methodologisches Vorgehen und seine Textanalysen korrekt sind, ganz unabhängig von den Schwerpunkten, die er bei der Interpretation der theologischen Bedeutung seiner Funde gelegt haben mag, ist es lediglich eine Sache der Vernunft wahrzunehmen, dass die frühislamischen Redaktoren, die Lüling am Werk sah, mit christlich-arabischen Hymnen in genau der gleichen Weise verfahren sind, in der, auch nach Annahme der modernen Koranstudien, der Formationsprozess des Korans vonstattengegangen ist, dass nämlich intertextuelles Material Ideen und Themen bereitstellte, die in den Koran integriert wurden. Diese Redaktoren schrieben nicht einfach ab, was sie vor Augen hatten, sondern schrieben den Inhalt der Kompositionen, die ihnen zur Verfügung standen, aktiv und bewusst um. Die genauen Umrisse oder Ebenen der Intensität und Transformation eines solchen Prozesses des Umschreibens können von der modernen Forschung natürlich nicht rückwärts in den voraufliegenden Text definiert oder diktiert, sondern müssen stattdessen wiederentdeckt werden. In einer ganz grundlegenden Weise entdeckte Lülings Arbeit der Rekonstruktion von christlich-arabischen Hymnen oder Abschnitten aus solchen Hymnen als Teil eines Ur-Korans gleichzeitig eine Fülle von Intertexten. Es ist also gerade im Raum der Öffnung eines beachtlichen Teils des Korans für Herangehensweisen an den

Text durch die Mittel intertextueller Fragestellungen, in dem Lülings Arbeit am Ur-Koran bleibenden und produktiven Wert sowie Inspiration für das wissenschaftliche Studium des Korans behält.

Angesichts der Konzentration meiner hier vorgelegten Arbeit auf hermeneutische und methodologische Fragestellungen empfiehlt es sich, die Besprechung konkreter Beispiele intertextueller Dimensionen der Rekonstruktionen einzelner Textabschnitte, die Lüling untersuchte, andernorts aufzugreifen. Hier scheint es dringender zu sein, die wissenschaftstheoretisch und methodologisch grundlegende Natur des Beitrags Lülings in seinem Buch über den Ur-Koran für die recht weitverbreitete und nützliche Arbeit des Wiederentdeckens von Intertexten anzusprechen, da diese unser Verständnis der frühen, formativen Geschichte des Korantextes, eines Untergebietes der Koranstudien, das im Augenblick klar im Trend der Zeit liegt, verbessern. Die sich anschließende Diskussion lokalisiert deshalb Lülings Ur-Koran innerhalb der begrifflichen, konzeptionellen und strukturellen Geschichte der Suche nach den intertextuellen Dimensionen des Korans, in der Form, in der er von der Überlieferung rezipiert oder aufgenommen wurde.

Lülings Ur-Koran und die Suche nach Intertextuellen Dimensionen des „überlieferten" Korans

Dass Texte sich explizit oder implizit aufeinander beziehen, ist keine neue Einsicht; weder in die Bedingungen der Produktion von Literatur, noch in die Natur von Texten. Man könnte ganz im Gegenteil argumentieren, dass die Qualität eines Textes, sich auf andere Texte zu beziehen, eine Eigenschaft von Texten ist, ohne die ein in Frage stehender Text gar nicht erst entstehen oder auch weiterbestehen könnte. Dank der Beteiligung am Prozess der Kommunikationsvorgänge zwischen Menschen, die entweder mündlich oder über den Weg des geschriebenen Wortes geschehen, nimmt jeglicher Text notwendigerweise an Beziehungen im Informationsaustausch teil. Selbst wenn man sich mit einem Textbegriff auf den Untersuchungsweg begibt, dessen Umfang so weit ist, dass er jegliche Art kultureller oder sozialer Interaktion einschließt, nimmt jeglicher Text und nehmen alle „Texte" wesentlich an kommunikativer Interaktion teil, ganz gleich welches die Wirksamkeitsebene oder die Ebene des Erfolgs dieser Kommunikation sein mag. Jegliche Kommunikationsform oder Kommunikationsstruktur, unabhängig vom Grad ihrer intentionalen Organisation, und somit auch jeglicher Text, insoweit er ein verkörperter Kommunikationsakt ist, ist in Beziehungen verwurzelt und eingebunden. Dies ist auch unabhängig davon wahr, ob ein bestimmter Sprecher, Autor oder Schöpfer einer Kommunikation sich dieser Beziehungen bewusst ist oder nicht. Man könnte in der Tat sagen, dass ohne diese innewohnende Qualität eines Textes, die man als „Relationalität" oder als „Referenzialität" bezeichnen könnte, sei sie nun explizit oder implizit, Texte weder existieren könnten noch würden.[7]

Auf die Zeit vor etwa fünfzig Jahren lassen sich die ersten Schritte datieren, die innerhalb des Rahmens der Entwicklung postmodernen Denkens unternommen wurden, ein Bewusstsein von Texten als relationalen Einheiten zu artikulieren. Im Jahr 1980 begann die bulgarisch-französische Literaturtheoretikerin, Psychoanalytikerin und Philosophin Julia Kristeva damit, sich mit dem kulturkritischen Werk des russischen Denkers Mikhail Bakhtin auseinanderzusetzen. Hierbei beschäftigte sie sich und interagierte sie mit der Entwicklung seiner Vorstellungen zum sozialen Kontext von Sprache. Kristeva fand sich im Besonderen von Bakhtins Idee des Dialogismus als einer Eigenschaft der Kultur angesprochen. Sie baute auch auf die Aussagen des schweizerischen Linguisten Ferdinand de Saussure bezüglich der systematischen Eigenschaften, die jeglicher Sprache inhärent sind, auf. Auf der Basis dieser Erfahrungen und Einflüsse artikulierte Kristeva wesentliche Aspekte eines heuristischen Herangehens an Texte, das sie „intertextualité" nannte.[8] Kristeva und Bakhtin bestanden darauf, dass Texte untrennbar in die Texthaftigkeit der weiteren kulturellen und sozialen Welten, die sie hervorbrachten, eingebunden waren. Texte tragen die sozialen Kämpfe und ideologischen Strukturen immer mit sich und reflektieren diese durch und in ihrem Diskurs. Das intertextuelle Herangehen an Texte, welches das „dass" und „wie" der Beziehungen zwischen Texten betont, gewann im Laufe der Zeit stark an Boden und Einfluss.

Für diejenigen, die ihr Hauptaugenmerk auf das Studium von Texten als Kommunikationswerkzeuge legen, hat eine Hermeneutik der verschiedenen Dimensionen intertextueller Methoden viel zu bieten.[9] Mit Blick auf das Studium der

---

7 Stefan Wild, Hg., *Self-referentiality in the Qur'ān. Diskurse der Arabistik 11* (Wiesbaden: Harrassowitz, 2006), sammelt Studien, die unter anderem aufzeigen, dass und wie der Korantext verschiedene Ebenen und Bewusstseinsebenen einer solchen Relationalität widerspiegelt.

8 Siehe Julia Kristeva, „Desire in Language: a Semiotik Approach to Literature and Art," in *European Perspectives: a Series in Social Thought and Cultural Criticism*, Hgg. Leon S. Roudiez, Thomas Gora und Alice Jardine (New York: Columbia University Press, 1980), 36. Hier formulierte Kristeva, dass ein Text „eine Umformung von Texten [ist], eine Intertextualität innerhalb des Raumes eines bestimmten Textes," in dem „mehrere Äußerungen, die von anderen Texten übernommen sind, sich überschneiden und einander neutralisieren."

9 Ich möchte Robert Phenix Jr. für zahlreiche, ausgiebige Gespräche und Diskussionen danken, in deren Verlauf seine Liebe zur Mathematik und ihren Methoden zur Formulierung der hier im

intertextuellen Dimensionen des Korans könnte man den Bogen der Herangehensweisen, die möglich sind, und auch derer, die von Forschern bereits angewandt wurden, als in drei Hauptkategorien von Intertextualität fallend klassifizieren. Hierbei sind relevante Untervarianten und drei wichtige, aber lediglich verwandte Vorgehensweisen der Erforschung des Phänomens der Intertextualität zu unterscheiden. Wenn man beobachtet, wie Koranleser das Phänomen der Intertextualität betrachtet haben, stellt man fest, dass die Kategorien von Intertext, die angewandt werden, recht direkt, geradlinig und einsichtig sind.

Eine erste Klassifizierung der Intertextualität, die geprüft werden könnte, ist die der *hermeneutischen Intertextualität*. In den Koranstudien handelt es sich bei dieser Klassifizierung um die Eingrenzung des Verortungsraums der Intertexte auf den Koran selbst, also eine Kategorie der Einzeichnung eines Teils des Korans auf einen anderen. Dies ist vielleicht die älteste Form intertextueller Studien in der Erforschung des Korans; man kann diese Art von Intertextualität bis ins Werk des islamischen Traditionsdenkers Muqātil b. Sulaymān aus dem achten Jahrhundert zurückverfolgen, wie auch ins Werk vieler anderer, einschließlich der Arbeiten des iranischen islamischen Wissenschaftlers Faḫr ad-Dīn ar-Rāzī aus dem zwölften Jahrhundert, ins Werk zu Sūra Paaren, das der indische Forscher Ḥamīd ad- Dīn ʻAbd al-Ḥamīd al-Farāhī und besonders sein Schüler, der pakistanische Wissenschaftler Amīn Aḥsan Iṣlāḥī (1322(4)–1415(7) / 1904(6)–1997), vorlegten, oder auch noch in neuester Zeit, beispielsweise ins Werk von Islam Dayeh, und zu einem großen Maß in die Arbeiten Angelika Neuwirths.[10] Solch eine hermeneutische Intertextualität besteht weiterhin als produktiver Aspekt koranischer Studien in der Gegenwart. Im Raum der biblischen Studien gehören zu dieser Kategorie von Untersuchungen auch die Werkzeuge und Instrumente der kanonischen Kritik,

---

Ansatz umrissenen neuen Grundstrukturen einer intertextuellen Hermeneutik die entscheidenden Impulse hervorgebracht hat.

10 Zu Muqātil b. Sulaymān und Faḫr ad-Dīn ar-Rāzī siehe Jane Dammen McAuliffe, „Text and Textuality: Q. 3:7 as a Point of Intersection," in *Literary Structures of Religious Meaning in the Qur'an*, Hg. Issa J. Boullata (London: Curzon Press, 2000), 56–76, hier 60 und 65. Zu Ḥamīd ad-Dīn ʻAbd al-Ḥamīd al-Farāhī und Amīn Aḥsan Iṣlāḥī, siehe Mustansir Mir, *Coherence in the Qur'ān. A Study of Iṣlāḥī's Concept of Naẓm in Tadabbur-i Qur'ān* (Indianapolis: American Trust Publications, 1406/1986); und Mustansir Mir, „Iṣlāḥī's Concept of Sūra-Groups," *Islamic Quarterly* 28.2 (1984): 73–85. Siehe weiterhin Islam Dayeh, „Al-Ḥawāmīm: Intertextuality and Coherence in Meccan Surahs," in *The Qur'ān in Context. Historical and Literary Investigations into the Qur'ānic Milieu*, Hgg. Angelika Neuwirth, Nicolai Sinai und Michael Marx (Leiden and Boston: Brill, 2010), 461–494; und beispielsweise Angelika Neuwirth, „Mary and Jesus—Counterbalancing the Biblical Patriarchs. A re-reading of *sūrat Maryam* in *sūrat Āl-ʻImrān* (Q 3:1–62)," *Parole de l'Orient* 30 (2005): 231–260.

der Form biblischer Hermeneutik also, die Textabschnitte der Bibel als ein- und desselben Gesamtwerkes miteinander vergleicht.

Eine zweite Klassifizierungskategorie ist die Eins-zu-eins-Identifizierung koranischer Wörter oder auch kürzerer oder längerer koranischer Textsegmente mit anderen Texten, die außerhalb des Korans liegen. Man könnte diese Klassifizierung als *Identitätsintertextualität* bezeichnen. Bei ihr handelt es sich auch um die Kategorie von Intertextualität, mit der der Autor arbeitet, der unter dem Pseudonym „Christoph Luxenberg" bekannt wurde.[11] Einige Aspekte der Rekonstruktionen vorislamischer christlich-arabischer Hymnen, die Lüling vorlegte und bei denen die rekonstruierten Hymnen als Bestandteile des Ur-Korans verstanden wurden, fallen gleichfalls in diese Kategorie der Intertextualität. Darüber hinaus gehören einige Aspekte der Suche nach und des Wiederentdeckens von Intertexten, bei denen Beitragende zum *Corpus Coranicum* Projekt sich engagieren, oder die von einigen der Teilnehmenden am Koranseminar unter der Leitung von Gabriel Reynolds durchgeführt werden, zu dieser Kategorie einer Identitätsintertextualität, insofern als jeglicher Intertext, der identifiziert wird, notwendigerweise mit mindestens einem seiner Wörter, aber besser noch mit einem seiner Ausdrücke oder Formulierungen, zu mindestens einem Wort oder einer Formulierung im Koran in Beziehung steht. Hier ist darüber hinaus auch noch anzumerken, dass die Identitätsintertextualität nicht auf den Vergleich von Texten in ein und derselben Sprache eingeschränkt ist. Es ist auch wichtig, klar zu formulieren, dass die Identitätsintertextualität und die Frage des Identifizierens eines Textes X als Quelle eines Textes Y miteinander in Beziehung stehen. Es ist in der Tat so, dass jegliche „Quelle" eines Textes A ein Teil der Untergruppe aller Intertexte ist, mit denen A in Beziehung steht. Eine umfassendere Diskussion der Frage, wie die Identitätsintertextualität sich zur Suche nach den Quellen eines bestimmten Textes verhält und wie sie sich von dieser unterscheidet, ist notwendig, kann hier jedoch nicht vorgelegt werden. Für die aktuelle Untersuchung mag als Formulierung ausreichen, dass die Identifizierung eines Textabschnitts als Intertext mit Identitätseigenschaften oder als Quelle, ohne die beiden miteinander gleichzusetzen, noch nicht auf die Artikulation hinausläuft, aber eine solche auch nicht im Vorhinein ausschließt, wie ein jeweiliger Autor einen jeweiligen Text als Quelle oder Intertext gebrauchte oder wie sie oder er diesen verstanden wissen wollte.

11 Siehe zum Beispiel Christoph Luxenberg [Pseudonym], *Die syro-aramäische Lesart des Koran: ein Beitrag zur Entschlüsselung der Koransprache* (Berlin: Das Arabische Buch, 2000; 3. Auflage: Berlin: Schiler, 2007).

Schließlich gibt es noch die dritte Klassifikationskategorie der *kontinuierlichen Intertextualität*, die für unsere unmittelbaren Zwecke der Evaluierung des Lülingschen Beitrags zu den Koranstudien die für die Diskussion zentrale Kategorie ist. Wenn man sich den Begriff der kontinuierlichen Intertextualität vor Augen hält, denkt man an die Identifikation von Textabschnitten im Koran mit Abschnitten aus dem Koran oder mit Parallelen in Texten außerhalb des Korans, wobei man Textbereiche im Koran dem weiteren kulturellen Raum des Korans zuordnet. Um dies besser zu verstehen, hilft es, die Idee des Grenzpunktes aufzunehmen. Ein Grenzpunkt ist ein Element eines Textes, das den Text in einem gewissen Sinn definiert, indem es ihn als genau bestimmten Gegenstand abschließt. Man mag sich einen solchen Grenzpunkt als einen wichtigen Zug oder eine wichtige Eigenschaft eines Textsegments, die in einem gewissen Sinne charakteristisch ist, vorstellen. Vom Begriff des Grenzpunktes her können wir eine kontinuierliche Zuordnung eines Textes zu einem anderen definieren. Eine kontinuierliche Zuordnung eines Textes A auf einen Text B bewahrt dabei alle Grenzpunkte des Textes A, das heißt, alle seine intuitiv wichtigen Aspekte, im Text B. Es ist jedoch nicht erforderlich, dass die Züge oder Eigenschaften, die als Grenzpunkte des Textes A identifiziert wurden, auch Grenzpunkte des Textes B sind; diese mögen anderen, wichtigeren Eigenschaften oder Zügen untergeordnet sein.

Die Klassifizierungskategorie der kontinuierlichen Intertextualität kann noch weiter unterteilt werden, indem man eine ihrer Unterkategorien bespricht, die wir hier als *homöomorphische Intertextualität* bezeichnen werden. Im Falle dieser homöomorphischen Intertextualität bewahrt jede Zuordnung eines Textes A auf einen Text B alle Grenzpunkte als Grenzpunkte: Es reicht hierbei nicht aus, dass die charakteristischen, markanten oder entscheidenden Züge oder Eigenschaften des Textes A auch in Text B enthalten sind; vielmehr müssen diese auch auf die eine oder andere Weise charakteristische, markante oder entscheidende Eigenschaften oder Züge im Text B sein, und nicht einfach anderem Material untergeordnet oder durch anderes Material überdeckt sein. Die Zusammenfassung eines wissenschaftlichen Aufsatzes in einer studentischen Semesterarbeit beispielsweise, die ohne weitergehende Analyse vorgelegt wird, wäre ein Homöomorphismus dieses wissenschaftlichen Aufsatzes in einem neuen Text. Im Raum studentischer Semesterarbeiten und akademischer Veröffentlichungen sind sowohl ordentlich dokumentierte Aufsätze wie auch fehlgeleitete Veröffentlichungen von Akademikern und Akademikerinnen, die sich des Plagiats schuldig machen, gute, wenn auch nicht die einzigen Beispiele für homöomorphische Intertextualität: Sowohl im Fall einer korrekt dokumentierten Repräsentation der Ideen eines anderen Autors in der eigenen Publikation wie auch im Fall einer durch Plagiate entstellten Publikation sind alle Schlüsselelemente eines bestimmten Arguments beibehalten; nichtsdestotrotz ist die Formulierung verändert worden, im Fall des Plagiats oft nur sehr leicht, wobei auch einzelne Textabschnitte mitunter lediglich in trivialer Weise neu angeordnet worden sind. Die korrekt dokumentierte Veröffentlichung identifiziert ihre Quellen oder Intertexte in den Fußnoten; die mit Plagiaten belastete tut dies nicht. Die Tatsache, dass der Fall des akademischen Plagiats hier als Beispiel aufgenommen wurde, um die Natur der homöomorphischen Intertextualität als einer Untergruppe der kontinuierlichen Intertextualität zu erklären, ist nicht so zu verstehen, als impliziere die hier vorgelegte Untersuchung, dass die Arbeit antiker und anderer älterer Autoren, die uns oft keine Fußnoten zu den Quellen ihrer Arbeit lieferten, sowie ihr Einsatz solcher kontinuierlicher intertextueller Praktiken in irgendeiner Weise unehrlich oder fragwürdig seien, oder dass man irgendwelche Schuld bei modernen Wissenschaftlern suchen sollte, die herauszufinden versuchen, was vorhergehende Autoren in ihren Fußnoten hätten niederschreiben sollen, wenn sie moderne Vorgehensweisen angenommen hätten. Diese Beispiele illustrieren lediglich recht effektiv das zentrale Phänomen, um das es geht.

Man könnte mittlerweile eine ganze Reihe von Wissenschaftlern, die sich um die Koranstudien bemühen, nennen, die verschiedene Fälle kontinuierlicher oder, noch spezieller, homöomorphischer Intertextualität in Gruppen von Abschnitten aus dem Koran und externen Textabschnitten offengelegt haben. Eine chronologisch geordnete Liste solcher Beiträge muss mit der Arbeit Günter Lülings beginnen, die Abschnitte des *textus receptus* des Korans über den Weg einer Rekonstruktion des Ur-Korans mit Abschnitten aus alter christlich-arabischer Dichtung passend nebeneinanderstellte. Eine solche Liste schließt auch Aspekte der Arbeit Angelika Neuwirths ein, die vorschlug, das *Shemaʿ* aus Deuteronomium 6:4 und das sogenannte Nicäno-Konstantinopolitanische christliche Glaubensbekenntnis als Intertexte mit *sūrat al-Iḫlāṣ* (112) zusammenzusehen.[12] Man hat beispielsweise die Arbeiten von Sidney Griffith und Mark Whitters anzuführen, die Linien der syrischen Hagiographie der Siebenschläfer oder der jüdischen Erzählung von Taxo und seinen sieben Söhnen im Text der *Himmelfahrt des Moses*

12 Angelika Neuwirth, „Two Faces of the Qur'ān: Qur'ān and Muṣḥaf," *Oral Tradition* 25.1 (2010): 141–156; siehe hierzu auch Mehmet Paçacı, „Sag: Gott ist ein einziger—ahad/æhād. Ein exegetischer Versuch zu Sure 112 in der Perspektive der semitischen Religionstradition," in *Alter Text—neuer Kontext. Koranhermeneutik in der Türkei heute*, Üb. Felix Körner (Freiburg: Herder, 2006), 166–203; ursprünglich veröffentlicht als „De Ki Allah 'Bir'dir: *'aḥad/'eḥād.* Sami Dini Geleneği Perspektifinden İhlas Sûresi'nin Bir Tefsiri Denemesi," in Mehmet Paçacı, *Kur'an ve Ben Ne Kadar Tarihseliz?* (Ankara: Ankara Okulu Yayınları, 2000).

als Intertexte für *sūrat al-Kahf* (18:9–26) identifiziert haben.[13] Die Liste könnte noch vielfältig erweitert werden. Hier wären unter anderem Arbeiten von Geneviève Gobillot zu Verbindungen zwischen dem Koran, der Bibel, hellenistischer und patristischer Literatur aufzunehmen.[14] Auch einige meiner eigenen Arbeiten, die eine ganze Bandbreite christlicher apokrypher Kindheitsevangelien und verwandter zusammengesetzter apokrypher Texte, besonders solcher, die mit dem Buch Mariens oder der Geschichte des Lebens Mariens in Verbindung stehen, als Intertexte zu Textabschnitten im Koran offengelegt und diskutiert haben, könnte man nennen.[15] Letztlich wäre jegliche Darstellung einer solchen Auflistung unvollständig, da die Arbeiten in diesem Forschungsbereich zurzeit noch sehr aktiv im Gang sind und letztlich vielleicht auch nie abgeschlossen sein können.

Im Zusammenhang der hier vorgelegten Diskussion ist es relevant, zwei Punkte dieses Szenarios eines in den letzten Jahren doch recht stark angestiegenen wissenschaftlichen Interesses am Phänomen der kontinuierlichen Intertextualität zu betonen. Der oder die aufmerksam Lesende mag bemerkt haben, dass es sich mit Ausnahme eines der aufgeführten Beispiele bei den Intertexten, die identifiziert worden sind, um Texte handelt, für deren Existenz, Gebrauch und relativ weitreichende Zirkulation es reichlich Nachweismaterial in den erhaltenen literarischen Monumenten gibt, die die spätantike Literatur dokumentieren. Für den Fall der vorislamischen christlich-arabischen Hymnen, die Lüling rekonstruierte, könnte man jedoch vielleicht als Einwand gegen ihre Behandlung als Intertexte vorbringen, dass bislang in alten Handschriften außerhalb des Korantextes keine Dokumentation bereitstehe, die Unterstützung dafür liefere, dass solche vorislamischen christlich-arabischen Hymnen in der Tat zirkulierten.

---

13 Sidney Griffith, „Christian Lore and the Arabic Qur'ān: The 'Companions of the Cave' in *Sūrat al-Kahf* and in Syriac Christian Tradition," in *The Qur'ān in Its Historical Context*, Hg. Gabriel Said Reynolds (London and New York: Routledge, 2008), 109–137; und Mark Whitters, „The Source for the Qur'ānic Story of the Companions of the Cave (*sūrat al-Kahf* 18)," in *The Bible, the Qur'ān, & Their Interpretation: Syriac Perspectives*. Eastern Mediterranean Texts and Contexts 1, Hg. Cornelia Horn (Warwick, Rhode Island: Abelian Academic, 2013), 167–187.

14 Geneviève Gobillot, „Le Coran, guide de lecture de la Bible et des textes apocryphes," *Pardès* 50 (2011): 131–154; und Geneviève Gobillot, „Grundlinien der Theologie des Koran. Grundlagen und Orientierungen," in *Schlaglichter, Die beiden ersten islamischen Jahrhunderte*, Hgg. Markus Groß und Karl-Heinz Ohlig (Berlin: Hans-Schiler-Verlag, 2008), 320–369.

15 Siehe zum Beispiel Cornelia Horn, „Syriac and Arabic Perspectives on Structural and Motif Parallels Regarding Jesus' Childhood in Christian Apocrypha and Early Islamic Literature: the 'Book of Mary,' the *Arabic Apocryphal Gospel of John*, and the Qur'ān," *Apocrypha. Revue internationale des littératures apocryphes* 19 (2008): 267–291; und Cornelia Horn, „Apocrypha on Jesus' Life in the Early Islamic Milieu: From Syriac into Arabic," in *Senses of Scriptures, Treasures of Tradition. The Bible in Arabic among Jews, Christians and Muslims*, Hg. Miriam Lindgren Hjälm (Leiden: Brill, 2017), 58–78.

Dieser *prima facie* vernünftige Einwand erhebt sich jedoch von einer Perspektive her, die man als positivistische Sicht auf eine historische Beweislage betrachten sollte. Positivistisch bezieht sich hier auf die erkenntnistheoretische Haltung des Positivismus, auf die Vorstellung also, dass sich alle Erklärungen auf Beweismaterial reduzieren und beschränken müssen, das bereits entdeckt worden ist; selbst wenn die offensichtlichste und deutlichste Erklärung eines Datensatzes zur Existenz einer Sache oder eines Zusammenhangs führt, die oder der bislang noch nicht aufgefunden worden ist, muss ein Argument einfach deshalb zurückgewiesen werden, weil sein Gegenstand bislang noch nicht als eigenständig existent vorgefunden oder festgestellt worden war. Im Raum der Logik, der jegliche wissenschaftliche Disziplin und Untersuchung untergeordnet sein muss, kann ein Syllogismus, bei dem eine oder beide der Prämissen negativ sind und der eine positive Schlussfolgerung präsentiert, nicht gültig sein; hier handelt es sich um den sogenannten Irrtum der affirmativen Schlussfolgerung aus einer negativen Prämisse. Man kann, mit anderen Worten gesagt, nicht auf der Grundlage eines fehlenden Beweises argumentieren. Für unseren Fall der Evaluierung des Nachweises, den Lüling durch seine Analyse des Korans erstellte, sowie der Schlussfolgerungen, zu denen er kam, dass es nämlich einen Ur-Koran christlichen Inhalts gegeben habe, der aus vorislamischen christlich-arabischen Hymnen bestand, bedeutet dies: Wenn man durch die und im Verlauf der Anwendung einer philologischen Methode in der Lage ist, auf systematische Weise mehrere Probleme in einem bestimmten Text zu lösen, und wenn man bei einem solchen Vorgehen Beweismaterial zusammenstellt, das die Existenz vorislamischer christlich-arabischer Hymnen, die ein Ur-Koran hätten sein können, nahelegt, ist dies Beweismaterial für solche Hymnen, wenn die Untersuchungsmethoden sowie ihre Anwendung gültig sind und richtig und solide angewendet wurden. Es ist jedoch kein gültiges Argument zu behaupten, die Methode oder ihre Schlussfolgerungen seien falsch, weil bislang kein physischer Nachweis solcher Hymnen zum Beispiel in alten Handschriften gefunden werden konnte. Dies wäre ein Argument auf der Grundlage des fehlenden Beweises, welches ein logischer Irrtum und ungültig ist. Die Grenzen der Sicherheit, mit der man arbeitet, haben keinen Einfluss auf das, was wahr ist, wenn sie auch einen Einfluss auf das haben können, was man als wahr zu erkennen in der Lage ist.

Auch aus dem Raum der wissenschaftlichen Untersuchungen des Neuen Testaments lässt sich ein recht gut bekannter Vergleichsfall heranziehen. Lülings Feststellung der Existenz eines strophischen christlich-arabischen Textes, der Teilen des Korans zugrunde lag, oder eines Ur-Korans ist im Wesentlichen nicht anders gelagert als die Feststellung einer Quelle „Q" für die Matthäus und Lukas zugeschriebenen Evangelien, die, zusammen mit dem Markusevangelium und dem für das Lukasevangelium und das Matthäusevangelium je eigenen Material, in der Zwei- oder Drei-Quellen-Theorie jeweils das Textmaterial für das Matthäusevangelium und das Lukasevangelium lieferte. Bislang ist auch hier kein unabhängiger Textzeuge für diese Q-Quelle außerhalb des Matthäusevangeliums und des Lukasevangeliums gefunden worden, wenn auch die Spruchquelle des Thomas, die weithin als *Thomasevangelium* bekannt ist, als möglicher Zeuge für Q vorgestellt worden ist. Argumente, die gegen die Existenz von Q vorgebracht werden, liegen ihrerseits hauptsächlich in Argumenten begründet, die sich mit der Komplexität der Daten in den synoptischen Evangelien befassen. Es hat jedoch, soweit ich sehe, bislang noch kein(e) Wissenschaftler(in) ernsthaft versucht zu argumentieren, dass die Tatsache, dass Q bislang noch nicht unabhängig vom Lukas- und vom Matthäusevangelium identifiziert worden sei, bedeute, dass Q nicht existierte und dass deshalb die Zwei- oder die Drei-Quellen-Hypothese der neutestamentlichen synoptischen Evangelien inkorrekt sei. Von daher ergibt sich, dass es, wenn man die Gültigkeit des methodologischen Vorgehens Lülings in der Rekonstruktion der vorislamischen christlich-arabischen Hymnen nicht widerlegen und auch keine bessere Lösung anführen kann, um schlüssig mit dem Material der entsprechenden Koranabschnitte umzugehen, sinnvoll ist, Lülings Rekonstruktionen zumindest als mögliche Beweise für diese Hymnen anzunehmen und sie als Intertexte für den Koran zu behandeln.

Es gibt noch einen zweiten Punkt, der betont werden sollte: In den wissenschaftlichen Analysen der kontinuierlichen Zuordnung entsprechend gepaarter Texte aus der christlichen oder jüdischen Tradition als Intertexte zu ihren passenden Abschnitten im Koran bemerkt man sowohl in den Arbeiten Lülings wie in denen Neuwirths eine anhaltende und starke Betonung der Diskussion deformativer oder entstellender Prozesse sowie auch eine Betonung der Prozesse des Um- und Neuschreibens und ihrer jeweiligen intellektuellen oder ideologischen, transformativen Agenden, die als recht radikale Neuinterpretationen des intertextuellen Materials im neuen Kontext des Korans verstanden werden. Damit soll nicht gesagt werden, dass andere Wissenschaftler nicht auch auf solche Prozesse geachtet haben, durch die Intertexte einer deutlichen Uminterpretation oder einem Um- oder Neuschreiben unterzogen wurden, als man sie in ihre neue, koranische Umgebung integrierte. Die Betonung der Intensität und der radikalen Neuheit der islamischen Repräsentation des jeweiligen Inhalts ist jedoch im Werk dieser beiden genannten Forscherpersönlichkeiten ein sehr deutlicher, ihnen gemeinsamer Zug.

Vielleicht ist es möglich, diese geteilte Schnittstelle einer gemeinsamen Betonung im Werk Lülings und Neuwirths durch eine weitere Nuancierung der Klassifizierung der kontinuierlichen Intertextualität und ihrer Untergruppe der homöomorphischen Intertextualität durch die Einführung der *holonomischen Intertextualität* als einer Untergruppe der homöomorphischen Intertextualität zu erklären. Hier gehen wir von einer Menge von Punkten, die jeweils neu zusammengestellt werden kann, zu einer Zusammenstellung von Räumen, die kontinuierlich deformiert oder umgeformt werden können, über. Wenn man nicht nur auf die Bewahrung aller Grenzpunkte beim Übergang von Text A zu Text B achtet, sondern auch auf die möglichen Umformungen, die dann vorkommen, wenn sich die Kontexte, in denen sich A und B bewegen, in Bezug auf die Texte ändern, dann beschreibt der Begriff der holonomischen Intertextualität die Zuordnung des Textes A auf den Text B in folgender Art und Weise: Wenn alle Grenzpunkte von Text A auch in Text B bewahrt bleiben, bezieht sich Text A durch den Prozess einer sich in mehreren Schritten vollziehenden Neuorientierung des Raumes, in dem beide Texte existieren, immer noch in seinen Grenzpunkten auf Text B, teilt aber nicht mehr die gleiche Orientierung mit Text B. Solch eine Klassifizierung ist vielleicht am besten in der Lage, von der Intensität und starken Intentionalität in der religiösen Differenz Rechenschaft abzulegen, die die Zuordnungen von Intertexten zum Koran wiedergeben, die in den Fällen erscheinen, die im Werk Lülings und Neuwirths vorgestellt werden. In der Tat bewegt man sich von der Beziehung zwischen Texten hin zur Beziehung zwischen Tendenzen und ihrer Auswirkung auf die Redaktion von Intertexten in ein Gesamtdokument oder einen ganzen Satz von Dokumenten.

Es ist offensichtlich, dass alle drei Hauptkategorien oder Hauptklassifizierungen der Intertextualität im Grunde genommen interreligiöse Diskurse offenbaren. Sogar im Fall der hermeneutischen Intertextualität, die sich mit dem Koran inhärenten Zuordnungen beschäftigt, eröffnen beispielsweise die Unterschiede in der islamischen Behandlung der Frage, wie islamische Perspektiven auf die christlichen Sichtweisen der Geburt Jesu darzustellen sind, interreligiöse Zusammenhänge. Doch ist die Relevanz solch interreligiöser Kontexte und ihres Einflusses, wenn sich der Übergang vom einen Kontext zum anderen ereignet, im Fall der holonomischen Intertextualität bedeutend betonter und wichtiger. Ein Beispiel sind Fälle, in denen Lüling argumentierte, dass vorislamische christlich-arabische Hymnen, die wenigstens einen Teil des Ur-Korans bildeten, in ihrer Orientierung so stark verformt und umgestaltet wurden, dass sie nicht länger und leicht als Ausdrucksformen des Christentums erkennbar blieben, sondern zu Ausdrücken der neuen Religion des Islams geworden waren, und dass sie in ihrer früheren Orientierung nur nach einem mehrstufigen Rückgewinnungsprozess wiederentdeckt werden können. Als weiteres Beispiel ist Neuwirths Entdeckung von sūra 112 als intentionale Gestalt und als Endpunkt eines Prozesses der Umorientierung zu nennen, in dem eine bekenntnishafte Glaubensaussage zum einen Gott als Intertext sich einer Neuorientierung durch Transformationen sowohl aus dem jüdischen wie aus dem christlichen Raum unterzogen hat. In solchen Fällen scheinen interreligiöse Kontexte und die jeweiligen Interessen, die sie an radikaleren und exklusiveren Formulierungen von Besitzansprüchen an religiöser Wahrheit repräsentieren, sehr viel wichtiger zu sein. Es bleibt somit als ein Punkt, der bei künftigen Diskussionen zu bedenken ist, in welchem Ausmaß die wissenschaftliche Wiederentdeckung von Fällen solcher holonomischer intertextueller Beziehungen alte Interessen miteinander im Wettstreit stehender Religionen offenlegt, ihre eigenen Profile so zu artikulieren, dass sie für ihre eigenen Zuhörerschaften in vergangenen Zeiten leichter zugänglich und erkennbar waren, und in welchem Ausmaß sie den Zuhörerschaften der heutigen Zeit dabei dienlich ist oder sein kann, die Unterschiede zwischen den beteiligten Religionen besser oder umfänglicher wahrzunehmen.

Bei der Klassifizierung der drei Hauptstränge der wissenschaftlichen Anfrage an und Untersuchung der Intertextualität mit Bezugnahme auf den Koran habe ich meine Besprechung der Kategorie der kontinuierlichen Intertextualität absichtlich dadurch erweitert, dass ich eine vollere Reihe von Beispielen von Repräsentanten aus dem zwanzigsten und einundzwanzigsten Jahrhundert für die unterschiedlichen Schulen und Herangehensweisen an das Studium des Korans, seiner Anfänge als literarischem Text und seines spätantiken literarischen, kulturellen und ideologischen Kontextes aufgeführt habe. Dies geschah, um zu signalisieren, dass meiner Sicht der Dinge nach alle Parteien, die beteiligt sind, sich in ihrer Arbeit deutlich überschneiden und dass sie ein starkes wissenschaftliches Interesse daran haben, sich in dieser besonderen Kategorie intertextueller Untersuchungen zu engagieren. Die Tatsache jedoch, dass Günter Lüling chronologisch der Erste in der Liste war, ist von Bedeutung. Sein Werk geht dem anderer deutlich voran, auch derer, von denen viele ihm keine oder lediglich eine blasse Anerkennung seiner Gedanken in ihrem eigenen Werk gezollt haben.[16] Vielleicht ist jetzt die Zeit gekommen, ihm Anerkennung für den richtungsweisenden Einfluss zukommen zu lassen, den seine Arbeit auf die Entwicklung der Koranstudien und im Besonderen auf die Entwicklung der Beschäftigung mit den intertextuellen Dimensionen des Korans, ihren Bedingungen in interreligiösen Kontexten und Beziehungen zwischen den Religionen und ihren Implikationen für diese ausübte.

---

16 Siehe zum Beispiel Günter Lüling, „Ein neues Buch zu einem alten Streit," *Zeitschrift für Religions- und Geistesgeschichte* 36 (1984): 56–67; neu abgedruckt in Günter Lüling, *Sprache und archaisches Denken. Aufsätze zur Geistes- und Religionsgeschichte* (Erlangen: Verlagsbuchhandlung Hannelore Lüling, 2., um zwei Aufsätze erweiterte Auflage, 2005), 181–189.

Fred M. Donner

Dīn, *Islām*, und *Muslim* im Koran

Vor mehr als 50 Jahren hat der berühmte kanadische Religionshistoriker Wilfred Cantwell Smith sein bahnbrechendes Buch *The Meaning and End of Religion* veröffentlicht.[1] In diesem Buch beschreibt Smith, wie die geistigen und ethischen Ideen verschiedener Prediger sich im Laufe der Zeit entwickelt haben, bis zu ihrer Kristallisierung in dem, was Smith „reifizierte Religionen" genannt hat. Smith war der Meinung, dass diese Prediger, die später oft als „Begründer einer Weltreligion" beschrieben wurden, ursprünglich nicht beabsichtigt hatten, eine neue Religion zu schöpfen. Sie waren eher vor allem mit ihrem eigenen inneren, geistigen Leben beschäftigt, sowie mit dem geistigen Leben ihrer Anhänger. Es war erst später, normalerweise mehrere Generationen später, dass man die geistigen Lehren und Ideen dieser „Begründer" in einer systematischen Weise zusammengeknüpft hat – ein Verfahren, aus dem die „reifizierten Weltreligionen" – Zoroastrianismus, Buddhismus, Judentum, Christentum, z. B. – schließlich entstanden sind.

Smith aber schlug vor, dass der Islam eine Ausnahme zu dieser Regel bildete, weil schon im Koran das Wort *al-islām* als Bezeichnung der neuen Religion zu finden ist. Diese Tatsache, seiner Meinung nach, erbringt den Beweis für das Vorhandensein des Konzepts des Islams als reifizierte Religion im Zeitalter des Propheten Muḥammads. Smith gibt aber zu, dass, obwohl das Konzept eines reifizierten Islams im Koran schon vorhanden ist, es jedoch dort noch relativ schwach entwickelt bleibt.[2] Durch eine Art statistischer Analyse sämtlicher Belegstellen im Koran, wo Wörter abgeleitet von dem Verbum *aslama* zu finden sind – d. h. das Partizip *muslim* und das Gerundium *islām* – hat Smith gezeigt, dass sie meistens „sich unterwerfen" oder „sich ergeben" [d. h., sich Gott ergeben] bedeuten, bzw. „jemand, der sich [Gott] ergibt" oder „ergeben hat." Relativ selten bedeuten sie „Islam", oder „Muslim" im Sinne eines Anhängers der reifizierten

Die Originalfassung dieses Beitrags wurde zum großen Teil während meines Aufenthalts als Marta Sutton Weeks Fellow am Stanford Humanities Center, Stanford University, 2014–2015, geschrieben. Ich möchte dem Stanford Humanities Center und seiner Direktorin, Prof. Caroline Winterer, sowie den anderen Fellows, für ihre intellektuelle und praktische Unterstützung meinen aufrichtigen Dank äußern.

1 Wilfred Cantwell Smith, *The Meaning and End of Religion: a New Approach to the Religious Traditions of Mankind* (New York: Macmillan, 1963).
2 Einen ähnlichen Gedankengang hat der bekannte Koranspezialist James Robson schon mehrere Jahre früher kurz verfolgt, in seinem Aufsatz „Islām as a term", *The Moslem World* 44 (1954): 101–109.

https://doi.org/10.1515/9783110599176-008

Religion. Normalerweise bewahren diese Wörter im Koran also ihre Verbindung mit der Urbedeutung „sich [Gott] ergeben" als eine persönliche, geistige Entscheidung. Smith zeigt aber, dass das Konzept von „Islam als reifizierter Religion", obwohl schwach im Koran, in den folgenden Jahrhunderten merklich stärker wurde. Er behauptet sogar, dass seit dem späten 19. Jahrhundert Islam, als Name der Religion, die frühere Bedeutung „sich [Gott] ergeben" im Arabischen und in die andere Sprachen der islamischen Welt fast völlig verdrängt hat.

Um den Sachverhalt konkreter zu machen, betrachten wir kurz einige Beispiele. Zuerst einen Satz, in dem das Wort *muslim* (hier im Dual, *muslimayna*) die Bedeutung „sich [Gott] ergeben" trägt: Sure 2, Vers 128 lautet: *rabba-nā wa-j'al-nā muslimayni laka*... „Und mach, Herr, dass wir (beide) Dir ergeben sind." Hier ist *muslimayni* offensichtlich als „sich [Gott] ergeben" zu verstehen, besonders weil es von der Präposition *li-* „zu" gefolgt ist: „mach uns Dir ergeben."

Ein zweites Beispiel, in dem das Gerundium *islām* in ähnlicher Weise vorkommt: in Sure 9, Vers 74 steht: *wa-la-qad qālū kalimata l-kufri wa-kafarū ba'da islāmi-him*... „Aber sie haben ja das Wort des Unglaubens gesagt und sind, nachdem sie sich [Gott] ergeben hatten, ungläubig geworden."

Andererseits gibt es Fälle, in denen das Wort *islām* als Hinweis auf die Religion des Islams im reifizierten Sinn erscheint. Sure 3, Vers 19 z. B. lautet: *inna d-dīn ʿinda llāh al-islām* oft übersetzt als „Wahrlich, die Religion [*dīn*] bei Gott ist der Islam." Wir kommen später auf diesen Vers zurück.

Smith hat auch die Rolle des Wortes *dīn* im Koran behandelt – aber nur in aller Kürze. Im Arabischen hat *dīn* drei Bedeutungen oder Nebenbedeutungen.[3] Die arabische Grundbedeutung von *dīn* scheint „Sitte" oder „übliches Verhalten", und daher auch „Dienst" und „Gehorsam" zu sein.[4] Es gibt aber zwei Nebenbedeutungen, zwei Homonyme, jede von einer anderen Fremdsprache abgeleitet: auf der einen Seite, kann *dīn* „Recht, Gesetz, Urteil" usw. bedeuten, abgeleitet vom aramäischen und gemeinsemitischen *dīn*. Wenn z. B. der Koran von *yawm ad-dīn*,

---

3 Übersicht in *Encyclopaedia of Islam* (2. Auflage), s.v. „Dīn" (L. Gardet). S. auch die Beobachtungen von Henri Lammens, „Le Califat de Yazid Ier", *Mélanges de la Faculté Orientale*, Université de Saint-Joseph de Beyrouth 5 (1911): 164 – 67, sowie die Überlegungen von Toshihiko Izutzu, *God and Man in the Koran* (Tokyo: Keio University, 1964), 219 – 29, und Jacques Waardenburg, „Towards a Periodization of Earliest Islam According to its Relations With Other Religions," in *Proceedings of the Ninth Congress of the Union Européenne des Arabisants et Islamisants*, Hg. Rudoplh Peters (Leiden: Brill, 1981), 304 – 26. Trotz des Titels, behandelt der berühmte Aufsatz von Ignaz Goldziher, „Muruwwa und Dîn," in *Muhammedanische Studien* I (Halle a. S.: Max Niemeyer, 1889), 1 – 39, nicht die Bedeutung von *dīn*, sondern benutzt das Wort (im Sinne von „Religion") einfach als Abzeichen für die neue islamische Moralvorstellungen, die im Gegensatz zu dem altarabischen *muruwwa*, „männliche Tugend", stehen. [S. insbesondere S. 13, Fußnote 2.]

4 Interessante Beispiele bei Lammens, a.a.o.

„Tag des Gerichts“ spricht, d. h. vom Jüngsten Tag, ist das Wort *dīn* offensichtlich in diesem Sinne zu verstehen. Auf der anderen Seite kann *dīn* auch vom Mittelpersischen *dēn* abgeleitet worden sein, was „Religion“ bedeutet. Smith war an dem Wort *dīn* (und an seinem mittelpersischen Vorgänger *dēn*) mit dieser Bedeutung interessiert, weil er glaubte, es äußere – vielleicht zum ersten Mal in der Geschichte der Menschheit – das Konzept einer reifizierten Religion. Und vom Vorhandensein des Wortes *dīn* in diesem Sinne im Koran, sowie von *islām*, ist Smith zu dem Schluss gekommen, dass der Islam, als Ausnahme unter den großen Weltreligionen, sich von Anfang an als reifizierte Religion verstanden hat.

Die Beobachtungen von Smith haben eine breite Rezeption unter den Studenten des Islams im Westen gefunden, symbolisiert vielleicht am klarsten in dem Titel eines bekannten Aufsatzes von D. Z. H. Baneth „What did Muḥammad mean when he called his religion „Islam“?“. Für gläubige Muslime ist dieser Titel von Baneth natürlich völlig unannehmbar, weil er implizit sagt, dass Muḥammad, und nicht Gott, den Koran verfasst hat. Aber fast alle Muslime, wie fast alle Orientalisten, stimmen mit Smith überein, dass schon der Koran bedeutungsvoll vom „Islam“ als reifizierte Religion spricht.

Heute aber möchte ich diese Frage noch einmal stellen. Können wir so sicher sein, dass im Zeitalter des Propheten und in der frühsten Gemeinde seiner Anhänger, das Konzept von „Islam“ als Religion in abstraktem Sinne schon vorhanden war? Und wurden die religiösen Ideen dieser frühen Gemeinde schon „der Islam“ genannt? Oder ist es möglich, dass was Günter Lüling den „Ur-Koran“ nannte – d. h. die heilige Schrift wie sie in der Zeit des Prophetens entstanden ist – nie vom „Islam“ und „Muslimen“ im reifizierten Sinne gesprochen hat? D. h., ist es möglich, dass die Koranstellen, die dieses reifizierte Konzept beweisen, Interpolationen eines späteren Zeitpunkts sind? Vielleicht Ergebnisse kleiner Veränderungen zu einzelnen Wörtern im „Urkoran“, oder der Einschub zusätzlicher Wörter, die nicht im Urtext zu finden waren? Ich stelle diese Möglichkeiten als Fragen, weil, wie ich glaube, ihre Antworten noch nicht bekannt sind. Aber ich möchte im Folgenden einige Hinweise zusammenstellen, die m. E. verlangen, dass wir diese Fragen ernst nehmen.

Lassen Sie uns wieder die Wörter *aslama, islām,* und *muslim* in Betracht ziehen. Insgesamt erscheinen diese Wörter im Koran ungefähr 70 Mal und, wie wir oben schon bemerkt haben, schwankt ihre Bedeutung zwischen dem reifizierten „Islam“ oder „Muslim“ und dem normalen „sich [Gott] ergeben.“ Ich nenne den letzteren Fall „normal“, weil die überwiegende Mehrheit unter den 70 Belegstellen am besten anhand dieser Bedeutung erklärt werden können. Sie deuten, wie oben gesagt, auf eine geistige Entscheidung des Gläubigen hin, sich Gottes Willen zu ergeben, und stellen über 90 % der Fälle dar, in denen Wörter abgeleitet von *aslama* zu finden sind. Merkwürdig ist, dass das Wort *islām* im Koran nur acht Mal auftaucht, von denen fünf ganz offensichtlich „sich Gott ergeben" bedeuten. Tatsächlich also gibt es nur *drei* Stellen im Koran, an denen die reifizierte Bedeutung „Islam", als Religion, unvermeidlich scheint. Lassen Sie uns diese drei Fälle näher überprüfen.

[1] Den ersten Fall haben wir schon oben erwähnt: Sure 3, Vers 19, die lautet: „Wahrlich, die Religion [*dīn*] bei Gott ist der Islam" [*inna d-dīn ʾinda llāhi l-islām*]. Die Passage erscheint eindeutig von Islam als reifizierte Religion zu sprechen, besonders weil sie *al-islām* mit *dīn* gleichsetzt, was hier normalerweise als „Religion" verstanden wird.

Man kann versuchen diese Passage im Sure 3, Vers 19 wegzuerklären, indem man den breiteren Zusammenhang von Versen 19 – 20 betont. Insgesamt sprechen diese zwei Verse von den „Leuten der Schrift" (*ahl al-kitāb*, d. h. Christen und Juden), und benutzen das Verbum *aslama* im Sinne von „sich Gott ergeben", was die Übersetzung dieses Teils von Vers 19 nicht als „die Religion bei Gott ist der Islam", sondern als „die Religion bei Gott ist sich ihm zu ergeben" rechtfertigen könnte. (In der Tat, Smith, S. 113, schlägt etwas Ähnliches vor.) Wir können, kurz gesagt, das Erscheinen von reifiziertem Islam hier umgehen, durch scharfsinnige Auslegung.

Ob eine solche Auslegung überzeugend ist, liegt natürlich im Auge des Betrachters. Es gibt aber noch einen anderen Faktor zu berücksichtigen, wenn wir den Vers 19 von Sure 3 betrachten. Die traditionelle islamische Literatur über die *qirāʾāt* oder „die kanonischen Lesarten" enthält eine Lesung für diesen Vers, dem Prophetengefährten Ibn Masʿūd zugeschrieben, die lautet: *inna d-dīna ʿinda llāhi l-ḥanīfiyya* „Religion bei Gott ist al-Ḥanifiyya."[5] Al-Ḥanīfiyya bezeichnet im Koran den vorislamischen Monotheismus, und wird als das Glaubensbekenntnis Abrahams beschrieben. Den Gläubigen wird mehrere Male im Koran empfohlen, am *millat Ibrāhīm*, dem Glaubensbekenntnis Abrahams, des *ḥanīf*, teilzunehmen. Dieser Unterschied zwischen den zwei Wörtern *al-islām* und *al-ḥanifiyya* im Vers 19 von Sure 3 ist offensichtlich nicht wie die vielen anderen kleineren Schwankungen, die man in einem Text erwartet, der mündlich oder schriftlich überliefert worden ist. Sie wirft daher die Frage auf: ist diese Variante das Ergebnis einer absichtlichen Veränderung des Textes des Ur-Korans? War *al-ḥanifiyya* die ur-

---

5 Arthur Jeffery, *Materials for the History of the Text of the Qur'ān. The Old Codices* (Leiden: E. J. Brill, 1937), 32. Eigenartigerweise, im arabischen Text des *Kitāb al-maṣāḥif* von Abū Dāwūd as-Siğistānī, im gleichen Band herausgegeben (arabisch S. 59), wird der Vers 3:19 als Variantentext notiert, die Variantenlesung erscheint aber nicht; stattdessen ist der kanonische Text, mit *al-islām*, zu finden. Stellt das ein Redaktionsversehen Jefferys dar? Nur eine Prüfung der Handschriften des *Kitāb al-maṣāḥif* kann die Sache klären.

sprüngliche Lesung, ersetzt durch *al-islām* vielleicht in der Zeit des Umayyadenherrschers ʿAbd al-Malik (r. 685–705), der allem Anschein nach den Islam als Identität seiner Glaubensgemeinde etablieren wollte, die sich bisher durchgehend als eine Gemeinde der „Gläubigen", *muʾminūn*, beschrieben hat? Wir bemerken, dass dieser Vers, Sure 3, Vers 19, in den Mosaikinschriften des Felsendoms in Jerusalem zu finden ist, gebaut auf ʿAbd al-Maliks Anordnung ungefähr im Jahre 692. Ich bin der Ansicht, dass ʿAbd al-Malik diesen Vers vom Koran mit dieser Lesung im Felsendom einbezogen hat, um seine Politik gegen das Christentum zu fördern, oder wenigstens gegen die christliche Trinitätslehre. Aber ist es vielleicht möglich, dass diese bestimmte Lesung des Verses (d. h. mit *al-islām* statt *al-ḥanīfiyya*) im Koran zu finden ist, weil der Vers Teil der Inschrift des Felsendoms war, und nicht umgekehrt?

[2] Wenden wir uns jetzt dem zweiten Vers, in dem das Wort *al-islām* im reifizierten Sinne vorkommt, zu! Sure 5 Vers 3 – ein sehr langer Vers – lautet:

> Verboten ist euch Fleisch von Verendetem, Blut, Schweinefleisch und das worüber ein anderes Wesen als Gott angerufen worden ist, und was erstickt, geschlagen, gestürtzt oder (zu Tod) gestoßen ist, und was ein wildes Tier geschlagen hat – es sei denn, ihr schächtet es— und was auf einem Opferstein geschlachtet worden ist, und mit Pfeilen das Los zu ziehen. So etwas ist Frevel. – Heute haben diejenigen, die ungläubig sind, hinsichtlich eurer Religion nichts zu hoffen. Darum fürchtet nicht sie, sondern mich! Heute habe ich euch eure Religion [*dīn*] vervollständigt und meine Gnade an euch vollendet, und ich bin damit zufrieden, dass ihr den Islam als Religion [*dīn*] habt. – Und wenn einer aus Hunger sich in einer Zwangslage befindet, ohne sich einer Sünde zuzuneigen, so ist Gott barmherzig und bereit zu vergeben.

Einige Aspekte dieses Verses laden ein, kommentiert zu werden. An erster Stelle ist er, wie schon bemerkt, ein sehr langer Vers. Er steht inmitten einer Gruppe von anderen langen Versen (Verse 2–6 von Sure 5), alle unter den längsten der 120 Verse dieser Sure. Alle diese Verse, wie Vers 3, behandeln rituelle Beachtungen und verbotene oder erlaubte Dinge. Aber die anderen Verse dieser Gruppe (und die anderen langen Verse dieser Sure, wie die Verse 106 oder 110) hängen stark zusammen in ihrem Inhalt; das heißt, sie behandeln ein einziges Thema und die Verslänge mag nur das Bedürfnis wiederspiegeln, ein begonnenes Thema oder eine Anordnung zu vervollständigen. Vers 3 aber behandelt ausnahmsweise nicht ein Thema, sondern mehrere. Er besteht aus vier Teilen. Er fängt mit einer erheblichen Liste von verbotenen Speisen an. Der zweite Teil verbietet in einem kurzen Satz die Anwendung von Pfeilen, um das Los zu ziehen —etwas, das wir vielleicht als eine natürliche Entwicklung ansehen können, von verbotenen Speisen im ersten Teil zu einer verbotenen Handlung im zweiten. Im dritten Teil aber finden wir etwas völlig Neues: dieser Teil mahnt den Gläubigen, nicht die

Ungläubigen, sondern nur Gott zu fürchten, und sagt dann: „Heute habe ich euch eure Religion [*dīn*] vervollständigt und meine Gnade an euch vollendet, und ich bin damit zufrieden, dass ihr den Islam als Religion [*dīn*] habt.“ Diese Bemerkung hat offensichtlich keine logische Beziehung zu dem, was vorangegangen ist. Abschließend, im vierten Teil, teilt der Vers den Gläubigen mit, dass Gott barhmerzig ist, wenn man durch Hunger gezwungen ist – das heißt, dass es erlaubt ist, verbotene Speisen zu essen um den Hungertod zu vermeiden, ein klarer Bezug auf die Speiseverbote des ersten Teils.

Wie sollen wir diese scheinbare Unstimmigkeit des Inhalts von Sure 5, Vers 3 verstehen? Zum Allermindesten können wir sagen, wie andere auch bemerkt haben, dass der dritte Teil nicht am rechten Platz zu sein scheint.[6] Auffällig ist auch, dass der Teil, welcher nicht am rechten Platz zu sein scheint, genau die Passage ist, die erklärt, dass der Islam die auserwählte Religion Gottes sei. Woher aber dieser Versteil kommen mag, wenn er ja nicht am rechten Platz ist, wagt niemand zu erklären. Man hat wahrscheinlich angenommen, er komme ursprünglich von einer anderen Stelle im Ur-Koran, d. h., von einem anderen Augenblick im Lebenslauf des Propheten. Aber wir dürfen auch fragen: ist es möglich, dass dieser Versteil ein kleiner Einschub aus einer späteren Zeit ist?

Noch dazu: es ist die Zusammenstellung des Wortes *al-islām* mit dem Wort *dīn*, häufig als „Religion“ übersetzt, die diese Passage als eine Beschreibung von Islam als reifizierte Religion erscheinen lässt. Wir werden das Wort *dīn* bald näher untersuchen, aber zuerst lassen Sie uns unsere Aufmerksamkeit einem dritten Koranvers widmen.

[3] In Sure 3, Vers 85, finden wir die folgenden Sätze: „Wer auch immer eine andere Religion [*dīn*] als den Islam wünscht [*wa-man yabtaghi ghayra l-islāmi dīnan*...], es wird nicht von ihm angenommen werden. Und im Jenseits gehört er zu denen, die den Schaden haben.“

Für sich genommen erscheint dieser Vers, das Wort *al-islām* eindeutig im reifizierten Sinne als „die Religion des Islams“ zu benutzen. Die zwei vorange-

---

6 Arthur Droge, *The Qur'ān: A New Annotated Translation* (Sheffield, UK and Bristol, CT: Equinox, 2015), 64, note 18, bemerkt, „Today...Today...: the following two sentences, which interrupt the regulations on food, are out of place in their present location.“ Michel Cuypers, *The Banquet: A Reading of the Fifth Sura of the Qur'an* (Miami: Convivium, 2009), 80, sagt, dieser Teil hat „a very different content and style“ von den benachbarten Teilen. (Wir können auch bemerken, dass laut der „Ring-Struktur“ die Cupyers in Sure 5 findet, dieser Versteil weggelassen werden könnte, ohne die Struktur zu stören.) Rudi Paret, *Der Koran: Kommentar und Konkordanz* (Stuttgart: Kohlhammer, 1980), 114: „Der Passus von *al-yawma ya'isa lladīna kafarū* bis *wa-raḍītu lakumu l-islāma dīnan* ist vielleicht aus einem anderen Zusammenhang hierher versprengt.“

henden Verse in Sure 3 aber bilden den Zusammenhang, in dem man Vers 85 verstehen muss; die Rahmung dieser drei Versen als eine Einheit wird klar durch das Erscheinen des eigenartigen Ausdrucks „ein *dīn* außer...", der am Anfang des Verses 83, und am Ende des Verses 85 benutzt wird, fast wie eine Klammer. Die drei Verse lauten:

> [83] „Können sie sich denn etwas anderes wünschen als die Religion Gottes [*dīn Allāh*], wo sich doch ihm – sei es freiwillig, sei es widerwillig – (alle) ergeben haben, die im Himmel und auf der Erde sind? Und zu ihm werden sie zurückgebracht. [84] Wir glauben an Gott und (an das) was auf uns, und auf Abraham, Ismael, Isaak, Jakob und die Stämme herabgesandt worden ist, und was Mose, Jesus, und die Propheten von ihrem Herrn erhalten haben, ohne dass wir bei einem von ihnen einen Unterschied machen. Ihm sind wir ergeben. [85] Wer auch immer eine andere Religion [*dīn*] als den Islam wünscht (*wa-man yabtaghi ghayra l-islāmi dīnan...*), es wird nicht von ihm angenommen werden. Und im Jenseits gehört er zu denen, die den Schaden haben.

Wir merken aber auch in dieser vereinigten Gruppe von drei Versen, dass die ersten zwei Verse, 83 und 84, das Wort *aslama* bzw. *muslimūn* im „normalen", unreifizierten Sinn benutzen, d.h., mit der Bedeutung „jemand, der sich [Gott] ergeben hat"; in Vers 83 sagt der Text „wo sich doch ihm...(alle) ergeben haben, die im Himmel und auf der Erde sind..."[*wa-lahu aslama man fī s-samawāt wa-l-arḍi...*], und in Vers 84, nachdem mehrere Propheten erwähnt worden sind, heißt es „ohne dass wir bei einem von ihnen einen Unterschied machen, und ihm sind wir ergeben" [*lā nufarriqu bayna aḥadin min-hum wa-naḥnu lahu muslimūn*]. Aber diese doppelte Verwendung von Wörtern mit einer Bedeutung abgeleitet von „sich [Gott] ergeben" – einmal das Verbum, einmal das Partizip – lässt das Auftauchen des Gerundiums *al-islām* im nachfolgenden Vers unpassend erscheinen, wenn es im reifizierten Sinn verstanden wird. Der Zusammenhang deutet eher an, dass *al-islām* in Vers 85 auch im Sinne von „sich [Gott] ergeben" verstanden werden sollte – oder, dass das Wort *al-islām* vielleicht eingeschoben worden ist, oder ein anderes Wort ersetzt hat, obwohl die Variantenliteratur kein Hinweis darauf bietet, dass hier einst ein anderes Wort zu finden war.

* * *

Die drei oben behandelten Koranpassagen – Sure 3, Vers 19; Sure 5, Vers 3 und Sure 3, Vers 85 – haben, außer ihrer Verwendung des Worts *al-islām* im reifiziertem Sinn, noch eine andere gemeinsame Besonderheit: in allen drei Versen ist das Wort *al-islām* eng mit dem Wort *dīn*, auch im reifizierten Sinne von „Religion," verknüpft. Wie oben gesehen, hat *dīn* drei Grundbedeutungen: (1) die altarabische Bedeutung „Sitte, Dienst, Gehorsam" (2) die Bedeutung „Recht, Gericht, Gesetz,

Urteil" vom Aramäischen abgeleitet; und (3) die Bedeutung „Religion" vom Mittelpersischen abgeleitet. Smith hat die Wichtigkeit der dritten Bedeutung betont, weil sie für ihn das Vorhandensein des Konzepts von „reifizierte Religion" im Koran überhaupt beweist.

Eine nähere Untersuchung der Koranstellen, die *dīn* benutzen, ist aber sinnvoll. Das Wort *dīn* erscheint insgesamt ungefähr 90 Mal im Koran. Weil die verschiedenen Bedeutungen von *dīn* manchmals überlappen, bleiben mehrere Verse doppeldeutig oder verschwommen (z. B., ist es in einem bestimmten Vers als „Sitte" oder „Gesetz" zu verstehen? Oder ist es „Dienst" oder „Religion"? u.s.w.). Nichtsdestoweniger ist eine grobe semantische Aufteilung dieser 90 Fälle möglich und bringt interessante Ergebnisse.

In einem solchen Verfahren wird es klar, dass die häufigste Bedeutung für *dīn* im Koran zweifellos die altarabische, „Sitte, Dienst, Gehorsam" ist; das macht insgesamt vielleicht 50 von den 90 Fällen aus, in denen *dīn* auftritt. Zum Beispiel, in Sure 2, Vers 132 sagt Abraham zu seinen Söhnen: „Gott hat für euch *ad-dīn* [Dienst; oder: Gehorsam?] gewählt. Ihr dürft ja nicht sterben, ohne (Gott) ergeben zu sein." [*inna llāha ṣṭafā la-kum ad-dīn fa-lā tamūtunna illā wa-antum muslimūn*]. Die Übersetzung „Gott hat für euch Religion erwählt" [oder: die Religion, im allgemein] ist unwahrscheinlich; viel natürlicher ist es, die Stelle mit „Gott hat für euch Dienst (gegenüber Gott)" oder „Gehorsam (gegenüber Gott) erwählt" zu übersetzen – besonders weil am Ende des Verses betont wird, dass die Zuhörer sich Gott ergeben sollen (*muslimūn* sein). Ein zweites Beispiel, wo *dīn* am besten als „Gehorsam" zu verstehen ist, bietet Sure 2, Vers 193: „Und kämpft gegen sie, bis es keine Versuchung (oder Zwietracht) mehr gibt [*fitna*], und Gehorsam [*dīn*] ist zu Gott..." [*wa-qātilū-hum ḥattā lā takūna fitnatun wa-yakūna d-dīnu li-llāhi...*]. Der Kontext des Verses macht es naheliegend, dass *dīn* hier eher „Gehorsam" (oder „Dienst") als „Religion" bedeutet, weil „Religion" in diesem Zusammenhang zu unbestimmt und unklar zu sein scheint. Ein drittes, und sehr interessantes Beispiel: in Sure 4, Vers 125 heißt es: „Wer ist besser im Dienst [*man aḥsanu dīnan*], als wer seiner Gesicht Gott ergibt [*mimman aslama wajha-hu li-llāhi*], während er rechtschaffen ist [*wa-huwa muḥsinun*] und das Glaubensbekenntnis Abrahams befolgt, als ein Ḥanīf? [*wa-ttabaʿa millata Ibrāhīma ḥanīfan...?*]." Wichtig ist hier die enge Verknüpfung der Wörter *dīn* und *islām*, beide aber im unreifiziertem Sinne; es geht eher um das persönliche Verfahren, sich Gott zu ergeben. Wenn in diesem Vers von einer reifizierten Religion überhaupt die Rede ist, wäre sie vielmehr mit dem *millat Ibrāhīm*, dem Glaubensbekenntnis Abrahams, das Ḥanīfentum, zu identifizieren.

Soweit die häufigste Bedeutung von *dīn* im Koran. Seine zweithäufigste Bedeutung erscheint die von Aramäischen abgeleitete als „Gesetz, Urteil" usw. zu sein, die ungefähr 30 bis 35 Fälle ausmacht. Dies schließt die 20 Verse ein, in denen von *yawm al-dīn*, wörtlich „Tag des Urteils" (oder des Gerichtes), d. h. dem jüngsten Tag, die Rede ist. Unter anderen Beispielen, die in diesem semantischen Bereich fallen, können wir Sure 12, Vers 76 erwähnen, die vom „Recht (oder Gesetz) des Königs", *dīn al-malik*, spricht. Sowie Sure 24, Vers 2, indem der Koran die Peitsche als Strafe für Ehebruch bestimmt, und seine Zuhörer mahnt, „Und lasst euch im Hinblick darauf, dass es um *dīn* Gottes geht, nicht von Mitleid mit ihnen erfassen..." Offensichtlich wird hier *dīn* im Sinne von „das Recht (oder Urteil) Gottes" benutzt. Es gibt noch etwa 10 andere Verse, die in ähnlicher Weise *dīn* im Sinne von „Recht", „Urteil", „Gericht" usw. benutzen. Das Problem der Doppeldeutigkeit scheint mit *dīn* als „Gesetz" usw. nicht so beträchtlich zu sein.

Das Problem der Doppeldeutigkeit erscheint am prominentesten, wenn wir das koranische *dīn* im Sinne von „Religion" betrachten. Wir haben schon gesehen, dass von den 90 Textstellen wo das Wort *dīn* erscheint, schon etwa 80 entweder mit der Bedeutung „Sitte, Dienst, Gehorsam" oder mit der Bedeutung „Recht, Urteil" usw. zu verstehen sind. Das heißt, dass *dīn* im Sinne von „Religion" – reifizierte Religion – relativ selten vorkommt, insgesamt nur etwa 10 Mal im Koran, und manche dieser Verse sind doppeldeutig. Die wenigen Fälle, in denen sich *dīn* in reifiziertem Sinne findet, schließen die drei reifizierten *islām*-Verse, die wir oben untersucht haben ein, und beide Wörter – *islām* und *dīn* – tragen in diesen Versen eine Bedeutung, die nicht ihre „normale" Bedeutung ist. Wir können also wenigstens sagen, dass insofern der Koran vom Islam als einer Religion im reifiziertem Sinne spricht, dies ein Randphänomen darstellt, kein zentrales Konzept der Offenbarung – nicht vergleichbar mit z. B. dem Konzept von „Glaube" (*īmān*, *mu'minūn*, usw.), das mehr als 1000 Mal im Koran auftaucht. Aber das scheinbar im Koran sehr schwache Vorkommen des „Islams" als Religion, sowie von *dīn* im Sinne von „reifizierter Religion" erlaubt uns die Frage zu stellen: hat der Ur-Koran überhaupt von dem Islam als Religion gesprochen? Und ist das Wort *dīn* im Ur-Koran vielleicht nur in den zwei „normalen" Bedeutungen zu verstehen, und nicht als „Religion" im reifiziertem Sinne?

In diesem Zusammenhang sind einige Hinweise aus dem ersten Jahrhundert nach der Zeit des Propheten (bzw. des Urkorans) erheblich. Auffällig ist, dass die Wörter „Islam" und „Muslim" in den frühesten Aufzeichnungen, die die neue Gemeinde erwähnen, nicht zu finden sind. Arabische Inschriften und Papyri des 7. Jahrhunderts, welche den Führer der Gemeinde erwähnen, nennen ihn stets *amīr al-mu'minīn*, „Befehlshaber der Gläubigen" und datierte arabische Urkunden aus dem 7. Jahrhundert beschreiben ihre Herrschaft als die „Gerichtsbarkeit der Gläubigen" (*qaḍā' al-mu'minīn*). (Die Datierungsformel „Jahre des Hidjras" erscheint in Urkunden erst im 9. Jahrhundert zum ersten Mal.) Diese Tatsachen zeigen eindeutig, dass die Mitglieder dieser neuen Gemeinde sich als „Gläubige", *mu'minūn*, verstanden haben, nicht als „Muslime" – das soll uns kaum erstaunen, gerade weil der Koran das Konzept der Gläubigen so kräftig betont. Wie die arabischen Quellen, so bieten auch die nichtarabischen Quellen dieser Zeit keinen Hinweis auf eine Identität der neuen Gemeinde als „Muslime." Im Altsyrischen, Griechischen, Mittelpersischen, Koptischen, und anderen Dokumenten oder Texten des 7. Jahrhunderts, finden wir eine Vielzahl von Wörtern für die Eroberer – *ṭayyāyē* („nomaden"), *mhaggrāyē* (von Arabischen *muhājirūn*, vielleicht „Einsiedler" oder „Soldaten"?), *Sarakēnoi*, *ʿArabēs*, usw. – aber wir begegnen keinem Wort, das ein Versuch zu sein scheint, das arabische Wort *muslim* wiederzugeben. Der Islam – als Religion, und so genannt – tritt zum ersten Mal in den Inschriften des Felsendoms in Jersualem auf, wo, wie wir oben gesehen haben, Sure 3, Vers 19 zitiert wird, mit seiner dramatischen und vielleicht erstmaligen Verkündigung, „wahrlich, die Religion bei Gott ist der Islam" (*inna d-dīn ʿinda llāh al-islām*). Aber wir haben auch schon die Fragen gesehen, welche die Lesungsvariantenliteratur in Bezug auf diesen Vers erhebt.

Es gibt noch einen Vers, der nicht das Wort *al-islām*, sondern das Partizip *muslim* in reifiziertem Sinn zu benutzen scheint – und nicht in enger Verbindung mit dem Wort *dīn*. Ich finde diesen Vers schwierig wegzuerklären, und deshalb stellt er vielleicht das Haar in der Suppe meiner Hypothese dar. Es geht um einen Ausschnitt aus Sure 22, Vers 78, der sagt: „Abraham hat euch vorher und in diesem (d. h. in dem Koran?) *al-muslimīn* genannt ..." Hier spricht der Text weder von einem Verhalten der Gläubigen, noch von einer persönlichen Entscheidung derselben, sondern von einer Benennung seitens Abrahams. Die Bedeutung „Muslime" erscheint deshalb vernünftiger für *al-muslimīn* als „jemand, der sich [Gott] ergibt." Haben wir aber hier noch einen Einschub späterer Zeit? Vielleicht die Tatsache, dass dieser Vers der allerletzte dieser Sure ist – wo zusätzliche Wörter am leichtesten einzuschieben wären – und die außerordentliche Länge des Verses, bieten Gründe, die zweite Hälfte des Verses (oder den ganzen Vers) unter Verdacht zu stellen. Es ist auch beachtenswert, dass dieser Vers 78 damit anfängt den Gläubigen zu ermutigen, das Glaubensbekenntnis Abrahams, „euer Vater" zu folgen [*millat abīkum Ibrāhīm*]; das klingt wie den Abschluss von dem, was in den vorangehenen Versen zu finden ist, nämlich die wiederholte Erinnerung der Gläubigen, an rituellen Pflichten wie dem Gebet festzuhalten. Dann aber plötzlich folgt der Satz, „Abraham hat euch *al-muslimīn* genannt...", der unvorbereitet die Identität der Gemeinde von *millat Ibrāhīm* zu Muslime – d. h., zu dem Islam, zu wechseln scheint. Und noch dazu erwähnt der Vers in der folgenden Zeile den Apostel (*ar-rasūl*, d. h. Muḥammad), was auch sehr selten im Koran passiert und sonst vorher in dieser Sure nicht zu finden ist. Zusammengenommen würde die Erwähnung von *muslimīn* im reifizierten Sinne, und dem Propheten, gut zum politischen Programm der Zeit ʿAbd al-Maliks passen, den Islam als Religion zu gründen, mit Schwerpunkt auf dem Koran als Schrift und Muḥammad als Prophet.

Es erscheint also, dass die Frage, die im Titel des bekannten Aufsatzes von D.Z.H. Baneth gestellt wird, „Was hat Muḥammad gemeint, als er seine Religion „Islam" nannte?" eine falsche Frage ist. Der Koran bietet uns kaum einen Hinweis – wenn meine Hypothese richtig ist, können wir sagen, überhaupt keinen Hinweis – darauf, dass der Ur-Koran wirklich von „Islam" im reifiziertem Sinne gesprochen hat. Die wahren Fragen erscheinen mir eher zu sein: Wann, und warum, und wie, wurden die koranischen Wörter *islām* und *muslim* – die ursprünglich eine persönliche Entscheidung, sich Gott zu ergeben, darstellten – umgedeutet, um als eine neue Bezeichnung für die Gemeinde Muḥammads und für die Mitglieder dieser Gemeinde zu dienen? Ich habe oben mehrere Male vorgeschlagen, dass die Zeit des Umayyadenherrschers ʿAbd al-Malik (r. 685–705) nähere Untersuchung verdient, aber die Fragen bleiben noch offen. Darüber hinaus scheint die Umdeutung der Wörter *islām* und *muslim* nur ein Beispiel eines breiteren historischen Verfahrens zu sein, indem Bezeichnungen für Institutionen und Vorgänge der sich entwickelnden Gemeinde mit koranischen Ausdrücken ersetzt wurden, ein Verfahren, das wir „Koranifizierung" nennen dürfen.[7] Zweck davon war, die Identität der Gemeinde und des Staats eindeutig als „islamisch" (im neuen, reifizierten Sinn) zu beweisen und dadurch die Gemeinde klar von anderen Gemeinden – besonders von den anderen monotheistischen Gemeinden, dem Judentum und dem Christentum – endgültig und zweifellos zu unterscheiden.

Zusammenfassung

Diese wenigen Passagen, die wir heute besprochen haben, erscheinen die einzigen zu sein, in denen die Wörter *islām* und *dīn* in ihrem reifizierten Sinne benutzt worden sind. Sie passen m. E. viel leichter in die Gedankenwelt des frühen 8. Jahrhunderts, als in die des frühen 7. Jahrhunderts. Wenn wir annehmen, dass der Koran im Grunde genommen ein Text des frühen 7. Jahrhunderts sei – und ich nehme das an – dann müssen wir irgendwie erklären, wie diese scheinbare Unstimmigkeit in der Bedeutung dieser Wörter entstehen konnte. Die Möglichkeit, dass der „Urkoran" im Laufe seiner Überlieferung manche kleinen Einschübe bekommen hat, oder kleine Wortveränderungen erlitten hat, um Teile des Texts

7 Fred M. Donner, „The Qurʾanicization of Religio-Political Discourse in the Umayyad Period," *Révue des Mondes Musulmans et de la Mediterranée* 129 (2011): 79–92.

besser an etwas spätere Konzepte der Gemeinschaft anzupassen, habe ich versucht im Vorangegangenen zu rechtfertigen. Wir können zumindest beschließen, dass wir sorgfältiger sein sollten, wenn wir diese Wörter im Koran, *islām, muslim,* und *dīn,* übersetzen. Wir müssen immer versuchen, die passendste von mehreren möglichen Bedeutungen für eine bestimmte Passage zu identifizieren – und nicht z. B. einfach gedankenlos *muslimūn* oder *al-islām* als „Muslime" und „Islam" zu übersetzen.

Diese Überlegungen bleiben natürlich hypothetisch, denn es gibt noch keinen urkundlichen Beweis dafür – wie z. B. eindeutige Spuren solcher Veränderungen in frühen Koranhandschriften, d. h. Exemplare des 7. Jahrhunderts.[8] Glücklicherweise, ist das Studium von frühen Koranhandschriften heute – nach fast einem Jahrhundert der Vernachlässigung – wieder ein wichtiger Teil der wissenschaftlichen Koranforschung. Wir können deshalb hoffen, dass künftige Forschung an den Handschriften diese Hypothese, und viele andere, entweder bestätigen oder widerlegen wird. Die reiche Ernte der heutigen Arbeit an den frühen Koranhandschriften ist aber ein riesengroßes Thema, und eine Auseinandersetzung damit muss auf einen anderen Tag warten.

---

8 David Powers, *Muhammad is Not the Father of Any of Your Men* (Philadelphia: University of Pennsylvania Press, 2009), 155–96, hat Beweise der Ersetzung eines Wortes durch ein anderes in einer sehr frühen Qur'ānhandschrift entdeckt, mit beträchtlichen theologischen und politischen Folgen. Ein solcher Prozess ist also nicht unbestätigt.

Marianus Hundhammer

Qur'ānic Studies between Revisionism and Reinvention

Reflections on the Methodology of Günter Lüling

More than forty years had passed by between the publication of the dissertation of Günter Lüling (1928–2014) in 1970 and the 2011 publication of the latest English edition of his work on the Qur'ān. Comparing the editions, considerable corrections and modifications of the author's theses become apparent. Despite these alterations, questions still remain concerning Lüling's methodical and theoretical approaches, particularly in the light of the current state of research in Qur'ānic Studies.[1] Therefore, the epistemological interest of this article is to examine these questions, whose answers can only be given by general reflections on the topic. The rationale for this very general approach is based on the extraordinary infrequent reception of Lüling's work in Qur'ānic Studies, which is commonly the basis for any approach that deals critically with the methods and sources in the main work of an author.[2]

---

1 Already in 1977, Maxime Rodinson, professor for oriental languages, summarized this problem in a review of Lüling, asking ironically, whether there was, besides the Ur-Qur'ān, also an "Ur-Lüling," that should be contrasted with a "Deutero-Lüling." See Maxime Rodinson. "Review of Günter Lüling. *Über den Ur-Qur'ān. Ansätze zur Rekonstruktion vorislamischer christlicher Strophenlieder im Ur-Qur'ān* (Erlangen: Verlagsbuchhandlung Hannelore Lüling, 1974)," *Der Islam* 54/2 (1977): 321–325, 322.

2 Up to this day, just a few reviews of Lüling's work have been published, most of them not by experts in Qur'ānic Studies (in the following, I will give reference to author and journal only). Erhart Kahle, *Zeitschrift der Deutschen Morgenländischen Gesellschaft* (ZDMG) 132/1 (1982): 182–184, Walter Beltz, *Zeitschrift für Religions- und Geistesgeschichte* (ZRGG) 27/2 (1975): 169–171, Sebastian Günther, *al-Qantara* 16 (1995): 485–490, Bernd Weischer, *Orientalistische Literaturzeitung* (OLZ) 74 (1979): 468–473, Theodor Lohmann, *Theologische Literaturzeitung* 103 (1978): 560–562, Georg Stadtmüller, *Una Sancta* 34 (1979): 266, Victor Poggi, *Orientalia Christiania Periodica* 41 (1975): 529–532, Mark Batunsky, *Narody Azii i Afriki* 6 (1987): 143–153, Heinrich Ringel, *Deutsches Pfarrerblatt* 74 (1974): 680–681, Claude Gilliot, *Arabica* 30 (1983): 16–37, Diana Steigerwald, *Journal of the American Oriental Society* (JAOS) 124/3 (2004): 621–623. The following articles discuss Lüling's work briefly: Karl Steenbrink, "New Orientalist Suggestions on the Origins of Islam," *The Journal of Rotterdam Islamic and Social Sciences* 1/1 (2010): 1, Raimund Köbert, "Frühe und spätere Koranexegese. Eine Ergänzung zu Or 35 (1966): 28–32," *Orientalia* (Nova Series) 55/2 (1986): 174–176, and Claude Gilliot, "Review of Günter Lüling. *Über den Ur-Qur'ān. Ansätze zur Rekonstruktion vorislamischer christlicher Strophenlieder im Ur-Qur'ān* (Erlan-

https://doi.org/10.1515/9783110599176-009

The scholarly responses to further works of Lüling, dealing largely with the history of religion, but which nevertheless obliquely reference his hypotheses on the genesis of the Qur'ān, are even fewer in number, and barely provide scholarly explanation regarding methodology and source material.[3] The same dynamic also applies to the comparatively numerous newspaper articles on the author's work, often containing reproaches of revisionism against the author.[4] Therefore, a short introduction to the theses of Lüling from a methodological perspective, along with a critical juxtaposition of these theses with the relevant methods in Qur'ānic Studies and related fields, will be covered at the beginning of this contribution. This paper argues that there is a great disparity between established scholarly approaches towards the Qur'ān and Lüling's method.

More precisely, I will discuss this disparity as it relates to the application of certain methodologies concerning Lüling's specific object of research. I focus most particularly on the use of primary and secondary literature in the author's work. Finally, these reflections will be highlighted through examining the central thesis of Lüling's work, that essential parts of the Qur'ān are grounded on a pre-Islamic Christian hymnodic ground layer.

The Ur-Qur'ān-Thesis: Methodology and Sources

In his first thesis, Lüling claims that the "Text of the Koran as transmitted by orthodox Muslims contains, hidden behind it as a ground layer and considerably scattered throughout it (together about one-third of the whole Koran text) an

gen: Verlagsbuchhandlung Hannelore Lüling, 1974)," *Revue du Monde Musulmane et de la Méditerranée* (REMMM) 70/1 (1993): 142–143.

3 For reviews on Günther Lüling, *Die Wiederentdeckung des Propheten Muhammad: Eine Kritik am "christlichen" Abendland* (Erlangen: Verlagsbuchhandlung Hannelore Lüling, 1981) see Annemarie Schimmel, *The Muslim World* 77/2 (1987): 140–141, A. A. Brockett, *International Journal of Middle East Studies* 13 (1981): 519–521, Gerald Hawting, *Journal of Semitic Studies* (JSS) 27 (1982): 108–112, and Theodor Sundermeier, *Beihefte zur Evangelischen Theologie* 30 (1985): 14–15. For reviews on Günter Lüling: *Der christliche Kult an der vorislamischen Kaaba als Problem der Islamwissenschaft und christlichen Theologie* (Erlangen: Verlagsbuchhandlung Hannelore Lüling, 1977), see Adel Theodor Khoury, *Orientalistische Literaturzeitung* (OLZ) 78 (1981): 150–151, and Walter Beltz, *Zeitschrift für Religions- und Geistesgeschichte* (ZRGG) 30/2 (1978): 181.

4 See e.g. Nicolai Sinai, *Neue Zürcher Zeitung*, February 19 (2004), Harald Vocke, *Frankfurter Allgemeine Zeitung*, June 18 (1979), Hans-Joachim Woitowitz, *Frankfurter Allgemeine Zeitung*, July 17 (1979), Wolfgang Günther Lerch, *Frankfurter Allgemeine Zeitung*, June 1 (2004), and Thomas Kapielski, *Frankfurter Rundschau*, March 10 (2005).

originally pre-Islamic Christian text."[5] In particular, this ground layer is constituted by a pre-Islamic "erstwhile" Christian-Arabic strophic Hymnody.[6] In his English edition of 2003, as well as in the second English edition of 2011, Lüling even claims that these texts would have been 200 years old by the time of the Prophet Muhammad.[7] As evidenced by this second part of Lülings first thesis, it appears that certain differences exist between the several German and English editions of his work on the Qur'ān. This kind of evolutionary process in the work of Günter Lüling can be seen *pars pro toto* for all of his theses, first and foremost concerning his religio-historical findings. Such an analysis, however, cannot fit into the epistemological frame of this article and is therefore beyond its scope. Yet for the question of methodology and the use of scientific sources, a diachronic perspective on Lüling's publications from his Dissertation 1970 up to his last Book, "A Challenge to Islam for Reformation" published in second edition in 2011, proves useful.

---

5 Günter Lüling, *A Challenge to Islam for Reformation*, 2nd ed. (Erlangen: Verlagsbuchhandlung Hannelore Lüling, 2011), 1 and Günter Lüling, *A Challenge to Islam for Reformation* (New Delhi: Motilal Banarsidass Publishers, 2003), 1. The second edition is a reprint of the first edition, therefore both will be cited in the following as Lüling, *Challenge*, first and second ed. See also Günter Lüling, *Über den Ur-Qur'ān. Ansätze zur Rekonstruktion vorislamischer christlicher Strophenlieder im Ur-Qur'ān*, 2nd ed. (Erlangen: Verlagsbuchhandlung Hannelore Lüling, 1993), 1 and Günter Lüling, *Über den Ur-Qur'ān. Ansätze zur Rekonstruktion vorislamischer christlicher Strophenlieder im Ur-Qur'ān* (Erlangen: Verlagsbuchhandlung Hannelore Lüling, 1974), 1. As in the previous case, the second edition is a reprint of the first edition: both will be cited as Lüling, *Ur-Qur'ān*, first and second ed. See also Günter Lüling, *Kritisch-exegetische Untersuchung des Qur'āntextes* (Erlangen: J. Högl, 1970), VIf.

6 Lüling, *Challenge*, first and second ed., 9. In his earlier Publications, Lüling treats the characteristics of these texts being Christian Arabic poetry on the one hand and Hymnody on the other Hand separately. See Lüling, *Ur-Qur'ān*, first and second ed., 2 and 8. In his Dissertation, he firstly calls the texts poetic and strophic (VI), then mentions Christian authors (VII), and finally defines them as Qur'ānic Christian hymns (VIII). See Lüling, *Untersuchung*, VIff.

7 See Lüling, *Challenge*, first and second ed., 21. In his book, Lüling presents three more consecutive theses, all of which correspond with the first thesis. In his second thesis, Lüling states that "According to the statements of Thesis 1 the transmitted text of the Koran contains four different kinds of layers of text" (11). Thirdly, "The transmitted Koran text is the final result of several successive editorial revisions" (Thesis three, 20), and finally "The findings within the Koran text are confirmed by an abundance of Muslim traditions and useful information apart from and beyond the Koran text itself. These important traditions and information have hitherto either not been understood in their original meaning or they have remained unexamined." (24). See ibid., 11, 20, and 24.

The Applicability of Methods and the Object of Research

Comparing texts has been and will always be a fascinating task for the scholarly endeavor. This is especially the case when common ideas, topoi, narratives, and even figures recur in different texts, of course in distinct functions and roles. The number of respective corpora is great, and the amount of relevant objects of comparison vast, if not uncountable. When dealing with sacred texts, scholars face certain limitations concerning the material, while a sharp distinction between sacred and profane texts generally proves very complicated. Such an approach has become even more difficult since post-modern approaches found entrance to the respective scholarly field. This is especially true in the case of Biblical Studies.[8]

To cover all the relevant approaches dealing with the object of research, namely methods of literary studies, history, religious studies and Islamic studies, as well as methods of Islamic and Christian theology, would go beyond the framework of this article. Günter Lüling's object of research, whose core issue is the comparison between parts of the Qur'ān and pre-Islamic Christian Arabic strophic Hymnody, requires interdisciplinary methods. This article will therefore focus on the historical-critical method. One decisive reason for this choice can be observed by going back to the origins of historical criticism, which can be traced primarily to the Scientific Revolution during the Age of Enlightenment and the subsequent birth of Bible Criticism. Due to the fact that Lüling's core thesis argues that the ground layer of the Qur'ān consists of pre-Islamic Christian Arabic strophic hymnody, this corpus must therefore be significantly influenced by biblical ideas, topoi, figures and references.

It seems to be possible, if not logical, to rely on methods of biblical criticism, whose origins also dealt with comparable scholarly issues. Dominated by the values of the Age of Enlightenment, philosophers and later theologians ceased to pursue a teleological epistemological interest in the scientific examination

8 For a discussion of the ongoing debate in this field since the early 1990s see Robert Fowler, "Postmodern Biblical Criticism," *Foundation & Facets Forum* 5 (1989): 3–30, Gary Phillips, "Exegesis as Critical Praxis: Reclaiming History and Text from a Postmodern Perspective," *Semeia* 51 (1990): 7–50, and Fred Burnett, "Postmodern Biblical Exegesis: The Eve of historical Criticism," *Semeia* 51 (1990): 51–80, as well as George Aichele et al., eds., *The Postmodern Bible* (New Haven: Yale University Press, 1995), A. K. M. Adam, ed., *Handbook of Postmodern Biblical Interpretation* (St. Louis: Chalice Press, 2000), and John Collins, *The Bible after Babel: Historical Criticism in a Postmodern Age* (Grand Rapids: Eerdmans, 2005).

of the Bible, and began to question the exclusively divine origins of the text.[9] The comparison of older, contextualizable texts with the Bible was now taken into account, and from the 19th century onwards additional results of science of religion, archaeology, and even cultural geography produced a blossoming of biblical scholarship. Already at the time of the publication of Lüling's dissertation 1970 and the publication of his second book "Über den Ur-Qur'ān" in 1974, these approaches had become part of the methodical canon of Christian Theology, especially as it concerned German Protestant theology, which Lüling studied originally at the University of Göttingen. Presently, the historical-critical approach to the Bible can be summarized in the following five canonical methods, which are, to a variable extent, suitable for the Object of Research, including the qur'ānic text:

> Textual and transmission criticism are concerned with the reconstruction of textual history. Methods of textual criticism are used to identify the various stages of textual development, with the aim of scientifically identifying its original phase. Transmission criticism focuses on the reconstruction of a text's complete developmental process examining possible preliterary and oral stages.[10]

---

9 One of the key figures in this regard was the Dutch Jewish philosopher Baruch de Spinoza (1632–1677). In his *Tractatus theologico-politicus*, published anonymously in 1670, he postulates historical – critical as well as linguistic methods as the basis for the interpretation of the Bible. Shortly thereafter, Christian Theology also was struck by this paradigm shift. Worth mentioning in this regard are among others the influential works of the French catholic priest and theologian Richard Simon (1638–1712) and the German Professor of Protestant Theology Johan Salomo Semler (1725–1791). See Baruch de Spinoza, *Theologisch-politische Abhandlung*, trans. Julius Hermann von Kirchmann, Philosophische Bibliothek 35 (Berlin: L. Heimann, 1870), especially chapters 7–13, 106–189, Richard Simon, *Histoire critique du Vieux Testament* (Rotterdam: Reinier Leers, 1685), Richard Simon, *Histoire critique du texte du Nouveau Testament* (Rotterdam: Reinier Leers, 1690), and Johan Salomo Semler, *Abhandlung von freier Untersuchung des Canon*, Texte zur Kirchen- und Theologiegeschichte 5, 4 Vols., 2nd ed., (Gütersloh: Gütersloher Verlagshaus, 1980).

10 Due to the complexity of the object of research, only proposals for methodical approaches can be made in this article. On textual criticism see for a general introduction Paul Maas, *Textual Criticism* (Oxford: Oxford University Press, 1958), and Jerome McGann, *A critique of modern textual criticism* (Chicago: University of Chicago Press, 1993). For textual criticism in Biblical research see the study by Peter McCarter, Jr., *Textual criticism: recovering the text of the Hebrew Bible* (Philadelphia: Fortress Press, 1986), and the articles in Barbara Aland, ed., *New Testament Textual Criticism, Exegesis and Church History. A Discussion of methods*, Contributions to Biblical Exegesis and Theology 7 (Kampen: Kok Pharos, 1994). For non-biblical Christian texts see Wim Weren et al., eds., *Recent developments in textual criticism: New Testament, other early Christian and Jewish literature* (Assen: Van Gorcum, 2003). For the Qur'ān see the contributions in Manfred Kropp, ed., *Results of contemporary research on the Qur'ān. The question of a historio-critical text*

Literary,[11] composition and redaction criticism[12] are devoted to the examination of a text's semantic, logical and syntactical coherency, along with textual development and the relationship between parts of the text and the entire text.

Form and genre criticism are methods aimed at comparing and analyzing forms and structures (genres) of texts, along with comparing the function and intention of a text with function and intention of a genre. [13]

Finally, motive and tradition criticism are devoted to the task of identifying the inherent motives in the text, the contextualization of these motives within existing traditions and analysis of their adaption and transformation.[14]

---

of the Qur'ān (Würzburg: Ergon, 2007), and the introduction in Keith Small, *Textual Criticism and Qur'ān Manuscripts* (Plymouth: Lexington, 2011), 1–30.

11 On the theoretical debate in Biblical studies and in particular literary criticism see the contributions in Stephen Moore, ed., *The Bible in theory. Critical and postcritical essays* (Leiden: Brill, 2011) and Jürgen Werlitz, *Studien zur literarkritischen Methode. Gericht und Heil in Jesaja 7,1–17 und 29,1–8*, Beihefte zur Zeitschrift für die alttestamentliche Wissenschaft 204 (Berlin: De Gruyter, 1992), 7–94. For questions of methodology see Jutta Krispenz, *Literarkritik und Stilstatistik im Alten Testament. Eine Studie zur literarkritischen Methode, durchgeführt an Texten aus den Büchern Jeremia, Ezechiel und 1 Könige* (Berlin: De Gruyter, 2001), 7–58. For applicable approaches concerning the object of research see Angelika Neuwirth, *The Qur'ān in context. Historical and literary investigations into the Qur'ānic milieu* (Leiden: Brill, 2010), and Gabriel Said Reynolds, *The Qur'ān and its biblical subtext* (London: Routledge, 2010).

12 For the composition of the Qur'ān see the Introduction in Angelika Neuwirth, *Studien zur Komposition der mekkanischen Suren*, 2nd ed. (Berlin: De Gruyter, 2007), 1–45. For a general introduction to redaction criticism see Norman Perrin, *What is Redaction Criticism?* (London: SPCK, 1970), and Klaus Berger, *Exegese des Neuen Testaments: Neue Wege vom Text zur Auslegung*, 3rd ed. (Heidelberg: Quelle & Meyer, 1991), 202–217. For a comprehensive theoretical discussion see Reinhard Wonneberger, *Redaktion. Studien zur Textfortschreibung im Alten Testament, entwickelt am Beispiel der Samuel-Überlieferung*, Forschungen zur Religion und Literatur des Alten und Neuen Testaments 156 (Göttingen: Vandenhoeck & Ruprecht, 1992), 39–179. For the redaction of the Qur'ān see Angelika Neuwirth, *Der Koran als Text der Spätantike: ein europäischer Zugang* (Berlin: Verlag der Weltreligionen im Insel Verlag, 2010), 235–275.

13 For form and genre criticism see the detailed studies of John Hayes, *Old Testament Form Criticism* (San Antonio: Trinity University, 1974) and Klaus Berger, *Formen und Gattungen im Neuen Testament* (Tübingen: Francke, 2005). Concerning hymnody see Frank Crüsemann, *Studien zur Formgeschichte von Hymnus und Danklied in Israel* (Neukirchen-Vluyn: Neukirchener Verlag, 1969). For the Qur'ān see the interesting approach in Karl-Friedrich Pohlmann, *Die Entstehung des Korans. Neue Erkenntnisse aus Sicht der historisch-kritischen Bibelwissenschaft* (Darmstadt: Wissenschaftliche Buchgesellschaft, 2012), 59–79.

14 See G.W. Coats, "Motive Criticism, OT," in *The Interpreter's Dictionary of the Bible*, ed. George Butterick et al., Vol. 5 (Nashville: Abingdon, 1961–1976), 607, Rolf Rendtorff, "Martin Noth and Tradition Criticism," in *The History of Israel's Traditions: The Heritage of Martin Noth*, Journal for the Study of the Old Testament Supplement Series 182, eds. Stephen McKenzie et al. (Sheffield: Sheffield University Press, 1994), 91–100, and the comprehensible introduction in James

Comparing the Incomparable: Reconsidering Lüling's Object of Research

As demonstrated in the last section, there exists a large variety of methods, some of them interdisciplinary, which are applicable to Lüling's specific object of research. Consequently, the object of research has to be examined and defined as precisely as possible in order to identify the most suitable method. Concerning the Qur'ān, Lüling postulates the existence of a pre-Islamic ground layer. However, in all his works dealing with the Qur'ān, he never defines the parts of the text that he examines exactly. In other words: he never limits his object of research to certain parts of the Qur'ānic text.[15] This makes it hard to identify an applicable method, especially due to the fact that the pertinent methods are generally limited to certain parts or units of text. To give an example, motive and tradition criticism can be employed as a tool to compare inherent motives both in Christian and Islamic tradition, but both methods rely on such compartmentalization of the analyzed corpora.

Even more surprising are the arguments of Lüling concerning the oldest texts that he postulates as forming the ground layer of the Qur'ān. If one examines all the editions of his works on Qur'ānic Studies beginning from the 1970 dissertation to the last English edition 2011 in light of the question of which primary texts of pre-Islamic Arabic strophic Hymnody Lüling examines, the answer is: None, they are "voluminous but lost".[16] Indeed, the current state of research concerning pre-Islamic Arabic Christian Hymnody reveals the same finding.[17]

In this perspective, Lüling's conclusion that "about one third of the present Koran text" originally consists of these pre-Islamic Arabic Christian texts without

---

Kugel, *Traditions of the Bible: A Guide to the Bible as it was at the start of the Common Era* (Cambridge: Harvard University Press, 1998), 1–42. For the Qur'ān see Heinrich Speyer, *Die biblischen Erzählungen im Qoran* (Gräfenhainichen: Schulze, 1931), Nadja Abott, *Studies in Arabic literary Papyri*, Vol. 1 (Chicago: University of Chicago Press, 1957), 1–60, and the recent Study by Viviane Comerro, *Les traditions sur la constitution du muṣḥaf de ʿUthmān*, Beiruter Texte und Studien 134 (Würzburg: Ergon, 2012). The arrangement of the Methods goes back to Christoph Dohmen, *Die Bibel und ihre Auslegung* (München: C. H. Beck, 1998), 58–61.

15 In fact, Lüling tries to verify his theses by analyzing just a few exemplary Surahs and Verses, while he states at the same time, that "about one third" of the Qur'ān consists of the aforementioned ground layer. See Kahle, *ZDMG* 132/1 (1982): 183, and Beltz, *ZRGG* 27/2 (1975): 170.

16 Lüling, *Challenge*, first and second ed., 8.

17 See e.g. Steigerwald, *JAOS* 124/3 (2004): 622–623.

having examined one of them is puzzling.[18] Lüling bridges this gap in his main thesis by using a *tertium comparationis*. Most interestingly, this *tertium comparationis* is not static in its diachronical perspective concerning the 40 years of his research on the Qur'ān. If we take a look at Lüling's dissertation from 1970, the message is clear. The texts he examines in order to analyze the Arabic Christian hymnodic ground layer of large passages of the Qur'ān are "Ethiopian Christian hymns of the sixth century".[19] Just a few years later in 1974, the object of his research becomes hardly recognizable. It is no more limited to a special corpus and even genre, but "a chain of tradition reaching from Old Egyptian, Old Testamentarian and Jewish, then Byzantine, Coptic, Syriac, (non-qur'ānic) Arabic and Ethiopic references to the late middle age Arabic strophic song *zağal*".[20]

This argumentation persisted for almost 30 years, until this chain of tradition was expanded by "pre-Islamic old Arabian" in 2003, for which he provides no further explanation in the book.[21] Finally, Lüling emphasizes the great importance of the aforementioned Ethiopic texts in relation with Coptic sources within this chain of tradition.[22] In summing up this metamorphosis regarding the use of the main primary texts, one could say that the *tertium comparationis* between the Christian-Arabic strophic texts and the Qur'ān consists of Ethiopian sources that represent a key part of a Middle Eastern literary tradition reaching from Early Antiquity to the Late Middle Ages.

Reasoning without References or References without Reasoning – Lülings *Tertium Comparationis*

As a rule, analyzing such broad, long-lasting streams of traditions is the work of generations of scholars, published over decades, if not centuries, in voluminous lexica. Of course, in some cases, specific objects of research can be analyzed within the stream of tradition, as demonstrated by the continuity of the topos of the great flood, reaching from the oldest parts of the Epic of Gilgamesh via

---

18 See Lüling, *Challenge*, first and second ed., 1, Lüling, *Ur-Qur'ān*, first and second ed., 1, and Lüling, *Untersuchung*, VII.
19 Ibid., VIIf.
20 Lüling, *Ur-Qur'ān*, first and second ed., 2.
21 Lüling, *Challenge*, first and second ed., 7–8.
22 See ibid., 8.

the Old Testament to the Qur'ān.[23] But in these and comparable cases, it is always one very distinct, describable object of research such as literary motives and topoi, which can be analyzed by the aforementioned methodologies.

The opposite is the case with Lüling's *tertium comparationis*. The only characteristics of the texts that he emphasizes are that they are Christian, strophic and hymnodic. There is no doubt that these structures can be well analyzed by methods of comparative form and genre criticism, as has been described above. But far more criteria are necessary for a scientific comparison of literary forms and genres. In the case of Biblical studies, relevant secondary literature defining the requirements for comparison concerning primary sources as well as methods, is vast. So which scientific primary and secondary sources are used by Lüling to prove his theory of a strophic-metric context between a supposed ground layer of the Qur'ān and Old Egyptian, Old Testamentarian, Jewish, Byzantine, Coptic, Syriac, old Arabic, (non-qur'ānic) Arabic and Ethiopic references to the late middle age Arabic strophic song *zağal?*

Examining all of Lüling's publications on Qur'ānic Studies between 1970 and 2011, one has to state that in the majority of the cases, there are no primary or secondary sources mentioned, and in the minority of the cases, Lüling refers mostly to only one source that is often one of his further publications.

Reasoning without References: The Post- and Prehistory of Koranic Strophe Poetry

Most interestingly, the author is at first glance not apprehensive towards problematizing this thesis of a milleniums-old form tradition in the main part of his book. He devotes a whole chapter "On the History of Koranic Strophe-Composition"[24] that even indicates methods of form and genre criticism in its German title in the editions of 1974 and 1993 ("Zur Formgeschichte des koranischen Strophenbaus").[25]

---

23 Even contextualizations within ancient Greek and Indian mythology seem to be plausible. See Speyer, *Erzählungen*, 89–116, Andrew George, *The Babylonian Gilgamesh Epic: Introduction, Critical Edition and Cuneiform Texts* (Oxford: Oxford University Press, 2003), 70, Philippe Wajdenbaum, *Argonauts of the Desert: Structural Analysis of the Hebrew Bible* (New York: Routledge, 2014), 104–108, and Thomas Trautmann, *Aryans and British India* (Berkeley: University of California Press, 1997), 58–59.

24 Lüling, *Challenge*, first and second ed., 174–191.

25 Lüling, *Ur-Qur'ān*, first and second ed., 139–161.

But in this section, Lüling generally writes that this core part of his thesis has "subordinate importance" and will be left to future research, although there is "no room for doubt that we consider the final verification of our koranic strophe-theory to be certain." But still, Lüling offers "some helpful hints as to the form-historical traditions in the chain of which the Koran's strophic poetry has its place."[26]

Lüling begins at the end of the chain of tradition that he himself presents, at the medieval Arabic strophic poetry *zağal*, treated in the subchapter "On the Post-History of the Koranic Strophe-Poetry".[27] In this chapter, he relies on Karl Voller's theory of the existence of an Arabic koiné in Arabia before and during the time of Muhammad, spoken by Mekkans and Medinans.[28] Because this language was popular Arabic without *iʿrāb*, he argues that there must have also existed a popular Arabic poetry.[29] Based on this assumption, he indicates another chain of literary tradition of Arabic poetry, reaching from pre-Islamic times to the Middle Ages and the *zağal*. As already mentioned, he grounds this chain with an unclear hypothetical origin and very few, only marginally relevant sources.

The connection between these nebulous beginnings and *zağal* lies in a millennium of darkness that is not enlightened by any reference to source material or secondary literature by the author. Instead, Lüling presents a lengthy explanation of the non-existence of these texts, their contextualization and interpretation:

> The reason is rather that this vernacular poetry was the particular medium on the internationally orientated Christians of central Arabia who were not at all interested in national classical Arabic – unless perhaps as a means for missionary activities. So when it became necessary religio-politically to deny the development of at least considerable parts of the Koran out of this pre-Islamic Christian vernacular strophic poetry, it seemed most effective to deny categorically the existence of such a vernacular poetry as a whole having existed in pre-Islamic times.

Apart from quoting few secondary sources on early and pre-Islamic Arabic strophic poetry, the author presents no further primary or secondary sources to explain the development of this genre, stretching from Late Antiquity to the Late Middle Ages. The only proof for these hypothetical findings is again the main

26 Lüling, *Challenge*, first and second ed., 174.
27 See ibid., 174–180.
28 Karl Vollers, *Volkssprache und Schriftsprache im alten Arabien* (Strasbourg: Trübner, 1907).
29 In this case, Lüling refers to Martin Hartmann, *Das arabische Strophengedicht I: Das Muwaššaḥ*, Semitistische Studien 13/14 (Weimar: Felber, 1897), 216–217. The source is problematic in this context, because Hartmann's analysis is limited to early Islamic times.

thesis of the author, which he, in a somewhat circular argumentation, intends to prove with these findings.

So if we return to the central issue of this article, the question of Lüling's methodology and his use of sources, we can deduce three main methodological approaches in Lüling's argumentation for his scholarly pronouncements. The first form can be described as pure speculation without any references. The second form is the derivation of arguments from very few, barely relevant or decontextualized citations from the secondary literature. And the last form is the provision of evidence for a speculative assertion via another speculative assertion, often both by Lüling himself.

The next chapter of this book is devoted to the origins of this chain of tradition ("On the Pre-History of the Koranic Strophe-Poetry"), where arguments for a continuity of oriental Christian strophic poetry reaching from Late Antique Syriac through Byzantine and onto Arabic traditions are presented.[30] The assumptions in this paragraph are again highly speculative, and the references to scientific literature do not verify this continuity. They are therefore in my opinion negligible, except for the case of the Ethiopic sources that will be treated by the end of this article.[31]

Millennia of Literary Tradition or References without Reasoning

After his attempts to analyze the proposed chain of literary tradition historically, Lüling aims at a structural and content-based analysis of the composition of the strophic ground layer of the "Ur-Qurʾān" in the following chapter. That is, quite appropriate to comparable research, subdivided into five chapters, dealing on the one hand with meter, composition, and rhyme, and on the other hand with performance and language of this poetry. These sections are subsumed under one main chapter with the title "Indirect Description of the Strophic Poetry contained in the pre-Islamic Koran".[32]

30 Lüling, *Challenge*, first and second ed., 180–184.
31 In fact, Lüling is compiling rather selectively works of different scholars and scientific disciplines to prove his line of thought of an old age of Christian strophe poetry reaching far into pre-Islamic times. These are in the most cases not relevant for the topic, including for example quotations without page reference (p. 180), generalizing single references (p. 180), quoting personal addresses (p. 184), and finally quoting his own further works (p. 182). See ibid., 180.
32 Ibid., 184–191.

In contradistinction to the way of scientific reasoning outlined above, the first three chapters dealing with meter, composition, and rhyme consist of a mere collage of direct citations, strung together by the author without any scientific assertion. The question as to why this part of the book is not substantiated in a scholarly fashion, given that it addresses core elements of thesis number one, remains unanswered.[33] Even the last sub-chapters dealing with "The Performance of Strophic Poetry" and "The Language of Strophic Poetry" once more consist of a mere compilation of references. Although the author comments on parts of the citations, they exhibit Lüling's paradigm of scientific reasoning. They are based on no or few questionable citations and sources, or on other, again hypothetical theses of the Author.[34]

Exemplifying Lüling's Study of Source Material: Ethiopian Hymns

After introducing the claim that the analysis of the chain of tradition proposed by Lüling is not verified scientifically in his works – neither by reference on primary texts, nor on respective methodological secondary literature – the focus is finally on the decisive link of this chain, Ethiopian hymns. In his dissertation 1970, these texts were the only *tertium comparationis*, or in other words, the missing link between the non-existent pre-Islamic Christian texts and the Qur'ān. In 2011, Lüling wrote:

> Today it stands beyond question that the rich Christian Ethiopian Hymnody of the early sixth century goes back in the main to Christian Coptic originals, sometimes corresponding word for word across hundreds of strophes, the sequence of which is neatly maintained. Frequent misunderstandings of the Coptic originals in the Ethiopic translations result without any possible doubt from typical misunderstandings of an ambiguous Arabic text minus its diacritical consonant-points and vowel-strokes. This indicates that these voluminous

33 Lüling explains this "indirect description" by clusters of citations "because a direct description before the reconstruction of all erstwhile Christian hymns hidden in the traditional Koran seems to us to be premature". See the Chapters "The Metre of Strophic Poetry" (185) "Composition and Strophe formation" (186–187) and "The Rhyme" (187) in Lüling, *Challenge*, first and second ed., 184–191. This argument is in my opinion questionable, in particular because these chapters are not part of Lüling's Dissertation from 1970, but have instead been inserted into the first edition of "Über den Ur-Qur'ān" four years later in 1974. These Chapters remained identical for all further editions of the book until 2011, including its quotations. No further results of research are considered. See Lüling, *Ur-Qur'ān*, first and second ed., 151–161.

34 Lüling, *Challenge*, first and second ed., 188–191.

> Ethiopic strophic texts of circa 500 CE which stem from Coptic sources must have passed through the central Arabian stage of a likewise voluminous but lost pre-Islamic Christian Arabic strophic Hymnody.[35]

Although the hypothesis of the literary chain of tradition was added to the "Ur-Qur'ān" 1974 and modified in the English edition of 2003, the core argument concerning the Ethiopian sources did not change over these four decades. For this reason, I analyzed all references to Ethiopic language, texts and hymns, taking the 2011 edition as a basis, and adding references from the editions of 2004, 1993, 1974 and 1970 when necessary. In the Edition of 2011, Ethiopic is mentioned 13 times in total, whereas ten of these passages deal with Ethiopian hymns.[36] Five of these parts are negligible, due to the fact that Lüling does not quote any sources. On the other five pages, where the author analyzes Ethiopic hymnody, several sources are quoted. Yet none of these sources are primary texts, and in none of the several German or English editions are such sources detectable in this context.

Analyzing Lüling's method, this is a crucial point in two accounts. First of all, he asserts that one third of the Qur'ān consisted originally of Christian Arabic strophic poetry, without examining primary sources, because they are "lost". Secondly, he argues that these Arabic texts were part of the aforementioned Middle Eastern literary tradition that presents Ethiopian Hymns as the key link in this chain. As a consequence, any imaginable method must rely at least on parts of primary Ethiopian texts.

But this is, in fact, not the case, and Lüling's five remaining quotations of secondary literature do also not always refer to relevant Ethiopic texts. The first quotation is for example not relevant in the scientific sense of the word, but should be mentioned for the sake of completeness: "The late Ethiopist and Islamicist Ernst Hammerschmidt, in a personal address classified our rediscovery of a voluminous pre-Islamic Christian strophe hymnody in the transmitted Koran as 'a revelation for all Ethiopists'."[37]

In the next passage, Lüling quotes the pertinent work of the German Semitist Anton Schall (1920–2007) on Ethiopic poetry.[38] But on the respective page of Schall's book, we find a discussion of the word "Tabor" in Ethiopic hymns,

35 Ibid., 8.
36 See ibid., 545.
37 Ibid., 184.
38 Ibid., 236.

which is not relevant for our inquiry.[39] The third passage deals with the age of the Ethiopian hymnodic poetry. In order to fit into Lüling's theory, it must be older than the Qur'ān. So Lüling quotes an article of the Swedish orientalist Oscar Löfgren (1889–1992), where the author states that "there is no doubt that the Arabic Gospel of John is the Model of the Ethiopian Ta'âmera lyasûs."[40]

At this point, we have the first direct reference to an Ethiopian text. But this quote does not make any statement about the structure, content, and genre of the primary source. Furthermore, it is not explained what this text dealing with the miracles of Christ, said to be an adaption of an Arabic translation of the New Testament, has to do with the Qur'ān. Finally, the translation from Arabic into Ethiopian must, according to Löfgren, have happened later than in the eighth century, and therefore cannot be contextualized with Lüling's pre-Islamic ground layer of the Qur'ān. Lüling doubts this age dating, referring to "questionable" arguments in another publication of Löfgren.[41] He does not, however, explicitly state these arguments or give any further justification of his doubts, be it by analytic reasoning or having recourse to research.

The next author that Lüling quotes in order to prove the old age of the Ethiopian hymns, is the German Orientalist and Semitist Carl Brockelmann (1868–1956).[42] But even though the quoted book is an old, and still a standard reference for Syriac and Christian-Arabic Literature, it is not in the case of Ethiopic literature, even at the time of its publication. In this note, we find vague Information that "some poetry of Jakob of Serûg (Syrian Bishop of Edessa around 500 CE) has come by procurement of the Arabs to the Ethiopians".[43] This source does not provide information regarding the content, structure, age and authorship of the aforementioned Ethiopian texts, which would be essential for a valid scientific analysis.

---

39 Anton Schall, *Zur äthiopischen Verskunst: eine Studie über die Metra des Qenē auf Grund der Abhandlung "al-Qenē laun min aš-ši ʿr al-ḥabašī von Murad Kamil"* (Wiesbaden: F. Steiner, 1961), 165.

40 Oscar Löfgren, "Ergänzendes zum apokryphen Johannesevangelium," *Orientalia Suecana* 10 (1961): 139–144, 140–141.

41 Oscar Löfgren, "Zur Charakteristik des apokryphen Johannesevangelium," *Orientalia Suecana* 9 (1960): 107–130.

42 See Lüling, *Challenge*, first and second ed., 183.

43 Carl Brockelmann, "Geschichte der syrischen und christlich-arabischen Literatur," in *Geschichte der christlichen Litteraturen des Orients*, Die Litteraturen des Ostens in Einzeldarstellungen 7, eds. Carl Brockelmann et al. (Leipzig: Amelang, 1907), 1–74, 26.

Weddāsē Māryām – The Ethiopic Key Texts for Understanding the Ur-Qur'ān?

If we summarize the examination of sources concerning Lüling's thesis, there is only one secondary source left to be analyzed, and this is the work of the Austrian Arabist and Semitist Adolf Grohmann (1887–1977) on the topic of special Ethiopic hymns devoted to Mary, the mother of Christ, published in 1919.[44] I want to emphasize at this point, that this source is already the main source in Lüling's dissertation in 1970, where he writes only of the Ethiopian texts as *tertium comparationis*, but not of the millenia-old near eastern literary tradition.

Moreover, in a period of more than forty years, in all editions of Lüling's work on the Qur'ān, Grohmann is the only author Lüling relied upon directly concerning his theory of the Ethiopic hymns as *tertium comparationis* to the Ur-Qur'ān. But still in 2011, Lüling wrote: "About the essential body of this old Ethiopian hymnody, – which is said to have been composed in the main by the famous priest Yârêd (first quarter of the sixth century) –, there is absolutely no doubt that it was translated into Ethiopian from Arabic copies, which once again can be traced back to the Coptic originals."[45]

At this point, Lüling quotes Grohmann's book "Äthiopische Marienhymnen", published in 1919, where Grohmann deals with the *Weddāsē Māryām*, which are undoubtedly Ethiopic hymns. But they are no more than a part, and not "the essential body" of old Ethiopian hymnody, and cannot be regarded as representative for the entire genre. Furthermore, Lüling presents a scientifically verified transmission history of the Ethiopian texts going back to Arabic and finally to Coptic sources, whereas Grohmann writes differently about a "translation of those seven hymns for the days of the week, that *may* [emphasis mine] have been the original text of the Coptic Theotokians.(..) The translation was *probably* [emphasis mine] made from Arabic."[46]

In fact, Grohmann even discusses the transmission history of the texts on that very page. He quotes Karl Fries, the author of the most important individual study on *Weddāsē Māryām* at that time, who advocated for a translation from Coptic, and not from Arabic, [47] and contrasts that with the opposite opinion

---

44 Adolf Grohmann, *Äthiopische Marienhymnen* (Leipzig: Teubner, 1919).

45 See Lüling, *Challenge*, first and second ed., 183.

46 Grohmann, *Marienhymnen*, 10. Compare also the reviews of Grohmann's Book by A. Walther, *Orientalistische Literaturzeitung* (OLZ) 25 (1922): 444–445, and Hugo Duensing, *Theologische Literaturzeitung* 47 (1922): 197–198, who do not support Lüling's assumptions.

47 Karl Fries, *Weddase Marjam. Ein äthiopischer Lobgesang an Maria* (Leipzig: G. Fock, 1892), 5.

of the German Orientalist Enno Littmann (1875–1958) in his standard work on the genre, "Geschichte der äthiopischen Literatur."[48] However, the most important point in this regard is found one page later, where Grohmann examines the age of the text. Contrary to Lüling's assumptions, Grohmann argues that, if the text was translated from Arabic, this must have happened "not before the ninth or 10th Century, but probably much later".[49] So how can Lüling argue against the findings of Grohmann while quoting his work as evidence for an earlier dating? This is only possible, because he links the texts to the "famous priest Yârêd", who – according to Lüling – is alleged to have lived in the sixth century.[50] Once again, Grohmann is quoted to underscore his argument, but as in the previous case, Grohmann quite contrarily offers a broad discussion of authorship, spanning from an early dating to the possibility that Yârêd was not even a historical figure at all.[51]

Lüling's final argument may be a good example for the way he construes his hypotheses and employs the relevant methods. Concerning the main issue discussed in this article, namely the thesis that one third of the Qurʾān consisted originally of lost Christian Arabic strophic poetry that is nevertheless part of a Middle Eastern literary tradition reaching from Early Antiquity to the Late Middle Ages (whereby the most important part and therefore *tertium comparationis* in this respect are Ethiopian hymns), Lüling concludes: "The hymnody of the pre-Islamic Koran rediscovered by means of a critical exegesis is uncontestable evidence for the soundness of the old Ethiopian tradition about the early origin of this Hymnody".[52]

The way Lüling describes and analyses the hymnody of the pre-Islamic ground layer, as well as scientific reasoning concerning "uncontestable" evidence, has already been discussed in this article. In conclusion, we should take a look at the source Lüling uses to underpin these assumptions. It is once again Grohmann, who compares the *Weddāsē Māryām* with another liturgical Ethiopic text, the *Weddāsē wa-Genāy*. He discusses the authorship on the

---

48 See Enno Littmann, "Geschichte der äthiopischen Literatur," in *Geschichte der christlichen Litteraturen des Orients*, Die Litteraturen des Ostens in Einzeldarstellungen 7, eds. Carl Brockelmann et al. (Leipzig: Amelang, 1907), 185–270, 205. For newer Research on the topic see Uwe-Karsten Plisch, "Zur Bedeutung der koptischen Übersetzungen für Textkritik und Verständnis des Neuen Testaments," in *Recent developments in textual criticism: new testament, other early Christian and Jewish literature*, eds. Wim Weren et al. (Assen: Gorcum, 2003), 95–108.
49 Grohmann, *Marienhymnen*, 11–12.
50 Lüling, *Challenge*, first and second ed., 183.
51 Grohmann, *Marienhymnen*, 11–12 and 22–23.
52 Lüling, *Challenge*, first and second ed., 184.

given page, but without indicating a final conclusion.[53] In the respective footnote, Lüling does not offer any further argument or reference besides this barely relevant quotation.[54]

Reinventing Qur'ānic Studies offside the academic discourse – a methodological conclusion

These kinds of expansive, but merely hypothetical assertions, in most cases no more than partially verified by one or a few quotes, can be seen as paradigmatic for the entire methodical approach of Lüling. This article has demonstrated that this trend applies most particularly to his use of source material and general methodology concerning his first thesis. To sum up the results of this examination briefly, Lüling proposes a Qur'ānic ground layer, consisting of pre-Islamic "erstwhile" Christian Arabic strophic hymnodic texts. These texts are 200 years older than Islam, and they have vanished, primarily because they fell victim to dogmatic Islamic censorship. But this poetry is part of a thousand-year-old Middle Eastern literary tradition, in which Ethiopic hymns feature prominently. Most importantly, the *Weddāsē Māryām* functions as the key link and tertium comparationis in this chain. They enable the researcher to reconstruct this Christian Arabic pre-Islamic ground layer of the Qur'ān.

All of these assertions are not verified by scientific evidence, neither by research on source material nor by referring to the pertinent secondary literature. In addition, Lüling did not consider the research progress that occurred over the span of nearly four decades in his last publication of 2011. If he does indeed quote the respective literature, the sources are on average more than 25 years old, and the few secondary sources he uses for the core arguments of his thesis of the Ethiopian texts as *tertium comparationis* all date back at least to the 1920's. This inobservance of the established field of Qur'ānic Studies, as well as other related disciplines, might have been a reaction to the marginality (and marginalization) of Lüling within and by German academia. So apart from the reproach of methodological revisionism, I would rather consider Lüling's approach as an attempt to reinvent Qur'ānic research.

53 Grohmann, *Marienhymnen*, 22.
54 Lüling, *Challenge*, first and second ed., 184.

Lüling was a Protestant theologian as well as an Arabist, and one might suppose that he did have recourse to the relevant literature and theory of both disciplines. But just the opposite was the case: Although the research in this regard, especially in Protestant theology, was extensive during the four decades of Lüling's scholarly life, his reception of these approaches was, however, marginal.

Finally, if one considers the current state of research, it does not support Lüling's approach. To this day, there are no texts available that can be verified as pre-Islamic Christian-Arabic strophic hymnody in the way Lüling imagined them. Furthermore, there are not enough contemporary and in particular pre-Islamic Arabic texts, that point to Lüling's proposed origins of the Qurʾānic text, neither concerning its content nor matters of form and genre. The literary tradition of strophe-metric poetry proposed by Lüling is constructed via the collection, compilation and citation of secondary literature. However, Lüling rarely discusses such material by commenting on established cited sources.

Especially with regard to the epistemological interest of verifying a Christian ground layer of the Qurʾān, this approach did not become, to my knowledge, the object of further research. The same applies to the Ethiopic texts that play a crucial role in Lülings first thesis. Few works on *Weddāsē Māryām* have been published up to the present day, none of them treating issues of Qurʾānic Studies.[55]

Nevertheless, Lüling did, in my eyes, pose many legitimate questions concerning the possible origins of parts of the Qurʾānic text. Unfortunately, they were not accompanied by scientifically satisfying answers. There is no doubt that the religious ideas of Jewish, Christian, Jewish-Christian, and other religious groups of Late Antiquity have had great influence on the Qurʾān. It is up to future research to find new texts and ways to analyze them, even though the epistemological interest in uncovering an "Ur-Qurʾān"-text does not seem to be realistic due to the present state of research.

---

55 Concerning references to secondary literature see Walther W. Müller, "Lobpreis Marias," in *Marienlexicon*, ed. Remigius Bäumer et al., Vol. 4 (St. Ottilien: EOS-Verlag, 1993), 137–138, Friedrich Heyer, *Die Kirche Äthiopiens: eine Bestandsaufnahme*, Theologische Bibliothek Töpelmann 22 (Berlin: De Gruyter, 1971), 90–98, and Walther W. Müller, "Weddase Maryam," in *Kindlers Neues Literatur Lexikon*, ed. Walter Jens, Vol. 19 (München: Kindler, 1992), 777–778.

Holger Zellentin

Q 96 *Sūrat al-ʿAlaq* Between Philology and Polemics: A (Very) Critical Assessment of Günter Lüling's Ur-Qurʾān

Günter Lüling fits the description of an intellectual hero. He trod on despite severe criticism, without support within the academy, and perhaps most painfully of all, in the face of being simply ignored by so many of his contemporaries. Such heroism can be essential to advance a field, yet it can be also, or even equally, the result of obstinacy, of hurt pride, or of tragic misunderstandings. The organizer of the symposium and editor of the present volume must be thanked for recognizing how important it is to celebrate the learning, the creativeness, and the fearlessness of one of our late colleagues, at the same as seeking to bring clarity regarding the possible value of Lüling's propositions.[1]

The writing of this article has been made possible with the generous support of the Philip Leverhulme foundation. My gratitude to Devin Stewart, who read an earlier draft of this paper, for his important comments and corrections.

1 A good example of the importance of persistence in the face of excruciating criticism may be a case in the sciences, namely that of Dan Shechtman. Despite being accused of having misunderstood the basics of physics after claiming the existence of so-called "quasicrystals" in 1981, Shechtman continued his work over years before being vindicated by a number of international awards, culminating in a Nobel Prize in 2011. There are, however, three important differences between Schechtman and Lüling. The former recognized that he must work in a team and published his findings collaboratively, whereas the latter worked almost exclusively on his own. Schechtman, moreover, completed his PhD and worked in the academy for a decade before advancing his revolutionary concept, whereas Lüling's unsuccessful revolution began with his PhD. While the first difference may indict the habits of the humanities more generally and the second one may contain but a cautionary tale, the third difference proves the most consequential. Schechtman defended a new finding with established and recognized methods, whereas Lüling tended to adopt methods to fit the needs of defending a construct largely conjured by intuition, as I will seek to establish in the following. While the fields of Shechtman and Lüling, physics and Islamic studies, diverge, the insights offered by both cases are transferable, and may even offer an unexpected disciplinary overlap in its material culture: it was mathematically sophisticated quasi-regular mosaic patterns known throughout the medieval Islamic world that reportedly led physicist to appreciate the design of quasicrystals in the first place, see Peter J. Lu and Paul J. Steinhardt, "Decagonal and Quasi-crystalline Tilings in Medieval Islamic Architecture," *Science* 315 (2007): 1106–1110; and Dan Shechtman et al., "Metallic Phase with Long-Range Orientational Order and No Translational Symmetry," *Physical Review Letters* 53 (1984): 1951–1953.

https://doi.org/10.1515/9783110599176-010

Scholarly clarity can be painful to establish in case of far-reaching criticism of the sorts in which I am about to engage. In general, I believe that intellectual charity is the best initial guide to appreciate any scholar's work, and I will introduce this contribution by establishing a few positive aspects of Lüling's methods. Exceptional circumstances, however, can necessitate the curtailment of indulgences, and I believe that the state of the field of Qur'ānic studies dictates a more forceful response than my comfort level (and my fear of chickens coming home to roost) would normally allow. The past ten or fifteen years have seen a burgeoning of scholarship in our field. We are, however, still in the midst of a precarious phase in our attempt to establish Qur'ānic studies as an independent subject both within Islamic studies and within the humanities more broadly. The work towards a scholarly consensus on basic questions of the Qur'ān's milieu and provenance is well underway, yet far from complete. I will thus not hesitate to dismiss the main ideas put forward by Dr. Lüling almost in their entirety, and invite scholars as well as the broader public to spend their energy on more mature approaches.

In short, in my view as well as in Lüling's, the Qur'ān participates in a late ancient discourse informed by formal and ideological features we can reconstruct with the help of previous texts. Lüling, however, reduced the Qur'ān to a hypothetical "Ur- Qur'ān" somewhere behind the extant text and allegedly reconstructible with the help of the methods of formal criticism and historical theology that was *en vogue* in biblical studies of his time. Egregiously, he limited his interest mainly to this elusive poetic document, positing that it should conform in all ways to his understanding of some form of Jesus' true (i.e. Jewish) Christianity, the half millennium of intellectual history in between Jesus and Muhammad notwithstanding. Instead, he posited that the discrepancies between his Ur-Qur'ān and the extant Qur'ān all stem from the posited textual falsification of the former by the hands of its early Muslim audience – a sort of inverted *taḥrīf* argument that turns the accusation of textual falsification not only against Muslims but even against the document in which we first find this concept in its Arabic iteration.[2] In my view, by contrast, the Qur'ān *responds* to previous discourses and appropriates them with literary integrity and ideological independence, covering a full spectrum of responsive modes ranging from the appreciative to the polemical. Pertinent previous discourses, moreover, should not be limited to Christian or "Jewish-Christian" traditions, as Lüling effectively did. In-

---

2 On the late antique context of the accusation of scriptural falsification see e.g. Gabriel Said Reynolds, "On the Qur'ānic Accusation of Scriptural Falsification (*taḥrīf*) and Christian anti-Jewish Polemic," *Journal of the American Oriental Society* 130 (2010): 189–202.

stead, in addition to addressing its primary pagan audience, we should realize that the Qur'ān is engaged in a well-informed trialogue with both Christians and Jews, all the while translating their Aramaic traditions into a worldview informed by a uniquely Arabic and Arabian perspective.[3]

In the following, I will begin with a brief survey of the genuine value that marks many of the aspects of Lüling's methodology, and raise the question why there is such a stark discrepancy between his potential and his eventual results. In a second part I will then discuss the example of Lüling's formal analysis and "reconstruction" of Qur'ān Q 96 *Sūrat al-ʿAlaq* in order to illustrate how effectively his methodology of reconstructing a putative original text can be debunked. This part will illustrate how Lüling reconstructs one line of this specific Qur'ānic text, namely verse 15, based on his highly selective and idiosyncratic reading of the rules of Arabic poetry. (He suppresses verse 16 as a later addition to the text.) The final third part of this contribution will consider Lüling's contextualization of his rewritten verse 15 in an equally idiosyncratic and selective cultural context of Late Antique religiosity in general. I suggest that the chosen example is symptomatic for his work as a whole, offering an alternative approach to the same Qur'ānic passage in which I will broaden the methodological inquiry to include Qur'ānic, Christian, and Jewish materials ignored by Lüling. It is my overall thesis that the form of the Qur'ān as it is traditionally read, i.e. the extant *muṣḥaf*, is much more closely related to the mainstream Jewish and Christian tradition as we know them than Lüling's reconstructions. There is then less need, and more importantly less reliable data, for any reconstruction of the Qur'ān if one only contextualizes it properly.

1 Günter Lüling's Inheritance: A Qualified Disclaimer

The extent to which Lüling's methodology pre-empted important developments in the field stands in tragic contrast to the dismissive ways in which his work is widely (and, in my view, justly) treated. Lüling, to begin with, avoided the cardinal sin of many of his orientalist or traditional predecessors: the cheap psycho-

3 On the Qur'ān's engagement of the Jewish and Christian tradition see now Holger Zellentin, "Trialogical Anthropology: The Qur'ān on Adam and Iblis in View of Rabbinic and Christian Discourse," in *The Quest for Humanity – Contemporary Approaches to Human Dignity in the Context of the Qur'ānic Anthropology* eds. Rüdiger Braun and Hüseyin Çiçek (Newcastle upon Tyne: Cambridge Scholars Publishing, 2017), 54–125.

logical, or respectively overly pious, focus on the figure of Muhammad, usually bolstered by an uncritical reliance on the *sīra* literature. Instead, Lüling offered a reading focused on the Qur'ān's text as our primary evidence, pre-empting the "Qur'ānist" approach that has become ever more popular.[4] Lüling equally recognized the importance of pre-Islamic Arabic poetry for the understanding of the Qur'ān, a trajectory which has in the meantime been further explored by Angelika Neuwirth and Nicolai Sinai.[5] Lüling's focus on the rhyme scheme and poetic structures in the Qur'ān was contemporary to the groundbreaking work by Friedrun Müller; apart from the ongoing contributions by Devin Stewart, Neuwirth, and Sinai, the topic has not found its true recognition to this day.[6] Perhaps most importantly, Lüling saw the importance of the Qur'ān's polemics against Christianity, but sadly not so much of Syriac Christianity, a theme that has gained dramatic insights in the recent work of Gabriel Reynolds, Joseph Witztum, and Sidney Griffith.[7] Lüling's evocation of pre-Qur'ānic Arabic Christian literature, however, finds at least a partial parallel in Griffith's own persuasive suggestion that parts of the Bible circulated orally in Arabic before the rise of Islam, and a

---

4 The volumes edited by Gabriel Reynolds and Angelika Neuwirth remain exemplary for the new directions in Qur'ānic studies, see Gabriel Said Reynolds, *New Perspectives on the Qur'ān: The Qur'ān in Its Historical Context 2* (Abingdon: Routledge, 2011); Angelika Neuwirth, Michael Marx and Nicolai Sinai, eds., *The Qur'ān in Context: Historical and Literary Investigations into the Qur'ānic Milieu* (Brill: Leiden, 2010); and Gabriel Said Reynolds, ed., *The Qur'ān in its Historical Context* (London: Routledge, 2008).

5 See for example Angelika Neuwirth, *Der Koran. Band 1: Frühmekkanische Suren* (Berlin: Verlag der Weltreligionen, 2011); Nicolai Sinai, "Religious Poetry from the Qur'ānic Milieu: Umayya b. Abī ṣ-Ṣalt on the Fate of the Thamūd," *Bulletin of the School of Oriental and African Studies* 74 (2011): 397–416; and Angelika Neuwirth, *Der Koran als Text der Spätantike. Ein europäischer Zugang* (Berlin: Insel Verlag, 2010); see also eadem, *Studien zur Komposition der mekkanischen Suren. Studien zur Sprache, Geschichte und Kultur des islamischen Orients* 10 (Berlin: Walter de Gruyter, 1981), see also the previous note.

6 See e.g. Devin Stewart, "Rhymed Prose," in Jane Dammen McAuliffe, *Encyclopaedia of the Qur'ān* (2015: online resource); idem, "*Saj*ʿ in the Qur'ān: Prosody and Structure," *Journal of Arabic Literature* 21 (1990): 101–39; and Friedrun R. Müller, *Untersuchungen zur Reimprosa im Koran* (Bonn: Selbstverlag des Orientalischen Seminars der Universität Bonn, 1969).

7 See e.g. Sidney H. Griffith, "Christian Lore and the Arabic Qur'ān: The 'Companions of the Cave' in *Sūrat al-Kahf* and in Syriac Christian Tradition," in *New Perspectives on the Qur'ān*, ed. Reynolds, 109–137; Joseph Witztum, *The Syriac Milieu of the Quran: The Recasting of Biblical Narratives* (PhD Dissertation, Princeton, NJ, 2011); Gabriel Said Reynolds, *The Qur'ān and its Biblical Subtext* (London: Routledge, 2010); and Sidney H. Griffith "Syriacisms in the 'Arabic Qur'ān': Who were those who said 'Allāh is third of three' according to al-Mā'ida 73?" in *A Word Fitly Spoken: Studies in Mediaeval Exegesis of the Hebrew Bible and the Qur'ān, Presented to Haggai Ben-Shammai*, ed. Meir M. Bar-Asher (Jerusalem: The Ben Zvi Institute, 2007), 83*–110*.

fuller one in Robert Hoyland's equally plausible hypothesis of the existence of written pre-Islamic Christian Arabic texts.[8] Lastly, much of Lüling's research is predicated on the idea that Islam, or at least the original version of the Qurʾān, offers us the last glimpse of "primitive" Jewish Christianity. The importance of Judaeo-Christian legal culture for an understanding of the Qurʾān is at the very centre of my own published work; the topic has also recently been pushed forward rather forcefully by Patricia Crone.[9]

More specifically, Lüling understood the use of the term *shirk* as a charge not of crude polytheism, but of what John of Damascus described as "heterism," of associating another being with God. This idea was much more fully developed by Gerald Hawting and Patricia Crone; it is in the view of many one of the keys to the Qurʾān's late Meccan and Medinan engagement with Christianity and Judaism.[10] Lüling's other real contribution may be the emphasis on the precarious-

---

8 See Sidney H. Griffith, *The Bible in Arabic: the Scriptures of the People of the Book* (Princeton: Princeton University Press, 2013); and Robert Hoyland, "Mount Nebo, Jabal Ramm, and the Status of Christian Palestinian Aramaic and Old Arabic in Late Roman Palestine and Arabia," *The Development of Arabic as a Written Language.* Papers from the Special Session of the Seminar for Arabian Studies held on 24 July, 2009. Proceedings of the Seminar for Arabian Studies Vol. 40, Supplement (Oxford: Archaeopress, 2010), 29–45.

9 In my own work I conceptualize Judaeo-Christian legal culture as a discourse within mainstream Syriac Christianity, and focus on its iterations in the fifth through the seventh centuries C.E., see Holger Zellentin, "Judaeo-Christian Legal Culture and the Qurʾān: The Case of Ritual Slaughter and the Consumption of Animal Blood," in *Jewish Christianity and the Origins of Islam* ed. Francisco del Río Sánchez (Turnhout: Brepols, 2018), 117–159; and idem, *The Qur'ān's Legal Culture: The Didascalia Apostolorum as a Point of Departure* (Tübingen: Mohr Siebeck, 2013). Patricia Crone argued for a more robust sense of an independent Jewish-Christian community, relying on inferential arguments from a broad number of topics, see eadem, "Jewish Christianity and the Qur'ān (Part Two)," *Journal of Near Eastern Studies* 75 (2016): 1–21; and eadem, "Jewish Christianity and the Qurʾān (Part One)," *Journal of Near Eastern Studies* 74 (2015): 225–253. See also note 18 below.

10 The useful expression coined, to the best of my knowledge, by John of Damascus, "heterists" (ἑταιριαστάς, *De Haeresibus* 100.60, cited according to P. Bonifatius Kotter, *Die Schriften des Johannes von Damaskos. Patristische Texte und Studien* 22 (Berlin: De Gruyter, 1981), vol. 4, ad. loc.) and describing Christian "associators," has regrettably been eclipsed in our language by the anthropological term for primitive promiscuity, "heterism," which derives from the same root. On "associationism" and "associators" see Gerald Hawting, *The Idea of Idolatry and the Emergence of Islam: From Polemic to History* (Cambridge: Cambridge University Press, 1999), e.g. 84 on John's term; see also Gerald Hawting, "Idolatry and Idolaters," in *Encyclopaedia of the Qurʾān*, ed. Jane Dammen McAuliffe. Missing here is Patricia Crone, "The Quranic *Mushrikūn* and the Resurrection (Part II)," *Bulletin of the School of Oriental and African Studies* 76 (2013): 1–20; *eadem*, "The Quranic *Mushrikūn* and the Resurrection (Part I)," *Bulletin of the School of Oriental and African Studies* 75 (2012): 445–72; and *eadem*, "The Religion of the Qurʾānic Paness of the early and especially pre-ʿUthmānic transmission history of the Qurʾān, and the possibility of error in the vocal or even consonantal interpretation of the unmarked (a.k.a. "skeletal") writing of the earliest Qurʾānic manuscripts, the *rasm* text. This aspect also informs the insistence of Christoph Luxenberg on an imaginary and allegedly reconstructible *Syriac* (i.e. Christian Aramaic) lectionary before, or better, at the real basis of the Qurʾān. Luxenberg's argument parallels to that of Lüling, yet pushes the idea of an "Ur-Qurʾān" beyond the linguistic barrier of the Arabic language. While Luxenberg's work has been dismissed as forcefully (and as rightly) as that of Lüling, there remain a few – indeed very few – adherents of the idea of accessing an earlier form of the Arabic Qurʾān that prove more philology sound than either Lüling or Luxenberg.[11] Among them we can for example count Munther Younes, who shares with Lüling the rather irrefutable idea that the Qurʾān offers quite a few grammatical difficulties.[12] Thus, as Sidney Griffith summarizes in the context of the present volume, Lüling already in the 1970s clearly tried to see the Qurʾān in its late Antique context, which puts him far ahead of his time.[13] In a sense, we have to admit that even if their ideas prove untenable, the field has been pushed into gear by people such as Lüling and Luxenberg.

---

gans: God and the Lesser Deities," *Arabica* 57 (2010): 151–200. Hartmut Bobzin, "Martin Werner und Albert Schweitzer und ihre Bedeutung für die Arbeiten von Günter Lüling," 23–32 in the current volume.

11 For criticism of Luxenberg see e.g. Walid Saleh, "The Etymological Fallacy and Qur'anic Studies: Muhammad, Paradise, and Late Antiquity," in *The Qurʾān in Context: Historical and Literary Investigations into the Qurʾānic Milieu*, eds. Michael Marx et al., 649–698 and, unfortunately *ad hominem*, François de Blois, "Review of 'Christoph Luxenberg, *Die syro-aramäische Lesart des Koran: Ein Beitrag zur Entschlüsselung der Koransprache*,'" *Journal of Qur'anic Studies* 5 (2003): 92–97; one of the notable exceptions to a wholesale dismissal of Luxenberg is Cornelia B. Horn, whose contribution in the present volume is also one of the most charitable ones towards Lüling, see eadem and Robert R. Phenix Jr. "Review of "Christoph Luxenberg, *Die syro-aramäische Lesart des Koran: Ein Beitrag zur Entschlüsselung der Koransprache*," *Hugoye: Journal of Syriac Studies* 6 (2003) and eadem, "Hermeneutische Dimensionen der Intertextualität und Interreligiöse Kontexte des Korans," 111–128 in the current volume. For Luxenberg's own publications see idem, *The Syro-Aramaic Reading of the Koran*, 2nd edition (Berlin: Hans Schiler, 2007); translation of *Die syro-aramäische Lesart des Koran: Ein Beitrag zur Entschlüsselung der Koransprache* (Berlin: Hans Schiler, 2000).

12 See Munther Younes, "Blessing, Clinging, Familiarity, Custom – or Ship? A New Reading of the Word *Īlāf* in Q 106," *Journal of Semitic Studies* 62 (2017): 181–189; and idem, "Angels, Stars, Death, the soul, horses, bows – or Women? The opening verses of Qur'ān 79," in *New Perspectives on the Qurʾān*, ed. Reynolds, 264–278.

13 Sidney Griffith, "Late Antique Christology in Qurʾānic Perspective," 33–68 in the current volume.

If Lüling has to be credited in so many instances with having his finger on the pulse of time, or rather twenty years ahead of his time, why then were his readings so disastrously unhinged? First of all, it has to be pointed out that nearly all the abovementioned enduring insights and impulses that Lüling channelled were widely available in the 1970s, and can in many cases be traced back to the foundational work by figures such as Theodor Nöldeke, Julius Wellhausen, Tor Andrae, and even Hans-Joachim Schoeps.[14] Thus, Lüling stood on firm ground in so far as we should follow his lead. When it comes to his true innovations, it seems that his theses were driven by a theological agenda rather than by historical inquiry. For once, while Lüling was reasonably well-read in Christianity, he hardly considers the Jewish context of the Qurʾān more than incidentally.[15] I will seek to illustrate the extent to which his dismissal of the Jewish record, hardly excusable in light of readily available studies such as those of Abraham Geiger and Heinrich Speyer, deprived Lüling of crucial comparative data.[16] More fundamentally, Lüling understood the difference between the Qurʾān and those Christian sources and ideas he did consider squarely to be the result of an editing hand intervening *after* the Qurʾān's fixation as a *rasm* text. He then dedicated much of his considerable creativity and intelligence to proving what he had posited. It seems that it never occurred to him that the differences between the Qurʾān and Christianity may be the result of the fact that the Qurʾān may simply not be, and never have been, a Christian text. More specifically, Lüling did not consider how pervasively the Qurʾān, as an explicitly anti-Christological text, points to the vast chasm between its own views on Christ and that of the Christians of its time. Lüling, in other words, did not even come close to appreciating

14 See for example Hans Joachim Schoeps, *Geschichte und Theologie des Judenchristentums* (Tübingen: Mohr Siebeck, 1949); Tor Andrae, *Der Ursprung des Islams und das Christentum* (Uppsala: Almqvist & Wiksells, 1926); Julius Wellhausen, *Reste arabischen Heidentums, gesammelt und erläutert von J. Wellhausen* (Berlin: Georg Reimer, 1897); and Theodor Nöldeke, *Geschichte des Qorâns* (Göttingen: Verlag der Dieterichschen Buchhandlung, 1860); the latest edition of this fundamental study has now been translated, see idem, Friedrich Schwally, Gotthelf Bergsträßer and Otto Pretzl, *The History of the Qurʾān, Edited and Translated by Wolfgang H. Behn* (Leiden: Brill, 2013).

15 Lüling explicates his view that Jews hardly mattered for the Qurʾān's (Meccan) prophet, claiming that "[d]ie mekkanischen Gegner des Propheten in der Hauptsache Christen waren, und zwar trinitarische Christen, die der Prophet im Gefolge judenchristlicher Tradition wegen dieser Trinitätslehre als Polytheisten bekämpfte," see idem, *Der christliche Kult an der vorislamischen Kaaba als Problem der Islamwissenschaft und christlichen Theologie* (Erlangen: H. Lüling, 1977), 41.

16 See Heinrich Speyer, *Die Biblischen Erzählungen im Qoran* (Gräfenhainischen: Schulze, 1931); and Abraham Geiger, *Was hat Mohammed aus dem Judenthume aufgenommen?* (Bonn: Baaden, 1833).

what Griffith so aptly calls the Qurʾān's "polemical corrective" of Judaism and Christianity.[17] Instead of analysing the Qurʾān's own voice, which is what I would consider the basic task of the scholar, Lüling offered us the theology of an "Ur- Qurʾān" that unsurprisingly inclines towards "Jewish Christianity" as he understood it, relying rather eclectically on marginal scholarship of his time.[18] As various contributions to this volume point out, Lüling uses philology

17 See e.g. Griffith, *The Bible in Arabic*, 23 and esp. 27. Especially, but not exclusively in the Medinan surahs, the Qurʾān repeats previous Jewish and Christian traditions with a difference, and generates meaning for an audience that is familiar with previous iterations of a tradition and capable of grasping the significance of the often subtle differences between the known, previous version and the slightly different new one. It functions thus in a parallel way to the radical reinvention of tradition we see for example in the Babylonian Talmud, but, unlike rabbinic literature, the Qurʾān does not usually value the playful or even humorous ways of dealing with the audience's expectations we find in the Talmud. Moreover, while the Talmud shows clear awareness of the intellectual development of tradition and lauds limited human participation in this process, the Qurʾān constructs its innovations fully in terms of a return to the true origins and polemicizes against any human intervention. Disregarding the intellectual history of both the Jewish and the nascent Islamic tradition, Lüling obliterates the differences between the Qurʾān and the Christian tradition as he imagines it, an action tantamount to the effective obliteration of the Qurʾān as a meaningful document of any literary or intellectual integrity. On the Talmud's use of the past see for example Moulie Vidas, *Tradition and the Formation of the Talmud* (Princeton: Princeton University Press, 2014) and Holger Zellentin, *Rabbinic Parodies of Jewish and Christian Literature* (Tübingen: Mohr Siebeck, 2010).

18 Lüling simply posits that "pre-Islamic Arabian Christianity, as far as dogma is concerned, had an archaic Jewish-Christian or quasi-Arianic character" (see Günter Lüling, *A Challenge to Islam for Reformation: The Rediscovery and Reliable Reconstruction of a Comprehensive Pre-Islamic Christian Hymnal Hidden in the Koran under Earliest Islamic Reinterpretations* (Delhi: Motilal Barnasidass Publishers, 2003), 67; and idem, *Über den Ur-Qur'ān: Ansätze zur Rekonstruktion vorislamischer christlicher Strophenlieder im Qur'ān* (Erlangen: H. Lüling, 1993 [1974]), 66), without citing any evidence for such a claim. The contribution of von Stosch in the present volume discusses and dismisses as ahistorical the putative angelic Christology of Martin Werner on which Lüling builds his theories, see Klaus von Stosch, "Eine urchristliche Engelchristologie im Koran?," 69–90 in the current volume. Note that the English translation of Lüling's work obliterates the crucial difference between the German terms "jüdisch-christlich," designating the collective of the Jewish and the Christian tradition, and "judenchristlich," designating a fusion of Jewish and Christian elements; both German terms are translated as "Jewish-Christian;" see idem, *A Challenge to Islam for Reformation*, e.g. 38, 49, 67–8, 168, 183, 206, 296 and 338; and idem, *Über den Ur-Qur'ān*, 41, 61, 97, 149, 165, 183, 198 and 355. At other times, the translation renders the German "wahrscheinlich Judenchristlich," i.e. "probably Jewish-Christian," as "early Christian," e.g. when claiming that "the Christian ground layer of the Koran, – at the lifetime of the Prophet most probably two hundred years old –, indisputably advocates an archaic ur-Christian ("wahrscheinlich Judenchristlich,") angel-Christology which had meanwhile been classified as heresy and therefore been condemned by all politically influential Christian confessions extant in Mecca," see idem, *A Challenge to Islam for Reformation*, 21 and idem, *Über den*

to polemicize against Christianity and Islam both in its reconstructable historical as well as in its practiced extant forms today.[19] While I am deeply sympathetic to Lüling's attempt to free the study of early Christianity and of the Qur'ān from the dictates of religious or academic orthodoxies, any attempt to do so must follow rigorous historical methods or be relegated to the footnotes of the history of scholarship, as I will now try to do.[20]

2 Rhyme and Reason: Formal Aspects of Lüling's Reconstructions

Lüling's main work offers a detailed analysis of *Sūrat al-ʿAlaq* 96, stretching over 69 pages.[21] A refutation of any work must always summarize what it seeks to dismiss, and by its very nature tends to be longer than its object of criticism. It is thus difficult to discuss the entirety of Lüling's many suggestions regarding surah Q 96 in the framework of one article; I will instead focus on his reconstruction of verse 15 and his dismissal of verse 16 as secondary addition. I will submit that, *pars pro toto*, the circularity of his specific suggestions regarding two verses translates into the fundamental fallaciousness of Lüling's method and thereby of his work on Islamic origins as a whole. The chosen example illustrates one of Lüling's central tools for identifying the alleged fallaciousness of the Qur'ān's *muṣḥaf.* In the verse under consideration, as throughout his book, his main argu-

Ur-Qur'ān, 10. Yet even within the German original, Lüling's use of the term "judenchristlich" is ill-defined and in my view historically vacuous, as von Stosch correctly points out, see also note eight above.

19 See for example, Bobzin, "Martin Werner und Albert Schweizer," 23–32, Horn, "Hermeneutische Dimensionen," 111–128, von Stosch, "Eine urchristliche Engelschristologie," 69–90, and Marianus Hundhammer, "Qur'ānic Studies between Revisionism and Reinvention," 141–158, all in the current volume.

20 The problems with Lüling's work should be stated much more clearly than do for example the more "objective" summaries given e. g. by Reynolds, "Introduction: The Qur'ānic Studies and its Controversies," in *The Qur'ān in its Historical Context,* ed. idem, 11; and Harald Motzki, "Alternative Accounts of the Qur'ān's Formation," in *The Cambridge Companion to the Qur'ān,* Jane Dammen McAuliffe (Cambridge: Cambridge University Press, 2006), 65–7. One should also note that the current Wikipedia entries on Lüling, especially on the German site, goes very far indeed in seeking to argue for the rehabilitation of his theses, see <https://de.wikipedia.org/wiki/Günter_Lüling> and <https://en.wikipedia.org/wiki/Günter_Lüling>, accessed September 3, 2018.

21 See Lüling, *A Challenge to Islam for Reformation*, 28–97 and idem, *Über den Ur-Qur'ān*, 25–77.

ment is of a poetic nature and depends on a broken rhyme scheme.[22] In order to prepare an assessment of Lüling's ideas, I will thus very briefly present the short surah as a whole in its traditional reading, establishing the symmetry and coherence of its traditional rhyme scheme – the alleged *absence* of which forms the basis of Lüling's reconstruction). The text of Qur'ān Q 96 *Sūrat al-ʿAlaq* of *ʿĀṣim* as transmitted by *Ḥafṣ* (but omitting the *basmala*) can be transliterated as follows:[23]

1.	*ʾiqraʾ bi-smi rabbika llaḏī ḫalaq*	Read in the Name of your Lord who created;
2.	*ḫalaqa l-insāna min ʿalaq*	created man from a clinging mass.
3.	*ʾiqraʾ wa-rabbuka l-ʾakram*	Read, and your Lord is the most noble,
4.	*llaḏī ʿallama bi-l-qalam*	who taught by the pen,
5.	*ʿallama l-insāna mā lam yaʿlam*	taught man what he did not know.
6.	*kallā ʾinna l-ʾinsāna la-yaṭġā*	Indeed man becomes rebellious
7.	*ʾan raʾāhu staġnā*	when he considers himself without need.
8.	*ʾinna ʾilā rabbika r-ruǧʿā*	Indeed to your Lord is the return.
9.	*a-raʾaita llaḏī yanhā*	Tell me, he who forbids
10.	*ʿabdan ʾiḏā ṣallā*	a servant when he prays,
11.	*a-raʾaita ʾin kāna ʿalā l-hudā*	tell me, should he be on guidance,
12.	*ʾau amara bi-t-taqwā*	or bid [others] to Godwariness,
13.	*a-raʾaita ʾin kaḏḏaba wa-tawallā*	tell me, should he impugn him and turn away
14.	*ʾa-lam yaʿlam bi-ʾanna llāha yarā*	– does he not know that God sees?
15.	*kallā la-ʾin lam yantahi*	No indeed! If he does not stop,
	la-nasfaʿan bi-n-nāṣiyah	We shall seize him by the forelock,
16.	*nāṣiyatin kāḏibatin ḫāṭiyah*	a lying, sinful forelock!
17.	*fa-l-yadʿu nādiyah*	Then let him call out his gang!
18.	*sa-nadʿu z-zabāniyah*	We [too] shall call the keepers of hell.
19.	*kallā lā tuṭiʿhu wa-sǧud wa-qtarib*	No indeed! Do not obey him, but prostrate and draw near [to God]!

22 Lüling makes pervasive use of "rhyme-criticism" in his analyses of all surahs of his volume; his chapter two, more specifically, is composed of and titled as "Comments on the Rules of Strophe Composition Applied in the Pre-Islamic Christian Hymnody as Contained in the Islamic Koran," see idem, *A Challenge to Islam for Reformation*, 174–91, and idem, *Über den Ur-Qur'ān*, esp. 139–61. The inadequacies of Lüling's sense of Arabic rhyme will have to be dealt with elsewhere, but see note 33 and Lutz Edzard, "Chances and problems with the morpho-syntactic analysis of the Qur'ān, based on a colometric representation," 187–198 in the current volume.

23 Arabic is transliterated according to the system of the ZDMG, i.e. DIN 31635 (1982). The suggested English translation follows that of Sayyid ʻAli Quli Qara'I, ed. and trans., *The Qur'an with an English Paraphrase* (Qom: Centre for Translation of the Holy Qur'ān, 2003) with very minor modifications. Syriac as well as Jewish Aramaic and Hebrew will be transliterated in accordance with the early defective (i.e. non-vocalized) tradition, as follows: *ʾ b g d h w z ḥ ṭ y k l m n s ʿ p ṣ q r š t*.

The topics of the surah are well known themes in the Qurʾān; the surah as a whole has been adequately dealt with in previous studies such as those of Angelika Neuwirth and Michel Cuypers.[24] Most western commentators on the surah, most recently Michel Cuypers and including Lüling, have divided it into three parts (as is common in the Qurʾān). Based on their understanding, the surah falls into an opening "hymn" focusing on scribal themes (verses 1–5), a "reprimand" against human beings forgetting their place (verses 6–8), and a "polemics" expressing a rebuke to an unnamed sinful yet socially powerful figure that apparently interferes with the worship of the Qurʾān's prophetic addressee (verses 9–18).[25] While this division certainly has some merits, one should never read the Qurʾān, or any literary text, only based on one formal criterion. Complex texts overlay multiple structural layers on top of each other, engaging the audience in a myriad of ways. The scholarly three-partite division, for example, disregards the surah's blatant rhyme scheme, which Devin Stewart and Angelika Neuwirth have duly noted.[26]

In detail, the traditional reading of *ʿĀṣim* here adopted already sets apart verses 6–14 through their continuous rhyme scheme; these verses all end with a long *alif*. This major middle segment thereby sets apart verses 1–5 as an opening and verses 15–19 as a closing frame around it. The opening and closing segments are both composed in a balanced way, each containing five verses exactly. Moreover, if one reads the text not strictly according to *ʿĀṣim*, as Lüling had, but according to its traditional recitation, taking into account the pausal forms of the words in *fāṣila* (i.e. end of verse) position, more phonetic repetitions emerge: the opening part, verses one to five, contains two independent rhymes, *-alaq* for

---

24 See Neuwirth, *Der Koran*, 264–79, and Michel Cuypers, "L'analyse rhetorique face a la critique historique de J. Wansbrough et de G. Lüling. L'exemple de la sourate 96," in *The Coming of the Comforter: When, Where, and to Whom?, Studies on the Rise of Islam and Various Other Topics in Memory of John Wansbrough. Orientalia Judaica Christiana 3*, eds. Carlos A. Segovia and Lourie Basil (Piscataway, NJ: Gorgias Press, 2012), 343–69. Note that Cuypers' criticism of Lüling mainly consists of substituting what he calls his own "rhetorical analysis" for the "historical criticism" of Lüling; he hardly engages Lüling's arguments directly.

25 See Cuypers, "L'analyse rhetorique," 348–50 and Richard Bell, *The Qurʾān. Translation, with a critical re-arrangement of the Surahs* (Edinburgh: T&T Clark, 1950), 667; as noted by Cuypers (ibid), the Islamic tradition, which considers 96:1–5 the beginning of the Qurʾānic revelation, thereby effectively maintains a bipartite structure dividing the surah into verses 1–5 and 6–19.

26 See Stewart, "Sajʿ in the Qurʾān," 137 (see also 111); Stewart correctly identifies only the last syllable of the first rhyme as "*-aq*," yet the fuller phonetic repetition extraordinarily extends over two syllables as *-alaq*. Neuwirth suggests a more elaborate tripartite structure based on rhyme scheme, i.e., verses 1–5, 6–18, and 19, with the first two units subdivided (as verses 1–2 and 3–5, and 6–8, 9–14 and 15–18, see eadem, *Der Koran*, 264–67), a reading upon which my own proposal below is partially based.

verses one and two, and *-am* for verses three, four and five.[27] The first four verses of the final part, verses 15–18, end with *-ah* (i.e. *āCiyah* according to Neuwirth), leading to the culminating exhortation in verse 19 that contains the only non-rhyming verse in the surah. The dominant rhyme of the final part (i.e. verses 15–18), *-ah*, thus offers only a minor, yet a consistent phonetic variation to the rhyme of the central part (i.e. verses 6–15), *-ā*. The "border" between these two nearly homophonous and remarkably persistent rhyme schemes of the middle and the closing part is located between verses 14 and 15. This brief consideration already offers at least a counterpoint to the division of the surah offered by Lüling, Cuypers and others: it corroborates the separation between their suggested "part one" and "part two," yet separates their suggested "part one" into two units, it fuses their suggested "part two" with "part three," and it divides their suggested "part three" into two sections. A division based on rhyme scheme, as proposed (slightly differently) by Neuwirth, along with a transliteration based on the pausal forms of a recitation, allows us to visualize this alternative segmentation of the surah:[28]

---

27 The rules and complexities of Qurʾānic *Sajʿ* are well sketched by Stewart; while often translated as "rhyming prose," his suggested translation of the term as "accent poetry" may be more astute; see Stewart, "Rhymed Prose;" idem, "Sajʿ in the Qurʾān;" and Neuwirth, *Studien zur Komposition der mekkanischen Suren.* Note that the pausal forms in recited Qurʾānic Arabic constitute a formal parallel to the traditional recitation of the Hebrew Bible: in the Masoretic text, the pausal form causes the stress to recede to the penultimate syllable, in which short vowels are either lengthened or otherwise altered, see e.g. Edward Lipiński, *Semitic Languages: Outline of a Comparative Grammar. Orientalia Lovaniensia Analaecta* 80 (Leuven: Peeters, 2001), 26:2 (191). On Lüling's discussion of Arabic poetry see above, note 22 and below, note 30.

28 Note that Neuwirth considers verses 15–18 as part of the middle part of the surah, thereby eclipsing the symmetry of five verses each in parts one and three and fusing the clearly separate rhymes of *-ā* and *-ah* into one unit, see eadem, *Der Koran*, 264–6.

Division established by Cuypers, Lüling, et al. / Division based on rhyme scheme

1. *iqraʾ bi-smi rabbika llaḏī ḫalaq*
2. *ḫalaqa l-ʾinsāna min ʿalaq*
3. *iqraʾ wa-rabbuka l-ʾakram*
4. *llaḏī ʿallama bi-l-qalam*
5. *ʿallama l-ʾinsāna mā lam yaʿlam*
6. *kallā ʾinna l-ʾinsāna la-yaṭġā*
7. *ʾan raʾāhu staġnā*
8. *ʾinna ʾilā rabbika r-ruǧʿā*
9. *ʾa-raʾaita llaḏī yanhā*
10. *ʿabdan ʾiḏā ṣallā*
11. *ʾa-raʾaita ʾin kāna ʿala l-hudā*
12. *ʾau ʾamara bi-t-taqwā*
13. *ʾa-raʾaita ʾin kaḏḏaba wa-tawallā*
14. *ʾa-lam yaʿlam bi-ʾanna llāha yarā*
15. *kallā la-ʾin lam yantahi*
la-nasfaʿan bi-n-nāṣiyah
16. *nāṣiyatin kāḏibatin ḫāṭiʾah*
17. *fa-l-yadʿu nādiyah*
18. *sa-nadʿu z-zabāniyah*
19. *kallā lā tuṭiʿhu wa-sǧud wa-qtarib*

The literary structure that emerges when reading the surah based on rhyme neatly divides the surah in three parts, the first and third of which both have five verses; *all* verses but the last one rhyme.[29] Lüling, by contrast, states regarding this surah that "attention should be paid to the fact that the traditional Arabic text ... is a prose text steadily continuing through extended lines and nowhere interrupted by rhymes."[30] This is of course as false as it is disingenuous, for

29 The discrepancy between the two possible divisions, one based on content and one based on rhyme, should not be taken as a reason to substitute one division for the other. We should also refrain from simply discarding the helpful exercise of establishing such divisions. Yet the discrepancy between the two segmentations is quite real, and we should take the fact that we reach such different results based on two quite objective criteria as a warning not to rely on any such divisions alone in order to "criticize" the Qurʾānic text, and certainly not to the extent of rewriting it. Yet this is of course exactly what Lüling did, based on considerations of both form and content, as we will now see.

30 See Lüling, *A Challenge to Islam for Reformation*, 90 and idem, *Über den Ur-Qurʾān*, 71.

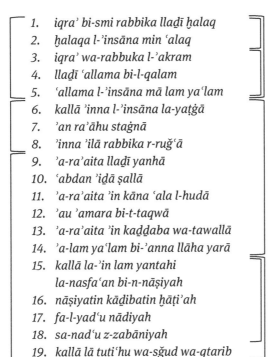

Lüling seems quite aware of some of the rules of recitation of what he calls "strophic poetry," including pausal forms.[31] The traditionally recited text includes precisely the rhymes of the pausal forms, accentuated by the subsequent pauses (*awqāf*) throughout the surah. Instead of paying attention to the existing rhymes, Lüling posits their absence in light of which he proposes a completely new rhymed poem which he argues to be the original form of surah 96.[32] While a full discussion of the proposed poem far exceeds the confines of this essay, one example should suffice to illustrate that the implementation of the method is as arbitrary as are its premises.

The speaker in the verses of the surah, according to the traditional reading, is God, who warns the sinful figure that should he not cease from his behaviour, then He, i.e., God, will "seize him" i.e. the human, "by the forelock." This reading is in line with the sense of divine power and human submission we find throughout the Qur'ān, as well more generally in antiquity (as will be corroborated in part three below). Lüling challenges the simple reading. Instead, he strips the *rasm* text from its diacritical marks and in two steps reinterprets it according to his own understanding of Qur'ānic rhyme and reason. In his first reinterpretation, Lüling engages the verse's rhyme scheme as follows:

> Since we have already had four strophes with the rhyme on long -ā (96:6–14), one is not mistaken in assuming that the two words *nasfa'ā̱* (96:15b) "we shall grab or seize" and *nāṣiyah̲* (96:15c), "shock, forelock" establish the rhyme-endings on long -ā̱ of the second and third strophe line of the complex 96,15abc. Thus the words لبن لم ينته *la-in lam yantahi̲* "if he does not cease" of the traditional interpretation of 96,15a must at all events end in a long -ā̱ to get the still missing rhyme on -ā for the first line-ending of the strophe. But to read the *rasm* ينته ending on an -ā is, according to the rules of Arabic, only possible if this word is read in the passive voice *yuntaha* (the grammatically short final -a becomes automatically a long -ā at the end of a verse because of metrical rules). This strophe-technically necessary passive voice can now be understood as an impersonal one: "If it (the praying) is not being stopped or ceased or given up". Alternatively it can be taken for a personal passive implying the subject of this passive verb to be God: "If He (God) is not being ceased or stopped or given up (by prayer)."

A few of the imprecise grammatical claims in Lüling's passage, such as the strange personal passive which is as incorrect in Arabic as it is in German, have already been dealt with adequately by one of the reviewers of Lüling's dis-

---

31 See note 22 above.
32 This text is summarized in Lüling, *A Challenge to Islam for Reformation*, 91–7 and idem, *Über den Ur-Qur'ān*, 70–7.

sertation, Anton Spitaler, and need not be repeated here.[33] A more interesting issue is that of the rhyme scheme. Lüling quite rightly points out that the rhyme scheme on *-ā* is dominant in verses 6–14; he divides this block into four subsections and thus speaks about "four strophes"[34]. Highlighting the continuity of the rhyme scheme in verses 6–14 is reasonable and even helpful (albeit it in tension with Lüling's own subdivision of the surah, as already pointed out). However, as Devin Stewart (based on *Ibn al-Athīr*) has clearly shown, *kallā la-in lam yantahi* should be considered an introductory phrase to verse 15, to which metrical constraints of the *sajʿ* colon proper do not apply. The phrase therefor does not have to rhyme with or be metrically parallel to the subsequent cola.[35] Lüling's claim that the verb *yantahi* would therefore need to confirm to the rhyme scheme on -ā, which forms the basis of his subsequent textual intervention, is simply false.

The subsequent verb in the same verse fifteen suffers the same fate by Lüling's hand. He again begins with a reasonable observation, yet then is carried away by his enthusiasm for rewriting the text. Lüling quite rightly points out that the Arabic verbal form transliterated as *la-nasfaʿan*, translated as "We shall seize *him*," offers a grammatical difficulty. The *rasm* text, لنسفعا, does not offer a clear indication of a suffix (or any other type of personal pronoun) that would explain who exactly is seized. Instead of offering a systematic inquiry into other cases in which the Qurʾān would elide a suffix, however, Lüling simply calls the omission a "serious mistake."[36] Then, instead of considering the mild

---

33 Lüling had submitted his yet unfinished dissertation as a writing sample along with his application for a position in modern Arabic at the University of Göteborg. Anton Spitaler served as one of the external referents, and saw fit to dedicate three additional pages to his criticism of the ungrammatical nature of many of Lüling's reconstructions and his idiosyncratic sense of Arabic poetry, see idem, "Besetzung des Lehrstuhls für die arabische Sprache, namentlich modernes Arabisch," Munich, January 29, 1970, addendum "Lüling," 2. Georges Tamer was kind enough to provide me with a copy of this document. On the academic and legal ramifications of Lüling's dissertation and unsuccessful habilitation see Georges Tamer, "Günter Lüling: Leben, Werk und Fall," 1–18 in the current volume. It should be mentioned that neither Lüling nor his *Doktorvater* saw Spitaler's weighty reservations before the submission of the thesis; Lüling does respond *ad hominem* against Spitaler in the English translation of his main book, see Lüling, *A Challenge to Islam for Reformation*, XVII–XIX and 117–9.

34 See Lüling, *A Challenge to Islam for Reformation*, 46–7 and idem, *Über den Ur-Qur'ān*, 42–3.

35 See Devin Stewart, "Sajʿ in the Qurʾan: Prosody and Structure," esp. 116–18. See also Edzard, "Chances and problems with the morpho-syntactic analysis of the Qurʾān," 197.

36 See Lüling, *A Challenge to Islam for Reformation*, 65; the argument is missing in the German first edition. Another case of the omission of a suffix (in Q 93:3) has been recorded by Ibn al-Ṣāʾigh al-Ḥanafī, see Devin Stewart, "Poetic License in the Qur'an: Ibn al-Ṣāʾigh al-Ḥanafī's *Iḥkām al-rāy fī aḥkām al-āy*," *Journal of Qur'anic Studies* 11 (2009): 36. Lüling does not note

textual ambiguity (resulting from the "missing" suffix) in its Qur'ānic context, Lüling again opts for a radical rereading, and proposes to change the verb (yet not the *rasm*) into another passive: *la-yusfaʿā*, "He," that is God himself, "will be seized," again for the simple reason that Lüling can then read the entire verse 15 three times as ending in *-ā*. There is, again, no reason to do so other than Lüling's claim that the rhyme scheme established in verses 6–14 ought to continue in the way he sees fit – with *-ā* instead of *-ah* and with a triple internal rhyme in verse 15![37] Yet perhaps even more startling than the missing grounds and guidelines for Lüling's textual intervention is his result, which he transliterates and translates as follows:

15.	*kallā la-'in lam yuntahā*	Not at all! If He is not ceased (not given peace) (by prayer)
	la-yusfaʿā	Truly He will be seized
	bi-n-nāṣiyati	By the forelock

that the root *s-f-ʿ* is a *hapax legomenon* in the Qur'ān even though this fact may have been marshalled to point to the verse's peculiarity; such terms are often soft markers of Semitic intertextuality. See von Rippin, "Foreign Vocabulary," in *Encyclopaedia of the Qur'ān*, ed. Dammen McAuliffe.

37 Lüling's full argument is perfectly circular, a fact which he remarkably admits in passing. It is worthwhile trying to consider his full wording: "This interpretation is now already an anticipation of our judgment on the traditional interpretation of 96,15b: the traditionally given first person plural *la-nasfaʿā* (of the first person pluralis) "truly we shall seize" has to be read (without a change of the *rasm*) as the passive of the third person singular *la-yusfaʿā* "truly He will be seized". In Arabic script this alteration is from لنسفعا to ليسفعا. To corroborate this reading we have to pay attention, in the meantime, to two important aspects: Firstly we have to consider that the peculiar writing of this verb (no matter whether in its traditional or in its reconstructed shape) with a final *alif* ا can only be explained correctly as the indication for the long *-ā* required because of its position as final sound in the strophe line having to rhyme on long *-ā* (according to the metric rules of Arabic poetry, every vowel finishing as vowel of the rhyme of the strophe line becomes long): The early (Christian) composer of this pre-Islamic strophic hymn gave this indication for the long rhyming *-ā* and all subsequent Islamic text editors, in spite of their having converted what is a highly poetic text into dry prose, retained it, but now without purpose. This seems to be the only reasonable explanation and it corroborates our thesis that 96,15 is a three-line strophe, each line ending with the rhyme on long *-ā*. This exceptional spelling of the last word of strophe line 96,15b̲ indicating its rhyme on long *-ā* proves, retroactively in a circulus hermeneutics, that, as we initially assumed, the vowel *-i* of the traditional interpretation at the end of the strophe line 96,15a̲ must also be read as a long *-ā* and that means that the last word of this line has uncontestably to be read as a passive voice on two accounts. We can therefore see that the arguments for our reconstructed interpretations grows [sic] more and more convincing," see Lüling, *A Challenge to Islam for Reformation*, 64–5. In the first edition of the German version, Lüling promises to return to the issue of his passive rendering, but then fails to do so in as far as I can follow his argument, see idem, *Über den Ur-Qur'ān*, 59.

The change in meaning is radical: God himself becomes the subject of the violent treatment of being seized by *His* forelock, so the worshipper threatens God. This, say, unusual statement would of course require the attribution of the "lying, sinful forelock" of the subsequent verse 16 to God Himself, which seems to violate even Lüling's sense of Late Antique religiosity. Verse sixteen, then, must have been added as part of the rewriting of the original text, he argues, for the very simple reason that it contains no definitive pronoun:

> If verse 96,15 and verse 96,16 had originally been a normal phraseological unit it would have been, – no matter whether in the traditional or in the reconstructed sense –, of the syntactically homogenous structure "We seize(d) by the forelock, the lying and sinful forelock", that is, all the nouns would have been constructed as definite nouns. This leads us immediately to the conclusion that these undefined three words of 96,16 originally did not belong to the text verses 96,1–19, that is: they are a gloss or a commentary introduced into the text of the Islamic reinterpretation of Sura 96, according to the frame-narrative which had been pressed on the *rasm*-text of Sura 96.[38]

Lüling does not specify what grammatical rule he is invoking, or where it may come from. He simply claims that the repetition of a noun that carries a definite article in the first instance must also carry one in the repetition, with no reference other cases in the Qurʾān where this would be the case. Yet even if one troubles oneself with considering such cases of repeated nouns (which do exist and point to the exceptional nature of the present one), I do not see any grammatical reason why the Qurʾān's text should need to conform to Lüling's sense of poetry and the use of definite articles, to his sense of the use of suffixes, or to his sense of the surah's rhyme scheme.[39]

In each of the three cases discussed so far, and in many others throughout his work, Lüling begins with a reasonable, even interesting observation, and in each case, he seeks to obliterate any perceived irregularity by rewriting the text. Yet not in a single one of the cases that Lüling brings, here or elsewhere in his work, is this necessary, let alone plausible, for irregularities are the stuff of literary production in general. Poetic licence, after all, is part of any literary text, and

---

38 See Lüling, *A Challenge to Islam for Reformation*, 68 and idem, *Über den Ur-Qur'ān*, 62.
39 Repetitions of the same word are not uncommon in the Qurʾān. One example of a repeated noun whose definite article *is* repeated can be found in Q57:27: *wa-aṣḥābu l-yamīni mā aṣḥābu l-yamīni* literally means "the companions of the right, what are the companions of the right?" Here, the repetition of the definitive article prepares the specification of the group of sinners in the next verse 28; see the similar cases e.g. in Q69:1–3 and Q101:1–4. All these examples, however, differ from Q96:15–16 in as far as they do not *immediately* repeat a noun, moreover, the meaning in all these examples would slightly change if the second article were omitted, which is not the case in the passage under consideration.

traditional Islamic scholarship has long treated this phenomenon in the Qur'ān.[40] I have, thus, not found any formal or grammatical basis for and no objective transparent guideline to Lüling's intuitive reconstruction of his Ur-Qur'ān, neither in this case nor in any other that I have studied. It may be a personal tragedy that he has not had any conversation partners that would have pointed out the insularity of his thought to him (a role at least his dissertation supervisor should have played), yet we need to disassociate any sympathy for the fate of the person from an assessment of his work. The result remains that nearly nothing of what Lüling published deserves further consideration, for any residual merit one could find in some of his initial observations is buried underneath a near impenetrable layer of arbitrary claims. We shall see that a similar case has to be made for his historical reconstructions in which he seeks to place his rewritten Qur'ān.

3 Normative Upheaval: Aspects of Lüling's Historical Reconstructions

One of the aspects of Lüling's suggestions that may have given them a slightly longer shelf life than they deserve is the fact that his methods mimic that of (mainly protestant) Biblical criticism as practiced in (mainly German) universities of his time. In line with this tradition, Lüling duly seeks to corroborate his "lower," or textual criticism with the "higher" historical-critical studies of the surroundings of the Qur'ān. Such an approach, of course, is not at all unsound. With regards to his rewriting of verse 15 and deletion of verse 16, Lüling recognized himself that a certain tension may persist between the idea of grabbing God by the forelock and the Islamic tradition. And again, while his initial impulse as a historian also makes good sense, Lüling immediately veers off course, as in the following observation:

> In the simile "to seize God by the forelock" there appears not only an anthropomorphism offensive to the Islamic understanding of God… but it expresses an attitude towards God which is foreign to the world of orthodox Islamic religious ideas…. It is however familiar in Jewish and Christian conceptions of God. This topos is one of the most central ideas car-

40 See Devin J. Stewart, "Poetic License in the Qur'an: Ibn al-Ṣā'igh al-Ḥanafī's *Iḥkām al-rāy fī aḥkām al-āy*," *Journal of Qur'ānic Studies* 11 (2009): 1–56; see also idem, "Divine Epithets and the Dibacchius: Clausulae and Qur'ānic Rhythm," *Journal of Qur'anic Studies* 15 (2013): 22–64; and cf. Friedrun R. Müller, *Untersuchungen zur Reimprosa im Koran*, which does not discuss the issue of poetic licence.

ried from the Old to the New Testament and into the basic of evangelical-protestant religious attitude.[41]

Lüling's claim that either the image of "seizing God by the forelock" or the alleged underlying "attitude" would be constitutive of, or even compatible with the Biblical or the Christian tradition is false. The image itself is as foreign to the Jewish and to the Christian tradition as it is to the Islamic one. To the best of my knowledge, the only deity ever to be seized by his forelock is Kairos, the Greek god of opportunity, whose image was indeed widespread throughout Late Antiquity. Yet the Greek god is but a personification of opportunity, whose very purpose it is to be seized – he has little relation to the fearsome monotheist deity whose very purpose it is to exercise His limitless power.[42] Lüling's placement of the seizing of God at the centre of Jewish and Christian theology is thus utter nonsense. For the present purpose, however, we should still appreciate to what lengths Lüling went to defend his claim, how intensely he marshalled his broad training to do so, and how absurd his reasoning became the more intensely he defended his theses.

The examples Lüling adduced to corroborate his idea of a violent struggle with God are Genesis 32, Jacob's nocturnal fight with "a man" whom Jacob later associates with the "face of God," and various passages in the prophetic literature and the New Testament in which God is allegedly challenged.[43] While the Biblical image of Jacob's fight, survival, and thigh injury is a remarkable one indeed, it does not support the argument: in Genesis, it is not clear who attacks whom, and while the "man" emerges unscathed, Jacob does not. All other Biblical or New Testament examples given simply emphasize persistent

41 See Lüling, *A Challenge to Islam for Reformation*, 66 and idem, *Über den Ur-Qur'ān*, 59. The citation is given in full, omitting three footnotes (indicated by …) referencing Arabic poetry (Lüling's note 65, to be discussed below), medieval Islamic magic (his note 66), and Martin Luther (his note 67).

42 As the fourth century rethorician Callistratus put it: "while the lock of hair on his (i.e. Kairos') forehead (τὴν δὲ κατὰ τοῦ μετώπου κόμην) indicated that he is easy to catch as he approaches, yet, when he has passed by, the moment of action has likely expired and that, if Kairos is neglected, it cannot be recovered," see Callistratus, *Descriptions* 6, text and translation by Arthur Fairbanks, *Elder Philostratus, Younger Philostratus, Callistratus, Loeb Classical Library*, vol. 256 (London: Harvard University Press, 1931), 398–99. On Kairos in Late Antique and medieval art see e.g. Simona Cohen, *Transformations of Time and Temporality in Medieval and Renaissance Art* (Leiden: Brill, 2014), 199–244.

43 See Lüling, *A Challenge to Islam for Reformation*, 66 and idem, *Über den Ur-Qur'ān*, 59; the examples he lists are the book of Job; Isaiah 62:6; Matthew 11:12 and parallels; and Matthew 7:7–11 and parallels.

prayer as a means of interceding with God, or "pressing" into the kingdom of Christ.

Unfortunately, Lüling was uninterested in most post-biblical literature. In order to corroborate the idea of challenging God, Lüling could have marshalled certain monastic and rabbinic traditions. Both in the *Mishna* and in the *Apophthegmata Patrum*, we find holy men who literally compel God to send rain.[44] According to the Talmud, Titus challenged God after destroying the Temple, and, in a different story, the rabbinic sages even manage to vanquish Him in a Scriptural argument. Titus, of course, is severely punished for his impudence, and even the rabbis, who only won with God's ultimate approval in the first place, have to pay dearly for their victory, almost bringing about utter destruction of the world.[45] These late antique traditions indeed discuss the issue of challenging God, but of course they are all quite different from threatening to seize God should he not listen to the prayer, as Lüling's Ur-Qur'ān would have it. While Lüling could be forgiven for his disregard of Jewish and monastic sources since he had no respective training, he also seems uninterested in the fact that the Qur'ān itself, albeit in a Medinan passage, openly *polemicizes* against the idea of compelling God. It accuses the Jews of claiming that "God's hand is tied," a passage in tension with his imagery of an alleged challenge of God that Lüling equally does not consider.[46]

---

44 See Mishna *Ta'anit* 3:8 and the *Apothtegmata Patrum* on Abba Moses 13 (*Patrologiae Graecae* 65:285); the Apothtegmata circulated as widely in Syriac as they did in Greek, see Michal Bar Asher Siegal, *Early Christian Monastic Literature and the Babylonian Talmud* (Cambridge: Cambridge University Press, 2013), 13–9.

45 The theme of challenging God is of course well-known from the Talmud, yet in a very different manner. In the famous episode in Bavli *Bava Metsi'a* 59, the rabbis overcome God's monopoly on scriptural interpretation. In another famous story in Bavli *Gittin* 56b, the Roman Emperor challenges God to a duel, and painfully loses. See e.g. Jeffery Rubenstein, *Talmudic Stories: Narrative, Composition, and Culture* (Baltimore: Johns Hopkins University Press, 1999), 34–63; and Joshua Levinson, "'Tragedies Naturally Performed': Fatal Charades, Parodia Sacra, and the Death of Titus," in *Jewish Culture and Society Under the Christian Roman Empire*, eds. Seth Schwartz and Richard Kalmin (Leuven: Peters, 2003), 349–82, see also the next note and note 52 below.

46 See Q5:64; the text rectifies this alleged Jewish claim by emphasizing that, to the contrary, it is the hands of the Jews that are tied, whereas God's hand spends openly. The context here is thus most likely the question of community finances and the support of the poor, a common theme in the Qur'ān. It should be noted that the Hebrew Bible and the mystical as well as the rabbinic Jewish tradition evoke the imagery of God's hand as possibly restrained. *Lamentation* 2:3 states that God has "drawn back his right hand (*hšyb 'ḥwr ymynw*) from before the enemy;" *Sefer Hekhalot* understands this as God's physical restraint of his hand after the destruction of the Temple, see Peter Schäfer et al., *Synopse zur Hekhalot-Literatur* (Tübingen:

Lüling was of course aware of the historical tension his image evoked, and went out of his way to "Biblicize" it, again in a rather perverse manner, as follows:

> .... Besides it should be remarked that our topos of Sura 96:15 "to seize God by his forelock" is at home in the sphere of the eschatologic-apocalyptic literature. This is corroborated by its appearance in Ezek. 8,3: "he took me by the lock of my head."
>
> Since the Hebrew for "lock" [*ṣyṣ*] used in this context also stands for a kind of ornament at the forehead of the Highpriest it is very likely that the "lock" of Ezek. 8,3 also has the positive meaning of "the seat of honour" as does the forelock in Sura 96,15."[47]

The geminate Biblical Hebrew term *ṣyṣt* (not *ṣyṣ*), along with its later Aramaic cognates *ṣwṣyt'*, designates curled hair, specifically that of the front of the head. Lüling did not comment on the fact that it is lexically related to the doubly defective Hebrew root *nwṣ'* as well as to the Arabic term *nāṣiya*, "forelock," which we find in surah Q 96:15–16, even though this lexical link – to which we shall return – may have rendered the Biblical evidence somewhat more pertinent.[48] Instead, Lüling claimed that someone being grabbed by his forelock in the Bible would constitute a historical parallel to his reading. It is of course the prophet Ezekiel, and not God, who is lifted by his forehead in the Bible, so the claim Lüling makes, that "our topos of Surah 96:15 "to seize God by his forelock"

J.C.B. Mohr (P. Siebeck), 1981), 68. In the well-known Talmudic passage, Bavli *Menahot* 29b, finally, Moses asks God, in a peculiar formulation, "who prevents your hand (*my mʿkb ʿl ydk*)?," i.e. from writing out later rabbinic law Himself, see Jeffrey Rubenstein, *Stories of the Babylonian Talmud* (Baltimore: Johns Hopkins University Press, 2010), 182–202. None of these sources, of course, share the specific financial context we find in *sūrat al-Māʾidah*, yet they still corroborate the potential pertinence of the Qurʾān's association of the Jewish tradition and the image of God's hand being somehow restrained. See also the previous note and note 52 below.

47 See Lüling, *A Challenge to Islam for Reformation*, 66 and idem, *Über den Ur-Qur'ān*, 59. Lüling here confuses *ṣyṣt*, which designates a forelock, and the admittedly related term *ṣyṣ*, which designates the high priest's "shining thing" or "plate of gold," which can be found in Exodus 28:36 and 39:30 and in Leviticus 8:9.

48 The underlying root *yṣ'* means to "go out," and variants of the term *nwṣ'* as designating types of "hair" or "feather growth" are attested for example in Hebrew, Jewish Aramaic, Syriac, Ethiopic, Assyrian and Acadian, see L. Koehler and W. Baumgartner, eds., *Hebräisches und aramäisches Lexicon zum Alten Testament* (Leiden: Brill, 1967–1990), 682; see also Michael Sokoloff, *A Dictionary of Jewish Babylonian Aramaic of the Talmudic and Geonic Periods* (Baltimore: The Johns Hopkins University Press, 2003), 955–6; idem, *A Syriac Lexicon: A Translation from the Latin, Correction, Expansion, and Update of C. Brockelmann's Lexicon Syriacum* (Winona Lake: Eisenbraun's, 2009); and Marcus Jastrow, *A Dictionary of the Targumim, the Talmud Bavli and Yerushalmi, and the Midrashic Literature* (New York: The Judaica Press, 1996 [1903]), 889 and notes 51 and 58 below.

is at home in the sphere of the eschatologic-apocalyptic literature" is again a false one. The image of the angelic figure taking Ezekiel on a tour "by a lock of my head (*bṣyṣyt r'šy*)," moreover, evokes the utter impotence of the prophet before God; the rabbis have understood the story accordingly.[49] Likewise, the marginal case of the headgear of the Israelite high priest, which indeed shares the same root in Biblical Hebrew as the term "forelock," has no relationship at all to the imagery of seizing *anyone* by the forehead, leave alone God. The Biblical cases here discussed could thus be made relevant only in order to support the traditional reading, yet not that of Lüling.

In a marginally more helpful attempt to buttress his findings as historically plausible, Lüling again tried to make the case that "this figure of speech.... "he will be seized by the forelock" is not as objectionable as one might think."[50] He recalls one instance in which an ancient Arabic poet spoke favourably about the "forelock" of a warhorse and cites Wellhausen's observation that the forelock was indeed a sign of the freeborn in pre-Islamic societies, whereas slaves had it cut off.[51] On the one hand, I do not think that evoking the forelocks of horses would do much to support the case that God should be imagined thus. The observation by Wellhausen, on the other hand, is very valuable, albeit again not for Lüling's understanding of the verse. As we have seen, the opponent in *Surah* 96 *al-'Alaq*, according to its traditional understanding, seems to be able to exercise some power over the Qur'ān's prophet; it is "he who forbids" the prayer (Q 96:9). It makes thus perfect sense for God to threaten the socially high ranking opponent of grabbing him by his "seat of honour" in the eschatological judgment. Wellhausen's observation thus buttresses the traditional reading of the verse, whereas Lüling did not bring a single case that would lend itself to support his claim that God had a forelock, or that one should attempt to seize Him by it.

To the contrary, there are several contemporary sources that further heighten the tension between Lüling's imagery and late antique literature. For God in the Bible indeed does have hair, but it would be rather impractical to seize Him by it. In addition to the classical topics of God's considerable size, His unknown or unreachable location, and the dangers of approaching Him in the first place, there

---

49 See for example the medieval midrash Exodus Rabbah 3:6, which paraphrase the incidence thus: "God said: When I so wish it, one of the angels who is a third of the world stretches out his hand from heaven and touches the earth, as it says: "And the form of a hand was put forth, and I was taken by a lock [*bṣyṣt*] of my head (Ezekiel VIII, 3)," see also Babylonian Talmud *Menahot* 42a and *Yoma* 76b.

50 See Lüling, *A Challenge to Islam for Reformation*, 66, note 65 and idem, *Über den Ur-Qur'ān*, 436, note 50.

51 See the previous note and Wellhausen, *Reste arabischen Heidentums*, 197–9.

is the issue of the fire surrounding His throne, about which the Book of Daniel already informed us as follows:

> While I looked, thrones were placed, and one who was ancient of days sat, whose garment was white as snow, and the hair of his head (*wsʿr rʾšh*) was like pure wool; his throne was like a fiery flame, its wheels like burning fire.

In parts of the Bible and in the Jewish and Christian traditions that arose in dialogue with Daniel God may have hair, yet the image of anyone seizing this hair violates even the most rudimentary sense of the "eschatologic-apocalyptic" tradition Lüling invokes. In Jewish literature in greater proximity to the time of the Qurʾān, moreover, the image of seizing someone by the forelock is indeed as highly negative as it seems in the Qurʾān, as the following short excerpt from Bavli *Sanhedrin* 82a illustrates. In this narrative expanding on Numbers 25, Zimri ben Salu, an Israelite prince, drags Cozbi, a Medianite princess, in front of Moses, where both are ultimately slain by Phineas:

> What did (Zimri) do? He arose and assembled twenty-four thousand Israelites and went unto Cozbi, and said unto her, "Surrender thyself unto me." She replied, "I am a king's daughter, and thus hath my father instructed me, 'Thou shalt yield only to their greatest man'." He said: "I too am the prince of a tribe; moreover, my tribe is greater than his [Moses'], for mine is second in birth, whilst his is third." He then seized her by her forelock (*tpsh bblwryth*) and brought her before Moses.[52]

Seizing a person by the forelock, thus, is degrading; forelocks, moreover, are now designated with a post-biblical term and associated with idolatry in rabbinic literature.[53] We can thus, from the point of view of the Jewish tradition, safely reject Lüling's idea that seizing God by His forelock would be "not as objectionable as one might think." To the contrary, doing so would invert the relationship of the eschatological judge-executioner on the one hand and of the convicted victim on the other. While aspects of normative upheaval and of the carnivalesque may be identifiable in certain late antique texts, none of them go as far

52 See Bavli *Sanhedrin* 82a–b. Note that Phineas then behaves "as though he argues with his maker" (*kbykwl šʿsh plylwt ʿm qwnw*) about the severity of the punishment of the Israelites in the story, incidentally illustrating another instance of the Talmudic argument with God, see notes 45 and 46 above.

53 See Christine Hayes, *Between the Babylonian & Palestinian Talmuds: Accounting for Halakhic Difference in Selected Sugyot from Tractate Avodah Zarah* (Oxford: Oxford University Press, 1997), 84–91.

as challenging God in the heavens.[54] If Lüling's Ur-Qur'ān appeals to certain post-modern sensitivities relating to the divine it is simply the result of the fact that his text is entirely a post-modern, more specifically late 20th century protestant fabrication.

In order to conclude the discussion, I want to shift away from the Late Antique to the Qur'ān's own context, which is of course the place in which Lüling would and could have started his inquiry. Doing so may have spared him from making his argument in the first place, for the seizing of forelocks is nowhere as well attested as here. Q 11 *Sūrat Hūd* 56, thus, states in general terms that "there is no living being but He holds it by its forelock (*āḫiḏun bi-n'āṣiyatihā*)." The image here shows God sovereignly supporting, or perhaps more likely controlling all his creatures. More closely related to our passage is Q 55 *Sūrat ar-Raḥmān* 41, where we learn that "the guilty will be recognized by their mark; so they will be held by the forelocks (*fa-yu'ḫaḏu bi-n-nawāṣī*) and the feet." The phrasing in *Surah* 96 *al-ʿAlaq* is thus fully in line with the Qur'ān's usage elsewhere, as is the imagery of God holding, or seizing His creatures by their forelocks. Did Lüling not know these passages, or did he exclude them from consideration in order to push his case? A comparable case in the sequel of his study may suggest the former, since Lüling does not shy away from citing evidence contradicting his readings as if they supported it.[55] In either case, the re-

54 See for example Joshua Levinson, "עולם הפוך ראיתי'–עיון בסיפור השיכור ובניו," *Jerusalem Studies in Hebrew Literature* 14 (1993): 7–23; Zellentin, *Rabbinic Parodies* esp. 51–94; and cf. Daniel Boyarin, *Socrates and the Fat Rabbis* (Chicago: University of Chicago Press, 2009).

55 As a result of his textual interventions, Lüling would also need to read Q96:17 as attributed to God, so he sets out to ameliorate the verse's connotations. When contextualizing the term *nādiyah* in Q96:17, Lüling claims that the same word in its one other occurrence in the Qur'ān, in Q29:29, would have "the profane meaning 'assembly of councillors.'" This is not entirely untrue, yet Lüling withholds the crucial information from his audience that the word *nādiyah* here describes the gatherings of the male inhabitants of Lot's city (i.e. Sodom) whom the Qur'ān accuses of what it sees as the most outrageous forms of criminal and sexual misconduct: "... and you (pl.) commit outrages in your gatherings (*wa-ta'tūna fī nādīkumu l-munkara*)?" The context in Q29 must not, of course, necessarily guide our understanding of the same term in Q96, yet it is also not as innocent as Lüling makes the unsuspecting reader believe. Again, the attempt of following Lüling's argument in detail reveals his train of thought: "But meanwhile it has become quite clear that the second frame-narrative of Sura 96, the story of the intruder, is actually the compass of later Koran editors pointing the way ahead for their interpretation of the third part (96.15–19) of the erstwhile Christian strophic hymn 96.1–19. So it is not surprising that on account of this later reinterpretation a typical abnormity becomes apparent also in 96.17, namely the application as well as the meaning of the word *nādī* "council".... The Arabic word stem *n-d-w* has throughout an especially noble and elevated meaning both in the secular as well as in the religious sphere.... The word *nādin* "council" appears only once in the Koran

sult is that Qur'ānic scholars who deprive themselves of the Qur'ān as guideline to assess their suggestions in various other contexts in the same text effectively deprive themselves of the most valuable hermeneutical guideline in their possession – the Jewish and Christian tradition, no matter how relevant, will never suffice as a sole guide for a truly critical reading of the Qur'ān.

The best I can say about Lüling's *Ur-Qur'ān*, then, is that Lüling has some residual respect for the Qur'ān as an Arabic document, unlike his contemporary successor Christoph Luxenberg. It may be astute in the present discussion to consider how Luxenberg deals with the term *nāṣiya*, "forelock," in our passage:

> It is astounding that, of our Koran translators, not one has objected to the expression *"forelock"* (Paret *"Schopf,"* Blachère *"toupet"*). Yet, what is meant here by the spelling ناصية (except for the secondarily inserted ا / ā) is Syro-Aramaic ... *naṣṣāyā*.... For this, the *Thes.* (II 2435) first gives the meaning: *contentiosus, rixosus* (*contentious, quarrelsome*) (said of a woman, as in Prov. 21:9, 19; 25:34).[56]

Here, Lüling's tragedy becomes a Luxenbergian comedy that is well worth savouring in detail. In his search for Syriac cognates in Qur'ānic Arabic, Luxenberg identifies the Syriac and Arabic verb *nṣy*, "to quarrel," as indicating the real meaning of the Qur'ānic term *nāṣiyat*, and insists that our verse Q 96:16 does not address the forelock after all, but the "adversary." He ridicules the *Lisān* (XV 327) for tracing the etymology of "quarrelling" back to two women who grab each other's hair, concluding that "it can be seen from this how little the later [i.e. medieval] Arabic philologists have understood the earlier Syriacisms and Aramaicisms."[57] It is of course Luxenberg himself who, in his selective approach to Semitic languages, had not noted that the verb *nṣy* is not only attested in Syriac and Arabic but also in Hebrew and Jewish Aramaic. He thereby missed the fact that it actually *does* etymologically relate to the widespread Semitic word for dishevelling each other's *hair* – as noted above, the Qur'ānic Arabic term *nāṣiya* in our surah is actually a full cognate to the Hebrew term *nwṣ'* and its later Aramaic variants, designating any type of "growth," and especially

---

apart from our reference 96.17 and that is Sura 29,29 where this word has the profane meaning "assembly of councillors," see Lüling, *A Challenge to Islam for Reformation*, 69–70 and idem, *Über den Ur-Qur'ān*, 63–4.

56 See Luxenberg, *The Syro-Aramaic Reading of the Koran*, 317 and idem, *Die syro-aramäische Lesart des Koran*, 325–6.

57 See Luxenberg, *The Syro-Aramaic Reading of the Koran*, 317 and idem, *Die syro-aramäische Lesart des Koran*, 325–6. Like Lüling, Luxenberg does not attempt to reconcile his findings here with other occurrences of the same term elsewhere in the Qur'ān, i.e. Q 11:56 and Q 55:41, nor does he inform his readers about these parallels in the first place.

"feathers," just as the *Lisān* has it.[58] The adversary in surah Q 96 is thus grabbed by his very human forelock, which may well evoke his cockscomb if one studies Semitic languages a little more carefully.

Unable as I am to conclude my considerations in any way on a positive note, I suggest instead concluding with the pensive remarks Munther Younes has attached to his own, linguistically much more rewarding wrestling with grammatical and lexical difficulties in the Qur'ān:

> The strongest argument in support of my reconstruction is that as they stand now, the verses of Qur'ān 79:1–5 [discussed in his article] are highly problematic, and all the interpretations and commentaries that have been proposed have failed to address their problems. In the absence of an account that addresses these problems in a convincing manner, I believe that my proposed reconstruction brings us closer to an understanding of the original structure, meaning, and character of these verses.[59]

I agree with Younes that there are several difficulties in the Qur'ān which "all the interpretations and commentaries" have indeed not explained. Younes' own reconstructions are much more reasonable and sound, linguistically as well as culturally, than those of Lüling and Luxenberg. Yet not even Younes' reconstructions add to our understanding of the text as long as we cannot verify or falsify them by outside means. Any attempt to reconstruct a text behind the text, in the absence of any objective tools such as manuscript variants, is by necessity circular. In the best of cases, such as that of Younes, the results of speculative philology are interesting; in the worst ones, such as those of Lüling and Luxenberg, they are vexing. Similar attempts have long been abandoned in cognate fields, such as biblical studies, and I suggest directing our attention to more feasible philological endeavours.[60] Instead of writing new texts, we should continue to

---

58 See notes 48 and 51 above.

59 Younes, "Angels, Stars, Death, the Soul, Horses, Bows – or Women?," 277.

60 A good case of comparison in the field of biblical studies, equally involving issues such as the reconstruction of a speculative *Urtexts* based on philological considerations, is that of the putative original Aramaic language of some of the sayings attributed to Jesus in the gospels. Aramaic was the most likely vernacular of first century Palestine, yet those Gospels that became canonical were very likely written in the internationally more adequate *koine* Greek. They were later re-translated into Christian Aramaic, i.e. Syriac. Some astonishing rhymes and word plays that do not work in the Greek Gospels can be appreciated in the (roughly fifth-century) Syriac *Peshitta* text of the gospels, inviting scholarly speculations that the ancient re-translation into a closely related Semitic dialect may well mirror aspects of Jesus "original" sayings. While the insights are fascinating and intellectually most rewarding, the same problem arises that we see in the work of Younes: how are we to determine how much of the recreated "original" is part of the genius of the scholar who recreated it, and how much is actually related to

read the traditional text as we have it and establish the historical context of the nascent Muslim community, and especially of the role of Syriac Christians and rabbinic Jews in seventh century Arabia with which this community stood in multiform and intimate dialogue. One can always return to speculative philology once a more robust consensus has been achieved.

Jesus, or, *mutatis mutandis*, to the Qurʾān? It should be noted that even one of the most capable scholars pursuing such reconstructions about the gospels has long abandoned the project, see e.g. Jan Joosten, "La tradition syriaqe des évangiles et la question du 'substrat araméen,'" *Revue d'Histoire de Philosophie Religieuse 77* (1997): 257–72.

Lutz Edzard

Chances and problems with the morpho-syntactic analysis of the Qur'ān, based on a colometric representation

Introduction

In the various extant versions of his dissertation, *Über den Ur-Qur'ān. Ansätze zur Rekonstruktion vorislamischer christlicher Strophenlieder im Qur'ān*, Günter Lüling adopted a colometric representation of the selected Qur'ānic passages that were subject to his critical approach. In such a representation, the Qur'ānic text is presented in transcription and in small syntactic/textual units that may also reflect the rhyme structure of the verses involved. Lüling's choice to use this textual representation was in line, at least implicitly, with the usual goals of a colometric representation, i.e. to provide an optically transparent structure as a basis for further quantitative and qualitative analysis (cf., e.g., Pawłowski 2008). Therefore, it is legitimate and meaningful to reflect on this method in connection with Lüling's œuvre and to discuss Lüling's suggestions in the framework of this theory. However, this article will not discuss the further-reaching claim by Lüling to the effect that the colometric presentation has a potential to reveal the strophic character of an alleged underlying or chronologically preceding (Christian) text layer.

The colometric method itself reaches back all the way to Greek antiquity. In general, the method is employed to highlight the poetic structure of texts. In the realm of Northwest-Semitic philology, especially Ugaritic, Biblical Hebrew, and Phoenician, important applications of the colometric method include Loretz 1976, 1979, and 1986, as well as Fecht 1990. In the years 1991–1993, the whole corpus of the Hebrew Bible, including the apocryphal book Ben Sira, appeared in a colometric representation edited by Wolfgang Richter (the present author had the honor to be involved as a research assistant in this task). Richter's goal was to present the text of the Hebrew Bible in a pre-Masoretic transcription in a colometric division aimed at elucidating the precise syntactic structure of the text (see below Section 3).

With respect to the Qur'ān, Lüling was the first to use the colometric method in an informal way. Neuwirth (1980, 1981), who was familiar with Richter's ap-

---

This paper is dedicated to the memory of Wolfgang Richter (1926–2015).

https://doi.org/10.1515/9783110599176-011

proach – already in the make at the time – applied the method with a view to enhance the text-linguistic and literary analysis of the Meccan suras. Edzard (2003) applied Richter's methodology to the whole corpus of the Qur'ān (see below Section 4), focussing exclusively on issues of syntax. The whole text of the Qur'ān is now available online in line with the tenets laid out in Edzard 2003.[1]

Excursus: Disjunctive and conjunctive accents in the Hebrew Bible

Contrary to the text of the Qur'ān, the text of the Hebrew Bible is accompanied by a sophisticated system of "cantillation marks" (*ṭəʿā̊mīm*, properly meaning "taste, sense") that indicates the precise syntactic structure of the individual verses.[2] As this system is highly relevant to the issue under discussion, here is a brief overview.

A group of "disjunctive accents" in a hierarchical four-level system, plus one type of "conjunctive accent" allows us to parse any verse in the Hebrew Bible in a successive binary partition as follows (there is one system for the 21 prose books, and one system for Job, Proverbs, and Psalms):

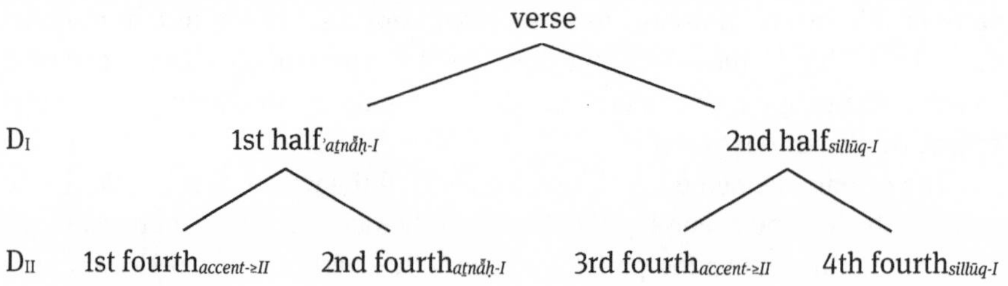

etc.

Here is an example (1):

---

1 Cf. https://www2.hf.uio.no/polyglotta/index.php?page=volume&vid=51.

2 For details, cf. Israel Yeivin, *Introduction to the Tiberian Masora (Mavo la-masora ha-ṭavranit)*, trans. and ed. E. J. Revell (Chico, CA: Scholars Press, 1980); Mark Aronoff, "Orthography and Linguistic Theory: the Syntactic Basis of Masoretic Hebrew Punctuation," *Language* 61 (1985): 28–72; and Lutz Edzard, "Oralité et écriture: les *ṭəʿā̊ mīm* comme représentation prosodique de la structure morpho-syntaxique de la Bible hébraïque," in *Oralité et écriture dans la Bible et le Coran*, ed. Pierre Larcher and Philippe Cassuto (Aix-en-Provence: Presses Universitaires d'Aix, Marseille, 2014), 41–52.

(1) Gen 1:1 structured by cantillation marks

בְּרֵאשִׁ֖ית בָּרָ֣א אֱלֹהִ֑ים אֵ֥ת הַשָּׁמַ֖יִם וְאֵ֥ת הָאָֽרֶץ׃

bə-rē(’)šīṯ bārā̊(’)’ĕlōhīm ’ēṯ haš-šā̊máyim wə-’ēṯ hā̊-’ā̊rɛṣ

In the beginning God created the heaven and the earth.

D_{I} D_{II} D_{III} D_{IV}

bə-rē(’)šīṯ$_{\textit{ṭip̄ḥā̊(’)-II}}$

[bā̊rā̊(’)$_{\textit{mūnaḥ}}$’ɛ̆lōhīm]$_{\textit{’aṯnā̊ḥ-I}}$

[’ēṯ$_{\textit{mērəḵā̊(’)}}$ haš-šā̊máyim]$_{\textit{ṭip̄ḥā̊(’)-II}}$

[wə-’ēṯ$_{\textit{mērəḵā̊(’)}}$ hā̊-’ā̊rɛṣ]$_{\textit{sillūq-I}}$

Here, the syntactic structure is unambiguous. In many cases, however, the very setting of the cantillation marks helps to disambiguate the internal syntactic structure of a verse. Again, here is an example (2):

(2) Ruth 2:14 structured by cantillation marks

וַיֹּאמֶר֩ לָ֨ה בֹ֜עַז לְעֵ֣ת הָאֹ֗כֶל גֹּ֤שִֽׁי הֲלֹם֙ וְאָכַ֣לְתְּ מִן־הַלֶּ֔חֶם ...

way-yṓ(’)mɛr l-ā̊h bō‘az lə-‘ēṯ hā̊-’ṓḵɛl gōšī hălōm wə-’ā̊ḵalt min-hal-lɛḥɛm ...

And Boaz said unto her at meal-time: ‘Come hither, and eat of the bread ...’,

D_{I} D_{II} D_{III} D_{IV}

[[way-yṓ(’)mɛr$_{\textit{təlīšā̊(’) qəṭannā̊(h)}}$ l-ā̊h]$_{\textit{’azlā̊(’)}}$ bō‘az]$_{\textit{gērēš-IV}}$

[lə-‘ēṯ$_{\textit{mūnaḥ}}$ hā̊-’ṓḵɛl]$_{\textit{rəḇīa‘-III}}$

[gōšī$_{\textit{məhuppā̊ḵ}}$ hălōm]$_{\textit{pašṭā̊(’)-III}}$

[wə-’ā̊ḵalt$_{\textit{mūnaḥ}}$ min-hal-lɛḥɛm]$_{\textit{zā̊qēp̄ qā̊ṭā̊n-II}}$

...

The representation clearly illustrates that one cannot read the verse as: *And Boaz said to her: ‘Come hither at mealtime, and eat the bread ...’

The colometric representation of the text of the Hebrew Bible by Wolfgang Richter (1991–1993)

It is the significant merit of Wolfgang Richter to have arranged the whole text of the Hebrew Bible in small syntactically independent units (“colon”, pl. “cola”). Richter (1991–1993) proceeded as follows: a colon is typically represented by a small, syntactically independent unit marked by a finite verb form. Additionally, topicalized phrases are marked by “P” (“casus pendens”), relative clauses by

"R", infinitive clauses by "I", and interjections by "J". What is more, Richter made an attempt at creating a transcription at a pre-Masoretic text level, not representing, for instance, segolation, but this latter point plays no role in our context. Here is the beginning of Genesis (3):

(3) Gen 1:1–5 in Richter's representation

1	P3a	_b°=rēšīt_	בְּרֵאשִׁית
	PR	_barā(ʾ) ʾilōhīm ʾ°at-ha-šamaym w°=°at ha=ʾarṣ_	בָּרָא אֱלֹהִים, אֵת הַשָּׁמַיִם, וְאֵת הָאָרֶץ
2	a	_w°=ha=ʾarṣ hay°atā tuhw wa=buhw_	וְהָאָרֶץ, הָיְתָה תֹהוּ וָבֹהוּ
	b	_w°=ḥušk ʿal p°anē t°ihōm_	וְחֹשֶׁךְ, עַל-פְּנֵי תְהוֹם
	c	_w°=rūḥ ʾ°ilō*hīm m°raḥ[ḥ]°ipt ʿal p°anē ha=maym_	וְרוּחַ אֱלֹהִים, מְרַחֶפֶת עַל-פְּנֵי הַמָּיִם
3	a	_wa=yō(ʾ)mir ʾ°ilō*hīm_	וַיֹּאמֶר אֱלֹהִים
3	b	_y°ihy ʾōr_	יְהִי אוֹר
3	c	_wa=y°ihy ʾōr_	וַיְהִי-אוֹר
4	a	_wa-y°irʾ ʾ°ilōhīm ʾat ha=ʾōr_	וַיַּרְא אֱלֹהִים אֶת-הָאוֹר
	b	_kī ṭōb_	כִּי-טוֹב
	c	_wa=yabdil ʾ°ilō*hīm bēn ha=ʾōr w°=bēn ha=ḥušk_	וַיַּבְדֵּל אֱלֹהִים, בֵּין הָאוֹר וּבֵין הַחֹשֶׁךְ
5	a	_wa-yiqraʾ ʾ°ilō*hīm l°=[h]a=ʾōr yōm_	וַיִּקְרָא אֱלֹהִים לָאוֹר יוֹם
	b	_w°=l°=[h]a=ḥušk qarā(ʾ) laylā_	וְלַחֹשֶׁךְ קָרָא לָיְלָה
	c	_wa=y°ihy ʿarb_	וַיְהִי-עֶרֶב
	d	_wa-y°ihy buqr_	וַיְהִי-בֹקֶר
	e	_yōm ʾ°aḥ⁺ad_	יוֹם אֶחָד

1 In the beginning God created the heavens and the earth. 2 Now the earth was formless and empty, darkness was over the surface of the deep, and the Spirit of God was hovering over the waters. 3 And God said, "Let there be light," and there was light. 4 God saw that the light was good, and he separated the light from the darkness. 5 God called the light "day," and the darkness he called "night." And there was evening, and there was morning – the first day.

The colometric representation (in Richter's sense) of the Qurʾān (Edzard 2003)

Edzard (2003) constitutes an application of Richter's (1991–1993) method to the whole text of the Qurʾān. In concord with Richter's syntactic nomenclature, the text is represented in both Arabic script and transcription in small syntactically independent units ("colon", pl. "cola"). Hence, topicalized phrases are represented by "P", relative clauses by "R" and interjections by "J".[3] In contrast to the strategy adopted in the publications by Neuwirth (1980, 1981, and later articles), no attempt is made at representing textual and/or poetic structure. Here is a short example that also allows for the representation of syntactic ambiguities (4):

(4) *Sūrat al-Falaq* (113) in a colometric representation

بِسْمِ اللَّهِ الرَّحْمَٰنِ الرَّحِيمِ

bi-smi llāhi r-raḥmāni r-raḥīmi

In the name of Allah, the Most Beneficent, the Most Merciful.

قُلْ أَعُوذُ بِرَبِّ الْفَلَقِ

1a *qul*
1b *ʾaʿūḏu bi-rabbi l-falaqi*

Say: I seek refuge in the Lord of the Daybreak

مِن شَرِّ مَا خَلَقَ

2 *min šarri mā ḫalaqa*

From the evil of that which He created

وَمِن شَرِّ غَاسِقٍ إِذَا وَقَبَ

3a *wa-min šarri ġāsiqin*
3b *ʾiḏā waqaba*

From the evil of the darkness when it is intense,

وَمِن شَرِّ النَّفَّاثَاتِ فِي الْعُقَدِ

4a *wa-min šarri n-naffāṯāti fī l-ʿuqadi*

And from the evil of malignant witchcraft,

وَمِن شَرِّ حَاسِدٍ إِذَا حَسَدَ

5a *wa-min šarri ḥāsidin*
5b *ʾiḏā ḥasada*

And from the evil of the envier when he envieth.

Already Goldziher (1920: 177) pointed out that *ʾāya* 2 allows for an alternative reading. While the standard reading of *ʾāya* 2 stipulates that God *also* created evil, with *mā ḫalaqa* functioning as the second term of an annexation (*ʾiḍāfa*), which makes *šarri* definite, the alternative reading (representing the view of the Muʿtazila) stipulates that God did *not* create evil. Thereby, *šarrin* represents an indefinite antecedent with a subsequent relative clause, in which *mā* has to

---

3 As there are no infinitives (or infinitive clauses) in Arabic, the category "I" is obviously absent in the colometric transcription.

be interpreted as a negator, as opposed to a relative marker. Hence, the structure of the alternative reading is the following (5):

(5) Alternative reading of *ʾāya* 2 in *Sūrat al-Falaq* (113)in a colometric representation

2 *min šarrin*

2R *mā ḫalaqa*

From evil that He did not create.

Examples discussed by Lüling (1973)

Among the relatively few examples discussed thoroughly by Lüling (1973) are *Sūrat ʿAbas* (80:1–22) and *Sūrat al-ʿAlaq* (96). Both follow in a colometric transcription. First, here is *Sūrat ʿAbas* (80:1–22) (6):

(6) *Sūrat ʿAbas* (80:1–22)

بِسْمِ اللَّهِ الرَّحْمَٰنِ الرَّحِيمِ

bi-smi llāhi r-raḥmāni r-raḥīmi

In the name of Allah, the Most Beneficent, the Most Merciful.

عَبَسَ وَتَوَلَّىٰ

1a *ʿabasa*

1b *wa-tawallā*

He frowned and turned away

أَن جَاءَهُ الْأَعْمَىٰ

2 *ʾan ǧāʾa-hū l-ʾaʿmā*

Because the blind man came unto him.

وَمَا يُدْرِيكَ لَعَلَّهُ يَزَّكَّىٰ

3a *wa-mā yudrī-ka*

3b *laʿalla-hū yazzakkā*

What could inform thee but that he might grow (in grace)

أَوْ يَذَّكَّرُ فَتَنفَعَهُ الذِّكْرَىٰ

4a *ʾaw yaḏḏakkaru*

4b *fa-tanfaʿa-hū ḏ-ḏikrā*

Or take heed and so the reminder might avail him?

أَمَّا مَنِ اسْتَغْنَىٰ

5 *ʾammā mani staġnā*

As for him who thinketh himself independent,

فَأَنتَ لَهُ تَصَدَّىٰ

6 *fa-ʾanta la-hū taṣaddā*

Unto him thou payest regard.

وَمَا عَلَيْكَ أَلَّا يَزَّكَّىٰ

7a *wa-mā ʿalay-ka*
7b *ʾal-lā yazzakkā*
Yet it is not thy concern if he grow not (in grace).

وَأَمَّا مَن جَاءَكَ يَسْعَىٰ

8a *wa-ʾammā man ǧāʾa-ka*
8b *yasʿā*
But as for him who cometh unto thee with earnest purpose

وَهُوَ يَخْشَىٰ

9 *wa-huwa yaḫšā*
And hath fear,

فَأَنتَ عَنْهُ تَلَهَّىٰ

10 *fa-ʾanta ʿan-hū talahhā*
From him thou art distracted.

كَلَّا إِنَّهَا تَذْكِرَةٌ

11a *kallā*
11b *ʾinna-hā taḏkiratun*
Nay, but verily it is an Admonishment,

فَمَن شَاءَ ذَكَرَهُ

12a *fa-man šāʾa*
12b *ḏakara-hū*
So let whosoever will pay heed to it,

فِي صُحُفٍ مُّكَرَّمَةٍ

13 *fī ṣuḥufin mukarramatin*
On honoured leaves

مَّرْفُوعَةٍ مُّطَهَّرَةٍ

14 *marfūʿatin muṭahharatin*
Exalted, purified,

بِأَيْدِي سَفَرَةٍ

15 *bi-ʾaydī safaratin*
(Set down) by scribes

كِرَامٍ بَرَرَةٍ

16 *kirāmin bararatin*
Noble and righteous.

قُتِلَ الْإِنسَانُ مَا أَكْفَرَهُ

17a *qutila l-ʾinsānu*
17b *mā ʾakfara-hū*
Man is (self-)destroyed: how ungrateful!

مِنْ أَيِّ شَيْءٍ خَلَقَهُ

18 *min ʾayyi šayʾin ḫalaqa-hū*
From what thing doth He create him?

مِن نُّطْفَةٍ خَلَقَهُ فَقَدَّرَهُ

19a *min nuṭfatin ḫalaqa-hū*
19b *fa-qaddara-hū*
From a drop of seed. He createth him and proportioneth him,

ثُمَّ السَّبِيلَ يَسَّرَهُ

20 P *ṯumma s-sabīla*
20 *yassara-hū*
Then maketh the way easy for him,

ثُمَّ أَمَاتَهُ فَأَقْبَرَهُ

21a *ṯumma ʾamāta-hū*
21b *fa-ʾaqbara-hū*
Then causeth him to die, and burieth him;

ثُمَّ إِذَا شَاءَ أَنشَرَهُ

22a *ṯumma*
22b *ʾiḏā šāʾa*
22a *ʾanšara-hū*
Then, when He will, He bringeth him again to life.

Regarding *ʾāya* 3 of *Sūrat ʿAbas* (Lüling 1973: 107, 109) suggested an alternative parsing, which is colometrically reproduced here, together with Lüling's translation (7):

(7) Alternative parsing of *ʾāya 3* of *Sūrat ʿAbas* (Lüling 1973: 107, 109)
3a *wa-mā yudrī-ka*
3b *laʿalla-hū*
3c *tazakka*
Was wird dich lehren? Fürwahr, vielleicht ER!
Läutere dich!

In the case of colon 3c, Lüling actually proposed a wrong imperative form **taz-zakkā*, a point which was also raised by Bernard Lewin, Frithiof Rundgren, and Anton Spitaler in an evaluation of an earlier version of Lüling's thesis (Lüling never reacted to this criticism in a constructive way).

One other case study developed by Lüling concerns *Sūrat al-ʿAlaq* (96). Again, here is the text in a colometric transcription (8):

(8) *Sūrat al-ʿAlaq* (96)

بِسْمِ اللَّهِ الرَّحْمَٰنِ الرَّحِيمِ

bi-smi llāhi r-raḥmāni r-raḥīmi

In the name of Allah, the Most Beneficent, the Most Merciful.

اقْرَأْ بِاسْمِ رَبِّكَ الَّذِي خَلَقَ

1 *iqraʾ bi-smi rabbi-ka*

1R *llaḏī ḫalaqa*

Read: In the name of thy Lord Who createth,

خَلَقَ الْإِنسَانَ مِنْ عَلَقٍ

2 *ḫalaqa l-ʾinsāna min ʿalaqin*

Createth man from a clot.

اقْرَأْ وَرَبُّكَ الْأَكْرَمُ

3a *iqraʾ*

3b *wa-rabbu-ka l-ʾakramu*

Read: And thy Lord is the Most Bounteous,

الَّذِي عَلَّمَ بِالْقَلَمِ

4(3R) *llaḏī ʿallama bi-l-qalami*

Who teacheth by the pen,

عَلَّمَ الْإِنسَانَ مَا لَمْ يَعْلَمْ

5 *ʿallama l-ʾinsāna mā lam yaʿlam*

Teacheth man that which he knew not.

كَلَّا إِنَّ الْإِنسَانَ لَيَطْغَىٰ

6a *kallā*

6b *ʾinna l-ʾinsāna la-yaṭġā*

Nay, but verily man is rebellious

أَن رَّآهُ اسْتَغْنَىٰ

7a *ʾan raʾā-hu*

7b *staġnā*

That he thinketh himself independent!

إِنَّ إِلَىٰ رَبِّكَ الرُّجْعَىٰ

8 *ʾinna ʾilā rabbi-ka r-ruǧʿā*

Lo! unto thy Lord is the return.

أَرَأَيْتَ الَّذِي يَنْهَىٰ

9 *ʾa-raʾayta llaḏī yanhā*

Hast thou seen him who dissuadeth

عَبْدًا إِذَا صَلَّىٰ

10a *ʿabdan*

10b *ʾiḏā ṣallā*

A slave when he prayeth?

أَرَأَيْتَ إِن كَانَ عَلَى الْهُدَىٰ

11a *ʾa-raʾayta*
11b *ʾin kāna ʿalā l-hudā*
Hast thou seen if he relieth on the guidance (of Allah)

أَوْ أَمَرَ بِالتَّقْوَىٰ

12 *ʾaw ʾamara bi-t-taqwā*
Or enjoineth piety?

أَرَأَيْتَ إِن كَذَّبَ وَتَوَلَّىٰ

13a *ʾa-raʾayta*
13b *ʾin kaḏḏaba*
13c *wa-tawallā*
Hast thou seen if he denieth (Allah's guidance) and is froward?

أَلَمْ يَعْلَم بِأَنَّ اللَّهَ يَرَىٰ

14 *ʾa-lam yaʿlam bi-ʾanna llāha yarā*
Is he then unaware that Allah seeth?

كَلَّا لَئِن لَّمْ يَنتَهِ لَنَسْفَعًا بِالنَّاصِيَةِ

15a *kallā*
15b *la-ʾin lam yantahi*
15c *la-nasfaʿā bi-n-nāṣiyati*
Nay, but if he cease not We will seize him by the forelock –

نَاصِيَةٍ كَاذِبَةٍ خَاطِئَةٍ

16 *nāṣiyatin kāḏibatin ḫāṭiʾatin*
The lying, sinful forelock –

فَلْيَدْعُ نَادِيَهُ

17 *fa-l-yadʿu nādiya-hū*
Then let him call upon his henchmen!

سَنَدْعُ الزَّبَانِيَةَ

18 *sa-nadʿu z-zabāniyata*
We will call the guards of hell.

كَلَّا لَا تُطِعْهُ وَاسْجُدْ وَاقْتَرِب

19a *kallā*
19b *lā tuṭiʿ-hu*
19c *wa-sǧud*
19d *wa-qtarib*
Nay, Obey not thou him. But prostrate thyself, and draw near (unto Allah).

Various suggestions to emendate the text were proposed by Lüling, none of which, however, directly touched upon the syntactic structure *per se*, e.g., regarding *ʾāyāt* 6 and 7 (9):

(9) Alternative reading of *'āyāt* 6 and 7 *of Sūrat al-ʿAlaq* (96) (Lüling 1973: 73, 75)
6a *kallā*
6b *'anna l-'insāna la-yaṭġā*
7a *'in ra'ā-hu*
7b *staġnā*
Keineswegs soll der Mensch sich unklug abwenden,
wenn er Gott hoch erhaben sieht.
Sieh! Zu Gott muß man sich wenden.

Interestingly, Luxenberg (2000: 283 f.) had also suggested an alternative reading of this passage : "Fürwahr, der Mensch vergißt [Syriac ܛܥܐ *ṭəʿā* instead of Arabic طغى *ṭaġā*], wenn er sieht, daß er reich geworden ist."

Another, even more problematic example of Lüling's approach concerns *'āya* 15 of *Sūrat al-ʿAlaq* (96) (10):

(10) Lüling's re-analysis of *'āya* 15 of *Sūrat al-ʿAlaq* (96)
15a *kallā*
15b *la-'in lam yuntaha*
15c *la-yusfaʿā bi-n-nāṣiyati*
Keineswegs! Wenn ER nicht in Ruhe gelassen wird,
wird ER gepackt
beim Schopf!

Not only has one to point out the wrong form **yuntahā*, as suggested by Lüling; the anthropomorphic semantics of Lüling's translation in this case is highly objectionable as well.

Conclusion

In principle, Lüling's colometric representation of the textual passages he analyzed constituted a step in the right direction. However, the present author arrives at the opinion that Lüling's specific suggestions hardly have any merit from a philological or linguistic perspective, legitimate as his research may have been in principle. As Lewin, Rundgren, and Spitaler (1970) have rightly stressed, Lüling's ideas are marred by suggestions of often ungrammatical forms. Lüling does not present any evidence for an alleged "Middle Arabic" character of such forms, even though he could have referred to the work of Karl Vollers (1906) in order to advance such ideas. Independently of the grammatically problematic character of his proposals, Lüling has, in the view of the present author, not presented any semantically convincing suggestions.[4]

In conclusion, it is important to heed the words formulated by Stefan Wild (2010: 645), referring to the work of Christoph Luxenberg (alias: Ephrem Malki) (2000), words that are also applicable to Lüling:

> The first issue is that scholarship has the right to ask all questions. There can be no academic censorship that precludes expressing and discussing certain ideas. Historical criticism, text-linguistic, and literary approaches to the text and other methods of modern scholarship cannot be banned from research on the Qur'ān.
>
> A second issue is that the religious or cultural background of a scholar must not be used to discredit his or her ideas.
>
> The third issue is that a contribution to a Qur'anic topic authored by a non-Muslim cannot be considered true just because it causes a scandal and is opposed by Muslim scholarship.

4 For a balanced evaluation of Lüling's theses, cf. Ibn Rawandi, "On pre-Islamic Christian Strophic Poetical Texts in the Koran: a Critical Look at the Work of Günter Lüling," in *What the Koran Really Says. Language, Text, and Commentary*, ed. Ibn Warraq (Amherst, NY: Prometheus Books, 2002), 653–710.

Bibliographie

Abott, Nadja. *Studies in Arabic literary Papyri*, Bd. 1, *Historical Texts.* Chicago: University of Chicago Press, 1957.

Abrahamov, Binyamin. „Signs." In *Encyclopaedia of the Qurʾān*, Hg. Jane Dammen McAuliffe. Brill Online: http://dx.doi.org/10.1163/1875-3922_q3_EQCOM_00182.

Acampora-Michel, Elsbeth, Hg. und Üb. *Liber de pomo / Buch vom Apfel.* Frankfurt am Main: Vittorio Klostermann, 2001.

Adam, A. K. M., Hg. *Handbook of Postmodern Biblical Interpretation.* St. Louis: Chalice Press, 2000.

Aellig, Jacob. *Evangelisches Seminar Muristalden: Jubiläumsschrift 1854–1954. Ein Beitrag zur bernischen Kirchen- und Schulgeschichte.* Muristalden: Verlag des Seminars, 1954.

Aichele, George et al., Hgg. *The Postmodern Bible.* New Haven: Yale University Press, 1995.

Aland, Barbara, Hg. *New Testament Textual Criticism, Exegesis and Church History. A Discussion of methods.* Contributions to biblical Exegesis and Theology 7. Kampen: Kok Pharos, 1994.

Andrae, Tor. *Der Ursprung des Islams und das Christentum.* Uppsala: Almqvist & Wiksells, 1926.

Andrae, Tor. *Mohammed: The Man and His Faith*, Üb. T. Menzel. New York: Scribner's, 1936.

Aouad, Maroun. „Aristote de Stagire: De Pomo." In *Dictionnaire des Philosophes Antiques*, Bd. 1, 537–541. Paris: CNRS, 1994.

Aronoff, Mark. „Orthography and Linguistic Theory: the Syntactic Basis of Masoretic Hebrew Punctuation." *Language* 61 (1985): 28–72.

Azaiez, Mehdi. *Le contre-discours coranique, Studies in the History and Culture of the Middle East.* Bd . 30. Berlin: Walter de Gruyter, 2015.

Al-Azmeh, Aziz. *The Emergence of Islam in Late Antiquity.* Cambridge, UK: Cambridge University Press, 2014.

Azraqī, Muḥammad Abū l-Walīd. *Aḫbār Makkah.* 2 Bde., Hg. Rušdī ṣ-Ṣāliḥ Malḥas. Beirut: Dār al-Andalus, 1389/1969.

Baker-Brian, Nicholas J. *Manichaeism: An Ancient Faith Rediscovered.* London: T & T Clark, 2011.

Baneth, D. Z. H. „What did Muḥammad mean when he called his religion 'Islam'?." *Israel Oriental Studies* 1 (1975): 183–190.

Bar-Asher Siegal, Michal. *Early Christian Monastic Literature and the Babylonian Talmud.* Cambridge: Cambridge University Press, 2013.

Barbel, Joseph. *Christos Angelos. Die Anschauung von Christus als Bote und Engel in der gelehrten und volkstümlichen Literatur des christlichen Altertums. Zugleich ein Beitrag zur Geschichte des Ursprungs und der Fortdauer des Arianismus.* Bonn: Peter Hannstein, 1941.

Barker, Margaret. *The great angel. A study of Israel's second God.* Westminster John Knox Press, 1992.

Batunsky, Mark. „Review of Günter Lüling. *Über den Ur-Qurʾān. Ansätze zur Rekonstruktion vorislamischer christlicher Strophenlieder im Ur-Qurʾān.* Erlangen: Verlagsbuchhandlung Hannelore Lüling, 1974." *Narody Azii i Afriki* 6 (1987): 143–153.

https://doi.org/10.1515/9783110599176-012

Bauckham, Richard. *God crucified. Monotheism and Christology in the New Testament.* Grand Rapids-Cambridge: Eerdmans, 1998.

Beck, Edmund. *Des heiligen Ephraem des Syrers Paschalhymnen; (de Azymis, de Crucifisione, de Resurrectione)*, CSCO. Bde. 248 & 249. Louvain: Peeters, 1964.

Bell, Richard. *The Qur'ān. Translation, with a critical re-arrangement of the Surahs.* Edinburgh: T&T Clark, 1950.

Beltz, Walther. „Review of Günter Lüling. *Über den Ur-Qur'ān. Ansätze zur Rekonstruktion vorislamischer christlicher Strophenlieder im Ur-Qur'ān.* Erlangen: Verlagsbuchhandlung Hannelore Lüling,1974." *Zeitschrift für Religions- und Geistesgeschichte* (ZRGG) 27/2 (1975): 169–171.

Beltz, Walther. „Review of Günter Lüling. *Zwei Aufsätze zur Religions- und Geistesgeschichte, 1. Der vorgeschichtliche Sinn des Wortes 'Metall', 2. Avicenna und seine buddhistische Herkunft*, Erlangen 1977. Ders.: *Der christliche Kult an der vorislamischen Kaaba als Problem der Islamwissenschaften und christlichen Theologie*, Erlangen: Verlagsbuchhandlung Hannelore Lüling, 1977." *Zeitschrift für Religions- und Geistesgeschichte* (ZRGG) 30/2 (1978): 181–181(1).

Berger, Klaus. *Exegese des Neuen Testaments: Neue Wege vom Text zur Auslegung* Heidelberg: Quelle & Meyer, 3. Auflage, 1991.

Berger, Klaus. *Formen und Gattungen im Neuen Testament.* Tübingen: Francke, 2005.

Bijlefeld, Willem A. „A Prophet and More than a Prophet? Some Observations on the Qur'ānic Use of the Terms 'Prophet' and 'Apostle'." *Muslim World* 59 (1969): 1–28.

Blume, Friedrich, Hg. *Die Musik in Geschichte und Gegenwart.* Bd. 12. München: Saur, 1965.

Bobzin, Hartmut. *Der Koran. Aus dem Arabischen neu übertragen*, unter Mitarbeit von Katharina Bobzin. Munich: C.H. Beck, 2010.

Bobzin, Hartmut. *Der Koran. Eine Einführung.* München: Beck, 2000.

Bobzin, Hartmut. „Theodor Nöldekes Biographische Blätter aus dem Jahr 1917." In *„Sprich doch mit deinen Knechten aramäisch, wir verstehen es!": Festschrift für Otto Jastrow zum 60. Geburtstag,* Hgg. Werner Arnold und Hartmut Bobzin, 91–104. Wiesbaden: Harrassowitz 2002.

Boyarin, Daniel. *Socrates and the Fat Rabbis.* Chicago: University of Chicago Press, 2009.

Brock, S.P. „Poetry." In *Gorgias Encyclopedic Dictionary of the Syriac Heritage* (Beth Mardutho The Syriac Institute: Piscataway), Hgg. S.P. Brock et al., 334–336. NJ: Gorgias Press, 2011.

Brockelmann, Carl et al. *Geschichte der christlichen Litteraturen des Orients.* Die Litteraturen des Ostens in Einzeldarstellungen 7. Leipzig: Amelang, 1907.

Brockelmann, Carl. „Geschichte der syrischen und christlich-arabischen Literatur." In *Geschichte der christlichen Litteraturen des Orients.* Die Litteraturen des Ostens in Einzeldarstellungen 7, Hgg. Carl Brockelmann et al., 1–74. Leipzig: Amelang, 1907.

Brockett, A. A. „Review of Günter Lüling. *Die Wiederentdeckung des Propheten Muhammad. Eine Kritik am „christlichen" Abendland.* Erlangen: Verlagsbuchhandlung Hannelore Lüling, 1981." *International Journal of Middle East Studies* 13 (1981): 519–521.

Budde, Karl. *Die Religion in Geschichte und Gegenwart.* Bd. 1. Tübingen: Mohr 3. Auflage, 1957.

Burnett, Fred. „Postmodern Biblical Exegesis: The Eve of historical Criticism." *Semeia* 51 (1990): 51–80.

Callistratus. „Descriptions 6." In *Elder Philostratus, Younger Philostratus, Callistratus*, Üb. und Hg. Arthur Fairbanks. Loeb Classical Library 256. London: Harvard University Press, 1931.

Carrell, Peter R. *Jesus and the Angels. Angelology and Christology of the Apocalypse of John.* Cambridge: CUP, 1997.

Casanova, Paul. *Mohammad et la fin du monde, étude critique sur l'Islam primitif.* 2 Bde. Paris: P. Geuthner, 1911–1924.

Coats, G. W. „Motive Criticism, OT." In *The Interpreter's Dictionary of the Bible.* Bd. 5, Hgg. George Butterick et al., 607. Nashville: Abingdon, 1976.

Cohen, Simona. *Transformations of Time and Temporality in Medieval and Renaissance Art.* Leiden: Brill, 2014.

Collins, John. *The Bible after Babel: Historical Criticism in a Postmodern Age.* Grand Rapids: Eerdmans, 2005.

Comerro, Viviane. *Les traditions sur la constitution du muṣḥaf de ʿUthmān.* Beiruter Texte und Studien 134. Würzburg: Ergon, 2012.

Conzelmann, Hans und Andreas Lindemann. *Arbeitsbuch zum Neuen Testament.* Tübingen: Mohr Siebeck, 1991.

Cragg, Kenneth. *Jesus and the Muslim; an Exploration.* London: George Allen & Unwin, 1985.

Crone, Patricia und Michael Cook. *Hagarism. The making of the Islamic world.* Cambridge: Cambridge University Press, 1977.

Crone, Patricia. „Jewish Christianity and the Qurʾān (Part One)." *Journal of Near Eastern Studies* 74 (2015): 225–253.

Crone, Patricia. „The Quranic *Mushrikūn* and the Resurrection (Part I)." *Bulletin of the School of Oriental and African Studies* 75 (2012): 445–72.

Crone, Patricia. „The Quranic *Mushrikūn* and the Resurrection (Part II)." *Bulletin of the School of Oriental and African Studies* 76 (2013): 1–20.

Crone, Patricia. „The Religion of the Qurʾānic Pagans: God and the Lesser Deities." *Arabica* 57 (2010): 151–200.

Crone, Patricia. „What do we actually know about Mohammed?" *Open Democracy* (10 June 2008): online: https://www.opendemocracy.net/faith-europe_islam/mohammed_3866.jsp.

Crüsemann, Frank. *Studien zur Formgeschichte von Hymnus und Danklied in Israel.* Neukirchen-Vluyn: Neukirchener Verlag, 1969.

Cuypers, Michel. „L'analyse rhétorique face à la critique historique de J. Wansbrough et de G. Lüling. L'exemple de la sourate 96." In *The Coming of the Comforter: When, Where, and to Whom?, Studies on the Rise of Islam and Various Other Topics in Memory of John Wansbrough.* Orientalia Judaica Christiana 3, Hgg. Carlos A. Segovia und Lourie Basil, 343–69. Piscataway, NJ: Gorgias Press, 2012.

Cuypers, Michel. *The Banquet: A Reading of the Fifth Sura of the Qur'an.* Miami: Convivium, 2009.

Dammen McAuliffe, Jane. „Text and Textuality: Q. 3:7 as a Point of Intersection." In *Literary Structures of Religious Meaning in the Qur'an*, Hg. Issa J. Boullata, 56–76. London: Curzon Press, 2000.

Dassmann, Ernst. *Kirchengeschichte I. Ausbreitung, Leben und Lehre der Kirche in den ersten drei Jahrhunderten.* Stuttgart-Berlin-Köln: Kohlhammer, 1991.

Dayeh, Islam. „Al-Ḥawāmīm: Intertextuality and Coherence in Meccan Surahs.“ In *The Qur'ān in Context. Historical and Literary Investigations into the Qur'ānic Milieu*, Hgg. Angelika Neuwirth, Nicolai Sinai und Michael Marx, 461–494. Leiden and Boston: Brill, 2010.

De Blois, François „Elchasai – Manes – Muḥammad: Manichäismus und Islam in religionshistorischen Vergleich.“ *Der Islam* 81 (2004): 31–48.

De Blois, François. „Naṣrānī (Ναζωραῖος) and ḥanīf (ἐθνικός): Studies on the Religious Vocabulary of Christianity and of Islam.“ *Bulletin of the School of Oriental and African Studies* 65 (2002): 1–30.

De Blois, François „Review of Christoph Luxenberg, *Die syro-aramäische Lesart des Koran: Ein Beitrag zur Entschlüsselung der Koransprache.*“ *Journal of Qur'anic Studies* 5 (2003): 92–97.

Dohmen, Christoph. *Die Bibel und ihre Auslegung.* München: C. H. Beck, 1998.

Donner, Fred M. „The Qur'anicization of Religio-Political Discourse in the Umayyad Period.“ *Révue des Mondes Musulmans et de la Mediterranée* 129 (2011): 79–92.

Droge, Arthur. *The Qur'ān: A New Annotated Translation.* Sheffield, UK and Bristol, CT: Equinox, 2015.

Duensing, Hugo. „Review of Adolf Grohmann. *Äthiopische Marienhymnen.* Leipzig: Teubner, 1919.“ *Theologische Literaturzeitung* 47/9 (1922): 197–198.

Edzard, Lutz. „Oralité et écriture: les *ṭəʿāmīm* comme représentation prosodique de la structure morpho-syntaxique de la Bible hébraïque.“ In *Oralité et écriture dans la Bible et le Coran*, Hgg. Pierre Larcher und Philippe Cassuto, 41–52. Aix-en-Provence: Presses Universitaires d'Aix, Marseille, 2014.

Edzard, Lutz. „Perspektiven einer computergestützten Analyse der qur'ānischen Morpho-Syntax und Satz-Syntax in kolometrischer Darstellung.“ *Arabica* 50/3 (2003): 350–380.

Elad, Amikam. *Medieval Jerusalem and Islamic Worship. Holy Places, Ceremonies, Pilgrimage.* Leiden: Brill, 1995.

Erichson, Alfred. *Das Marburger Religionsgespräch über das Abendmahl im Jahre 1529 nach ungedruckten Straßburger Urkunden.* Straßburg, 1880.

Erichson, Alfred. *'Ein feste Burg'. Entstehung, Inhalt und Geschichte des Lutherliedes dem protestantischen Volk erklärt.* Straßburg: Schmidt, 1883.

Erichson, Alfred. *L'Eglise Française de Strasbourg au seizième siècle d'après des documents inédits.* Straßburg: Schmidt, 1886.

Erichson, Alfred. *Zwingli's Tod und dessen Beurtheilung durch Zeitgenossen.* Straßburg: Schmidt, 1883.

Fecht, Gerhard. *Die Metrik des Hebräischen und Phönizischen.* Wiesbaden: Harrassowitz, 1990.

Fisher, Greg. *Between Empires: Arabs, Romans, and Sasanians in Late Antiquity.* Oxford: Oxford University Press, 2011.

Fowden, Elizabeth K. „Sharing Holy Places.“ *Common Knowledge* 8 (2002): 124–46.

Fowden, Garth. *Before and after Muḥammad: The First Millennium Refocused.* Princeton, NJ: Princeton University Press, 2014.

Fowden, Garth. *Empire to Commonwealth: Consequences of Monotheism in Late Antiquity.* Princeton, NJ: Princeton University Press, 1993.

Fowler, Robert. „Postmodern Biblical Criticism.“ *Foundation & Facets Forum* 5 (1989): 3–30.

Friedmann, Yohanan. „Finality of Prophethood in Sunnī Islam.“ *Jerusalem Studies in Arabic and Islam* 7 (1986): 177–215.

Fries, Karl. *Weddase Marjam. Ein äthiopischer Lobgesang an Maria.* Leipzig: G. Fock, 1892.

Gallez, Édouard-Marie. *Le messie et son prophète : Aux origines de l'islam.* 2 Bde., Studia Arabia 1 & 2. Paris: Éditions de Paris, 2. Auflage, 2005.
Gallo, Maria, Üb. *Palestinese anonimo; Omelia arabo-cristiana dell'VIII secolo.* Roma: Città Nuova Editrice, 1994.
Gardet, L. „Dīn." In *Encyclopaedia of Islam*, 2. Auflage, Hgg. P. Bearman et al. Brill Online: http://dx.doi.org/10.1163/1573-3912_islam_COM_0168.
Geiger, Abraham. *Was hat Mohammed aus dem Judenthume aufgenommen?* Bonn: Baaden, 1833.
George, Andrew. *The Babylonian Gilgamesh Epic: Introduction, Critical Edition and Cuneiform Texts.* Oxford: Oxford University Press, 2003.
Gibson, Margaret Dunlop, Hg. *An Arabic Version of the Acts of the Apostles and the Seven Catholic Epistles from an Eighth or Ninth Century MS in the Convent of St Catharine on Mount Sinai, with a Treatise on The Triune Nature of God, with Translation, from the Same Codex.* Bd. VII, Studia Sinaitica. Cambridge: Cambridge University Press, 1899.
Gieschen, Charles A. *Angelomorphic Christology. Antecedents and early evidence.* Leiden-Boston-Köln: Brill, 1998.
Gil, Moshe. „The Creed of Abū ʿAmīr." *Israel Oriental Studies* 12 (1992): 9–57.
Gilliot, Claude. „Deux études sur le Coran." *Arabia* 30 (1983): 1–37.
Gilliot, Claude. „Review of Günter Lüling. *Über den Ur-Qurʾān. Ansätze zur Rekonstruktion vorislamischer christlicher Strophenlieder im Ur-Qurʾān.* Second ed. Erlangen: Verlagsbuchhandlung Hannelore Lüling, 1993." *Revue du Monde Musulmane et de la Méditerranée* (REMMM) 70/1 (1993): 142–143.
Gnilka, Joachim. *Die Nazarener und der Koran: Eine Spurensuche.* Freiburg: Herder, 2007.
Gobillot, Geneviève. „Grundlinien der Theologie des Koran. Grundlagen und Orientierungen." In *Schlaglichter, Die beiden ersten islamischen Jahrhunderte*, edited by Markus Groß and Karl-Heinz Ohlig, 320–369. Berlin: Hans-Schiler-Verlag, 2008.
Gobillot, Geneviève. „Le Coran, guide de lecture de la Bible et des textes apocryphes." *Pardès* 50 (2011): 131–154.
Goldziher, Ignaz. *Die Richtungen der islamischen Koranauslegung.* Leiden: Brill, 1920.
Goldziher, Ignaz. „Muruwwa und Dîn." In *Muhammedanische Studien* I. Halle a. S.: Max Niemeyer, 1889.
Goodman, William R. „Allegory." In *Eerdmans Dictionary of the Bible*, Hg. David N. Freedman, 43–44. Grand Rapids: W.B Freedman, 2000.
Grabar, Oleg. *The Formation of Islamic Art.* New Haven: Yale University Press, 1987.
Grabar, Oleg. *The Shape of the Holy.* Princeton: Princeton University Press, 1996.
Gräßer, Erich. „Schweitzer, Albert." In *Deutsche Biographische Enzyklopädie der Musik.* Bd. 2. München, 2003.
Griffith, Sidney H. „Christian Lore and the Arabic Qur'ān: The 'Companions of the Cave' in *Sūrat al-Kahf* and in Syriac Christian Tradition." In *The Qur'ān in Its Historical Context*, Hg. Gabriel Said Reynolds, 109–137. London and New York: Routledge, 2008.
Griffith, Sidney H. „Disclosing the Mystery: The Hermeneutics of Typology in Syriac Exegesis: Jacob of Serūg on Genesis XXII." In *Interpreting Scriptures in Judaism, Christianity, and Islam: Overlapping Inquiries*, Hgg. Mordechai Cohen, Adele Berlin et al. Cambridge, UK: Cambridge University Press, 2016.

Griffith, Sidney H. „Ephraem the Exegete (306–373): Biblical Commentary in the Works of Ephraem the Syrian." In *Handbook of Patristic Exegesis: The Bible in Ancient Christianity.* Bd. II, Hg. Charles Kannengiesser, 1395–1428. Leiden: Brill, 2004.

Griffith, Sidney H. *'Faith Adoring the Mystery': Reading the Bible with St. Ephraem the Syrian.* The Père Marquette Lecture in Theology 1997. Milwaukee, WI: Marquette University Press, 1997.

Griffith, Sidney H. „Holy Spirit." In *Encyclopaedia of the Qur'ān*, Hg. Jane Dammen McAuliffe. Brill Online: http://dx.doi.org/10.1163/1875-3922_q3_EQSIM_00193.

Griffith, Sidney H. *„Al-Naṣārā* in the Qur'ān: A Hermeneutical Reflection." In *New Perspectives on the Qur'ān.* The Qur'ān in its Historical Context 2, Hg. Gabriel Said Reynolds, 301–332. London & New York: Routledge, 2011.

Griffith, Sidney H. „Syriacisms in the Arabic Qur'ān: Who Were 'Those who said Allāh is Third of Three', according to *al-Mā'idah* 73?" In *A Word Fitly Spoken: Studies in Mediaeval Exegesis of the Hebrew Bible and the Qur'ān Presented to Haggai Ben-Shammai*, Hgg. Meir M. Bar-Asher et al., 83–110. Jerusalem: The Ben-Zvi Institute, 2007.

Griffith, Sidney H. *The Bible in Arabic: The Scriptures of the „People of the Book" in the Language of Islam.* Princeton, NJ: Princeton University Press, 2013.

Griffith, Sidney H. „The Melkites and the Muslims: The Qur'ān, Christology, and Arab Orthodoxy." *Al-Qanṭara: Revista de Estudios Arabes* 33 (2012): 413–443.

Griffith, Sidney H. „The Qur'ān's 'Nazarenes' and Other Late Antique Christians: Arabic-Speaking 'Gospel People' in Qur'ānic Perspective." In *Christsein in der islamischen Welt: Festschrift für Martin Tamcke zum 60. Geburtstag*, Hgg. Sidney Griffith und Sven Grebenstein, 81–106. Wiesbaden: Harrassowitz, 2015.

Griffith, Sidney H. „The '*Sunna* of Our Messengers': The Qur'ān's Paradigm for Messengers and Prophets; a Reading of Sūrat ash-Shu'arā' (26)." In *Qur'ānic Studies Today*, Hgg. Angelika Neuwirth und Michael Sells, 203–223. London & New York: Routledge, 2016.

Grohmann, Adolf, Hg. *Äthiopische Marienhymnen.* Abhandlungen der philosophisch historischen Klasse der Sächsischen Akademie der Wissenschaften 33, Nr. 16. Leipzig: Teubner, 1919.

Guggisberg, H. „Martin Werners Werk im Spiegel seines Briefwechsels." In *Weg und Werk Martin Werners. Studien und Erinnerungen*, Hg. F. Sciuto. Bern u. Stuttgart: Paul Haupt in Komm, 1968.

Guinot, Jean-Noël. „La frontière entre allégorie et typologie: école alexandrine, école antiochienne." *Recherches de Science Religieuse* 92 (2011): 207–228.

Günther, Sebastian. „Muḥammad, the Illiterate Prophet: An Islamic Creed in the Qur'ān and Qur'ānic Exegesis." *Journal of Qur'anic Studies* 4 (2002): 1–26.

Günther, Sebastian. „Review of Günter Lüling. *Über den Ur-Qur'ān. Ansätze zur Rekonstruktion vorislamischer christlicher Strophenlieder im Ur-Qur'ān.* Second ed. Erlangen: Verlagsbuchhandlung Hannelore Lüling,1993." *al-Qantara* 16 (1995): 485–490.

Hafner, Johann Ev. *Angelologie.* Gegenwärtig Glauben Denken 9. Paderborn u. a.: Schöningh, 2010.

Hainthaler, Theresia. *Christliche Araber vor dem Islam.* Eastern Christian Studies 7. Leuven: Peeters, 2007.

Hainthaler, Theresia. „La foi au Christ dans l'Eglise éthiopienne. Une synthèse des élèments judéo-chrétiens et helléno-chrétiens." *Revue des sciences religieuses 71* (1997): 330–331.

Hannah, Darrell D. *Michael and Christ. Michael Traditions and Angel Christology in Early Christianity.* Wissenschaftliche Untersuchungen zum Neuen Testament 2. Nr. 109. Tübingen: Mohr Siebeck, 1999.

Hartmann, Martin. *Das arabische Strophengedicht I: Das Muwaššaḥ.* Semitistische Studien 13/14. Weimar: Felber, 1897.

Hawting, Gerald R. „Idolatry and Idolaters." In *Encyclopaedia of the Qur'ān*, Hg. Jane Dammen. Brill Online: http://dx.doi.org/10.1163/1875-3922_q3_EQSIM_00206.

Hawting, Gerald R. „Review of Günther Lüling. *Die Wiederentdeckung des Propheten Muhammad: Eine Kritik am 'christlichen' Abendland.* Erlangen: Verlagsbuchhandlung Hannelore Lüling, 1981." *Journal of Semitic Studies* (JSS) 27 (1982): 108–112.

Hawting, Gerald. *The Idea of Idolatry and the Emergence of Islam: From Polemic to History.* Cambridge: Cambridge University Press, 1999.

Hayek, Michel. *Le Christ de l'Islam.* Paris: Éditions du Seuil, 1959.

Hayes, Christine. *Between the Babylonian & Palestinian Talmuds, Accounting for Halakhic Difference in Selected Sugyot from Tractate Avodah Zarah.* Oxford: Oxford University Press, 1997.

Hayes, John. *Old Testament form criticism.* San Antonio: Trinity University, 1974.

Heyer, Friedrich. *Die Kirche Äthiopiens: eine Bestandsaufnahme.* Theologische Bibliothek Töpelmann 22. Berlin: De Gruyter, 1971.

Hoffmann, Thomas. *The Poetic Qur'ān. Studies on Qur'ānic Poeticity.* Wiesbaden: Harrassowitz, 2007.

Holtzmann, Heinrich Julius *Das messianische Bewußtsein Jesu. Ein Beitrag zur Leben-Jesu-Forschung.* Tübingen: Mohr, 1907.

Holtzmann, Heinrich Julius. *Die Religion in Geschichte und Gegenwart.* Bd. 2. Tübingen, 1928.

Holtzmann, Heinrich Julius. *Die Synoptischen Evangelien, ihr Ursprung und geschichtlicher Charakter.* Leipzig: Engelmann, 1863.

Holtzmann, Heinrich Julius. *Lehrbuch der Neutestamentlichen Theologie.* Tübingen: J. C. B. Mohr, 2. Auflage, 1911 [1st Ed. 1897].

Horn, Cornelia. „Apocrypha on Jesus' Life in the Early Islamic Milieu: From Syriac into Arabic." In *Senses of Scriptures, Treasures of Tradition. The bible in Arabic among Jews, Christians and Muslims*, Hg. Miriam Lindgren Hjälm, 58–78. Leiden: Brill, 2017.

Horn, Cornelia B. und Robert R. Phenix Jr. „Review of „Christoph Luxenberg, *Die syro-aramäische Lesart des Koran: Ein Beitrag zur Entschlüsselung der Koransprache.*" *Hugoye: Journal of Syriac Studies* 6 (2003): 164–178.

Horn, Cornelia. „Syriac and Arabic Perspectives on Structural and Motif Parallels Regarding Jesus' Childhood in Christian Apocrypha and Early Islamic Literature: the 'Book of Mary,' the *Arabic Apocryphal Gospel of John*, and the Qur'ān." *Apocrypha. Revue internationale des littératures apocryphes* 19 (2008): 267–291.

Hoyland, Robert. „Mount Nebo, Jabal Ramm, and the Status of Christian Palestinian Aramaic and Old Arabic in Late Roman Palestine and Arabia." *The Development of Arabic as a Written Language. Papers from the Special Session of the Seminar for Arabian Studies held on 24 July, 2009, Proceedings of the Seminar for Arabian Studies Vol. 40, Supplement*, 29–45. Oxford: Archaeopress, 2010.

Huber, Konrad. *Einer gleich einem Menschensohn. Die Christusvisionen in Offb 1,9–20 und Offb 14,14–20 und die Christologie der Johannesoffenbarung.* Neutestamentliche Abhandlungen, N.F. 51. Münster: Aschendorff, 2007.

Ibn Abī Šaybah. *Muṣannaf.* 15 Bde. Karachi: Idārat al-Qur'ān wa-l-'ulūm al-islāmiyyah, 1406/1986.

Ibn al-Atīr, 'Izz al-Dīn. *Al-Kāmil fī l-ta'rīḫ.* 13 Bde., Hg. C.J Tornberg. Leiden: Brill, 1867.

Ibn Rawandi. „On pre-Islamic Christian Strophic Poetical Texts in the Koran: a Critical Look at the Work of Günter Lüling." In *What the Koran Really Says. Language, Text, and Commentary*, Hg. Ibn Warraq, 653–710. Amherst, NY: Prometheus Books, 2002.

Izutzu, Toshihiko. *God and Man in the Koran.* Tokyo: Keio University, 1964.

Jahn, Bruno, Hg. *Deutsche Biographische Enzyklopädie der Musik.* Bd. 2. München: Saur, 2003.

Jastrow, Marcus. *A Dictionary of the Targumim, the Talmud Bavli and Yerushalmi, and the Midrashic Literature.* New York: The Judaica Press, 1996 [1903].

Jeffery, Arthur. *Materials for the History of the Text of the Qur'ān. The Old Codices.* Leiden: E. J. Brill, 1937.

Jeffery, Arthur. *The Foreign Vocabulary of the Quran.* Baroda: Oriental Institute, 1938.

Jeffery, Arthur. *The Qur'ān as Scripture.* New York: Russell F. Moore Company, 1952.

Joëlle, Françoise Briquel-Chatonnet und Christian Julien Robin, Hgg. *Juifs et Chrétiens en Arabie aux Ve et VIe siècles: regards croisés sur les sources.* Collège de France – CNRS, Centre de Recherche d'Histoire et Civilisation de Byzance, Monographies 32. Paris: Association des amis du Centre d'Histoire et civilization de Byzance, 2010.

Joosten, Jan „La tradition syriaqe des évangiles et la question du 'substrat araméen." *Revue d'Histoire de Philosophie Religieuse 77* (1997): 257–72.

Jüngel, Eberhard et. al, Hgg. *Die Religion in Geschichte und Gegenwart.* Vol. 7. Tübingen: Mohr Siebeck Verlag, 4. Auflage, 2004.

Kahle, Erhart. „Review of Günter Lüling. *Über den Ur-Qur'ān. Ansätze zur Rekonstruktion vorislamischer christlicher Strophenlieder im Ur-Qur'ān.* Erlangen: Verlagsbuchhandlung Hannelore Lüling, 1974." *Zeitschrift der Deutschen Morgenländischen Gesellschaft* (ZDMG) 132/1 (1982): 182–184.

Kahle, Erhart. „Review of *Über den Ur-Qur'ān.*" *Zeitschrift der Morgenländischen Gesellschaft 132* (1982): 182–184.

Kapielski, Thomas. „Tief gestapelt: Bibelforscher." *Frankfurter Rundschau*, March 10, 2005.

Khalidi, Tarif. *The Muslim Jesus; Sayings and Stories in Islamic Literature.* Cambridge, MA: Harvard University Press, 2001.

Khoury, Adel Theodor. „Review of Günter Lüling. *Der christliche Kult an der vorislamischen Kaaba als Problem der Islamwissenschaft und christlichen Theologie.* Erlangen: Verlagsbuchhandlung Hannelore Lüling, 1977." *Orientalistische Literaturzeitung* (OLZ) 78 (1981): 150–151.

Köbert, Raimund. „Frühe und spätere Koranexegese. Eine Ergänzung zu Or 35 (1966) 28–32." *Orientalia* (Nova Series) 55/2 (1986): 174–176.

Koehler, L. and W. Baumgartner, eds. *Hebräisches und aramäisches Lexicon zum Alten Testament.* Leiden: Brill, 1967–1990.

Kofsky, Arieh. „Mamre: a case of regional cult?" In *Sharing the Sacred: Religious Contacts and Conflicts in the Holy Land, First-Fifteenth Centuries*, Hgg. Arieh Kofsky und Guy G. Stroumsa, 19–30. Jerusalem: Yad Ben-Zvi Press, 1998.

Kotter, P. Bonifatius. *Die Schriften des Johannes von Damaskos.* Patristische Texte und Studien 22. Bd. 4. Berlin: De Gruyter, 1981.

Kraemer, Jörg. „Das arabische Original des pseudo-aristotelischen ‚Liber de pomo'." In *Studi orientalistici in onore di Giorgio dell Vida.* Bd. 1. Rom: Istituto per l'Oriente, 1956): 484–506.

Krispenz, Jutta. *Literarkritik und Stilstatistik im Alten Testament. Eine Studie zur literarkritischen Methode, durchgeführt an Texten aus den Büchern Jeremia, Ezechiel und 1 Könige.* Berlin: De Gruyter, 2001.

Kristeva, Julia. „Desire in Language: a Semiotic Approach to Literature and Art." In *European Perspectives: a Series in Social Thought and Cultural Criticism*, Hgg. Leon S. Roudiez, Thomas Gora und Alice Jardine. New York: Columbia University Press, 1980.

Kropp, Manfred, Hg. *Results of contemporary research on the Qurʾān. The question of a historio-critical text of the Qurʾān.* Würzburg: Ergon, 2007.

Kugel, James. *Traditions of the Bible: A Guide to the Bible as it was at the start of the Common Era.* Cambridge: Harvard University Press, 1998.

Kümmel, Georg Werner. *Das Neue Testament. Geschichte der Erforschung seiner Probleme.* München/Freiburg: Karl Alber, 2. Auflage, 1970 [1. Auflage 1953].

Kümmel, Georg Werner, Hg. *Einleitung in das Neue Testament.* Heidelberg, 1965.

Lammens, Henri. „Le Califat de Yazid Ier." *Mélanges de la Faculté Orientale.* Université de Saint-Joseph de Beyrouth 5 (1911): 79–268.

Lane, Edward William. *An Arabic – English Lexicon.* 8 vols. London: Williams and Norgate, 1863–93.

Lawson, Todd. *The Crucifixion and the Qurʾān: A Study in the History of Muslim Thought.* Oxford: One World, 2009.

Leirvik, Oddbjørn. *Images of Jesus Christ in Islam.* New York: Continuum, 2. Auflage, 2010.

Lerch, Wolfgang Günther. „Über christliche Strophen im Koran." *Frankfurter Allgemeine Zeitung*, June 1, 2004.

Levinson, Joshua. „'עולם הפוך ראיתי'–עיון בסיפור השיכור ובניו" *Jerusalem Studies in Hebrew Literature* 14 (1993): 7–23.

Levinson, Joshua. „'Tragedies Naturally Performed': Fatal Charades, Parodia Sacra, and the Death of Titus." In *Jewish Culture and Society Under the Christian Roman Empire*, Hgg. Seth Schwartz und Richard Kalmin, 349–82. Leuven: Peters, 2003.

Lewin, Bernard, Frithiof Rundgren und Anton Spitaler. *Sakkunnigutlåtanden rörande sökande till professuren i arabiska, särskilt modern arabiska vid Göteborgs universitet år 1970* [Comparative evaluation of the candidates Mahmoud Hussein, Günter Lüling, Heikki Palva und Christopher Toll for a professorship in Arabic], 1970.

Lipiński, Edward. *Semitic Languages: Outline of a Comparative Grammar.* Orientalia Lovaniensia Analaecta 80. Leuven: Peeters, 2001.

Littmann, Enno „Geschichte der äthiopischen Literatur." In *Geschichte der christlichen Litteraturen des Orients.* Die Litteraturen des Ostens in Einzeldarstellungen 7, Hgg. Carl Brockelmann et al., 185–270. Leipzig: Amelang, 1907.

Löfgren, Oscar. „Ergänzendes zum apokryphen Johannesevangelium." *Orientalia Suecana* 10 (1961): 137–144.

Löfgren, Oscar. „Zur Charakteristik des apokryphen Johannesevangeliums." *Orientalia Suecana* 9 (1960): 107–130.

Lohmann, Theodor. „Review of Günter Lüling. *Über den Ur-Qurʾān. Ansätze zur Rekonstruktion vorislamischer christlicher Strophenlieder im Ur-Qurʾān.* Erlangen: Verlagsbuchhandlung Hannelore Lüling, 1974." *Theologische Literaturzeitung* 103 (1978): 560–562.

Loretz, Oswald. „Die Analyse der ugaritischen und hebräischen Poesie mittels Stichometrie und Konsonantenzählung.“ *Ugarit-Forschungen* 7 (1976): 265 – 269.

Loretz, Oswald. *Die Psalmen, Teil II: Beitrag der Ugarit-Texte zum Verständnis von Kolometrie und Textologie der Psalmen – Psalm 90 – 150.* Kevelaer: Neukirchener Theologie, 1979.

Loretz, Oswald. „Kolometrie ugaritischer und hebräischer Poesie: Grundlagen, informationstheoretische und literaturwissenschaftliche Aspekte.“ *Zeitschrift für die Alttestamentliche Wissenschaft* 98 (1986): 249 – 266.

Lu, Peter J. und Paul J. Steinhardt. „Decagonal and Quasi-crystalline Tilings in Medieval Islamic Architecture.“ *Science* 315 (2007): 1106 – 1110.

Lüling, Günter *A Challenge to Islam for Reformation: The Rediscovery and Reliable Reconstruction of a Comprehensive Pre-Islamic Christian Hymnal Hidden in the Koran under Earliest Islamic Reinterpretations.* Delhi: Motilal Banarsidass Publishers, 2003.

Lüling, Günter. *A Challenge to Islam for Reformation. The Rediscovery and reliable Reconstruction of a comprehensive pre-Islamic Christian Hymnal hidden in the Koran under earliest Islamic Reinterpretations.* Erlangen: Verlagsbuchhandlung Hannelore Lüling, 2. Auflage [englische Übersetzung, umgearbeitet und erweitert, der 2. deutschen Edition (1993) der Studie *Über den Ur-Koran*], 2011.

Lüling, Günter. *Der christliche Kult an der vorislamischen Kaaba als Problem der Islamwissenschaft und christlichen Theologie.* Erlangen: Verlagsbuchhandlung Hannelore Lüling, 2. Auflage, 1992 [1. Auflage 1977].

Lüling, Günter. *Die Wiederentdeckung des Propheten Muhammad. Eine Kritik am „christlichen“ Abendland.* Erlangen: Verlagsbuchhandlung Hannelore Lüling, 1981.

Lüling, Günter. „Ein neues Buch zu einem alten Streit.“ *Zeitschrift für Religions- und Geistesgeschichte* 36 (1984): 56 – 67; reprint in *Sprache und archaisches Denken. Aufsätze zur Geistes- und Religionsgeschichte*, Hg. Günter Lüling, 181 – 189. Erlangen: Verlagsbuchhandlung Hannelore Lüling, zweite um zwei Aufsätze erweiterte Auflage, 2005.

Lüling, Günter. *Kritisch-exegetische Untersuchung des Qur'āntextes.* Erlangen: J. Högl, 1970.

Lüling, Günter. *Sprache und archaisches Denken. Aufsätze zur Geistes- und Religionsgeschichte.* Erlangen: Verlagsbuchhandlung Hannelore Lüling, zweite um zwei Aufsätze erweiterte Auflage, 2005.

Lüling, Günter. *Über den Ur-Qur'ān: Ansätze zur Rekonstruktion vorislamischer christlicher Strophenlieder im Qur'ān.* Erlangen: Verlagsbuchhandlung Hannelore Lüling, 3. Auflage, 2004 [2. Ed. 1993; 1. Ed. 1974].

Luxenberg, Christoph. *Die syro-aramäische Lesart des Koran: Ein Beitrag zur Entschlüsselung der Koransprache.* Berlin: Das Arabische Buch, Berlin: Schiler, 3. Auflage, 2007 [2000].

Luxenberg, Christoph. *The Syro-Aramaic Reading of the Koran*, Hg. Tim Mücke. Berlin: Hans Schiler, 2007.

Maas, Paul. *Textual Criticism.* Oxford: Oxford University Press, 1958.

Al-Maḥallī, Jalāl ad-Dīn und Jalāl ad-Dīn as-Suyūṭī. *Tafsīr al-Jalalayn li-Imāmayn al-Jalīlayn*, Hg. Ṣafī ar-Raḥmān al-Mubārakfūrī. Riyadh, Saudi Arabia: Dār as-Salām li-n-Nashri wa-t-Tawzīʿ, 2002/1422.

Marshall, David. *God, Muhammad, and the Unbelievers: A Qur'ānic Study.* Richmond, Surrey, UK: Curzon Press, 1999.

McCarter Jr., Peter. *Textual criticism: recovering the text of the Hebrew Bible.* Philadelphia: Fortress Press, 1986.

McGann, Jerome. *A critique of modern textual criticism.* Chicago: University of Chicago Press, 1993.

Meier, Bernhard, *Gründerzeit der Orientalistik. Theodor Nöldekes Leben und Werk im Spiegel seiner Briefe.* Bd. 29. Würzburg: Ergon, 2013.

Michaelis, Wilhelm. *Zur Engelchristologie im Urchristentum. Abbau der Konstruktion Martin Werners.* Basel: Verlag Heinrich Majer, 1942.

Mimouni, Simon Claude. *Le judéo-christianisme ancien. Essais historiques.* Paris: Cerf, 1998.

Mir, Mustansir. *Coherence in the Qur'ān. A Study of Iṣlāḥī's Concept of Naẓm in Tadabbur-i Qur'ān.* Indianapolis: American Trust Publications, 1406/1986.

Mir, Mustansir. „Iṣlāḥī's Concept of Sūra-Groups." *Islamic Quarterly* 28.2 (1984): 73–85.

Montgomery, James E. „The Empty *ḥijāz*." In *Arabic Theology, Arabic Philosophy; from the Many to the One: Essays in Celebration of Richard M. Frank.* Orientalia Lovaniensia Analecta 152, Hg. J. E. Montgomery, 37–97. Leuven: Uitgeverij Peeters en Departement Oosterse Studien, 2006.

Moore, Stephen, Hg. *The Bible in theory. Critical and postcritical essays.* Leiden: Brill, 2011.

Motzki, Harald. „Alternative Accounts of the Qurʾān's Formation." In *The Cambridge Companion to the Qurʾān*, Hg. Jane Dammen McAuliffe. Cambridge: Cambridge University Press, 2006.

Mourad, Suleiman. „From Hellensim to Christianity and Islam: The Origin of the Palm-Tree Story concerning Mary and Jesus in the Gospel of Pseudo-Matthew and the Qurʾān." *Oriens Christianus* 86 (2002): 206–216.

Mourad, Suleiman. „Mary in the Qurʾān: A Reexamination of Her Presentation." In *The Qurʾān in Its Historical Context*, Hg. Gabriel Said Reynolds, 163–174. London & New York: Routledge, 2008.

Mourad, Suleiman. „On the Qurʾānic Stories about Mary and Jesus." *Bulletin of the Royal Institute for Inter-Faith Studies* 1 (1999): 13–24.

Mourad, Suleiman. „The Death of Jesus in Islam: Reality, Assumptions, and Implications." In *Engaging the Passion: Perspectives on the Death of Jesus*, edited by Oliver Larry Yarbrough, 357–379. Minneapolis, MN: Fortress Press, 2015.

Mozart, Wolfgang Amadeus. *Mozart. Briefe und Aufzeichnungen, gesammelt und erläutert von Wilhelm A. Bauer und Otto Erich Deutsch.* Bd. II: 1777–1779, Nr. 503. Kassel: Bärenreiter, 1962.

Müller, Friedrun R. *Untersuchungen zur Reimprosa im Koran.* Bonn: Selbstverlag des Orientalischen Seminars der Universität Bonn, 1969.

Müller, Walther W. „Lobpreis Marias." In *Marienlexicon.* Bd. 4, Hgg. Remigius Bäumer et al., 137–138. St. Ottilien: EOS-Verlag, 1993.

Müller, Walther W. „Weddase Maryam." In *Kindlers Neues Literatur Lexikon.* Bd. 19, Hg. Walter Jens, 777–778. München: Kindler, 1992.

Muqātil ibn Sulaymān, Abū l-Ḥasan. *Tafsīr Muqātil ibn Sulaymān.* 3 Bde., Hg. Aḥmad Farīd. Beirut: Dār al-Kutub al-ʿAqliyyah, 2002.

Neuwirth, Angelika. *Der Koran als Text der Spätantike. Ein europäischer Zugang.* Berlin: Verlag der Weltreligionen im Insel Verlag, 2010.

Neuwirth, Angelika. *Der Koran. Band 1: Frühmekkanische Suren.* Berlin: Verlag der Weltreligionen, 2011.

Neuwirth, Angelika. „Locating the Qurʾān in the Epistemic Space of Late Antiquity." In *Christsein in der islamischen Welt*, Hgg. Sidney Griffith und Sven Grebenstein, 65–79. Wiesbaden: Harrassowitz Verlag, 2015.

Neuwirth, Angelika. „Mary and Jesus – Counterbalancing the Biblical Patriarchs. A re-reading of *sūrat Maryam* in *sūrat Āl-ʿImrān* (Q 3:1–62)." *Parole de l'Orient* 30 (2005): 231–260.

Neuwirth, Angelika. *Scripture, Poetry and the Making of a Community: Reading the Qurʾān as a Literary Text*. Oxford: Oxford University Press / London: The Institute of Ismaili Studies, 2014.

Neuwirth, Angelika. *Studien zur Komposition der mekkanischen Suren. Studien zur Sprache, Geschichte und Kultur des islamischen Orients* 10. Berlin: Walter de Gruyter, 2. Auflage, 2007 [1981].

Neuwirth, Angelika. „Two Faces of the Qur'ān: Qur'ān and Muṣḥaf." *Oral Tradition* 25.1 (2010): 141–156.

Neuwirth, Angelika, Michael Marx und Nicolai Sinai, Hgg. *The Qurʾān in Context: Historical and Literary Investigations into the Qurʾānic Milieu*. Brill: Leiden, 2010.

Neuwirth, Angelika. „Zum neueren Stand der Koranforschung." In *XXI. Deutscher Orientalistentag, vom 24. bis 29. März 1980 in Berlin, Supplement 5*, Hg. Fritz Steppat, 183–189. Wiesbaden: Franz Steiner Verlag, 1983.

Neuwirth, Angelika. „Zur Struktur der *Yūsuf*-Sure." In *Studien aus Arabistik und Semitistik. Anton Spitaler zum siebzigsten Geburtstag von seinen Schülern überreicht*, Hgg. Werner Diem und Stefan Wild, 123–152. Wiesbaden: Harrassowitz, 1980.

Ninow, Friedbert. „Typology." In *Eerdmans Dictionary of the Bible*, Hg. David N. Freedman. Grand Rapids MI: William B. Eerdmans Publishing Company, 2000.

Nöldeke, Theodor, Friedrich Schwally, Gotthelf Bergsträßer und Otto Pretzl. *The History of the Qurʾān*, Üb. und Hg. Wolfgang H. Behn. Leiden: Brill, 2013.

Nöldeke, Theodor. *Geschichte des Qorâns*. Göttingen: Verlag der Dieterichschen Buchhandlung 1860; reprint 2. Auflage, Hildesheim und New York: Georg Olms, 1970.

O'Shaughnessy, Thomas. *The Development of the Meaning of Spirit in the Koran*. Orientalia Christiana Analecta 139. Rome: Pont. Institutum Orientalium Studiorum, 1953.

Paçacı, Mehmet. „De Ki Allah 'Bir'dir: *ʾaḥad/ʾeḥād*. Sami Dini Geleneği Perspektifinden İhlas Sûresi'nin Bir Tefsiri Denemesi." In *Kur'an ve Ben Ne Kadar Tarihseliz?*, Mehmet Paçacı. Ankara: Ankara Okulu Yayınları, 2000.

Paçacı, Mehmet. „Sag: Gott ist ein einziger—ahad/æhād. Ein exegetischer Versuch zu Sure 112 in der Perspektive der semitischen Religionstradition."In *Alter Text—neuer Kontext. Koranhermeneutik in der Türkei heute*, Üb. Felix Körner, 166–203. Freiburg: Herder, 2006.

Paret, Rudi. *Der Koran: Kommentar und Konkordanz*. Stuttgart: Kohlhammer, 1971; [1980].

Parrinder, Geoffrey. *Jesus in the Qurʾān*. New York: Oxford University Press, 1977.

Pawłowski, Adam. „Prolegomena to the History of Corpus and Quantitative Linguistics. Greek Antiquity." *Glottotheory* 1 (2008): 48–54.

Perrin, Norman. *What is redaction Criticism?* London: SPCK, 1970.

Phillips, Gary. „Exegesis as Critical Praxis: Reclaiming History and Text from a Postmodern Perspective." *Semeia* 51 (1990): 7–50.

Plisch, Uwe-Karsten. „Zur Bedeutung der koptischen Übersetzungen für Textkritik und Verständnis des Neuen Testaments." In *Recent developments in textual criticism: new testament, other early Christian and Jewish literature*, Hgg. Wim Weren et al., 95–108. Assen: Gorcum, 2003.

Poggi, Victor. „Review of Günter Lüling. *Über den Ur-Qur'ān. Ansätze zur Rekonstruktion vorislamischer christlicher Strophenlieder im Ur-Qur'ān.* Erlangen: Verlagsbuchhandlung Hannelore Lüling, 1974." *Orientalia Christiania Periodica* 41 (1975): 529–532.

Pohlmann, Karl-Friedrich. *Die Entstehung des Korans. Neue Erkenntnisse aus Sicht der historisch-kritischen Bibelwissenschaft.* Darmstadt: Wissenschaftliche Buchgesellschaft, 2012.

Porten, Bezalel, Hg. *The Elephantine Papyri in English: Three Millennia of Cross-Cultural Continuity and Change.* Leiden: Brill, 1996.

Powers, David. *Muhammad is Not the Father of Any of Your Men.* Philadelphia: University of Pennsylvania Press, 2009.

Qara'I, Sayyid 'Ali Quli, Üb. und Hg. *The Qur'an with an English Paraphrase.* Qom: Centre for Translation of the Holy Qur'ān, 2003.

Qara'I, Sayyid 'Ali Quli. *The Qur'an: With a Phrase-by-Phrase English Translation.* Elmhurst, NY: Tahrike Tarsile Qur'an, Inc., 2011.

Rendtorff, Rolf. „Martin Noth and Tradition Criticism." In *The History of Israel's Traditions: The Heritage of Martin Noth.* Journal for the Study of the Old Testament Supplement Series 182, Hgg. Stephen McKenzie et al., 91–100. Sheffield: Sheffield University Press, 1994.

Reynolds, Gabriel Said. *New Perspectives on the Qur'ān.* The Qur'ān in its Historical Context 2. Abingdon: Routledge, 2011.

Reynolds, Gabriel Said. „On the Qur'ānic Accusation of Scriptural Falsification (*taḥrīf*) and Christian anti-Jewish Polemic." *Journal of the American Oriental Society* 130 (2010): 189–202.

Reynolds, Gabriel Said. „The Muslim Jesus: Dead or Alive?" *Bulletin of the School of Oriental and African Studies* 72 (2009), 237–258.

Reynolds, Gabriel Said. *The Qur'ān and its Biblical Subtext.* London: Routledge, 2010.

Reynolds, Gabriel Said, Hg. *The Qur'ān in its Historical Context.* London: Routledge, 2008.

Richter, Wolfgang. *Biblia Hebraica transcripta BH^t, das ist das ganze Alte Testament transkribiert, mit Satzeinteilungen versehen und durch die Version tiberisch-masoretischer Autoritäten versehen, auf der sie gründet,* 16 Bde. St. Ottilien: EOS Verlag, 1991–1993.

Richter, Wolfgang. *Transliteration und Transkription. Objekt- und metasprachliche Metazeichensysteme zur Wiedergabe althebräischer Texte.* Arbeiten zu Text und Sprache im Alten Testament 19. St. Ottilien: EOS-Verlag, 1983.

Ringel, Heinrich. „Review of Günter Lüling. *Über den Ur-Qur'ān. Ansätze zur Rekonstruktion vorislamischer christlicher Strophenlieder im Ur-Qur'ān.* Erlangen: Verlagsbuchhandlung Hannelore Lüling, 1974." *Deutsches Pfarrerblatt* 74 (1974): 680–681.

Rippin, Andrew. „Foreign Vocabulary." In *Encyclopaedia of the Qur'ān*, Hg. Jane Dammen McAuliffe. Brill Online: http://dx.doi.org/10.1163/1875-3922_q3_EQCOM_00068.

Rizzardi, Giuseppe. *Il problema della cristologia coranica: Storia dell'ermeneutica Cristiana.* Milano: Istituto Propaganda Libraria, 1982.

Robin, Christian Julien. „Ethiopia and Arabia." In *The Oxford Handbook of Late Antiquity,* Hg. Scott Fitzgerald Johnson, 247–332. Oxford: Oxford University Press, 2012.

Robinson, Neal. *Christ in Islam and Christianity.* Albany, NY: State University of New York Press, 1991.

Robson, James. „Islām as a term." *The Moslem World* 44 (1954): 101–109.

Rodinson, Maxime. „Review of Günter Lüling. *Über den Ur-Qur'ān. Ansätze zur Rekonstruktion vorislamischer christlicher Strophenlieder im Ur-Qur'ān.* Erlangen: Verlagsbuchhandlung Hannelore Lüling, 1974." *Der Islam* 54/2 (1977): 321–325.
Roggema, Barbara. *The Legend of Sergius Baḥīrā: Eastern Christian Apologetics and Apocalyptic in Response to Islam.* The History of Christian-Muslim Relations 9. Leiden: Brill, 2009.
Rubenstein, Jeffrey. *Stories of the Babylonian Talmud.* Baltimore: Johns Hopkins University Press, 2010.
Rubenstein, Jeffery. *Talmudic Stories: Narrative, Composition, and Culture.* Baltimore: Johns Hopkins University Press, 1999.
Saleh, Walid. „The Etymological Fallacy and Qur'anic Studies: Muhammad, Paradise, and Late Antiquity." In *The Qur'ān in Context: Historical and Literary Investigations into the Qur'ānic Milieu*, Hgg. Angelika Neuwirth, Michael Marx und Nicolai Sinai, 649–698. Leiden: Brill, 2009.
Samir, Samir Khalil. „The Earliest Arab Apology for Christianity (c. 750)." In *Christian Arabic Apologetics during the Abbasid Period (750–1258).* Studies in the History of Religions 63, Hgg. Samir Khalil Samir und Jørgen S. Nielsen, 57–114. Leiden: E.J. Brill, 1994.
Samuelson, Francine E. „Messianic Judaism: church, denomination, sect, or cult?" *Journal of Ecumenical Studies 37* (2000): 106–186.
Saritoprak, Zeki. *Islam's Jesus.* Gainesville, FL: University Press of Florida, 2014.
Sauvaget, Jean. *Introduction to the History of the Muslim East: A Bibliographical Guide. Based on the Second Edition as Recast by Claude Cahen.* Berkeley and Los Angeles: University of California Press, 1965.
Schäfer, Peter. *Jesus in the Talmud.* Princeton, NJ: Princeton University Press, 2007.
Schäfer, Peter et al. *Synopse zur Hekhalot-Literatur.* Tübingen: J.C.B. Mohr (P. Siebeck), 1981.
Schall, Anton. *Zur äthiopischen Verskunst: eine Studie über die Metra des Qenē auf Grund der Abhandlung „al-Qenē laun min aš-ši ʿr al-ḥabašī von Murad Kamil."* Wiesbaden: F. Steiner, 1961.
Schedl, Claus. *Muhammad und Jesus: Die christologisch relevanten Texte des Koran neuübersetzt und erklärt.* Wien, Freiburg, Basel: Herder, 1978.
Schimmel, Annemarie. „Review of Günter Lüling. *Über den Ur-Qur'ān. Ansätze zur Rekonstruktion vorislamischer christlicher Strophenlieder im Ur-Qur'ān.* Erlangen: Verlagsbuchhandlung Hannelore Lüling, 1974." *The Muslim World* 77/2 (1987): 140–141.
Schlatter, Adolf, Hg. *Religion in Geschichte und Gegenwart. Handwörterbuch für Theologie und Religionswissenschaft.* Bd. 7. Tübingen: Mohr Siebeck, 4. Auflage, 2004.
Schoeps, Hans-Joachim. *Jewish Christianity: Factional Disputes in the Early Church*, Üb. Douglas R. A. Hare. Philadelphia, PA: Fortress Press, 1969.
Schoeps, Hans-Joachim. *Theologie und Geschichte des Judenchristentums.* Tübingen: J.C.B. Mohr/Paul Siebeck, 1969 [1949].
Schulze, Reinhard. *Der Koran und die Genealogie des Islam.* Basel: Schwabe, 2015.
Schweitzer, Albert. *Aus meinem Leben und Denken.* Autobiographie. Bern und Leipzig: Richard-Meiner-Verlag, 1931.
Schweitzer, Albert. *Aus meinem Leben und Denken.* Stuttgart: Stuttgarter Hausbücherei, 1960.
Schweitzer, Albert. *Das Abendmahl im Zusammenhang mit dem Leben Jesu und der Geschichte des Urchristentums.* Erstes Heft: *Das Abendmahlsproblem auf Grund der*

wissenschaftlichen Forschungen des 19. Jahrhunderts und der historischen Berichte. Tübingen u. Freiburg: Mohr, 1. Auflage, 1901, 2. Auflage, 1929.

Schweitzer, Albert. *Das Abendmahl im Zusammenhang mit dem Leben Jesu und der Geschichte des Urchristentums.* Zweites Heft: *Das Messianitäts- und Leidensgeheimnis. Eine Skizze des Lebens Jesu.* Tübingen u. Freiburg: Mohr, 1. Auflage, 1901, 2. Auflage, 1929.

Schweitzer, Albert. *Die Mystik des Apostels Paulus.* Tübingen: J.C.B. Mohr & Paul Siebeck, 1930.

Schweitzer, Albert. *Die Religionsphilosophie Kants von der Kritik der reinen Vernunft bis zur Religion innerhalb der Grenzen der bloßen Vernunft.* Leipzig u. Tübingen: Mohr, 1899; reprint Hildesheim u. New York: Olms, 1974.

Schweitzer, Albert. *Geschichte der Leben-Jesu-Forschung.* Tübingen: J.C.B. Mohr & Paul Siebeck 1913.

Schweitzer, Albert. *Geschichte der paulinischen Forschung von der Reformation bis auf die Gegenwart.* Tübingen: J. C. B. Mohr, 1911.

Schweitzer, Albert. *Jean Sébastien Bach, le musicien poète.* Leipzig: Breitkopf &Härtel, o.J. [Vorwort 1904 datiert; zahlreiche Nachdrucke]; deutsche Fassung ebd., 1908.

Schweitzer, Albert. *Joannis Calvini opera quae supersunt omnia.* 59 Bde., Hgg. Guilielmus Baum, Eduardus Cunitz, Eduardus Reuss und Alfred Erichson. Braunschweig und Berlin: C. A. Schwetschke und Sohn, 1863–1900.

Schweitzer, Albert. *Von Reimarus zu Wrede. Eine Geschichte der Leben-Jesu-Forschung.* Tübingen: J.C.B Mohr, 1913.

Semler, Johan Salomo. *Abhandlung von freier Untersuchung des Canon.* Texte zur Kirchen- und Theologiegeschichte 5. Gütersloh: Gütersloher Verlagshaus, 1980.

Shechtman, Dan et al. „Metallic Phase with Long-Range Orientational Order and No Translational Symmetry." *Physical Review Letters* 53 (1984): 1951–1953.

Siddiqui, Mona. *Christians, Muslims, & Jesus.* New Haven, CT: Yale University Press, 2013.

Siegert, Folker. „Das Judenchristentum in der Antike: ein neuer Ansatz zu seiner Erforschung." In *Grenzgänge. Menschen und Schicksale zwischen jüdischer, christlicher und deutscher Identität. Festschrift für Diethard Aschoff'.* Münsteraner Judaistische Studien 11, Hg. Folker Siegert, 117–128. Münster: LIT, 2002.

Simon, Richard. *Histoire critique du Vieux Testament.* Rotterdam: Reinier Leers, 1690 [1685].

Simon, Robert. „Mānī and Muḥammad." *Jerusalem Studies in Arabic and Islam* 21 (1997): 118–141.

Sinai, Nicolai. „Auf der Suche nach der verlorenen Vorzeit: Günter Lülings apokalyptische Koranphilologie." *Neue Zürcher Zeitung*, February 19, 2004.

Sinai, Nicolai. „Religious Poetry from the Qurʾānic Milieu: Umayya b. Abī ṣ-Ṣalt on the Fate of the Thamūd." *Bulletin of the School of Oriental and African Studies* 74 (2011): 397–416.

Small, Keith. *Textual Criticism and Qurʾān Manuscripts.* Plymouth: Lexington, 2011.

Smith, R. Payne. *Thesaurus Syriacus*, fascicle, X, cols. 3871–3875. Oxford: Clarendon Press, 1897, reprint: Hildesheim: Georg Olms Verlag, Bd. II, cols. 3871–3875.

Smith, Wilfred Cantwell. *The Meaning and End of Religion: a New Approach to the Religious Traditions of Mankind.* New York: Macmillan, 1963.

Sokoloff, Michael. *A Dictionary of Jewish Babylonian Aramaic of the Talmudic and Geonic Periods.* Baltimore: The Johns Hopkins University Press, 2003.

Sokoloff, Michael. *A Syriac Lexicon: A Translation from the Latin, Correction, Expansion, and Update of C. Brockelmann's Lexicon Syriacum.* Winona Lake, IN & Piscataway, NJ: Eisenbrauns & Gorgias Press, 2009.

Sozomen. *The Ecclesiastical History of Sozomen*, Üb. Edward Walford. London: Henry G. Bohn, 1855.

Speyer, Heinrich. *Die Biblischen Erzälungen im Qoran.* Gräfenhainichen/Breslau: Schulze, 1931.

Spinoza, Baruch de. *Theologisch-politische Abhandlung,* Üb. Julius Hermann von Kirchmann. Philosophische Bibliothek 35. Berlin: L. Heimann, 1870.

Stadtmüller, Georg. „Der Ur-Koran – ein Zeugnis urchristlicher Engelschristologie'." *Una Sancta* 34 (1979): 266.

Steenbrink, Karl. „New Orientalist Suggestions on the Origins of Islam." *The Journal of Rotterdam Islamic and Social Sciences* 1/1 (2010): 154–165.

Steigerwald, Diana. „Review of Günter Lüling. *A Challenge to Islam for Reformation.* New Delhi: Motilal Banarsidass Publishers, 2003." *Journal of the American Oriental Society* (JAOS) 124 (2004): 621–623.

Stewart, Devin J. „Divine Epithets and the Dibacchius: Clausulae and Qurʾānic Rhythm." *Journal of Qur'anic Studies* 15 (2013): 22–64.

Stewart, Devin J. „Poetic License in the Qur'an: Ibn al-Ṣāʾigh al-Ḥanafī's *Iḥkām al-rāy fī aḥkām al-āy.*" *Journal of Qurʾānic Studies* 11 (2009): 1–56.

Stewart, Devin J. „Rhymed Prose." In *Encyclopaedia of the Qurʾān,* Hg. Jane Dammen McAuliffe. Brill Online: http://dx.doi.org/10.1163/1875-3922_q3_EQSIM_00359.

Stewart, Devin J. „*Sajʿ* in the Qurʾān: Prosody and Structure." *Journal of Arabic Literature* 21 (1990): 101–39.

Strecker, Georg. „Judenchristentum." *Theologische Realenzyklopadie 17* (1988): 320–325.

Stroumsa, Gedaliahu G. „'Seal of the Prophets': The Nature of a Manichaean Metaphor." *Jerusalem Studies in Arabic and Islam* 7 (1986): 61–74.

Stroumsa, Guy G. „Jewish Christianity and Islamic Origins." In *Islamic Cultures, Islamic Contexts: Essays in Honor of Professor Patricia Crone*, Hgg. Behnam Sadeghi et al., 72–96. Leiden: Brill, 2015.

Sundermeier, Theodor. „Review of Günter Lüling. *Die Wiederentdeckung des Propheten Muhammad. Eine Kritik am „christlichen" Abendland.* Erlangen: Verlagsbuchhandlung Hannelore Lüling, 1981." *Beihefte zur Evangelischen Theologie* 30 (1985): 14–15.

As-Suyūṭī, Ǧalāl ad-Dīn. *Al-Itqān fī ʿulūm al-qurʾān*. 289–297. Madīna, o. J.

Aṭ-Ṭabarī, Muḥammad b. Ǧarīr Abū Ǧaʿfar. *Tafsīr (Jāmiʿ al-bayān ʿan taʾwīl āy al-Qurʾān*, Hg. Maḥmūd Šākir. 16 Bde. Beirut, 1421/2001.

Aṭ-Ṭabarī, Muḥammad b. Ǧarīr Abū Ǧaʿfar. *Taʾrīkh ar-rusul wa-l-mulūk*, Hgg. M.J. de Goeje et al. 16 Bde. Leiden: Brill, 1879–1901.

Aṭ-Ṭabarī, Muḥibb ad-Dīn. *Al-Qirā li-qāṣid Umm al-Qurā*, Hg. Muṣṭafā as-Saqqā. Cairo, 1390/1970.

Tardieu, Michel. *Manichaeism*, Üb. M.B. De Bevoise. Urbana & Chicago: University of Illinois Press, 2008.

Taylor, David G.K. „The Disputation between a Muslim and a Monk of Bēt Ḥālē: Syriac Text and Annotated English Translation." In *Christsein in der islamischen Welt*, Hgg. Sidney Griffith und Sven Grebenstein, 187–242. Wiesbaden: Harrassowitz Verlag, 2015.

Trautmann, Thomas. *Aryans and British India.* Berkeley: University of California Press, 1997.

Van den Velden, Frank. „Kontexte im Konvergenzstrang – die Bedeutung textkritischer Varianten und christlicher Bezugstexte für die Redaktion von Sure 61 und Sure 5, 110–119." *Oriens Christianus* 92 (2008): 130–173.

Van den Velden, Frank. „Konvergenztexte syrischer und arabischer Christologie: Stufen der Textentwicklung von Sure 3, 33–64." *Oriens Christianus* 91 (2007): 164–203.

Van den Velden, Frank. „Relations between Jews, Syriac Christians and Early Muslim Believers in Seventh-Century Iraq." *The Bulletin of Middle East Medievalists* 19 (2007): 27–33.

Vidas, Moulie. *Tradition and the Formation of the Talmud.* Princeton: Princeton University Press, 2014.

Vocke, Harald. „Wenn Ihr Ungläubige trefft. Untersuchungen über den Urkoran – Ein Thema voll Brisanz." *Frankfurter Allgemeine Zeitung*, June 18, 1979.

Vollers, Karl. *Volkssprache und Schriftsprache im alten Arabien.* Straßburg: Verlag von Karl J. Trübner, 1906 [reprint 1981. Amsterdam: APA-Press].

Von Stosch, Klaus. „Jesus im Qurʾān. Ansatzpunkte und Stolpersteine einer qurʾānischen Christologie." In *Handeln Gottes – Antwort des Menschen. Beiträge zur Komparativen Theologie 11*, Hgg. Klaus Stosch und Muna Tatari, 109–133. Paderborn: Schöningh, 2014.

Waardenburg, Jacques. „Towards a Periodization of Earliest Islam According to its Relations With Other Religions." In *Proceedings of the Ninth Congress of the Union Européenne des Arabisants et Islamisants*, Hg. Rudolph Peters. Leiden: Brill, 1981.

Wajdenbaum, Philippe. *Argonauts of the Desert: Structural Analysis of the Hebrew Bible.* New York: Routledge, 2014.

Walther, A. „Review of Adolf Grohmann. *Äthiopische Marienhymnen.* Leipzig: G. Teubner, 1919." *Orientalistische Literaturzeitung* (OLZ) 25 (1922): 444–445.

Wansbrough, John. *Qur ʾānic Studies: Sources and Methods of Scriptural Interpretation.* Oxford: Oxford University Press, 1977.

Wansbrough, John. *The Sectarian Milieu: Content and Composition of Islamic Salvation History.* Amherst: Prometheus Books, 1978.

Watson, W.G.E. „Unit Delimitation on the Old Testament: an Appraisal." In *Method in Unit Delimitation*, Hgg. Marjo Korpel, Josef Oesch und Stanley Porter, 162–184. Leiden: Brill, 2007.

Watt, William Montgomery. *Bell's Introduction to the Qurʾān.* Edinburgh: Edinburgh University Press, 1970.

Wehnert, Jürgen. „Ebioniten." *LThK 3* (1995): 431.

Weischer, Bernd. „Review on Lüling, Günter. *Über den Ur-Qurʾān. Ansätze zur Rekonstruktion vorislamischer christlicher Strophenlieder im Ur-Qurʾān.* Erlangen: Verlagsbuchhandlung Hannelore Lüling, 1974." *Orientalistische Literaturzeitung* (OLZ) 74 (1979): 468–473.

Wellhausen, Julius. *Reste arabischen Heidentums, gesammelt und erläutert von J. Wellhausen.* Berlin: Georg Reimer, 2. Auflage, 1897.

Weren, Wim et al., Hgg. *Recent developments in textual criticism: new testament, other early Christian and Jewish literature.* Assen: Gorcum, 2003.

Werlitz, Jürgen. *Studien zur literarkritischen Methode. Gericht und Heil in Jesaja 7,1–17 und 29,1–8.* Beihefte zur Zeitschrift für die alttestamentliche Wissenschaft 204. Berlin: De Gruyter, 1992.

Werner, Martin. *Der protestantische Weg des Glaubens.* Bern: Haupt und Tübingen: Katzmann, 1955–1962.

Werner, Martin. *Die Entstehung des christlichen Dogmas. Problemgeschichtlich dargestellt.* Bern: Haupt, 1941 [2. Auflage Bern: Haupt und Tübingen: Katzmann, 1954].

Werner, Martin. *Die Entstehung des christlichen Dogmas. Problemgeschichtlich dargestellt. Mit einer Bildbeilage.* Urban Bücher Nr. 28. Stuttgart: Kohlhammer, 1959.

Werner, Martin. *The Formation of Christian Dogma. An Historical Study of Its Problem, by Martin Werner*, Üb. S. G. F. Brandon. New York: Harper & Brothers, 1957.

Werner, Martin. *The Formation of Christian Dogma. Rewritten in shortened form by the author from his Die Entstehung des christlichen Dogmas*, Üb. S. G. F. Brandon. London: Verlag A. & G. Black, 1957.

Whitters, Mark. „The Source for the Qur'ānic Story of the Companions of the Cave (*sūrat al-Kahf* 18)." In *The Bible, the Qur'ān, & Their Interpretation: Syriac Perspectives.* Eastern Mediterranean Texts and Contexts 1, Hg. Cornelia Horn, 167–187. Warwick, Rhode Island: Abelian Academic, 2013.

Wild, Stefan, Hg. *Self-referentiality in the Qur'ān.* Diskurse der Arabistik 11. Wiesbaden: Harrassowitz, 2006.

Wild, Stefan. „Lost in Philology? The Virgins of Paradise and the Luxenberg Hypothesis." In *The Qur'ān in Context. Historical and Literary Investigations into the Qur'ānic Milieu*, Hgg. Angelika Neuwirth, Nicolai Sinai und Michael Marx, 625–647. Leiden: Brill, 2010.

Witztum, Joseph. „The Foundations of the House (Q2: 127)." *Bulletin of the School of Oriental and African Studies* 72 (2009): 25–40.

Witztum, Joseph. *The Syriac Milieu of the Quran: The Recasting of Biblical Narratives.* PhD Dissertation, Princeton, NJ, 2011.

Woitowitz, Hans-Joachim. „Akademische Trivialität." *Frankfurter Allgemeine Zeitung*, July 17, 1979.

Wonneberger, Reinhard. *Redaktion. Studien zur Textfortschreibung im Alten Testament, entwickelt am Beispiel der Samuel-Überlieferung.* Forschungen zur Religion und Literatur des Alten und Neuen Testaments 156. Göttingen: Vandenhoeck & Ruprecht, 1992.

Woytt-Secretan, Mary. *Albert Schweitzer baut Lambarene.* Königstein: Langewiesche, 1959.

Yeivin, Israel. *Introduction to the Tiberian Masora (Mavo la-masora ha-ṭavranit)*, Üb. und Hg. E. J. Revell. Chico, CA: Scholars Press, 1980.

Younes, Munther. „Angels, Stars, Death, the soul, horses, bows – or Women? The opening verses of Qur'ān 79." In *New Perspectives on the Qur'ān*, Hg. Reynolds, 264–278. London/New York: Routledge, 2011.

Younes, Munther. „Charging Steeds or Maidens Doing Good Deeds? A Re-Interpretation of Qur'ān 100 (*al-ʿādiyāt*)." *Arabica* 55 (2008): 362–386.

Zellentin, Holger M. „*ʾaḥbār* and *ruhbān:* Religious Leaders in the Qur'ān in Dialogue with Christian and Rabbinic Literature." In *Qur'anic Studies at the University of Chicago*, Hgg. Angelika Neuwirth und M. Sells. Routledge Studies in the Qur'an. New York: Routledge, 2016.

Zellentin, Holger M. *Rabbinic Parodies of Jewish and Christian Literature.* Tübingen: Mohr Siebeck, 2010.

Zellentin, Holger M. *The Qur'ān's legal culture. The Didascalia Apostolorum as a point of departure.* Tübingen: Mohr Siebeck, 2013.

Ziegler, Theobald. Indexeintrag: *Meyers Konversations-Lexikon.* Bd. 17, 1017. Leipzig und Wien: Bibliographisches Institut, 5. Auflage, 1897.

Zinner, Samuel. *The Abrahamic Archetype: Conceptual and Historical Relationships between Judaism, Christianity and Islam*. Bartlow: Camb. UK: Archetype, 2011.

Websites

http://www.hls-dhs-dss.ch/textes/d/D10911.php.
http://www.mechon-mamre.org/.
https://de.wikipedia.org/wiki/Günter_Lüling, accessed December 28, 2015.
https://en.wikipedia.org/wiki/Günter_Lüling, accessed December 28, 2015.
https://www.biblegateway.com/passage/?search=Genesis%201:1-5.
https://www.deutsche-biographie.de/pnd118567640.html.
https://www2.hf.uio.no/polyglotta/index.php?page=volume&vid=51.

Personenregister

https://doi.org/10.1515/9783110599176-013

Sachregister

https://doi.org/10.1515/9783110599176-014

CPSIA information can be obtained
at www.ICGtesting.com
Printed in the USA
LVHW091816120720
660467LV00004B/557